THE
THIRD REICH
1919-1939

THE
THIRD REICH
1919-1939

THE NAZIS' RISE TO POWER

ANDREW RAWSON

SPELLMOUNT

AUTHOR'S NOTE

The aim of this book is to explain the turbulent years in Germany between the First World War and the Second World War, covering the events leading to the demise of the Weimar Republic and the rise of the Third Reich. It is for historical reference only and no expression of political or philosophical beliefs is intended or should be assumed.

I would like to thank the staff of the images archive working for the National Archives and Records Administration, Maryland, USA, for helping me to source many of the photographs in this book. They come from collection reference 242-HB, known as the Hoffmann Collection.

First published 2010 by
Spellmount Publishers, an imprint of
The History Press Ltd
The Mill, Brimscombe Port
Stroud, Gloucestershire, GL5 2QG
www.thehistorypress.co.uk

British Library Cataloguing in Publication Data.
A catalogue record for this book is available from the British Library.

ISBN 978 0 7524 5570 9

Typesetting and origination by The History Press
Printed in Great Britain by Scotprint

CONTENTS

ONE   POST-WAR CHAOS IN GERMANY   7

TWO   THE RISE TO POWER   25

THREE   ADOLF HITLER – THE FÜHRER   49

FOUR   THE PARTY   65

FIVE   THE SEIZURE OF POWER   85

SIX   SECURING POWER   97

SEVEN   THE NAZI STATE   105

EIGHT   THE NAZI CALENDAR   115

NINE   LAW AND ORDER   123

TEN   THE ECONOMY AND LABOUR   141

ELEVEN   RELIGION AND SCIENCE   161

TWELVE   THE PRESS, RADIO AND PROPAGANDA   169

THIRTEEN   CULTURE   179

FOURTEEN   THE FAMILY, WELFARE AND HEALTH   189

FIFTEEN   EDUCATION, YOUTH AND SPORT   197

SIXTEEN   RECLAIMING GERMANY'S BORDERS   217

SEVENTEEN   CREATING A GREATER GERMANY   223

EIGHTEEN   GERMANY'S ARMED FORCES   239

NINETEEN   MILITARY HARDWARE   257

TWENTY   THE STORM DIVISON, STURM ABTEILUNG, SA   273

TWENTY-ONE   THE PROTECTION ECHELON, SCHUTZSTAFFEL, SS   279

TWENTY-TWO   ENEMIES OF THE STATE   291

TWENTY-THREE   RESISTANCE   307

                INDEX   314

CHAPTER ONE

POST-WAR CHAOS IN GERMANY

Germany went to war against France, Russia and Great Britain in August 1914, in a flurry of patriotic fervour. After early successes in France and Russia, the fighting became deadlocked in a mass of trenches on both fronts. Germany went on the defensive in the west for the next three-and-a-half years, only attacking at Verdun in 1916 and the war was going in its favour by the end of 1917. Although the US had entered the war on the Allied side in April 1917, the armies of France and Great Britain were exhausted. Russia had also surrendered in March 1918, under the Treaty of Brest-Litovsk, allowing Germany to move large numbers of troops to the Western Front. Victory was in sight but it had to be accomplished before large numbers of American troops reached France. Ludendorff made three successive attacks on the Western Front in the spring of 1918 but the Allied line held each time; the attacks exhausted Germany's reserves.

The German Army fell back across France in the autumn, in the face of relentless Allied attacks. The German people were suffering from food shortages, leading to riots across the country, and Berlin was in a state of revolution by November 1918. After the Kaiser had been forced to abdicate, the new government accepted the Allied armistice terms.

Hundreds of thousands of soldiers returned home to find Germany in turmoil.

Although the guns fell silent across the Western Front on 11 November 1918, rioting increased across Germany. The Allies were now looking for revenge for the war and it was going to cost the people of Germany dearly. There were troubled times ahead and the nationalists placed the blame for Germany's problems firmly on the shoulders of the men who had signed the Armistice, the men they called the November Criminals.

THE TREATY OF VERSAILLES

The Peace Treaty which formally brought the First World War to an end was signed in Versailles in France on 28 June 1919. The terms forced Germany to give up territories, recognise her war guilt and pay compensation to the Allies.

Germany had to surrender fifteen per cent of its territory and ten per cent of its population. Allied troops also occupied the Rhineland and the Saar region, two of the country's coal producing regions, limiting the output of iron and steel; many armament factories were also closed down. Alsace and Lorraine, the provinces taken from France following the Franco-Prussian War of 1870–71, were also returned. Germany also handed over territory to Belgium and Denmark. Large tracts of the country's eastern territories were given to Poland. Many of Germany's overseas colonies were also divided up between the Allies.

New countries were established on Germany's borders. Czechoslovakia, Poland, Hungary and Lithuania were created, while Austrian independence was assured; Danzig was also made into a free city. Many German-speaking areas would now be administered by new governments.

The German armed services were also severely restricted. The army was reduced to 100,000 men, conscription was abolished, tanks and heavy artillery were banned. The navy was limited to a small number of capital ships and there were to be no U-Boats. Germany was not allowed to have a military air force.

The treaty was held in contempt by political parties and individuals across Germany. Political slogans called it the 'Versailles Diktat'. In December 1918 an English reporter writing in the *New Zürich* newspaper noted that 'as far as the German Army is concerned the general view is summarised in these words: it was stabbed in the back by the civil population.'

Nationalists and anti-Semites blamed the 'stab in the back' on traitors, black marketeers, Communists, Social Democrats and the Jewish community. The idea of betrayal appealed to soldiers returning from the trenches because many had marched home with their units to find their homeland in disarray. The German generals also wanted to believe that they had been defeated by forces beyond their control.

A Reichstag investigation later concluded that the morale of the Germany Army had been undermined by many internal and external factors. Although morale had fallen after the spring 1918 offensives, defeatists, pacifists, revolutionaries and corruption in Germany had reduced it further. The investigation concluded that the 'stab in the back' was a myth but it was a myth that the National Socialists exploited.

THE LEAGUE OF NATIONS

Towards the end of the war, plans were underway to prevent future conflicts. President Woodrow Wilson advocated the League, a group of nations formed to guarantee political independence and territorial integrity for all states, as part of his Fourteen Points of Peace. Although the formation of the League was approved at the Paris Peace Conference in January 1919, Wilson could not get the US to join; he was however, awarded the Nobel Peace Prize for helping to establish it. On 28 June 1919, 44 countries signed up to the League and on 16 January 1920 the first meeting was held. By the mid-1920s its role expanded beyond its original remit and the number of members increased.

THE WEIMAR REPUBLIC

Germany needed a new government and the first National Constituent Assembly planned to draw up a new constitution in Berlin in February 1919. Battles between communists and paramilitary units forced the assembly to relocate to Weimar, 150 miles to the south-west, where it drew up the constitution in the city's National Theatre. The system of government in Germany between 1919 and 1933 became known as the Weimar Republic.

The constitution provided for an elected president in place of the Kaiser, who would serve for seven years. There was a bicameral legislature, involving two debating chambers, the national Reichstag and the Reichrats representing the states. The system allowed proportional representation and, for the first time, women had the vote. Delegates were returned by percentage of votes, making it difficult for a single party to gain full control. The system favoured minority parties and resulted in many unstable coalition governments. There would be twenty cabinets between February 1919 and January 1933.

The system curbed the powers of the states, particularly the largest state, Prussia, which had used its size to block many decisions. The Reichrat could veto Reichstag bills. In turn the Reichstag could overrule a veto if it had a two-thirds majority, an unlikely occurrence in the multi-party politics of the era.

Although the constitution was one of the most advanced and democratic in the world at that time, it had been written to both appease the Allies and serve the Germans; in trying to do both it did neither. It had serious weaknesses, including the fact that the President could use Article 25 to dissolve the Reichstag while Article 48 gave him the right to define and declare a national emergency. He could then suspend civil rights, rule by decrees (temporary laws) and use the army to restore order. The clause was intended to protect Germany if there was an internal revolution but it was also open to exploitation.

FRIEDRICH EBERT (1871–1925)

Chairman of the Social Democrats since 1913, Ebert was elected first President of the Republic in February 1919. He had to contend with many problems as economic difficulties and political confusion ravaged Germany. While the continued Allied naval blockade and the occupation of industrial areas undermined the weak economy, spiralling inflation dealt a severe blow to the middle classes. The delay in sending prisoners of war home also affected the labour market. Widespread rioting in many cities threatened to bring down the government and the small army had to rely on paramilitary Free Corps units to suppress uprisings.

Political activists fought the army and the police across the country.

Attempts to stabilise German politics and economics were disrupted by all sides and Ebert had to use Article 48 (see above) over 130 times to deal with uprising and force legislation through. Veteran politicians were too timid to shake off old traditions and their attempts to forge links with the generals and the industrialists failed. New politicians, ranging from left-wing communists to right-wing nationalists, promoted civil unrest on the streets and tried to topple the government.

GUSTAV STRESEMANN (1878–1929)

Stresemann opposed the Weimar Republic's form of democracy but he accepted that it was the only option. He was appointed Chancellor of a coalition government in August 1923 and had to endure opposition from the left and right. The National Socialists made their own attempt to topple the government in Munich in November 1923. Stresemann was forced to resign two weeks later when the Social Democrats left his coalition. He would eventually negotiate Germany's repatriation into Europe through the Locarno Treaty and entry to the League of Nations. He died suddenly in Berlin on 3 October 1929.

THE WAR REPARATIONS

A major part, and a major contention, of the Versailles Treaty was the compensation Germany had to repay the Allies. Article 231 blamed Germany for the war and the reparations were meant to be a payment for war guilt; many Germans called it the 'war guilt lie':

> The Allied and Associated Governments affirm and Germany accepts the responsibility of Germany and her allies for causing all the loss and damage to which the Allied and Associated Governments and their nationals have been subjected as a consequence of the war imposed upon them by the aggression of Germany and her allies …

The cost of the damage was difficult to quantify and initial estimates were outrageous. Allied debts, in particular France's $4,000 million debt to the US and another $600 million to Britain, had to be taken into account. The Soviet government also refused to settle the debts incurred under the Tsar with France, complicating the calculations.

The Allied Supreme Council set the figure at 132,000 million gold Marks or $31.5 billion ($400 billion in 2007) in January 1921, and it was estimated that it would take 70 years to pay off. Although the amount was halved four months later to account for Germany's severe economic problems, the debt still threatened to cripple the country's economy. All the German political parties immediately denounced the reparations and the right-wing Germany Workers' Party made it one of its key points.

The collapse of the German Mark led to hyperinflation. Germany was unable to make payments and French troops marched into the Ruhr, Germany's industrial heartland, in January 1923 seeking to find alternative ways to settle the debt. Demanding payment was useless as the exchange rate spiralled from 8 Marks to 4,200,000 million Marks to 1 US dollar between November 1918 and April 1922. The highest denomination German banknote was 100,000,000 million Marks. Money meant nothing and people needed baskets to carry wages straight to the shops to buy food before it devalued. Prices changed by the hour and wages meant nothing after a few days. Germany could not afford imports and shops hoarded their stock to make money; the result was widespread food riots. No one could afford to pay their workers while savings, war bonds and state loans were wiped out. However, large loans and mortgages became worthless and property could be acquired for very little. The situation had turned the economy upside down. People were reduced to selling possessions for food, there was a nationwide crime wave and black marketeering flourished as people tried to stay alive. Germany needed a new repayment plan to prevent total economic collapse and the inevitable social unrest.

Charles Dawes, Director of the United States Bureau of the Budget, chaired a committee which looked for ways to balance Germany's budget and stabilise the Mark. On 9 April 1924 it made several recommendations:

Set the repayments at 2,000 million gold Marks a year

Return funds from mortgages on railways and industries and a transport tax

Use foreign loans to stabilise the German currency

Restore German fiscal and economic unity

The plan would control inflation but it did hand over control of Germany's finances and industry to other countries while the repayments were paid. The Dawes Plan became another point of contention for political parties, in particular the right-wing nationalists. The head of the Reichsbank, Dr Hjalmar Schacht, introduced the Rentenmark tied to gold price to settle currency and it was soon known as the Reichsmark (RM).

The worldwide economic recovery between 1924 and 1929 eased the reparation payments but Germany's economy was suffering, prompting Chancellor Stresemann to ask to renegotiate the settlement. American lawyer and financier Owen D. Young chaired a second committee, which made the following recommendations in June 1929:

The fixed capital value of the reparations was 37,000 million gold Marks

Payment would be made in 58 ½ annual instalments, ending in 1983

Identity of the number of instalments with the number of inter-Allied debt instalments

A Bank of International Settlements would handle all payments

There were protests across Germany, particularly from the communists and the National Socialists. Hjalmar Schacht resigned in protest and the leader of the Nationalist Party, Alfred Hugenberg, formed an opposition alliance called the Harzburg Front. Despite the protests, the Reichstag voted in favour of the Young Plan and President Hindenburg signed the bill on 13 March 1930.

However, the Wall Street Crash in October 1929 had already wrecked Germany's weak economy, which been reliant on short-term American loans. Germany was unable to make any repayments in 1931 and further reparations claims were written off at an international conference at Lausanne in Switzerland the following year.

COMMUNIST UPRISINGS

The Communist Party and the Independent Social Democrats called a general strike on 7 January 1919, creating havoc across Berlin. After three days of inactivity the Spartacist League called for armed action while President Ebert called upon paramilitary Free Corps units to help the army restore order. Over 1,000 were killed or executed in the violence that followed, including the communist leaders Karl Liebknecht and Rosa Luxemburg. Communists also declared a republic in the city Bremen; it too was also quickly crushed.

In Munich, Kurt Eisner (1867–1919), a Jewish theatre critic, declared Bavaria a free state and a republic on 8 November 1918. He enthusiastically called for reason but he alienated the Bavarian people by declaring that Germany was responsible for the war. The new government failed to operate and Eisner was defeated in the January 1919 elections. Count Arco-Valley murdered Eisner on 21 February 1919; reprisal killings and a general strike followed.

Bavaria was declared a Soviet Republic on 6 April but the government leaders refused to deal with the army and they formed their own paramilitary units. Chaos reigned until 9,000 soldiers and 30,000 Free Corps troops retaliated on 3 May; over 600 people were killed and several thousand were injured in the street battles.

Hitler was still serving with his regiment in Munich and he was disgusted by the anarchy and violence across Bavaria. Anton Drexler, Dietrich Eckart and Karl Harrer had also just formed the Germany Workers' Party in the city.

Armed Communist Party supporters take to the streets.

The government relied on Free Corps units to restore order.

THE FREE CORPS, FREIKORPS

Many officers organised demobilised soldiers into paramilitary units following the Armistice, to protect their towns and cities from political activists. Many ex-soldiers still had their weapons while army sympathisers provided right-wing nationalists with guns. The German Army, the Reichswehr, had been limited to 100,000 men under the Versailles Treaty and at first the army generals welcomed support from the Free Corps. Units broke up communist uprisings in Berlin, Bremen and Munich in violent confrontations; they also suppressed left-wing activists in the Ruhr industrial area.

Many Free Corps leaders supported the NSDAP during its early days and many members transferred to the SA when it started to grow in popularity. Once the Nazis seized power in 1933, many ex-Free Corps leaders were seen as potential troublemakers and while some were offered lucrative posts, others were forced into exile.

FREE CORPS ORGANISATIONS

THE STEEL HELMET, THE STAHLHELM

Franz Seldte (1882–1947) formed the national ex-serviceman's organisation in December 1918. With the help of Theodor Duesterberg (1875–1950) it expanded until it became the largest Free Corps organisation. The 'Wolf Force' was a smaller version of the 'Steel Helmet' based in Thuringia; most members eventually transferred to the SA.

By 1930 President Hindenburg was president of the Steel Helmet and it had over 800,000 members, twice the size of the SA. In October 1931 the organisation was represented in the Harzburg Front, the right-wing alliance opposed to the Young Plan. Duesterberg stood for president on behalf of the Nationalist Party in March 1932 but he came last in the elections following false accusations made by the NSDAP that he had a Jewish grandfather.

Hitler apologised to Duesterberg in January 1933 and he offered him a cabinet post, hoping for the Steel Helmet's support. When he refused the slur was resurrected. At the same time Hitler embraced Seldte as his Labour Minister, making him a Prussian State Minister; it split the leadership in two. Steel Helmet units in Prussia formed an auxiliary police force alongside the SA.

In December a decree absorbed the Steel Helmet into the SA, an unpopular move for many, and while younger men transferred to the SA, older men joined the SA Reserve. The SA Reserve was renamed the National Socialist German Veterans' Organisation in March 1934 with Seldte as its leader. Duesterberg's troubles continued when he was imprisoned during the June 1934 Blood Purge.

THE BAVARIAN FREE CORPS

Over 30,000 ex-soldiers joined the Free Corps across Bavaria and they helped the army to overthrow the communist uprising in Munich in May 1919 and a workers' revolt in the industrial Ruhr a few months later. The commander Franz von Epp (1868–1947) was an early NSDAP supporter and he raised money to buy the *People's Observer* newspaper for the party in 1921. Although he did not take part in the 1923 Beer Hall Putsch, he became Bavaria's SA commander when it reorganised in 1926. Epp eventually joined the NSDAP in 1928 and he was elected to the Reichstag for Upper Bavaria-Swabia; he was appointed head of the NSDAP's Military Political Office, promoting party politics in the military. In March

A Free Corps unit patrols the streets.

1933 he was appointed Bavaria's Governor, the Nazis' first head of state, and the leader of the Colonial Policy Office in May. He was sidelined after the SA's leadership was decimated during the Blood Purge in June 1934. Epp's influence faded and he was made Master of the Bavarian Hunt in August 1934 and General of the Infantry the year later.

THE EHRHARDT BRIGADE OR VIKING LEAGUE

Hermann Ehrhardt (1881–1971) was an ex-naval officer and members of his brigade painted the swastika symbol on their helmets. It helped to topple the Communist government in Munich in 1919 and led the Kapp Putsch in Berlin in 1920. The brigade was also used as an auxiliary police force in Bavaria. Many members eventually transferred to the SA but Hitler was suspicious of Ehrhardt's political ambitions. He was forced to escape to Austria following the Blood Purge in June 1934.

THE ROSSBACH GROUP

The Group fought against the Latvian Army in 1919 and took part in the Kapp Putsch in 1920. It was banned and its leader, Gerhard Rossbach (1893–1967), was arrested, but members continued to fight together under different organisations. Rossbach joined the NSDAP in 1922 and was appointed commander of the Munich SA. The flamboyant and notorious homosexual led his infantry cadets during the Beer Hall Putsch in November 1923, escaping to Austria after it failed. Rossbach returned to Germany with a supply of surplus brown uniforms made for the East African campaign when the NSDAP reformed in 1925. The brown shirts gave the SA its nickname. Rossbach avoided arrest during the June 1934 Blood Purge and he left the SA to make a living as a businessman.

THE ARTAMAN LEAGUE

This *Völkisch* wing of the nationalist youth movement was devoted to the concept of 'Blood and Soil'. Many were anti-Slav and they petitioned for Polish farmers to return to their own country, so they could work on farms in lieu of military service. Heinrich Himmler was a member until the organisation was absorbed into the NSDAP.

THE END OF THE FREE CORPS

It soon became clear that many Free Corps units were armed gangs seeking personal gain and the Weimar Republic dismissed many of them to comply with the limits set by the Treaty of Versailles. The 5,000-strong Ehrhardt's Brigade refused to lay down their arms and marched on Berlin on 12 March 1920, parading through the Brandenburg Gate the following morning. There were only 2,000 soldiers in the city and while the leader of the Reichswehr, General Hans von Seeckt, was adamant that the 'Reichswehr does not fire on Reichswehr', other military leaders privately supported the Putsch.

Wolfgang Kapp, a right-wing journalist, was appointed Chancellor but he soon discovered that the coup was unpopular when the Reichswehr refused to give its support. Government delegates had called for a general strike before going into hiding and striking transport workers brought the city to a standstill. After five days, Kapp resigned and fled to Sweden.

Many Free Corps supporters headed to Munich, a hotbed of nationalist politics and they took part in the NSDAP uprising in November 1923. The Nazis acknowledged the part played by the Free Corps in November 1933, on the tenth anniversary of the Putsch. A roll call of their units was made during the memorial service and their flags were displayed in the Brown House, the NSDAP's headquarters.

Police escort an early NSDAP parade.

THE GERMAN WORKERS' PARTY
THE *DEUTSCHE ARBEITERPARTEI*

The NSDAP started life as the German Workers' Party (DAP), a small fringe political party meeting in the backstreet bars of Munich. It was formed from the merger of Anton Drexler's Committee of Independent Workmen and Karl Harrer's Political Workers' Circle on 5 January 1919; they were joined by Dietrich Eckart. The small group met regularly in the Hofbräuhaus Beer Hall over the months that followed but they failed to attract much interest for their nationalist and anti-Semitic views.

In September 1919, Major Konstantin Hierl of the Army's Political Department ordered Adolf Hitler to monitor the Germany Workers' Party meetings, to gauge their support. He found that the party had no plan of action, little money and poor speakers. However, their views matched his own feeling of resentment at the state of the country, and he joined. He soon discovered that he was a talented and energetic speaker, helping to increase the membership over the winter.

The party opened a permanent office in December and on 24 February 1920 a large audience heard Drexler and Feder announce its 25-point political programme. Two months later the party was renamed the National Socialist German Workers' Party, the *Nationalsozialistische Deutsche Arbeiterpartei*, or NSDAP.

Hitler and Gregor Strasser sit at the head of the table at an early NSDAP meeting.

THE PARTY'S FOUNDING MEMBERS

ANTON DREXLER (1884–1942)

A Munich machine fitter who was forced to work as a musician in a Berlin restaurant after failing to make his fortune. After he was rejected as unfit for military service in 1914 he joined the Fatherland Party but fell out with the committee. In March 1918 he formed his own party, the Committee of Independent Workmen. Hitler felt that Drexler was a poor leader and he soon took over as head of the party. Drexler was appointed honorary chairman when it was renamed the NSDAP. He was imprisoned for a short time following the 1923 Munich Putsch and elected to the Bavarian Landtag in April 1924. He did not return to the NSDAP when it reformed and was forgotten by the Nazis.

DIETRICH ECKART (1868–1923)

A journalist and poet who introduced Hitler – the coarse Austrian peasant and ex-soldier – to an influential circle of friends in Munich. They met General Erich Ludendorff in Berlin in 1920 and persuaded him to support the NSDAP. Eckart also helped the party buy the *People's Observer* in December 1920 and he became an editor on the newspaper. Health problems stemming from alcoholism and a past morphine addiction continued to trouble Eckhart; he had also spent time in a mental asylum. He was briefly imprisoned following the Munich Putsch but was released due to illness and died suddenly on 23 December 1923.

HERMANN ESSER (1900–1981)

An ex-soldier and a rowdy anti-Semitic thug with an unsavoury private life. He was also an effective speaker and a gifted propagandist, specialising in producing anti-Semitic slander for the *People's Observer*. He fell out with Hitler after feigning illness during the 1923 Munich Putsch and fleeing to Austria. Esser was jailed briefly on his return but was shunned by other Nazis while Hitler was in prison and he joined forces with Julius Streicher. Hitler took Esser back on his release and he became the NSDAP's chief representative on Munich's city council. He edited the *Illustrated Observer* until he was elected to the Bavarian Landtag in 1932, becoming the state Minister of Economics. Although he was sacked in March 1935 following a scandal, he was appointed Head of the Tourist Division in the Propaganda Ministry and President of the Reich Group for Tourist Traffic.

GOTTFRIED FEDER (1883–1941)

A labourer who was convinced that Germany's economic problems had been caused by the bankers; he also wanted to abolish interest payments, using a theory called 'Interest Slavery'. When no one became interested in his political party – the German Alliance for the Destruction of Interest Slavery – he turned to the German Workers' Party and became a close friend of Hitler. He was appointed editor of the party's library. Feder was elected to the Reichstag in 1924 but his bizarre economic theories became unpopular when the party started to look for financial support from industrialists. He was appointed undersecretary of the Reich Ministry of Economics, in 1933, a minor post. His attempt to organise urban-style rural settlements near cities proved to be unpopular and he was dismissed in December 1934.

THE PARTY'S POLITICAL INFLUENCES

The German Workers' Party adopted their nationalist and anti-Semitic political ideals from a number of individuals and groups. Several nineteenth-century German scholars had developed ideas on nationalism, a corporate state, anti-Semitism and living areas for a pure Nordic race. The Nazis either adapted them to suit the current situation or took them out of context to gain political or financial support.

INFLUENTIAL INDIVIDUALS

FRIEDRICH MULLER (1823–1900)
Muller invented the term Aryan as a description for a group of Indo-European languages. Despite his caveats, the term was later used to refer to race.

PAUL ANTON DE LAGARDE (1827–1891)
De Lagarde promoted racism, anti-Semitic ideals and moral cleansing.

FRIEDRICH NIETZSCHE (1844–1900)
Nietzsche scorned the chaos in Germany and although he openly admired the Jews, the Nazis were eager to adopt his call to train a race of supermen.

HOUSTON CHAMBERLAIN (1855–1927)
Chamberlain explained his race theories, including the dominant role the German people had to play, in his book *The Foundation of the Nineteenth Century*. Chamberlain believed that Hitler was destined to lead Germany when the two met in Bayreuth in 1923.

ARTHUR VAN DEN BRUCK (1876–1925)
Den Bruck opposed democracy, communism and international law and promoted nationalism and a superior Nordic race to restore German values. He also believed that Germany had to be an authoritarian state with centralised control and a planned economy.

OTHMAR SPANN (1878–1950)
Spann was an Austrian economist who advocated the German version of the corporate state, relating the individual to nationality and class whilst protecting the rights of the individual against cartels.

EWALD BANSE (1883–1953)
Banse wrote *Living Areas and Race in World War* stating that while internationalism was degenerate, war was an inevitable method of solving national problems. He also advocated the need for the unification of national living areas and living space (*Lebensraum*).

INFLUENTIAL GROUPS

THE THULE SOCIETY
The Munich branch of a Teutonic Order which used elaborate rituals and mystical symbols, including the swastika. It was named after Thule, the legendary kingdom of Nordic mythology

and homeland of the ancient German race. The branch had been founded during the First World War and had over 1,500 members in Bavaria. The society studied ancient Germanic literature while promoting a powerful Germany, nationalism, race mysticism, anti-Semitism and occultism. Members included Dietrich Eckart, Gottfried Feder, Rudolf Hess and Alfred Rosenberg.

THE GEORGE CIRCLE

An exclusive literary group which revered the poet Stefan George (1868–1933) as a prophet. George wore cleric-style clothes and his members were called Cosmics. Hitler attended George's Munich lectures and listened to him talk of Nietzsche's philosophy for ruthless, unlimited power and a revival of ancient Teutonic lore; he also heard him talk of a hero who would step forward to lead Germany's takeover of the world. To George's dismay, Alfred Schuler, one of the members, promoted anti-Semitism.

VÖLKISCH GROUPS

The *Völkisch* or 'Of the People' movements, wanted to promote the country's culture and eliminate foreign influences. There were over 75 *Völkisch* organisations across Germany after the First World War advocating a mixture of extremist nationalism, race mysticism, and anti-Semitism. The *Völkisch* movement was the ideological starting point for National Socialism and while Hitler identified with their beliefs, he distanced himself from the movement.

THE YEARS OF TURMOIL: 1920–1923

The NSDAP fielded candidates for the Reichstag election in June 1920 but did not win any seats. Hitler became increasingly disillusioned with the party's committee and by the end of the year he was working with Ernst Röhm, Rudolf Hess and Hermann Göring to increase support. Meetings were often rowdy and Emil Maurice formed a security group, known as the

Crowds gather to hear Hitler's rallying call for a strong Germany.

Storm Group, the *Sturmabteilung*, in October, to protect the speakers. Meanwhile, Ernst Röhm persuaded General von Epp to raise money to buy the *People's Observer* so the party could present its views to the public. General Ludendorff also introduced Hitler to Gregor and Otto Strasser, two talented organisers in Berlin.

The first NSDAP National Congress was held in Munich in January 1921 but Hitler was becoming increasingly dissatisfied with how the party was being run. He eventually offered his resignation in the spring after Drexler planned to merge the NSDAP with the German Socialist Party. The Committee realised that Hitler was vital for the party and he returned on his own terms as sole leader. In September he spent a month in prison after a rival party leader was badly beaten.

Hitler speaks to a sparse gathering at the first NSDAP rally.

Captain Hermann Ehrhardt's Free Corps joined the NSDAP in August 1921 and Julius Streicher offered his Nuremberg-based membership in October 1922, doubling the party's size. The rest of the political parties across Germany took part in a political amnesty while the country's financial affairs were assessed in 1923, but the NSDAP carried on campaigning. 20,000 attended the first Party Day in Munich in January and 80,000 the second in Nuremburg in August.

AN EARLY NAZI MARTYR

French troops occupied the Ruhr in January 1923 following Germany's inability to pay the war reparations. Nationalist activists retaliated and in May, the Free Corps officer Albert Schlageter (1894–1923) was arrested for espionage and sabotage by the French police. He was executed on 26 May 1923, on Golzheimer Heath, near Düsseldorf. The NSDAP turned him into their first martyr. The Rossbach group sought revenge and an execution squad, believed to have included Martin Bormann and Rudolf Höss (the future commandant at the Auschwitz concentration camp) killed Walther Kadow, Schlageter's betrayer. A monument was erected in Schlageter's honour in 1931.

THE BEER-HALL PUTSCH
MUNICH, 8-9 NOVEMBER 1923

By the autumn of 1923, Hitler and the leaders of the NSDAP believed the time was right to stage a coup in Munich. A meeting by three key Bavarian officials, Gustav Ritter von Kahr, the Bavarian State Commissioner, General Otto von Lossow, the commander of the Bavarian armed forces, and Colonel Hans von Seisser, the chief of the Bavarian State Police, was planned for the evening of 8 November in the Bürgerbraukeller beer hall. It was the anniversary of the 1919 revolution. Armed groups would seize key buildings around the

Himmler carries the flag at one the barricades thrown up across Munich.

Ernst Röhm was a supporter of the Munich Putsch.

city, and Röhm was tasked with taking the army headquarters. Meanwhile, Hitler and the party leaders would take the statesmen hostage and hold them until their demands were met.

Over 600 SA men surrounded the building, placing a machine gun outside the front door, while Hitler and more SA men infiltrated the 3,000-strong crowd inside. As Kahr spoke to the audience, SA men blocked the exits. Hitler then jumped on a chair and fired a shot into the ceiling to silence the crowd. After declaring that 'the national revolution has broken out!' he explained that his supporters had already seized the army barracks and police headquarters. While the SA men kept watch on the uneasy crowd, Kahr, Lossow and Seisser were bundled into a side room where Hitler informed them that a new government led by General Erich Ludendorff was going to be formed.

All three refused to cooperate and Hitler burst into a rage and stormed back onto the stage, declaring that 'tomorrow will find a national government in Germany, or it will find us dead!' General Ludendorff's appearance on the stage was greeted with a huge cheer, relieving the tension. However, the three prisoners escaped in the confusion.

Across the city the plan to seize key buildings was not going to plan and news of the coup had reached the Reichswehr commander, General Hans von Seeckt. Troops were already being mobilised to help the Munich authorities restore control.

Hitler became increasingly depressed as the night hours passed but as 9 November dawned, Ludendorff convinced him to stage a march through the city. If he could get the support of the crowds gathering around the beer hall, they could lead them to the Ministry of War and hold an impromptu rally.

At midday, Hitler, Ludendorff, Göring and Julius Streicher led 2,000 SA men, NSDAP supporters, right-wing groups and hangers-on towards the centre of the city. The guard on the bridge over the River Isar stood aside and the crowd headed towards the town hall where more people were waiting, swelling the number of marching to 3,000 as it headed past the Bavarian palace.

A Free Corps unit drives through the crowds gathered outside Munich City Hall.

An armed police cordon blocked the street leading into Odeonplatz and the crowd came to a standstill. The uneasy standoff was broken when Hitler called upon the police to let them past. They refused and pandemonium broke out when shots were fired. Sixteen NSDAP supporters (see below) and three policemen were killed in the gun battle that followed. Göring was wounded while Hitler fell to the ground, injuring his shoulder. Ludendorff was one of the few to stand his ground and he successfully called upon the police to hold their fire.

The panicked crowd quickly dispersed and Hitler was hurried to safety at Ernst Hanfstangl's house. He was arrested two days later and held awaiting trial. Although Hitler initially thought that the failure of the Putsch was the end of his political ambitions, the newspapers were full of stories about it. The NSDAP had the attention of the German people it desired.

A funeral cortege carries the martyrs' coffins through Munich to their new resting place.

THE NAZI 'MARTYRS'

Felix Alfarth
Andreas Bauriedl
Theodor Casella
Wilhelm Ehrlich
Martin Faust
Anton Hechenberger
Oskar Korner
Karl Kuhn
Karl Laforce
Kurt Neubauer
Klaus von Pape
Theodor von der Pfordten
Joh Rickmers
Max von Scheubner-Richter
Lorenz Ritter von Stransky
Wilhelm Wolf

After the Nazis came to power, the martyrs' sarcophagi were placed in two purpose-built Temples of Honour in Königsplatz, next to Hitler's office in the centre of Munich. They were often used as a focal point during ceremonies, particularly during the ceremonies held on the anniversary of the Putsch.

THE BAVARIAN STATE COMMISSIONER

GUSTAV VON KAHR (1862–1934)

Kahr was head of the right-wing nationalist Bavarian People's Party. He was President of Upper Bavaria in 1917 and Prime Minister of Bavaria from 1920 to 1921. When President Friedrich Ebert declared a state of emergency in September 1923, Kahr was appointed General State Commissioner. Two months later he was taken hostage during the Munich Putsch but escaped after refusing to cooperate with Hitler. Kahr became the target of Nazi political slurs and he resigned from the post of commissioner in February 1924. Hitler never forgot how he had undermined the Munich Putsch. The 71-year-old Kahr was murdered during the June 1934 Blood Purge and his body was dumped in a swamp.

HITLER'S CONSPIRATOR

ERICH LUDENDORFF (1865–1937)

Ludendorff served in the Cadet Corps before joining the General Staff in 1908. After spending four years working on the Schlieffen Plan, Germany's war plan, he commanded an infantry brigade. In August 1914 he made a name for himself by leading the capture of the Belgian fortress of Liege. Ludendorff went on to become General Paul von Hindenburg's chief of staff, and they defeated the Russia's attacks against East Prussia in August and September 1914.

The two transferred from the Eastern Front to France in August 1916, where they eased the German Army's situation by withdrawing to the Hindenburg Line, a shortened line of

The accused; Heinz Pernet, Dr Friedrich Weber, Wilhelm Frick, Hermann Kriebel, Erich Ludendorff, Adolf Hitler, Wilhelm Brückner, Ernst Röhm and Robert Wagner.

prepared trenches. Ludendorff also worked to agree the Treaty of Brest Litovsk with Bolshevik Russia in March 1918.

The German offensives in the spring of 1918 failed to defeat the Allies and Ludendorff became increasingly despondent, urging for peace in the autumn. He was dismissed by Prince Max of Baden and went into exile in Sweden in October 1918.

Ludendorff returned to Germany in 1919 as a supporter of right-wing nationalist causes. He took part in the Kapp Putsch in 1920 and the NSDAP Putsch in 1923, heading the fateful march through the city. He was acquitted at the subsequent trial. Ludendorff formed the National Socialist Freedom Party with Gregor Strasser while Hitler was in jail. He was a delegate in the Reichstag from 1924–1928 and stood as the National Socialist Presidential delegate in 1925. He founded the Tannenberg League in 1926, an anti-communist, anti-Semitic and anti-Masonic organisation but it was overshadowed by the expanding NSDAP. Ludendorff became an eccentric pacifist towards the end of his life and became bitter enemies with Hitler and President Hindenburg, his old commanding officer.

THE MUNICH TRIAL

The trial of the Putsch leaders began on 24 February 1924 in Munich's Infantry Officers' School. The ten defendants, including Adolf Hitler, Erich Ludendorff, Wilhelm Frick and Ernst Röhm, appeared before two judges and three laymen, charged with conspiracy to commit treason. Over the next 24 days, Judge Georg Neithardt allowed Hitler to make several political speeches. Hitler knew he could implicate politicians and generals alike but he took the blame, portraying himself as Germany's saviour. The trial received a large amount of publicity across Germany; crowds gathered around the court room, and dozens of reporters gave it extensive coverage in the newspapers.

Nine of the ten were convicted of high treason when the verdict was announced on 1 April 1924. Only Ludendorff was acquitted. Hitler was facing a maximum life imprisonment but he was only given the minimum term, five years. He was also held as someone acting from honourable motives and given celebrity treatment in prison. He had his own cell, was allowed to wear his own clothes, choose his food and have numerous visitors. He also dictated of the first volume of his book, *Mein Kampf*, to his secretary Rudolf Hess during his stay. Hitler was released after only nine months in Landsberg prison.

THE NSDAP IN HITLER'S ABSENCE

Alfred Rosenberg stood in as leader of the NSDAP while Hitler was in prison, but he was neither a leader nor an administrator and the party splintered. The National Socialist Freedom Party was formed in April 1924 and a month later it won nearly two million votes and 32 of its 34 delegates – including Gregor Strasser, General Ludendorff and Ernst Rohm – won seats in the Reichstag elections. The SA also continued under the name *Frontbann*, and members met under the guise of sports clubs, singing clubs and rifle clubs.

Hitler contemplates
his future in
Landsberg Prison.

CHAPTER TWO

THE RISE TO POWER

DECEMBER 1925 TO JANUARY 1933

There were a large number of elections between 1925 and 1933 and they fell into three categories; the Presidential elections, the *Reichstag* elections and the state elections for the *Reichsrat*. The campaigns were inextricably linked, particularly during the politically turbulent early 1930s. While Hitler stood against President Hindenburg in the Presidential elections in 1932, the NSDAP focused on winning a majority in the Reichstag.

THE OPPOSITION PARTIES

KPD	German Communist Party
DDP	German Democratic Party
SPD	Social Democratic Party
DVP	German People's Party
Centre	Catholic Centre Party
BVP	Bavarian People's Party
DNVP	German Nationalist Party
NSDAP	National Socialists

THE GERMAN COMMUNIST PARTY (KPD) AND ERNST THÄLMANN (1886–1944)

Opposition to the war and food shortages at the end of the First World War led to riots and strikes across Germany. The Independent Social Democrats and the Spartakus League broke away from the mainstream Social Democrats and they called for action after Friedrich Ebert became Chancellor. The Spartacists seized power in Berlin in January 1919 but they failed to win army support and the Free Corps crushed their uprising; the revolution leaders, Karl Liebknecht and Rosa Luxemburg, were murdered. Bavaria becoming a short-lived Soviet state following another uprising, but the Free Corps again restored order.

The Moscow-based international communist organisation was called the Comintern and the first Communist Party congress in 1920 inspired Walther Ulbricht (1893–1973) to form the United Communist Party of Germany. It was renamed the German Communist

Communist leader, Ernst Thälmann.

Party and grew into the strongest communist party outside the Soviet Union. The Comintern initially insisted that the party side with the NSDAP in the fight against the Social Democrats and members supported the Munich Beer Hall Putsch.

Ernst Thälmann encouraged cooperation with the NSDAP and the communist paramilitary Red Front Fighters fought alongside the SA troopers against the Social Democrats. The KPD doubled their support as Germany's economic situation deteriorated in 1930 and it became the third strongest party in the Reichstag elections; Thälmann also came third in the 1932 presidential elections.

The Communist Party was the Nazis' first target after they seized power. On 25 February 1933 SA troopers broke into the KPD's Berlin headquarters and seized documents allegedly calling for a communist uprising against the government. Two nights later the Reichstag was set on fire and the NSDAP leaders blamed the communists. Hundreds of KPD members – including Ernst Thälmann and Ernst Torgler – were arrested and held in concentration camps. A few, including Walther Ulbricht, escaped to Russia.

Raising support for the Nazis at a university. (NARA-242-HB-00077)

THE GERMAN DEMOCRATIC PARTY (DDP)

The left-wing liberal party was founded in November 1918 and it soon had around eighteen per cent of the vote. It supported a democratic, republican form of government and while it advocated nationalism it also called for international collaboration and the protection of ethnic minorities. Popularity fell steadily and the adoption of a new name, the German State Party, in 1930 did not stop its share of the vote falling to one per cent.

Members were generally middle-class entrepreneurs, civil servants, teachers, scientists and craftsmen; right-wing nationalists often referred to it a party of Jews and professors. Prominent members were Hugo Preuss, the main author of the Weimar constitution, the sociologist Max Weber and Hjalmar Schacht, president of the Reichsbank. Schacht defected to the NSDAP when they came to power in 1933.

THE SOCIAL DEMOCRATIC PARTY (SPD)

The party had a central bias but many members left after it voted in favour of going to war in 1914. The defectors formed the Communist Party and the intense rivalry between the two parties continued throughout the 1920s. The Social Democrats became part of the Weimar Coalition, leading many of the short-lived cabinets between 1919 and 1933. The party continuously wrestled between supporting moderate policies (to appeal to the middle classes), and radical policies (to appeal to the working classes).

OTTO WELS (1873–1939)
Wels was a veteran member of the Reichstag when he became chairman of the SPD in 1931. His pleas to oppose the Enabling Act on 23 March 1933 failed and he escaped to Prague when the party disintegrated in May. He had to flee again when the Germans occupied Czechoslovakia. He died in Paris on 16 September 1939.

OTTO BRAUN (1872–1955)
Braun was the Minister-President of Prussia and led a coalition of Social Democrats and Central Parties from 1925 until he was ousted from office by Franz von Papen in July 1932. He went into exile in Switzerland in March 1933, fearing for his life.

JULIUS LEBER (1891–1945)
Leber was a leading member of the SPD who stood up to the National Socialists in the Reichstag for over ten years. He survived an assassination attempt the day after Hitler was appointed Chancellor in January 1933 and he was arrested following the Reichstag fire a month later; he spent the next four years in concentration camps.

THE GERMAN PEOPLE'S PARTY (DVP) AND GUSTAV STRESEMANN (1878-1929)

Gustav Stresemann and his right-wing liberal party represented the interests of the great German industrialists. While it advocated Christian family values and lower tariffs it opposed welfare spending and farming subsides. The party only had around eight per cent of the vote

SA troopers mingle with the public during a meeting. (NARA-242-HB-00202)

and while it initially opposed the Weimar Coalition, it eventually cooperated with the centre and left-wing parties. Stresemann was the Weimar Republic's only statesman of international standing and he served briefly as Chancellor, resigning shortly after the Munich Putsch in November 1923. He continued to serve as Foreign Minister until his death in October 1929. The party shifted further towards the right but its influence declined and it lost a third of its Reichstag seats in September 1930.

THE CATHOLIC CENTRE PARTY (CENTRE) AND MONSIGNOR LUDWIG KAAS (1881–1952)

The Centre Party was the second largest party in Germany in 1919. It formed coalition governments with the Social Democrats and the German Democrats and provided four chancellors. It did, however, have internal problems. While the centre of the party was loyal to the Church, the left had ties with Christian trade unions and the right had ties with nationalist movements. The party's share of the vote fell to ten per cent and in 1928 Monsignor Ludwig Kaas was elected in the hope that he would unite the party; it soon became clear that he was more concerned with defending the Church.

Although the party retained its share of the vote, it fell behind the communists and the Nazis after 1930. It supported Chancellor Brüning's government in 1932 but rejected Franz von Papen later in the year, accusing him of distorting the party's ideals; Papen left shortly afterwards. The party had campaigned against the NSDAP but it started its own negotiations with Hitler after Papen's attempts failed. It did not support Chancellor Schleicher's administration at the end of 1932.

Monsignor Kaas had hoped to form a coalition with the NSDAP and he fell for Hitler's false offers of cooperation. The March 1933 election gave the NSDAP and the Nationalist Party a majority, dashing the Centre's hopes for a coalition. Kaas wanted to preserve the rights of the Church and he believed Hitler's promise to guarantee civil liberties; the promise was never kept. The party disbanded in July 1933 and Kaas emigrated in disgust. He was appointed to a senior post in the Vatican with responsibility for Germany.

THE BAVARIAN PEOPLE'S PARTY (BVP)

The BVP split from the Centre Party in 1919 to pursue state politics. Bavaria refused to follow Berlin's instructions during the 1923 inflation crisis but the NSDAP Putsch in November 1923 finally forced Gustav von Kahr to cooperate. The party became increasingly moderate under the leadership of Heinrich Held and he became Prime Minister of Bavaria in 1924. He continued to work against separatism but his party never had more than five per cent of the Reichstag vote. The Bavarian government was forcibly removed by the Nazis on 9 March 1933. While Held fled to Switzerland, his son was held in Dachau concentration camp.

THE GERMAN NATIONALIST PEOPLE'S PARTY (DNVP)

Alfred Hugenberg (1865–1951) built up a huge business empire during the First World War and used his personal wealth to combine business with politics. Newspapers, publishing houses and the UFA film company were added to his portfolio and he became the main player in the German film and press industries.

Hardly anyone notices as an SA unit parades through the streets. (NARA-242-HB-00101)

Hugenberg became chairman of the DNVP in 1928 when it had over 70 delegates in the Reichstag and it opposed the Young Plan. The party's popularity suffered over the next five years and Hugenberg became increasingly involved in political intrigues. He tried to form a right-wing alliance opposition to the government at the Harzburg Front meeting in October 1931 but Hitler refused to join.

The DNVP was the only party to support Franz von Papen when he was defeated in July 1932. Hugenberg then supported Schleicher's cabinet but he quickly became disillusioned and transferred his support to Hitler, playing an important role in negotiating his chancellorship. He had hoped to control the Nazis, and while he was made the Reich Minister of Economy and Agriculture in Hitler's first cabinet, his party's share of the vote fell to eight per cent in March 1933. After seeing SA troopers attacking party members, Hugenberg resigned in June 1933 and dissolved the party.

REFORMING THE NSDAP
DECEMBER 1924 TO FEBRUARY 1926

Hitler was released from Landsberg Prison on 20 December 1924 after serving only nine months of his five-year sentence; he was lucky not to be repatriated to Austria. The ban on the NSDAP was lifted on 16 February but their leader was still barred from speaking in public in many states. Six days later 100 district leaders pledged their loyalty to Hitler and over 3,000 people attended the first party meeting in the Bürgerbräukeller in Munich on 27 February. Bavaria banned Hitler from speaking in public a few days later.

George Strasser joined the NSDAP in Berlin in March 1924 and he spent the summer raising the NSDAP's profile across northern Germany. The first 'defence echelon' unit, the *Schutzstaffel*, was formed in April from Hitler's personal bodyguard; it was the first SS unit.

President Friedrich Ebert had died on 28 February and Field Marshal Hindenburg was elected the second President of the Weimar Republic in a runoff election on 26 April. Hitler had persuaded General Ludendorff to stand but he only returned one per cent of the vote.

Hitler spent the summer of 1924 writing the second volume of his book in the Bavarian mountains. Strasser spent the summer campaigning across northern Germany, increasing the number of branches under his control to 250 by the end of the year. He was becoming disillusioned with the Bavarian-dominated party leadership and he made his grievances clear

Hitler on his early release from Landsberg Prison.

Hitler resumed leadership of the NSDAP after it fell to pieces under Alfred Rosenberg.

to the northern leadership on 10 September; it would not be the last time he argued with them. While he represented the urban, socialist, revolutionary side of politics, the south was advocating rural, racial and populist politics. Strasser also drew up a new party programme in November 1924.

Over the winter, differences between north and south intensified and Hitler finally called a party congress so they could be settled. While he tended to support the southerners view, he needed the northerners' support. The congress was held on 14 February in Bamberg, Franconia, but only two northern leaders attended: Gregor Strasser and his new assistant, Dr Joseph Goebbels.

Hitler made it clear that he was looking for support from both sides and that he would only use legal means to gain political and financial support. He also agreed to exclude Hermann Esser, the corrupt propagandist based in Munich, to gain northern support. While Strasser agreed to party unity and withdrew his programme, he was still dissatisfied with the outcome of the meeting. Goebbels, however, had been impressed by Hitler's performance and he switched his allegiance to support the party leader. He was appointed Berlin's *Gauleiter* as a reward.

NORTHERN OPPOSITION

GREGOR STRASSER (1892–1934) AND OTTO STRASSER (1897–1974)

Gregor was a decorated officer of the First World War and served in the Free Corps before joining the NSDAP in 1920. He was imprisoned for leading an SA detachment during the Munich Putsch and he joined Ludendorff's National Socialist Freedom Movement on his release. Although he was elected to the Bavarian Landtag in 1924, the Movement dissolved when Hitler was released from prison.

Otto joined the NSDAP in 1925 and worked alongside his older brother to increase NSDAP support across northern Germany. They founded the *Berlin Workers' Paper* and the newsletter *National Socialist Letters,* appointing Dr Paul Joseph Goebbels as their editor. The brothers became increasingly estranged from the Munich side of the party and although Gregor was

The strength of the NSDAP in the north: Gregor Strasser and Joseph Goebbels.

an able organiser and a shrewd politician, he was a poor speaker. He reluctantly agreed to follow the party line after the Bamberg Party Congress in February 1926.

The brothers continued to call for sweeping nationalisation and strikes, angering Hitler who was looking to gain political and financial support from industrialists. Hitler retaliated by arranging to buy shares in the Strassers' publishing house before closing it down. When it reopened, the *Berlin Workers' Paper* was only printed once a week while Goebbels' rival publication, *The Attack*, became a daily publication.

The brothers continued to stir up trouble in the party by presenting their own style of politics until Hitler confronted them on 21 May 1930. While Gregor agreed to cooperate, Otto refused and he was expelled from the party in July. Otto formed the Union of Revolutionary National Socialists, or the Black Front, with Walther Stennes the following year. It soon folded and Strasser went into exile in Prague, Czechoslovakia.

Gregor was appointed the Reich Organisation Leader in June 1932 but he disagreed with Hitler's decision to appoint Göring as President of the Reichstag when the NSDAP finally gained the majority. On 7 December 1932, Chancellor Kurt von Schleicher offered Strasser the vice-chancellorship and the Premiership of Prussia in the hope of splitting the Nazis. Hitler was furious when he found out and Strasser resigned in the argument that followed.

Gregor Strasser quit politics but Hitler never forgot the trouble he had caused over the years. He was arrested and executed in the Berlin Gestapo headquarters during the Blood Purge on 30 June 1934. Otto had to flee when German troops entered Czechoslovakia, and he went via Switzerland into France, pursued by agents from the German Security Service. He wrote an account of the Night of the Long Knives and published it in memory of his brother.

THE STRUGGLE FOR SUPPORT
MARCH 1926 TO OCTOBER 1929

In the summer of 1926, Hitler made it clear that the party membership had to unify behind him as their leader if the NSDAP was to succeed. On 3 and 4 July around 7,500 members met for the Annual Party Day in Weimar, Thuringia, one of the few cities where Hitler was allowed to speak. The SS paraded for the first time; there were 116 men. Afterwards, Hitler retired to the mountains above Berchtesgaden for a summer break.

Gregor Strasser was appointed Party Propaganda Leader in September 1926 while Goebbels was appointed Gauleiter of Berlin in December. Their tireless activities increased

Top: An early
meeting of the
NSDAP leadership.

Above: The SA
poster supports
'Death to Marxism'.

membership to 75,000 and over 30,000 attended the August 1927 Annual Party Day in Nuremberg. The spring of 1928 was spent preparing for the Reichstag elections and while Hitler spoke to thousands across Bavaria, Strasser and Goebbels continued their work in the north. The party was also restructured into 35 areas, or *Gau*, to match the delegate system across Germany.

On 20 May 1928 the NSDAP only returned 810,000 votes, 2.6 per cent of the vote, but they returned twelve delegates.

Party	SPD	DNVP	DVP	Centre	DDPS	BVP	KPD	Others	Nazis
Delegates	153	73	24	62	25	16	54	44	12

The Nazis analysed their support and discovered that while they had failed to make inroads into the communist-dominated urban areas, they had gained support in Protestant rural areas. They concluded that they could get more votes for less money in rural areas. A new agrarian programme was announced to capitalise on the protest vote against the Nationalist Party.

The party could not afford an annual rally and after another summer in the Bavarian mountains, Hitler met his Gauleiters in Munich on 31 August 1928. The future was looking bleak but they made plans to appeal to the people and increase the membership above 100,000. The only good news was that Prussia lifted its speaking ban on Hitler on 28 September, the last state to do so.

VIOLENT POLITICS

German politics between the wars was marred by violence. While political meetings were interrupted by spontaneous violence in the early days, the parties soon realised the political value of disrupting a rival's meeting. Heckling speakers and starting fights became a regular feature at political meetings.

Parties were forced to organise protection squads for their meetings and the Germany Workers' Party's Hall Defence Detachment became known as the NSDAP's Gymnastics and Sports Division, a group of tough war veterans who were not afraid of brawling. They were later called Monitor Troops, *Ordnertruppe*, and they were eventually renamed the Storm Detachment, the *Sturmabteilung* or SA, after one notable fight at the Hofbräuhaus in November

Injured fighting for the cause. (NARA-242-HB-00096)

1921. Party officials also needed protection teams to escort them through the crowds and guard them during meetings. The NSDAP formed Shock Troops, the *Stosstruppen* or SS to escort them and the Stosstrupp-Adolf Hitler became well known in the Munich area.

The Communist Party founded the Red Front Fighters' Association in 1924 and it expanded to over 150,000 men. They often fought alongside the SA. Members wore a green uniform and a red armband. The Social Democrats formed the Black-Red-Gold Banner of the Reich in 1924. Some members of the Centre Party and the Democratic Party also joined. Membership had risen to three million by 1932.

A CHANGE OF FORTUNE
NOVEMBER 1929 TO OCTOBER 1930

As the NSDAP struggled to increase their support, finances were running low and popularity was waning. The Germany economy was also suffering and by the end of 1928 unemployment was almost 3 million, having risen by 50 per cent over the previous twelve months. Chancellor Stresemann renegotiated the reparations settlement but the announcement of the Young Plan in June was attacked by all political parties.

At the end of June the NSDAP was able to celebrate when it took control of its first town council in Coburg, northern Bavaria, but it was usually only returning around five per cent in votes. The size of the crowds at the third Annual Party Day in Nuremberg in August had risen slightly to 40,000 but membership had stagnated at 130,000. The leaders recognised that the NSDAP needed a miracle if it was to become anything more than a fringe party. The miracle started two months later when the stock market crashed.

The Wall Street Crash began with panic selling on 24 October. On 29 October 1929, Black Tuesday, sixteen million shares were traded on the New York Stock Exchange as their value collapsed. Ten billion dollars were wiped off companies, twice the amount of money in circulation in the US; it was the same value as the cost of America's war effort. Over the months

A crowd watches as the Berlin SA parade through the Brandenburg Gate. (NARA-242-HB-00625)

that followed the world was plunged into a long depression, one in which Germany's economy was particularly vulnerable due to its reliance on large investments and short-term American loans. When the US called in all its loans, it placed Germany deeper into debt.

Production in German industry fell 40 per cent in three years. Two major banks failed and credit was in danger of collapsing. As farmers went bankrupt and the cost of imports rose, the spectre of food shortages appeared once again. Six million were unemployed by the end of 1931 but many more were on short hours and reduced wages. Trained people were taking unskilled jobs. Tens of thousands of homeless wandered Germany looking for work, and as

Goebbels plans the next stage of the party's propaganda campaign. (NARA-242-HB-00726)

crime, begging and prostitution rose, everyone was looking for someone to blame.

As taxes from income fell, unemployment benefits rose, placing a huge burden on the economy. Germany's mainstream political parties struggled to provide a solution and the left and right wing parties benefited from their inability to do so. While the Communist Party recruited the unemployed working classes, raising fears of an uprising, the NSDAP targeted the middle classes. A combination of popular politics, new propaganda and publicity brought thousands of members to the party.

Germany was facing financial ruin. In March 1930, Chancellor Hermann Müller resigned over increasing employer contributions to unemployment insurance. Hjalmar Schacht removed the Reichsmark from the gold standard but he refused to print more money and called for wages to be slashed, fearing inflation. He resigned as President of the Reichbank over the Young Plan reparation payments.

Heinrich Brüning, the Catholic Centre Party leader, was appointed Chancellor on 30 March because of his financial expertise. His cabinet was filled with experts and it ruled by decree in an attempt to solve the crisis quickly. He proposed cutting government expenditure and slashing unemployment benefits to balance the books. The Reichstag refused to accept his proposals and he was forced to dismiss the cabinet on 18 July.

Meanwhile, the economic mess allowed the NSDAP to continue attacking the main political parties for failing to solve Germany's financial problems. Voters started switching their allegiance to the NSDAP and in January 1930 Wilhelm Frick became the first party delegate to be appointed to a State Ministry in Thuringia as Minister of the Interior and Minister of Education. He quickly implemented nationalist and anti-Semitic policies across the state, a warning of what the future held.

Dr Joseph Goebbels was promoted to head the NSDAP's propaganda on 27 April and one of his first projects was to create a new Nazi martyr. Horst Wessel had joined the NSDAP and the SA in 1926. While earning a living as a pimp, he was killed on 23 February 1930 after an argument with communist sympathisers over the rent on his Berlin slum. Goebbels adopted a song he had written about the SA, the 'Horst Wessel Lied', as the party anthem and it would become as popular as the national anthem. The leader of Wessel's killers was murdered a few days after the Nazis seized power in 1933.

Goebbels and Strasser spent the summer campaigning and all the party leaders worked hard, addressing local concerns at key hustings. Most were youthful and energetic, still in their late thirties, far younger than other politicians, and they attracted young first time voters; they also targeted women voters. Their efforts were rewarded in spectacular fashion in the September 1930 Reichstag election. The NSDAP returned 107 delegates with 6,371,000 votes, a huge increase, making it the second largest party.

Party	SPD	DNVP	DVP	Centre	DDPS	BVP	KPD	Others	Nazis
Delegates	143	41	30	68	20	19	77	51	107

The economic crisis was forcing voters to the extremes of the political spectrum. While the NSDAP had again won landslide support in many Protestant farming communities, the communists had benefited in working-class urban areas.

On 5 October 1930 Chancellor Brüning asked the NSDAP for cooperation in the Reichstag, while it worked to ease Germany's problems. Hitler, Frick and Strasser refused; the NSDAP was benefiting from the political unrest. Meanwhile, the Nazi and Communist delegates were turning the Reichstag into a rabble. Chancellor Brüning responded by defining the situation as a national emergency and he implemented Article 48 of the Weimar Constitution. The Reichstag was adjourned in February 1931 for six months. The number of times it met fell from an average of twice a week in 1930 to once a fortnight by end of 1932. Nothing was being solved. Political intrigues were revolving around the man who could appoint ministers, dismiss cabinets and issue decrees – the ailing President Hindenburg.

A small audience listens to a speaker announcing 'Germany Awake!' (NARA-242-HB-00025)

POLITICAL MEETINGS

The basis of the NSDAP's success in the election campaigns was the endless succession of political meetings, and the party leaders toured the country speaking to the public (it was particularly important in these pre-television days). The Nazis became masters at holding mass meetings and they used stage managers to control the lighting and sound to turn the crowd's suspense into a frenzy. Indoor and outdoor political rallies also raised large amounts of revenue and local members were encouraged to help organise local events.

While the local NSDAP office hired a large hall and placed announcements in the newspapers, local leaders urged members to put up posters and hand out leaflets to advertise the meeting. On the day, people queued outside the flag-draped hall waiting to buy their ticket, and they were prepared to wait for hours if the speaker was a senior party official. As they waited, SA troopers paraded and sang party songs to entertain the crowds and raise the unit's profile. Street sellers also sold newspapers, pamphlets and song books.

When the doors finally opened, the crowd filed in and took their places on the rows of benches. The speakers' platform was draped with swastika flags at the front of the hall while pine branches and bunting dressed up the stage. While a military band played, the crowd read the newspapers and leaflets, while noting the political banners hanging from the balconies. Security was low-key; while SA men lined the walls of the hall, NSDAP

Crowds pack into the Berlin Sports Palace to hear Hitler speak. (NARA-242-HB-00764)

members mingled with the crowd looking for troublemakers.

Suddenly a fanfare of trumpets and drums heralded the speaker's arrival and the doors were flung open. NSDAP members in the crowd jumped up, shouting '*Sieg Heil*', spurring the audience to echo the rallying call. SA troopers held the crowd back as they strained to catch a glimpse of the speaker, while a cordon of SS troopers escorted him to the stage. As the speaker took his seat in the front row, the band and the crowd fell silent allowing the local party chairman to open the meeting and make the introductions.

The speaker then took his place at the rostrum and began to speak as the crowd strained to hear his words. Hitler was a master at working the crowd. He started quietly, almost pleading to the audience to listen. He worked himself up into a passionate crescendo of demands, shouting while flailing his arms. By the end of the speech, the crowd were on their feet, saluting and shouting '*Heil, Heil, Heil!*'

The rousing verses of '*Horst Wessel Lied*' brought the meeting to a close as the SS troopers escorted the speaker to safety. As the crowds queued to leave the SA troopers distributed membership forms and rattled collection tins, raising money for the next meeting.

BECOMING THE LARGEST PARTY
NOVEMBER 1930 TO JULY 1932

After the success of September 1930, the NSDAP had to be taken seriously in the Reichstag. They had risen from nothing to the second largest party in a short space of time. The only setback came on 18 September 1931 when Angela Raubal, or Geli, Hitler's niece and companion, committed suicide in his Munich apartment. The party's popularity had placed extra demands on Hitler's time and pressures on their close friendship. There were rumours that she had been murdered but they were never proved. Hitler fell into a deep depression after her death but the rest of the party leadership rallied round to keep up the momentum.

The leader of the German Nationalists, Alfred Hugenberg, had already tried to get the NSDAP's support in opposing the Young Plan back in 1928. He tried again on 11 October 1931, meeting right-wing nationalists, landowners, industrialists and the Steel Helmet in Bad Harzburg, Brunswick. This time he wanted to bring down Chancellor Brüning's government but Hitler again refused to offer support, fearing that it could undermine his political position. The Harzburg Front failed without the support of the NSDAP Reichstag delegates.

Hitler was determined to go it alone but the NSDAP needed extra money to finance its election campaigns, and on 27 January 1932 he spoke to 650 Rhineland industrialists in Düsseldorf. He attacked communism and the trade unions in an attempt win their backing and their money. Although the response was not as enthusiastic as he wanted, the party received enough money to help it through the two crucial elections in 1932.

THE PRESIDENTIAL ELECTIONS

Friedrich Ebert, the first President of the Weimar Republic, died on 28 February 1925. Candidates for the new presidential election could either represent a single political party or a coalition of parties. Field Marshal Paul von Hindenburg represented a coalition of right wing parties and he beat Wilhelm Marx on 26 April 1925. Although Hindenburg intended to remain out of politics, Otto Meissner, Chief of the Presidential Chancellery, persuaded him to step in when the economic crisis deepened in 1930. Although Meissner's intentions were sound, the ailing President was soon bombarded with ideas from scheming politicians and army officers, particularly General Kurt von Schleicher and Franz von Papen.

Hitler votes. (NARA-242-HB-04121)

The Weimar Republic President had to face re-election after seven years and Hindenburg's turn came in the spring of 1932, in the middle of Germany's financial crisis. Although Hitler was asked to confirm Hindenburg to avoid a presidential election, he declined. He saw it as another opportunity to showcase the party and he announced his intention to stand on 22 February. Hitler did not have German citizenship but four days later he was nominated to be a civil servant, granting him the necessary paperwork.

The Social Democrats and the centre parties formed the Iron Front to support Hindenburg and although he won the vote on 13 March, he narrowly failed to secure the required 50 per cent majority.

Hindenburg	Centre coalition	18.7 million
Hitler	NSDAP	11.3 million
Thaelmann	Communist	5.0 million
Dusterberg	Nationalist	2.6 million

Dusterberg was eliminated from the second election. Hitler took the opportunity to fly to twenty locations across Germany, speaking to nearly one million people. While Hindenburg secured a majority on 10 April 1932 with 53 per cent of the vote, Hitler had increased his share of the vote and his exposure to the public. Even though he had won, Hindenburg was angry that the nationalist parties had supported Hitler rather than him.

Hindenburg	Centre coalition	19.4 million
Hitler	NSDAP	13.4 million
Thaelmann	Communist	3.7 million

BANNING THE BROWNSHIRTS
THE SUMMER OF 1932

Franz Pfeffer von Salomon had been head of the SA since September 1927 but he was sacked during the August 1930 election following disagreements with Hitler. Hitler asked Ernst Röhm to return from Bolivia in January 1931, offering him leadership of SA, and the latter accepted. Röhm introduced military training and increased recruitment, quadrupling membership to 400,000 by the end of the year.

The SA presence on the streets was becoming a concern as political unrest increased and thousands of storm troopers were brought to trial for violent behaviour. Over 400 SA men were killed while hundreds more were injured during this turbulent period, as were an equal number of political opponents. Martin Bormann administered the National Socialist Relief Fund, an insurance plan for members injured fighting for the cause. The NSDAP portrayed fallen SA men as matyrs, and the party leaders turned their funerals into political rallies, portraying their killers as brutal thugs.

The street violence was getting out of hand by early 1932 and when plans for a military-style government if the NSDAP won the upcoming election were discovered, action had to be taken. The SA reacted to a ban on political uniforms by marching in white shirts; the effect was the same. The SA and the communist Red Front Fighters had to be banned by Wilhelm Groener, the Minister of the Interior, on 14 April, in the hope of restoring order on the streets. At the same time the police raided SA offices, confiscating weapons, flags and banners.

WILHELM GROENER (1867–1939)
Groener had been the first quartermaster general in the German Army when the Armistice was declared. He was appointed Minister of Defence in 1928 and acting Minister of the Interior in 1931, with the help of his benefactor, General von Schleicher. Göring and other Nazi deputies fiercely attacked Groener's decision to ban the SA and the SS even though he was suffering from a serious illness. He retired immediately afterwards and died in May 1939.

The SS protection squadron surrounds the stage; Röhm stands behind Hitler. (NARA-242-HB-00969)

CHANCELLOR BRÜNING RESIGNS

The ban on the SA did not have time to have an impact on the state elections on 24 April 1932. The NSDAP had started promoting Hitler as the face of the party and it won 36 per cent of the vote in Prussia, increasing its number of seats from 9 to 162. It also returned 32 per cent in Bavaria and 26 per cent in Wurttemberg. Their biggest victory was 41 per cent of the vote in Saxony-Anhalt, south-west of Berlin, where the first Nazi State President was appointed.

On 7 May, General Kurt von Schleicher asked the NSDAP for help in attempting to remove Brüning; in return he would lobby for the removal of the ban on the SA. The cabinet's deflationary policies were proving unpopular while the deepening economic crisis

was a cause for concern. The NSDAP supported Schleicher's suggestion and Brüning eventually resigned on 30 May on Hindenburg's request.

The new Chancellor was Franz von Papen, another Centre Party politician, but he accepted the post without the permission of his party; he resigned from the party two days later. Papen formed a new conservative cabinet called the 'Cabinet of Barons' because of the high number of titled ministers appointed to it. They had little experience and few party affiliations. Papen was also anxious to secure Hitler's support and on 16 June he lifted the ban on the SA and SS. It allowed the Nazis to start their Reichstag election campaign, a six-week campaign marred by violence; dozens were killed and hundreds were injured as political riots erupted across the country. The Prussian police were unable to control the violence and Papen was forced to wrest control from the Social Democrats and declare a state of emergency in Berlin as the army stepped in to quell the spectre of civil war.

Hitler led the exhaustive campaign, visiting 53 towns and cities in July. Mass rallies were another feature of the NSDAP's campaign and 120,000 people heard him speak while another 100,000 listened via loudspeakers at the Grunewald Stadium in Berlin alone. The hard work paid off and on 31 July the NSDAP doubled its number of voters, from 6.4 to 13.8 million. It was now the largest party in the Reichstag with 230 delegates and 37 per cent of the vote:

Party	SPD	DNVP	DVP	Centre	DDPS	BVP	KPD	Others	Nazis
Delegates	133	37	7	75	4	22	89	2	230

The biggest losers had again been the Social Democrats and the Centre parties but the NSDAP had also secured a large proportion of first-time voters due to its tireless electioneering.

THE STRUGGLE FOR LEGITIMATE POWER

The 1923 Beer Hall Putsch had proved that armed revolution was not the way to seize power and Hitler always vowed to use legal means to win political power, even if his view on what

The SA practise military drill. (NARA-242-HB-00995)

was legal was twisted. Once in power, the law could be changed to suit the NSDAP policies. Although this lawful approach could take years to accomplish, Hitler was determined to pursue it. Some of the SA commanders condemned his views and believed they were doomed to failure. Hitler emphasised his desire to support the law when he stood as a witness when Reichswehr officers who were NSDAP members were put on trial in Ulm in 1930.

In November 1931, senior NSDAP members, led by Werner Best, drew up emergency plans on how to seize power if there was a local communist uprising. The plans included the drastic proclamations and emergency decrees a provincial government needed to restore order quickly. While perpetrators would be tried before special courts martial, anyone resisting arrest would be executed. Property rights would be suspended and interest debts would be annulled. Unpaid work would be made compulsory while soup kitchens would be deployed.

A public scandal erupted when the documents were discovered in Boxheim House, near Worms, where the meetings had been held. Hitler denied knowledge of the plans but he was forced to reassure the party's financial backers that he was still dedicated to using legal means.

Hitler gave an insight into his real views on legality in the autumn of 1932. On 9 August five Nazis were arrested after beating Konrad Pietrzuch to death in Potempa, Upper Silesia. Hitler telegrammed the court, giving the men support while denouncing the dead man as a communist, a Pole and an enemy of Germany. The five men were jailed and sentenced to death. The Nazis announced an amnesty for any crimes committed 'for the good of the Reich during the Weimar Republic' on 21 March 1934 and the five men were released.

FALLING FROM FAVOUR
AUGUST 1932 TO NOVEMBER 1932

The July 1932 election left Chancellor Papen in a difficult position. While his cabinet was unconstitutional, most of the ministers supported it. However, Hitler was demanding the chancellorship behind the scenes. He spoke to Schleicher on 6 August but Hindenburg vehemently refused to agree to his appointment. On 11 August Schleicher and Papen offered Hitler the vice-chancellorship but Hitler refused. Two days later, a meeting between Hindenburg and Hitler ended abruptly when Hitler refused the President's offer of a cabinet post. He wanted the chancellorship or nothing.

The first Reichstag sitting on 30 August resulted in a coup for the Nazis when Hermann Göring was voted in as President, giving the NSDAP a degree of control over the turbulent chamber. Although Hindenburg had already given Papen a dissolution order, there was an unconstitutional postponement due to the country's difficult position. Germany needed a stable Reichstag but it was not going to get one. The Communists proposed a vote of no confidence against Papen's cabinet at the second Reichstag sitting on 12 September and there were no objections. As the cabinet walked out of the chamber, Papen ordered Göring to dissolve the Reichstag. Göring ignored the Chancellor and proposed a vote of no confidence after he had left. It was passed 512 to 42. The Nazis now had another election to plan for.

Hitler made his fourth flying visit around Germany, speaking to hundreds of thousands in 50 cities, exhausting the party coffers. However, the voters were becoming disillusioned by the constant campaigning and the election on 6 November was a disappointment. The NSDAP only returned 196 deputies, a loss of two million votes and 34 seats.

Party	SPD	DNVP	DVP	Centre	DDPS	BVP	KPD	Others	Nazis
Delegate	121	52	11	70	—	20	100	—	196

To make matters worse, the Communists had returned 750,000 votes, increasing their number of delegates. Although the NSDAP was still the largest political party in the Reichstag, it could not command an overall majority even if it allied with the nationalists. The future was looking bleak for the NSDAP.

THE FINAL INTRIGUING
NOVEMBER 1932 TO JANUARY 1933

Hitler rejected Papen's request to cooperate with the government on 16 November and the cabinet resigned the following day. Attempts to get Hitler to cooperate with the government three days later also failed. The Weimar government was now incapable of functioning. Papen considered ruling by decree and changing the constitution while the army and the police kept the peace on the streets. Schleicher also suggested securing an alliance with Strasser and 60 NSDAP deputies who were disillusioned with Hitler's all or nothing plan for the chancellorship.

Hindenburg was also coming under increasing pressure. Industrialists, led by Wilhem Keppler, were petitioning him to appoint Hitler as Chancellor. Hindenburg again refused. He was, however, concerned by Papen's plan to rule by decree. He was not convinced that the army would stand by him if there was a civil war, a view developed by General von Schleicher.

Faced with choosing between a Nazi dictatorship or an army-backed regime, Hindenburg chose Schleicher as Chancellor on 2 December 1932. Although he was the army's favourite it would be the start of 57 days of political backstabbing. Rumours that Schleicher was going to mobilise the army to bypass the Reichstag and restore order undermined his attempts to stabilise the situation. The intriguing around the President resumed.

Schleicher offered Hitler the vice-chancellorship and the Presidency of Prussia the following day in an attempt to get the NSDAP's support. Hitler refused but Gregor Strasser thought it was a worthwhile offer. On 5 December they argued bitterly over it. Strasser knew that the NSDAP did not have the enough money to pursue the bid for the chancellorship and wanted them to take what they could get. When Hitler refused, Strasser resigned. It made bitter enemies of the two and the party leaders rallied around Hitler, portraying Strasser as a traitor. Strasser did not react and left politics.

On 4 January 1933, Papen met Hitler at the home of the Cologne banker Kurt von Schroeder. Papen was seeking political revenge and he intended use Hitler and the NSDAP to bring down Schleicher's cabinet. Between them they would have the support of the industrialists and the landowners, a powerful combination. Six days later, Hitler ended a second meeting at Joachim von Ribbentrop's house when it became clear that Hindenburg still refused to appoint him Chancellor. Although the meetings were held in secret, news of them soon leaked out.

Schleicher was beginning to feel the pressure from all sides. While land reforms angered Hindenburg, talk of nationalisation angered industrialists. After hearing that Hitler had withdrawn from talks with Papen, Schleicher discussed the dissolution of the cabinet and a postponement of the imminent elections. However, Hitler once again demanded to head the cabinet on 18 January. Just as it appeared that all roads to the chancellorship had been closed, Ribbentrop suggested that it was time to meet President Hindenburg's son, Oskar, and discuss a small matter of tax fraud involving the President.

THE EASTERN AID SCANDAL

The estates in East Prussia had suffered badly during the deteriorating economic situation in the early 1920s. Their separation from the rest of Germany by the Polish Corridor had limited exports. The Reichstag had introduced considerable subsidies to help the estate owners but many had abused them for personal gain.

In 1927 a number of landowners and industrialists had collected funds to buy Hindenburg's ancestral estate in Rosenberg from the President's impoverished brother. The Stahlhelm presented the Neudeck Estate to the President on his eightieth birthday in October, expecting political influence in return. Although the house and the land were legitimate gifts, the estate title was bestowed on Oskar von Hindenburg (1883–1960) to avoid future death duties. The impending fraud had come to the Nazis' attention and they were about to use it in their negotiations for the chancellorship.

On 22 January, Hitler, Frick and Göring met Hindenburg's son and Otto Meisner of the Office of the Presidential Chancellery. They made it clear that the information would be leaked to the public unless Hitler was appointed Chancellor. Oskar had to break the news to his father and the President prepared to submit to Hitler's demands. (Seven months later the Nazis granted another 5,000 acres to the Hindenburg's estate, tax-free.)

On 22 January, Hindenburg's troubles increased when Schleicher made it clear that there was an impending vote of no confidence. The opportunity to appoint Hitler as Chancellor was in sight and on 27 January Ribbentrop held further discussions with Papen. Several cabinet members also made it clear that while they would serve under Hitler they refused to serve under Alfred Hugenberg of the National People's Party. All the political options had been exhausted and when Schleicher was forced resigned on 28 January, Hitler's chance came. Two days later he was appointed Chancellor at the head of a new cabinet.

THE PRESIDENT

PAUL VON HINDENBURG (1847–1934)

Hindenburg was a veteran of the Austro-Prussian War of 1866 and the Franco-Prussian War of 1870–1871. He had retired in 1911 as commander of Fourth Army but was recalled to active duty in August 1914 and served as Supreme Commander on the Eastern Front with General Erich Ludendorff as his chief of staff. The early victories at Tannenberg and the Masurian Lakes were rewarded with promotion to field marshal and he became a favourite commander in the German Army.

Hindenburg succeeded General Erich von Falkenhayn as chief of the General Staff, and he transferred to the Western Front. After supervising the withdrawal to the Hindenburg Line in the spring of 1917, the German Army struck back in the spring of 1918, nearly breaking the Allies. The success was short lived and by October the military situation was hopeless. After urging Kaiser William II to abdicate, Hindenburg led the withdrawal of the German Army into the homeland before retiring. Although he was due to be tried as a war criminal under the Treaty of Versailles, he was never summoned to appear.

Hindenburg was encouraged to return to public life following the death of President Ebert in 1925, and he was elected President in April. Although he intended to stay out of politics, he became increasingly involved in Germany's affairs as the country's economic and political situations descended into chaos, following the Wall Street Crash. By 1930 he had lost faith in democracy and did not support it.

Hindenburg was re-elected in April 1932, beating Hitler into second place but he soon found himself caught between the intrigues of Franz von Papen and General Kurt von Schleicher. Although Hindenburg's mental powers were waning, he repeatedly refused to give Hitler – the man he referred to as the 'Bohemian corporal' – the chancellorship.

Pressure from Papen, Schleicher and industrialists forced Hindenburg into a corner over the chancellorship. He finally conceded when Hitler confronted his son, Oskar, over tax evasion issues relating to the family estate. Hindenburg was finally forced to accept Hitler as Chancellor on 30 January 1933 with Papen as his Vice-Chancellor.

Hindenburg's political influence declined under the Nazis and he retired to his Neudeck home, a sick man. Initially, Hitler treated the ailing President with

Below: The day the NSDAP had campaigned for: Chancellor Hitler and Vice-Chancellor Papen. (NARA-242-HB-00560)

Bottom: Hitler remembers the old days in the Nazi Party museum. (NARA-242-HB-04070a)

respect but he quickly disregarded him once the Nazis had secured their own political position. Hindenburg died at Neudeck on 2 August 1934 and was buried in a new mausoleum called the Marshal's Tower at Tannenberg, the site of his greatest victory.

THE CHANCELLORS

All three chancellors in the early 1930s were engaged in political intrigues, undermining each other and repeatedly encouraging President Hindenburg to change the Chancellor or the cabinet. Brüning, Papen and Schleicher all courted the idea of using the NSDAP in a coalition government but Hitler was adamant that that he had to be Chancellor. His demands were ignored to begin with but the President and the politicians had to take notice as the NSDAP's share of the vote increased.

HEINRICH BRÜNING (1885–1970)
Brüning was named Chancellor in March 1930 as Germany's economy collapsed in the wake of the Stock Market Crash. Hindenburg wanted him to use his financial skills to set a budget but strong opposition forced him to ask for permission to override the need for a Reichstag majority. The Reichstag reacted strongly and Brüning dismissed the assembly in July 1930. He had to resort to ruling by decree but the deepening recession and rising unemployment undermined his support.

Brüning brought the war reparations to an end in 1932, easing Germany's situation, but he was faced with growing opposition from the Communists and the Nazis as both parties benefited from the country's difficulties. General Kurt von Schleicher's influence over Hindenburg weakened his position and the President eventually asked for his resignation on 30 May 1932. It was a serious setback for the Weimar Republic. Brüning emigrated to the US, fearing for his life, after the Nazis came to power.

Franz von Papen. (NARA-242-HB-22487a13)

FRANZ VON PAPEN (1879–1969)
Papen had served as a military attaché in Mexico and Washington DC during the First World War until he was forced to leave for spying. He ended the war serving on the Turkish staff in Palestine. He then joined the Catholic Centre Party and while he was relaxed about politics, he was also narrow-minded and convinced that the highly conservative Gentlemen's Club would eventually control Germany.

Papen was never elected to the Reichstag but three connections helped him up the political ladder. He was a Catholic nobleman with connections in the clergy and a retired staff officer with connections in the Reichswehr. He then married into money and his father-in-law provided connections to the Rhineland industrialists. He was also chairman of *Germania*, the leading

Catholic daily newspaper. Above all, Papen was an intriguer, always looking to further his own political ambitions.

Papen supported Hindenburg in the 1932 presidential elections rather than the Centre Party candidate, and he accepted the Chancellorship in June 1932 following Brüning's resignation, against the party wishes. He left the party shortly afterwards and appointed a conservative 'Cabinet of Barons' which was criticised for being out of touch with the working classes.

Papen then called an election and lifted the ban on Nazi paramilitaries to secure the NSDAP's support; the Nazis became the largest party in the Reichstag. A second election in November 1932 undermined Papen's cabinet, especially when Schleicher refused to support it. Papen was furious when Schleicher was appointed Chancellor. Papen sought his revenge with Hitler's help and on 4 January 1933 he promised the NSDAP the chancellorship. He then suggested appointing Hitler as Chancellor with himself Vice-Chancellor to Hindenburg. Hitler was appointed Chancellor on 30 January 1933 after further intriguing.

Although he had intended to use Hitler, Papen was shocked by the swift implementation of the Reichstag Fire Decree, the Enabling Act and the end of democracy. He also denounced the Nazis' brutality on 17 June 1934 at Marburg University. His speechwriter and assistants were murdered two weeks later, during the Night of the Long Knives, and he was fortunate to escape with his own life. A few weeks later he accepted the post of Minister to Vienna and worked for the Anschluss. He became the German Ambassador to Austria in 1936 but was recalled to Germany following the Anschluss in March 1938. A year later he was appointed Germany's Ambassador in Turkey.

KURT VON SCHLEICHER (1882–1934)

Schleicher served on Hindenburg's staff in the First World War and went on to organise Free Corps units and the Black Reichswehr, secret army units, after the Armistice. He was appointed head of the Armed Forces Division of the Reichswehr Ministry in February 1926, and he arranged secret training for tank and air officers in Russia. In 1929 he was appointed head of the new Ministry Bureau, taking charge of political and press affairs for the army and navy.

Schleicher (right) and Papen (left) visit President Hindenburg at his Neudeck estate.

Schleicher became the Reichswehr's political intriguer but he was often promoting himself rather than the armed forces. He was always pressurising Hindenburg to make changes in the Reichstag. He convinced the President to appoint Brüning as Chancellor in March 1930 and then replace him with Papen in May 1932. As Minister of Defence, he wanted to dissolve the Reichstag and introduce a military dictatorship to restore order across Germany towards the end of the year.

Schleicher proceeded to bring down Papen and he was appointed Chancellor in December 1932. He failed to split the Nazi vote or combine the Reichswehr and the trade unions. After less than two months in power, Schleicher resigned in January 1933, complaining that he had been undermined by political intrigue, and he retired from politics. He worked part time in the University of Berlin but Hitler correctly guessed that he was still plotting. On 30 June 1934, the Night of the Long Knives, Schleicher was shot dead at his home by an SS murder squad; his wife was mortally injured.

THE HOHENZOLLERN PRINCES

CROWN PRINCE WILHELM (1882–1951)

The eldest son of Kaiser William II, Wilhelm commanded the Fifth Army and the Crown Prince Army Group during the First World War. He resigned on 11 November 1918, the day of the Armistice, and went into exile in the Netherlands. Three weeks later he surrendered his rights the throne of the German Reich and the Kingdom of Prussia. After fours year in exile, he was invited to return home by Chancellor Gustav Stresemann where he remained in the shadow of his domineering father. Wilhelm assumed that the Nazis would restore the monarchy and he gave Hitler his support, particularly during the 1932 Presidency elections, but he did not actively engage in party activities. He retired from political activities following the Night of the Long Knives in June 1934.

PRINCE AUGUST (1887–1949)

Wilhelm's younger brother, August, was fascinated by Hitler and he joined the Steel Helmet, the NSDAP, and finally the SA. The Nazis used him to curry favour from monarchists and he often accompanied Hitler on speaking tours. When the Nazis came to power, August became a member of the Reichstag and he was given a post in the Prussian State. His secret desire to restore the monarchy would never be realised and he was cast aside, his influence no longer required. Although he was appointed an SA-Obergruppenführer in June 1939, he never regained his place in Hitler's inner circle.

President Hindenburg speaks to the crowds. (NARA-242-HB-115a5)

CHAPTER THREE

ADOLF HITLER – THE FÜHRER

CHILDHOOD (1889–1907)

Hitler's grandparents came from the Waldviertel region of northern Austria, near the Czech border. His father, Alois Schickelgruber, was raised by his uncle, Johann Hiedler. He wanted to change his surname to his mentor's in 1876 but a mistake by the priest resulted in the surname Hitler. Hitler's third wife Klara Poelzl was a peasant girl, 23 years his junior, and he worked as a customs official in the village of Braunau-am-Inn on the German border. The couple had five children but only two survived, Adolf who was born on 20 April 1889, and a younger sister, Paula, born in 1896. While Alois Hitler was a drunk who controlled his children with corporal punishment, his hardworking wife doted on her children. Hitler developed a hatred for his father and a devotion for his mother.

The family moved to Hafeld in 1895 and Adolf attended Fischlham Village School, transferring to Lambach Monastery School at the age of eight, but he was a resentful child and soon

Hitler's school class; he stands, with arms folded and a defiant look, in the centre of the top row.

expelled. The family moved to Leonding, near Linz, where Adolf attended Linz High School and Steyr Senior School. He continued to be a difficult student and only Dr Leopold Poetsch caught his attention when he spoke about nationalism. Hitler failed to graduate when he left school at sixteen and he spent the next two years drifting between the fields and the library with his only friend, August 'Gustl' Kubizek; he also deliberated over his ambition to be an artist.

YOUTH (1907–1914)

Eighteen-year-old Adolf was dealt a double blow in 1907. While coming to terms with rejection by the Vienna Fine Arts Academy in the autumn, his mother died before Christmas. A few months later he left for Vienna and joined Kubizek who was studying music. Hitler spent the summer of 1908 exploring the city only to be turned down by the Academy for a second time. After another twelve months living with Kubizek, he decided to find cheaper lodgings but within weeks he was on the streets. A cold and lonely Hitler found shelter in a poor-house, scratching a meagre living painting and selling postcards with a new friend, Reinhold Hanisch. He moved into a hostel in the spring and applied to the Arts Academy for a third time; he was rejected in the autumn.

Hitler's future was looking bleak until his godmother gave him money before she died. He preferred to live in the hostel for the next three years, living off his painting and doing odd jobs. In May 1913 he moved to Munich, where he continued to live a lonely and impoverished life.

MILITARY SERVICE (1914–1918)

Hitler (circled) celebrates the news that Germany has gone to war in Munich's Odeonplatz.

The Austrian military service summoned Hitler in January 1914 and although he went home to enlist, he was rejected as medically unfit. He returned to Munich and in July 1914 joined the crowds demanding action following Russia's mobilisation. Germany declared war on Russia and France. Hitler joined the 16th Bavarian Infantry Regiment and he was at the front line after only a few weeks of training.

Hitler served as an orderly during the First Battle of Ypres in October 1914 and he was awarded the Iron Cross Second Class. He later volunteered to be a regimental messenger, a dangerous role, and although he was offered promotion he refused to advance beyond the rank of corporal, preferring to stay in the ranks. He was injured in the thigh on 7 October 1916 on the Somme and returned to his regiment in March 1917, taking part in the Allied offensive at Arras.

In April 1918, Hitler was awarded the Iron Cross First Class for capturing an enemy officer and fifteen men. He was gassed and temporarily blinded near Ypres in October 1918 and as he lay in a hospital bed, he was disgusted to hear that the Armistice had been signed. Hitler was discharged in November 1918 and posted back to the Munich barracks.

PRE-PUTSCH YEARS
(1919–1923)

Hitler watched the political unrest in Munich with revulsion, witnessing the Communists seizing power and Free Corps troops resuming control. His frustration with the Weimar government made him turn to politics and while serving as an army political education officer, Major Konstantin Hierl ordered him to observe the new German Workers' Party in September 1919. The party was in disarray, with no plan of action, no political programme and little money, but Hitler was impressed by the speakers' ideas.

Hitler the soldier.

Hitler joined the small party and he was soon capturing the audience's attention with his energetic oratory, discovering he had a talent for public speaking. His speeches improved as the audiences grew and before long he had left the army to become head of the party. In February 1920 it announced a range of policies, based on nationalism, anti-Semitism and resentment.

The party was renamed the National Socialist German Workers' Party, the NSDAP, in September 1920. Membership grew as smaller right-wing parties joined and by the autumn of 1923, Hitler was convinced that the time was ripe for a revolution. On the evening of 8 November, Hitler's supporters seized senior political figures in a Munich beer hall, announcing the start of a new revolution. Their prisoners escaped and the army was roused but the next day they marched through the streets of Munich to hold a public rally. They found police blocking their route and nearly twenty supporters and police were shot dead in the gun battle that followed.

Hitler's NSDAP membership card; it states he joined as member 555 on 1 January 1920.

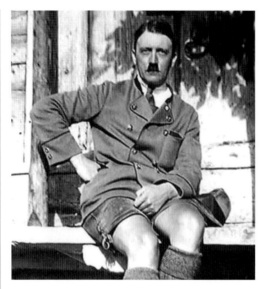

A young Hitler enjoys the mountain air as he relaxes and writes on Obersalzberg mountain in the Alps.

Hitler was injured in the skirmish and was taken to the house of a friend, Ernst Hanfstaengl, where he was seized a few days later. On 26 February 1924 he was brought to trial and defended himself against a charge of high treason. He used the opportunity to make political speeches and the newspaper reports increased his profile and support. Hitler was sentenced to five years' imprisonment but he only served nine months of his sentence in Landsberg-am-Lech prison, living in a comfortable cell surrounded by fellow conspirators. He was treated as an honoured guest, receiving many visitors while dictating the first volume of his biography, *Mein Kampf*.

REBUILDING THE PARTY (1924–1929)

A passionate Hitler speaks to the party. (NARA-242-HB-04547)

Hitler was released on 20 December 1924 and he immediately set to work rebuilding the NSDAP. As the membership grew, the party began to split as supporters in northern Germany

followed the Strasser brothers. Hitler out-manoeuvred them at the Bamberg party conference in February 1926, attracting followers from the left and right. Hitler's oratory skills, highly motivated party leaders and Joseph Goebbels' propaganda was aimed to attract a range of voters. However, Germany was enjoying an economic upturn and there were little support for the NSDAP's policies and they only gained twelve seats in the 1928 Reichstag elections.

THE RISE TO POWER (1929–1933)

By the time the economic depression started in 1929, Hitler was the undisputed leader of the NSDAP. Steps were also taken to widen the party's views to the whole of Germany. Hitler joined Nationalist Alfred Hugenberg in a united campaign against the Young Plan and he addressed a national audience through his newspapers. He also flew around the country during an energetic campaign, bringing himself to the attention of the German electorate. The NSDAP benefited from the recession and over six million voters returned 107 delegates in the September 1930 Reichstag elections, making the NSDAP the second largest party.

After acquiring German citizenship on 25 February 1932, Hitler stood against the aging incumbent, Paul von Hindenburg for the presidency, using the opportunity to promote the party. He came second in the initial election in March 1932 and in the re-run a month later, but in the July Reichstag elections the Nazis returned 230 delegates, becoming the largest political party in Germany. The following November Hitler received a slight setback when the number of Nazi deputies dropped to 196, as that of the Communists rose to 100.

The cabinet developed into a power struggle between the eastern landowners, the western industrialists and the Reichswehr officers. Neither Franz von Papen nor General Kurt von Schleicher could control them and both failed to enrol Hitler's support; he was determined to be Chancellor. Hindenburg refused until a small matter of tax evasion was raised by the Nazis. On 30 January 1933, Hitler was appointed Chancellor of the German Cabinet. He had achieved his goal through the ballot box but the German people soon discovered what the NSDAP had in mind for their country.

The party faithful gather to hear their leader speak at Nuremburg. (NARA-242-HB-22637)

CHANCELLOR, 1933–1934

The NSDAP only had a foothold in the cabinet but a new election would give them the chance to improve it. After only a month as Chancellor, the Reichstag was damaged during an arson attack on 27 February and in the police actions that followed many of the Nazis' political enemies were arrested. The election on 5 March gave the Nazis a slender majority but it was increased by taking advantage of the imprisoned delegates and by breaking the Reichstag rules.

On 24 March 1933, the Enabling Act took away from the Reichstag the powers of legislation and the Nazis set about implementing their own style of governing. Political parties were banned, Nazi governors were placed in control of the German states, trade unions were dissolved and the Church was undermined. All the changes were consolidated with the help of the new powers of the police.

Hitler relaxes as he is briefed. (NARA-242-HB-12078)

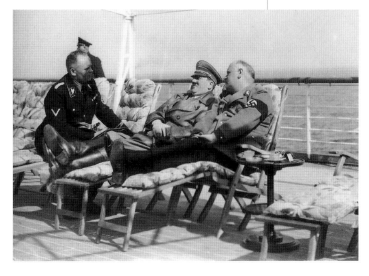

CONSOLIDATING THE DICTATORSHIP

The Nazi alliance with industrialists and generals had paved the road to power and Ernst Röhm's calls for a Second Revolution involving the SA were unnerving. Hitler was looking to consolidate his dictatorship and he did so by having his opponents murdered. On 30 June 1934 Röhm, other SA leaders and a variety of opponents were killed. It was a strong warning to anyone who wanted to resist the Nazi regime.

The death of President Hindenburg on 2 August 1934 allowed Hitler to assume the titles of Führer and Chancellor, fusing party and state, making him the undisputed leader of Germany. Army officers also had to take an oath of allegiance to their new Führer. Despite his new position, Hitler became less and less interested in domestic affairs, leaving his ministers to pursue vague strategies and policies. This loose style of governing often caused internal friction as Nazi officials vied for the Führer's approval.

HITLER THE DIPLOMAT AND THE ROAD TO WAR: 1935–1939

Everyone wanted to be pictured with the Führer. (NARA-242-HB-14568)

Having consolidated his position in Germany, Hitler began his campaign to restore Germany's power in Europe. While pursing an aggressive foreign policy, Hitler withdrew Germany from the League of Nations in October 1933. The following summer he attempted a union with Austria but he was forced to withdraw when Benito Mussolini mobilised troops on Italy's frontier. Hitler resorted to arranging a referendum in the Saar, returning the resource rich area to German control.

The German armed forces had also secretly been expanding, in violation of the Treaty of Versailles. Finances were provided for rearmament and industry increased production, while the unemployed were conscripted into the armed forces. In March 1935, Germany announced it had an army of 550,000 men and an air force of 1,900 warplanes; the world was both surprised and concerned by Germany's new military strength.

In March 1936, Hitler gave the order to send troops into the demilitarised Rhineland. Four months later he sent German troops to aid nationalist forces in Spain's civil war. In October he agreed the Rome-Berlin Pact with Mussolini, countering an alliance between Britain, France and the Netherlands.

Hitler often took the lead in diplomacy and he would lull politicians and diplomats into a false sense of security, speaking of peace while arming and preparing for war. On 5 November 1937 he declared his plans for war at the Hossbach Conference and when the head of the armed forces and the head opposed them, they were both replaced. In March 1938, Germany manipulated a crisis in Austria until the Chancellor resigned. The new German-approved Chancellor invited the German Army across the border. A union, or *Anschluss*, of the two countries followed.

Similar underhand tactics were used to cause problems in Czechoslovakia and the German-speaking Sudetenland on Germany's border, in September. The British and French became involved in the negotiations, but Hitler discussed, argued and negotiated the Munich Agreement. German troops entered the Sudetenland. The following March they occupied the rest of Czechoslovakia after the government conceded to Hitler's threats. Ten million people had been added to the Third Reich in twelve months.

Germany then turned her attention to the Polish Corridor and Danzig knowing that Britain and France had guaranteed Polish independence. Hitler spent the summer soothing Marshall Josef Stalin and the Soviet Union and on 23 August 1939 Germany and Russia signed a pact of friendship. They also signed a secret agreement to divide Poland between them. On 1 September 1939, German troops unleashed their *Blitzkrieg* on Poland. Two days later Britain and France declared war on Germany.

Hitler and Goebbels relax amongst friends for late night conversation. (NARA-242-HB-24800)

Hitler's postal vote confirming himself as Reich Chancellor in August 1934. (NARA-242-HB-07631)

CITIZENSHIP

Hitler was Austrian by birth, born in the old Austro-Hungarian Empire. He was turned down by the Austrian Army in the spring of 1914 but he was accepted by the German Army when he volunteered on the outbreak of war a few months later. He was still an Austrian citizen when he led the 1923 Munich Putsch but the Bavarian government imprisoned him rather than deport him.

Hitler renounced Austrian citizenship in April 1925 and he was without nationality during the years that the NSDAP grew into the most powerful party in the Reichstag. He needed German citizenship to stand in

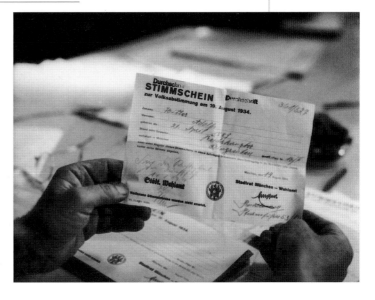

the presidential election in March 1932. Although Willhem Frick, Minister of the Interior for Thuringia, offered to make him an official in a local police force, Hitler chose to be appointed councillor on the state of Brunswick legation in Berlin. Nine months later he was the Chancellor of Germany.

THE LEADERSHIP PRINCIPLE

Hitler wanted to turn Germany into an authoritarian state, led by a dictator and an elite group of leaders using the Leadership Principle, the *Führerprinzip*. The title 'Führer' was first used in public by Hermann Esser in 1923 and its use increased rapidly. Joseph Goebbels made it a compulsory in 1931, creating the rally call 'One People! One Government! One Leader!' Following Hindenburg's death in August 1934, Hitler combined the offices of Chancellor and President and used the word Führer as his official state title.

Hitler believed that he was carrying out the will of the people and he encouraged them to cooperate. The NSDAP worked towards creating an orderly state based on discipline and a military-style leadership. Anyone he did not cooperate fell foul of the law.

Hitler was presented as a superhuman idol to the people as the cult of Führer Worship grew. Goebbels' propaganda campaign portrayed him as a teetotaller, a vegetarian, a non-smoker and an asexual bachelor with only one desire; the desire to lead Germany. His image was displayed everywhere and his birthday became a national holiday when the German people were encouraged to worship their saviour.

Hitler quietly contemplates his next speech. (NARA-242-HB-21229)

CLOSE AIDES

EMIL MAURICE (1897–1972)

Maurice was a watchmaker who joined the German Workers' Party in 1919 and he was the first leader of the SA. He became commander of Hitler's protection squad in 1923 and was imprisoned following the 1923 Beer Hall Putsch. He was Hitler's secretary in Landsberg prison, and took the dictation for *Mein Kampf* until Rudolf Hess took over.

On his release, Maurice reformed Hitler's protection squad as Stosstrupp Adolf Hitler; it would be renamed the *Schutzstaffel* at the end of 1925. Maurice worked as Hitler's chauffeur and they remained close until Hitler accused him of having an affair with his niece, Geli Raubal. The two drifted apart following her suicide in September 1931.

Maurice accompanied Hitler during the Blood Purge on 30 June 1934, shooting SA leader Edmund Heines and his homosexual companion. He also killed Father Bernhard Stempfle because he knew too much about Raubal's suicide. His lack of promotion in the SS was due to rumours of Jewish ancestors, a rumour that Himmler tried to prove. Maurice was eventually appointed the head of the Munich society of professional handicraft workers in 1937 and SS-Oberführer.

ERICH KEMPKA (1910–1975)

Kempka of the SS–Leibstandarte Adolf Hitler became Hitler's chauffeur in 1934. He was also the transport officer at Hitler's headquarters, organising the large fleet of cars used by the Führer and his guests.

Hitler's team: Joseph Dietrich looks over his shoulder, Julius Schreck drives, Otto Dietrich and Julius Schaub sit in the back. (NARA-242-HB-06328)

Julius Schaub, Hitler and Julius Schreck view the result of the 12 November 1933 election; 92 per cent were in favour of the NSDAP. There were no opposition parties. (NARA-242-HB-04130)

FRITZ WIEDEMANN (1891–1870)

Wiedemann was Hitler's officer in the First World War and he retired after the war to farm. He joined the NSDAP in 1934 and served as Hitler's personal adjutant until 1938. He was sent to London to inform the British Foreign Minister of Hitler's demands on the Sudetenland and he attended the 1938 Munich conference. He fell from favour after *Kristallnacht* and he was sent to San Francisco as German Consul General in 1939.

PAUL SCHMIDT (1889–1970)

Schmidt studied languages after the First World War and worked as an interpreter in the Foreign Ministry. He worked in many

important meetings including the Locarno Treaty and became Hitler's interpreter in 1933. He was present at many meetings with Mussolini, Franco and Chamberlain.

CLOSE FRIENDS

AUGUST (GUSTL) KUBIZEK (1888–1956)

Kubizek met Hitler in Linz in 1904, when they were teenagers. They both moved to Vienna in 1907 but while Kubizek was accepted by the Academy of Music, Hitler was refused by the Academy of Arts. After lodging together the two arranged to re-let rooms after Gustl's summer vacation. Hitler was again rejected by the Academy and he left, leaving no messages or a forwarding address. The two did not meet again in Linz until April 1938, by which time Hitler was the Führer and the Third Reich included Austria.

ULRICH GRAF (1878–1950)

Graf was a butcher who joined the NSDAP in 1920, becoming a member of Hitler's bodyguard. He was badly injured during the 1923 Munich Putsch, shot while protecting Hitler. After he recovered he was made a member of the Munich City Council. Graf became a Reichstag delegate in 1936 and an SS-Oberführer in 1937.

ERNST (PUTZI) HANFSTAENGL (1887–1975)

Hanfstaengl graduated from Harvard University in 1909 and after spending the First World War in the US, returned to Munich in 1922. The accomplished pianist was impressed by Hitler's speaking, and the two became close friends as he introduced him to the Munich world of art and culture. Hitler fled to Hanfstaengl's house in the Bavarian Alps after the 1923 Beer Hall Putsch.

Close friends Max Amann and Ernst Hanfstaengl accompany Hitler during a visit to Ignaz Westenkirchner, an old comrade from the trenches. (NARA-242-HB-03528)

Hanfstaengl helped Hitler restart his political career after his release, providing funds for the *People's Observer*. He was the light hearted comedian who provided relaxation during political campaigns; he also served as the NSDAP's foreign press chief. Hanfstaengl tried to moderate Hitler's views after he became Führer, and their arguments strained the friendship. He made an enemy of Goebbels and eventually fled Germany, fearing for his life.

HEINRICH HOFFMANN (1885–1957)

Hoffmann served as a photographer in the Bavarian Army and published his first book of photographs – *A Year of Bavarian Revolution* – in 1919. Two years later he was working for Hitler and the NSDAP and he was the only person to photograph the 1923 Beer Hall Putsch. He introduced Hitler to Munich's intellectual society, offering his house to entertain.

Hoffmann became the official photographer for the NSDAP and for some time he had the exclusive rights to take pictures of Hitler. Hoffmann's picture books of Hitler, titled *Germany*

Awakened, *The Brown House*, and *Hitler Unknown*, made a considerable amount for both of them. Hoffmann employed Eva Braun in his Munich photography shop and he introduced her to Hitler. Meanwhile, Hoffman's own daughter, Henny, married the Hitler Youth leader Baldur von Schirach.

The party photographer was elected to the Reichstag in March 1933 and he made a fortune from photographing party events. Although Hitler conferred the title of 'Professor' on him in 1938, in private he was nicknamed 'National Drunkard in Chief' because of his heavy drinking.

ROMANTIC ATTACHMENTS

Hitler only had fleeting early contacts with the opposite sex and although he admired a number of women, it is doubtful if he pursued any. As the NSDAP grew in popularity, so did his influence over women. He was referred to as 'Handsome Adolf' by women who were attracted to his powerful position, particularly after he was appointed Chancellor in 1933. He was loosely connected with a number of women, three of whom committed suicide:

Angela Raubal, niece
Winifred Wagner, daughter-in-law of Richard Wagner
Henny Hoffmann, daughter of the photographer Heinrich Hoffmann
Leni Riefenstahl, film director
Eva Braun, Heinrich Hoffmann's assistant
Renate Müller, actress
Mary Rahl, actress
Anny Ondra, actress
Unity Valkyrie Mitford, English aristocrat

ANGELA (GELI) RAUBAL (1908–1931)

Angela Raubal senior, Hitler's half sister, became his housekeeper at his Obersalzberg chalet

Hitler's half-sister Angela, and her daughter Geli.

in 1925. She was accompanied by her two daughters, Friedl and Angela. Hitler was attracted to his younger niece and over the next four years the two became close companions. The Raubals joined him when he rented a large apartment on Prinz Regentenstrasse in Munich, but gossip about the two dismayed Hitler and concerned the NSDAP hierarchy.

Despite appeals to distance himself from his niece, they were inseparable. As her independence grew, the arguments increased and she was soon planning to leave. Neighbours heard their final argument as Hitler left the apartment on 17 September; the following morning Geli was found dead in the apartment, having died of gunshot wounds.

A verdict of suicide was recorded, but her death was surrounded with suspicion. Some thought that Hitler had murdered her in a fit of rage, others believed that Himmler had her murdered. Whatever the truth, Hitler was grief stricken for a long time.

WINIFRED WAGNER (1897–1980)
Winifred Williams was born in England and was adopted by Karl Klindworth, a pupil of Franz Liszt. In 1915 she married Richard Wagner's son, Siegfried, who was 25 years her senior. She met Hitler in the spring of 1923 and he visited the Wagner home in Bayreuth, meeting the family, in the autumn, just before the Munich Putsch. He kept in contact with the family, becoming close to Winifred and her children when Siegfried died in 1930.

EVA BRAUN (1912–1945)
After Geli Raubal committed suicide, Hitler refused to become closely attached to any women, until Hoffmann introduced him to Eva Braun. Braun was a tall, slim, pretty Bavarian girl from Simbach on the Austrian border. She was working in Heinrich Hoffmann's photographic studio in the early 1930s when she was introduced to Hitler. He was enthralled by the shy athletic girl who loved dancing, swimming, gymnastics, skiing and mountain climbing. She in turn was devoted to Hitler and before long she had been moved into a flat near his own.

Eva Braun at the Eagle's Nest at Obersalzberg.

She later moved to the Berghof in Berchtesgaden and she was treated as the Führer's mistress. She was kept out of sight when visitors came and although she was part of Hitler's intimate circle of friends, servants were not allowed to talk to her. Very few people knew of the Führer's mistress and she remained at the Berghof, reading, exercising, writing letters and diaries. Her isolation heightened her depression and she attempted suicide several times. Her sisters, Ilse and Gred, often kept her company.

UNITY VALKYRIE MITFORD (1914–1948)
Mitford was a lively, statuesque woman from an eccentric background; the British fascist leader, Sir Oswald Mosley, was her brother-in-law. The rebellious English aristocrat was studying art in Munich when she was introduced to Hitler in 1935 and she soon became a member of his close circle of friends.

She fell in love with Hitler, and although he was attentive and polite, it was an unrequited love. She became distraught on the day that Great Britain declared war on Germany and attempted to commit suicide in Munich's Englischer Garten. She failed and Hitler made sure that she was cared for until she was able to return home in a specially organised train. She never recovered.

HITLER'S DOCTORS

KARL BRANDT (1904–1948)

Brandt was called upon to treat Hitler's niece, Geli, and his adjutant, Wilhelm Bruckner, in August 1933. The doctor made such a favourable impression that he was invited to become Hitler's escort physician in 1934. Brandt was appointed the Reich Commissioner for Health and Sanitation and he worked with Philip Bouhler on the euthanasia programme, starting in September 1939. Brandt was suspicious of the large number of drugs and vitamins Dr Morell was giving to Hitler and he recommended rest and exercise. The Führer ignored his warnings but he did continue to use both doctors.

THEODOR MORELL (1886–1948)

Morell practised in Berlin and treated many well-known actors and film stars. Heinrich Hoffmann recommended the doctor to Hitler in 1935 and after some time he was asked to carry out an examination. His diagnosis was exhaustion of the intestinal system, due to stress, and he suggested a course of injections. The cocktail of drugs temporarily improved the Führer's health and Morell injected more drugs each time the symptoms returned, increasing Hitler's dependency. While the doctor took advantage of his situation, many, including Brandt, distrusted him.

HITLER'S RESIDENCES

THE REICH CHANCELLERY

Hitler's Berlin base as Chancellor was the Reich Chancellery. The original building had opened in 1878 and a new extension was added in 1930. Hitler chose architects Paul Troost and Leonhard Gall to redesign the interior to suit his tastes in 1935. One of their projects was a garden conservatory complete with a bombproof cellar. It would eventually expand into the Führerbunker where Hitler committed suicide with his new wife, Eva Braun on 30 April 1945.

Following Troost's death, Hitler commissioned Albert Speer to rebuild a new Reich Chancellery in January 1938. Although the plans had already been finalised, the building had to be completed in twelve months, in time for annual diplomatic reception. 4,000 workers worked round the clock to complete the building on time but the cost was 90 million Reichsmarks (RM), a huge amount of money.

The original chancellery building remained the Chancellor's official residence but it was redesigned with huge halls and offices; Hitler's office alone was 400m² and the reception gallery was 145m long. The cabinet room was never used.

The completed
Berghof.

BERCHTESGADEN AND OBERSALZBERG

Hitler first visited the mountains above Berchtesgaden in search of Dietrich Eckart, in April 1923. His visit filled him with inspiration and went on to plan the Beer Hall Putsch in November. Following his release from Landsberg prison, he returned to Obersalzberg in July 1925 and rented a small chalet where he worked on the second volume of *Mein Kampf*. He continued to visit and eventually rented a small chalet in 1928 where his half-sister Angela Raubal lived as his housekeeper.

Hitler bought the nearby Haus Wachenfeld in September 1932 and had a terrace and a veranda added, the first stage of his new alpine home. Architect Alois Degano planned a huge extension and work began in 1935. The centrepiece was a huge window which could be lowered for views of Untersberg Mountain and Salzberg. The budget was unlimited and the Führer filled the rooms with large pieces of furniture, huge paintings and expensive carpets. The building reopened in 1936 with a new name – the Berghof.

LIFE AT THE BERGHOF

Hitler was attended to by a large staff of housekeepers, cooks and secretaries when he relaxed at the Berghof. While adjutants and orderlies dealt with administration, chauffeurs and a fleet of cars were on hand. Eva Braun became the informal lady of the house in 1936.

Daily life at the Berghof was monotonous. Hitler appeared late morning and started his day with a long lunch. A short walk down the mountainside to a nearby private 'teahouse' followed and guests politely listened to the Führer's monologues. Dinner was followed by films, music and discussions around the fireside late into the night.

The Berghof was often used for important meetings and guests included kings, premiers, dictators, foreign ministers and ambassadors. A small airport was opened nearby in 1933 and the railway station was enlarged. Visitors stayed at Berchtesgadener Hotel while Nazi officials stayed in one of the specially built hotels on the mountain.

THE OBERSALZBERG COMPLEX

Martin Bormann, Party Treasurer and manager of Hitler's private fortune, ran the Obersalzberg estate. After the Nazis took power in 1933, work started on a complex of buildings capable of accommodating government officials during Hitler's visits. Over 50 farms were replaced by administrative buildings, accommodation blocks and barracks. The 6,000 strong workforce spent four years building them and costs soared to 980 million RM.

Martin Bormann's house overlooked the Berghof and Göring's alpine manor was nearby. Albert Speer also had a house and an architectural studio. They all had air raid shelters. Other senior party officials stayed in the Party Guest House while junior party officials lodged in the palatial Platterhof Hotel. There were staff quarters, garages and a kindergarten. Fruit and vegetables were grown in a large greenhouse but the alpine climate was too harsh for the animals or crops on the Gutshof Farm.

The crowning glory of the Obersalzberg complex was the Eagle's Nest, a teahouse on the summit of Klienstein Mountain.

Hitler and Göring talk during a walk to the teahouse; Bormann and Baldur von Schirach follow. (NARA-242-HB-24102)

Cars took visitors up the twisting road and then walked down a tunnel into the centre of the mountain. A lift took them up to the teahouse. Over 3,000 workers were involved and the Nazi Party paid the 30 million RM bill.

As Hitler's popularity grew, so did the Berghof complex, and thousands flocked to see the Führer. A new barrack block was built for the 2,000 SS guards, and while miles of fences surrounded the mountain, roadblocks cordoned off the area. SS-Obersturmbannführer Bernhard Frank, one of the members of Himmler's inner circle, ran security on the complex.

HITLER THE AUTHOR: *MEIN KAMPF*

Hitler started writing in Landsberg prison, dictating to Emil Maurice and then Rudolf Hess. The original title was *My Struggle for Four and a Half Years against Lies, Stupidity and Cowardice* but Max Amann cut it to *My Struggle* or *Mein Kampf*. The first volume was published in 1925 and Hitler wrote a second volume on the Obasalzberg; it was published in 1928.

Although the book was tedious and crudely written, it did explain Hitler's political programme for a strong Aryan nationalist state, which united the Germanic people, suppressed dissident political parties and exiled the Jews. Germany could conquer lands in Eastern Europe and the Ukraine, replacing the Slavs with German peasants. His plans also called

A Dutch copy of 'My Struggle'. (NARA-242-HB-39881)

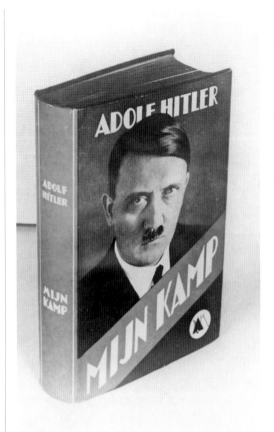

for alliances with Britain and Italy and together they could destroy France, which he believed was the stronghold of international Jewry.

Sales increased in proportion to the fortunes of the NSDAP. Over one million copies had been sold by 1933 and five million by 1939, making Hitler a wealthy man. It was translated into over ten languages but few Americans or Britons read it. There were plans for a sequel but rumours about a 'second book' were false.

Admirers crowd around Hitler hoping for his autograph. (NARA-242-HB-13229a)

CHAPTER FOUR

THE PARTY

THE NSDAP LEADERS

THE DEPUTY FÜHRER

RUDOLF HESS (1894–1987)

Hess emigrated from Egypt and served alongside Hitler in the German Army in the First World War. While studying at Munich University he joined the Thule Society and served in the Free Corps under General von Epp. He was arrested for taking part in the 1923 Munich Putsch and was imprisoned with Hitler for seven months, taking notes for him while he dictated *Mein Kampf*.

The tall, dark-browed Hess was an introverted man with few talents, but his absolute loyalty to Hitler meant that he served as his private secretary from 1925 to 1932. He was elected to the Reichstag in 1932 and was appointed chairman of the Central Political Commission during the reorganisation of the party in December 1932; he was also promoted to SS-Obergruppenführer.

Hess was appointed Deputy Führer in April 1933 and Reich Minister without Portfolio in June 1933. He appointed the Führer's Deputy for Party Affairs to stop in-fighting between civil servants and party officials in December 1933 and his office dealt with all laws and decrees after July 1934. After 1935 Hess was also made responsible for appointing all Reich employees, civil servants, local govern-

ment officers, lawyers and university lecturers. The party was now controlling the state. After September 1935 he also appointed all senior party officials, including *Gaulieters* and *Kreisleiters*.

In February 1938 Hess joined the Secret Cabinet Council and also became a member of the Ministerial Council for the Defence of the Reich in August 1939. He was named the second in line successor to the Führer after Hermann Göring.

THE DEPUTY FÜHRER'S CHIEF OF CABINET

MARTIN BORMANN (1900–1945?)

After serving briefly in the First World War, Bormann was employed as a farm inspector. He joined the Rossbach Free Corps and then the SA, transferring to the Frontbann when the SA was banned following the 1923 Munich Putsch. He gained notoriety after murdering Walther Kadow, the man who had betrayed Albert Schlageter, the Nazi martyr.

Martin Bormann on the left, lines up next to Robert Ley, Joseph Goebbels, Hermann Göring and Julius Streicher at the Nuremberg Rally. (NARA-242-HB-22628a15)

After serving only one year in prison, Bormann became Thuringia's regional press officer for the NSDAP and he was promoted to be the area Gauleiter and business manager in 1928. He was also a member of the SA's supreme command and he set up the National Socialist Welfare Fund to care for members injured while fighting for the party; it was the start of a lucrative career in fund raising. It is also believed that he bribed the police inspector investigating the death of Geli Raubal, Hitler's niece.

Once the Nazis were in power, Bormann was appointed Chief of Cabinet for the Deputy Führer, Rudolf Hess. He was also elected to the Reichstag in October 1933.

Although he kept out of the limelight, Bormann was an expert at using internal politics and intrigue to improve his position. While Hess had no personal ambitions, Bormann did, and he carefully attended to state and party appointments. He also ran the alpine complex surrounding Hitler's Berghof at Obersalzberg. He was able to act as the Führer's personal secretary on the mountain, isolating him from everyone including Hans Lammers' Reich Chancellor's Office.

Bormann also controlled the Führer's financial affairs and the *Adolf Hitler-Spende*, a fund financed by suggesting that industry make financial contributions in return for favours.

THE 25 POINT PROGRAMME

The German Workers' Party programme was drawn up by Anton Drexler, Gottfried Feder and Adolf Hitler in February 1920 and it was announced in the Hofbräuhaus in Munich. Heitler reaffirmed them after the 1926 confrontation with Gregor Strasser in Bamberg and they remained the party programme until the end of the Third Reich.

1   The union of all Germans in a Greater Germany.
2   The rejection of the Treaty of Versailles and the affirmation of the right of Germany to deal with other nations.
3   The demand for additional territories for additional food production and to settle excess German population.
4   Citizenship to be determined by race; no Jew to be a German.
5   Non-Germans in Germany are only guests and they are subject to appropriate laws.
6   Official posts are not to be filled by political favouritism, they are only to be filled according to character and qualification.
7   The livelihood of citizens must be the state's first duty. Should the state's resources be over-stretched, non-citizens must be excluded from the state's benefits.
8   Non-German immigration must be stopped.
9   Equal rights and duties for all citizens.
10 Each citizen must work for the general good.
11 All income not earned by work must be confiscated.
12 All war profits must be confiscated.
13 All large business trusts must be nationalised.
14 Profit-sharing must be introduced in all larger industries.
15 There must be adequate provision for old age.
16 Small businessmen and traders must be strengthened and large department stores must be be handed over to them.

'Blood and Soil', the nationalist concept merging people's ancestry and their homeland. (NARA-242-HB-05982)

17 A reform of land-ownership and an end to land speculation.
18 Ruthless prosecution of serious criminals and death for profiteers.
19 'Roman law', which is materialist, must be replaced by 'German law'.
20 A thorough reconstruction of the national education system.
21 The state must assist motherhood and encourage the development of the young.
22 The paid professional army must be abolished and replaced by a national army.
23 Newspapers must be German-owned; non-Germans will be banned from working on them.
24 There must be religious freedom, except for religions which endanger the German race; the party does not bind itself exclusively to any creed, but it is determined to fight against Jewish materialism.
25 A strong central government is needed for the execution of effective legislation.

THE NAZI IDEOLOGIES

The NSDAP used a variety of ideals to motivate different areas of society. Many of them were nineteenth-century ideologies which had been updated or adapted to take advantage of the poor economic conditions in post-war Germany.

THE NEW ORDER AND THE WORLD VIEW

Once the NSDAP had achieved a political victory, the party had to convince the German people to accept their 'New Order' and 'world view'. Nazi propaganda proclaimed that the party would bring prosperity and worldwide recognition to the German people. In reality it would take over every aspect of government administration, removing the powers of the Reichstag and the Reichrats while fusing the powers of the party and the state to further its own ends.

The New Order would be a totalitarian police state headed by the Führer and would coordinate all aspects of family life, employment, education, youth, law and order. Once the Nazis had convinced the German people to adopt their new order, Germany had to expand and seek world domination or ruin. The call for aggressive expansion was supported with slogans like 'Today Germany … Tomorrow the World!'

EXPANSIONISM

The Nazis adopted an early nineteenth-century call to expand Germany's borders to reunite all the German-speaking people and create a Greater German Empire. It was used to justify plans to occupy Austria and the Sudetenland in Czechoslovakia. Hitler particularly referred to the lands of the Slav peoples of Poland and Russia.

New farms built for Aryan families; the plan was to build many more in Eastern Europe. (NARA-242-HB-13570a30)

Before the First World War, the term 'living space', '*lebensraum*', referred to the new colonies around the world, particularly those in Africa. These colonies were confiscated under the Treaty of Versailles and the term was then used to demand their return. The NSDAP adopted the term 'People without Space' from the title of Hans Grimm's 1926 book and claimed that Germany was overpopulated to justify plans for aggressive territorial expansion. Hitler also called for a drive for self-sufficiency, or autarky, in raw materials and food stuffs.

RACIAL PURITY

The Nazis wanted to rid Germany of the mixture of impure races they called the 'Chaos of Peoples'. They believed that Germans were the 'master race' and while ethnic Germans were called *Volksdeutsche,* ex-patriot Germans were called *Volksgruppe.*

On 12 December 1935 Heinrich Himmler announced the Lebensborn Registered Society to promote 'The Fountain of Life' program, an attempt to create a superior German race. Women were repeatedly reminded of their duty to bear racially pure children while chosen girls were encouraged to father the children of SS men.

THE CLASS SYSTEM

Nazi ideology promoted a classless society and Hitler repeatedly referred to the front-line comradeship of the trenches. Both the wealthy and the educated middle classes were early Nazi targets. Once the Nazis were in power, the SA called for a 'Second Revolution' and it looked to merge the SA with the Reichswehr. Hitler had attained power with the help of the industrialists and the generals and he did not want to lose their support; he wanted national unity. He responded by murdering many SA leaders during the 'Night of the Long Knives' on 30 June 1934.

THE SWASTIKA

The Weimar *Reichsbanner* was a tri-colour of black, red and gold and it became an object of hatred for the Nazis. The four-armed hooked cross known as the swastika was the ancient symbol chosen as the Nazi Party's powerful emblem. The swastika had been associated with nationalistic and anti-Semitic movements for many years and the Ehrhardt Free Corps had painted swastikas on their helmets in the post-war period. The NSDAP version was a black cross on a white circular background set centrally on a red background; the three colours of German nationalism. It was officially adopted as the national flag during the 1935 Nuremberg Rally.

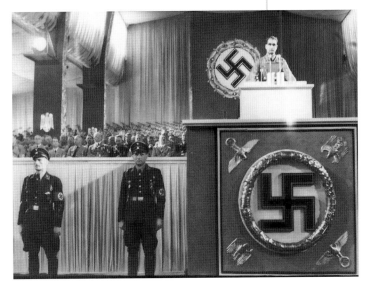

The unmistakable swastika, displayed in two ways. (NARA-242-HB-15022a39)

THE NSDAP ORGANISATIONS

The NSDAP was split into seven controlled organisations, eight affiliated organisations and six supervised organisations. The branches of the party were NSDAP-controlled party organisations and members could belong to one or more of them (NS – National Socialist; HJ – *Hitler Jügend*).

NS Elite Corps: SS
NS Storm Troops: SA
NS German Lecturers' League
NS German Students' League
HJ: Hitler Youth
NS Women's Organisation
NS Motor Corps: NSKK

The eight NSDAP-affiliated organisations each controlled a professional body and membership was mandatory; they were adult male dominated organisations.

NS German Doctors' League
NS People's Welfare Organisation
NS Legal Officials' League
German Civil Service
NS School Teachers' League
NS League for German Technology
German Labour Front
NS War Victims' Welfare Service

The party leadership gather in a smoky room to discuss policy in private. (NARA-242-HB-10589)

Women and students were encouraged to belong to a NSDAP-supervised organisations:

German Women's Work
Reich Family League
German Communal Congress
NS Physical Exercise League
German Students' Society
NS Former German Students League

The two remaining NSDAP organisations were the Reich Labour Service and the NS Flying Corps.

THE ORGANISATION OF THE NSDAP

The NSDAP was highly organised on all levels. Everyone took orders from, reported to, and was responsible to their immediate leader. The hierarchy stretched from the Führer right down to the lowly Party Comrade. Every year several manuals were published so that members could keep up to date with changes. The *Party Organisation Book* detailed the changing structure of the NSDAP while the *National Socialist Year Book* detailed the year's achievements. The party Who's Who, the *Führerlexikon*, listed many senior members and supporters.

THE REICH LEADERSHIP, THE REICHSLEITUNG

Adolf Hitler was the undisputed leader of the party. His deputy was Rudolf Hess. The Reich leadership were the senior party officials or Reich leaders, *Reichsleiters*. Once the NSDAP was in power, they served as heads of government departments or committees, agencies of the state, or ministers with specific portfolios. Others were heads of party formations, affiliated organisations and supervised organisations. The Reich leadership delegated tasks to various offices and Reich leaders worked together on committees to decide policies. They kept in close contact with the people through the party hierarchy, and are listed below:

Head of the Führer's Chancellery	Philipp Bouhler
Party Finance	Franz Schwarz
Chief of Staff of Deputies	Martin Bormann
Party Propaganda	Gregor Strasser to 1929, then Joseph Goebbels
Head of the Party Court	Walter Buch
Deputy of the Party Court	Wilhelm Grimm
Party Press	Max Amann
Press Chief	Otto Dietrich
Army Politics Office	Franz von Epp
Agriculture Office	Walther Darré
Reichstag Parliamentary Party	Wilhem Frick
NSDAP Secretary	Karl Fiehler
Party Foreign Affairs Department	Alfred Rosenberg

Party Law	Hans Frank
Political Organisation	Gregor Strasser until 1932 then Robert Ley
Reich Leader of the SS	Heinrich Himmler
Reich Youth Leader	Baldur von Schirach
Chief of Staff of the SA	Ernst Röhm until 1934 then Viktor Lutze

Hitler relaxes in the background while Goebbels and Hess talk economics with Hjalmar Schacht, President of the Reichsbank, on board a cruise ship. (NARA-242-HB-12078a3)

The party leadership line up to explain their policies to the people at Nuremberg. (NARA-242-HB-15026a16)

THE SOVEREIGNTY BEARERS, THE HOHEITSTRAEGER

The NSDAP had a strict vertical structure organised to carry out orders, supervise the membership and report on the public. Party officials were known as Sovereignty Bearers and each one was responsible to the next highest official in the Nazi hierarchy:

The *Gauleiter* was subordinate to the Führer
The Circle Leader, *Kreisleiter*, was subordinate to the *Gauleiter*
The Local Group Leader, *Ortsgruppenleiter*, was subordinate to the *Kreisleiter*
The Cell Leader, *Zellenleiter*, was subordinate to the *Ortsgruppenleiter*
The Block Leader, *Blockleiter*, was subordinate to the *Zellenleiter*

The Führer appointed Reichsleiters, Gauleiters and Kreisleiters. He also appointed Gau Office Leaders, *Gauamtsleiters*, the organisational heads of Gau offices. The Reich Leaders and Sovereignty Bearers together made the people conform to the National Socialist laws and ideologies, and they could rely on the party machinery to carry out their plans. They could also request assistance from the SA, SS, HJ or NSKK.

CORRUPTION

While the NSDAP campaigned against the Weimar republic's corruption, the party leaders quickly raised corruption to new levels when they were in power. Tax evasion and misuse of state funds from private enterprises became normal practice. The party leaders led the corruption, and they used their position of influence to acquire properties before diverting government funds to extend, redesign and run them.

Hitler acquired the President's funds after Hindenburg's death in August 1934 and his personal fortune increased with royalties from *Mein Kampf* and from using his image on stamps. As the Führer he was not accountable, and Reichleiters and Gauleiters were only answerable to him. Accountability went on down the chain, resulting in corruption, patronage, bribery and favouritism.

The NSDAP's old boys' network worked on a massive scale and ability played little part in appointments. While party members and SA troopers found work easy to come by, members of other political parties found it difficult.

DISTRICTS AND DISTRICT LEADERS

The NSDAP originally divided Germany into nine regions, or *Lands* and each one had four districts. The 36 districts, or *Gau*, were based on the Reichstag electoral districts and they usually covered a province such as Saxony or Swabia. Regional inspectors administered each *Land* until the posts were disbanded in 1933.

Hitler personally approved each Gauleiter and the Gau leadership, the *Gauleitung*, was responsible for coordinating political, cultural and economic control over its area on behalf of the NSDAP. The number of Gau increased to 44 as Germany annexed Austria, the Sudetenland and Danzig.

GAU AREAS

Baden	Essen	Wartheland	Westmark
Hamburg	Mark Brandenburg	Weser-Ems	Saxony
Bayreuth	Franconia	East Prussia	Pomerania
Hesse-Nassau	Mecklenburg	Styria	Upper Silesia
Berlin	Halle-Merseberg	Westphalia North	Lower Silesia
Carinthia	Main-Franconia	Westphalia South	Vienna
Danzig	Moselland	Swabia	Upper Danube
Cologne-Aachen	Upper Bavaria	Thuringia	Lower Danube
Hesse-Kassel	East Hanover	Weser-Ems	Tyrol-Vorarlberg
Dusseldorf	South Hanover	Salzburg	Sudetenland
Magdeburg-Anhalt	Wurttemberg-Hohenzollern	Schleswig-Holstein	Organisation for Foreigners

GERMANS LIVING OVERSEAS

National Socialism appealed to many Germans living overseas, especially those living in the US and Argentina. Ex-patriot communities were collectively known as the 43rd Gau and by 1939 over 60,000 Germans living in Argentina had joined. The Organisation for Foreigners kept them informed through a worldwide news service; it also controlled several shipping lines and ran a student exchange program.

ORGANISING THE RANK AND FILE

In the early 1920s the Nazi Party established a system of Street Cells based on the Communist Party organisation and each cell had four or five men. They were led by a chairman, or *Obman*, and he kept his men informed about party instructions and actively working for the party.

Muchow Reinhold (1905–1933) successfully organised the cell system in Greater Berlin Gau District I and Gauleiter Goebbels promoted him to city leader in 1928 so he could expand his system across the capital. He divided Berlin into local groups, each responsible for several blocks, while block leaders controlled several cells. The system allowed the city leaders to keep in touch with the rank and file. The system was quickly copied across Germany. Muchow transferred to the German Labour Front in May 1933 and implemented the same system in the work place; he killed in an accident in the Rhineland on 12 September 1933.

The banner screams 'the Jews are our misfortune!' to the audience. (NARA-242-HB-16352)

Thousands gather to see the Führer pass through Nuremberg while film crews capture the moment for the newsreels. (NARA-242-HB-15006)

Each District, *Gau* was split into a number of Circles, *Kreisen*. Most Gau had around fifteen Circles, each covering a city district, a single town or a rural area. Each Circle was headed by a Circle Leader, a *Kreisleiter* and they were the lowest ranking salaried NSDAP official. Circles were split into Local Groups, *Ortsgruppen*. There could be as few as 140 or as many as 3,100 Local Groups in a Circle but most had between 300 and 700. A Local Group covered part of a town or a small section of city, several villages or a small rural district; each one covered between 1,500 and 3,000 households. The Gauleiter appointed the Local Group Leader, *Ortsgruppenleiter.*

The next level down was the Cell, *Zellen*, and they were led by Cell Leaders, *Zellenleiters.* A cell could cover a village and in towns they were based around a neighbourhood or a factory. City cells covered between four to eight blocks of houses or apartments. The final level was the Block which monitored a street, or an apartment block, of around 50 households. The Block Warden, *Blockwart* or *Blockleiter*, reported on the people in his area to the party office. They made sure that members paid their subscriptions, contributed to charities, joined the right organisations and turned out for demonstrations. They organised local meetings and accommodation for visiting members. They would also report on their neighbours.

The ordinary member of the Nazi party was known as the Party Comrade, the *Parteigenosse,* and was expected to be a 'self-coordinator', *Selbstgleichschlater,* a disciplined citizen who coordinated his own family's activities in accordance with the party ideals.

THE PARTY HEADQUARTERS

The NSDAP headquarters was always based in Munich. It started with a few rooms in Sternacker-Brau Brewery in 1920 and two years later it moved to a small building on

Corneliusstrasse. When the party reformed in January 1925, after the Putsch, its new head-quarters were in the Eher publishing house on Thierstrasse. Six months later it hired rooms in Schellingstrasse and took over the entire building when the party expanded.

In 1928 the party bought Barlow Palace, a large house on Briennerstrasse, next to Köenigsplatz, using money donated by Rhineland industrialists. The mansion was rede-signed by the architect Paul Troost and he added intermediate floors, splitting the palatial rooms into smaller offices. Hitler, Hess, Goebbels, Strasser and Röhm had offices on the second floor and there was a restaurant in the basement. It was opened on New Year's Day 1931 and was known as the Brown House.

The new Party Administration Office in the centre of Munich. (NARA-242-HB-16972)

Over the years that followed, the Nazi Party headquarters expanded until it occupied several dozen buildings across a city block. Two Temples of Honour were built next to the Brown House for the sarcophagi of the martyrs killed in the Munich Putsch. Two huge office blocks were built either side of the memorials. One was Hitler's offices, the Führerbau, while party operations were coordinated in the Party Administration Building. The Papal Nuncio occupied the build-ing opposite the Brown House.

Martin Bormann, Hermann Göring and Rudolf Hess had palatial offices in Meiserstrasse. The party's leadership offices, the SA headquarters and Hitler Youth headquarters were on Barerstrasse along with Heinrich Hoffmann's pho-tographic studio where Eva Braun worked. Karlstrasse housed the SS headquarters, the Students' Association, the propaganda office, and the post and press offices. The buildings on Karolinenplatz housed the legal offices, the Supreme Court and the audit and accounts offices. Heinrich Himmler's police headquarters and Reinhard Heydrich's Security Service had their offices and cells in nearby Türkenstrase. Extensive meeting rooms and apartments were available for visiting members.

FINANCING THE NSDAP

The party needed a constant source of money to pay officials, rent offices, hire meeting halls and cover travelling expenses. The NSDAP spent far more on propaganda – including newspapers, posters and banners – than any other party. Political parties usually conceal where their money comes from and the NSDAP treasurer made sure that the party accounts were kept a secret. However, estimates can be made on how much the party needed and where it could have raised the money. It is estimated that the NSDAP spent fifteen million RM in 1930, fifteen times what the Communist Party spent, and the cost increased as the party's popularity grew.

PARTY TREASURER

FRANZ SCHWARZ (1875–1947)

After serving in the First World War, Schwarz was an accountant for Munich city council. The stout, bald man joined the NSDAP in 1922 and he became the party's National Treasurer when it reformed in 1925 after the Munich Putsch. He was also elected to the Munich City Council in 1929.

Schwarz had to carefully balance the party finances to stop it going bankrupt; income came from membership subscriptions, collections and private donations, and money was spent on officials' expenses, propaganda and office rentals. The accounting became more difficult at the start of the 1930s when the membership increased dramatically. In September 1931 he was called upon to help cover up Geli Raubal's suspicious death in Hitler's Munich flat.

Enrolment of the NSDAP was suspended in May 1933, with one and half million applications outstanding. Contributions were taxed through the German Labour Front in future, superseding the need for membership fees. Schwarz was returned as a Reichstag delegate for the Franconia Constituency in 1933.

Franz Schwarz and Hitler on the balcony of the Brown House. (NARA-242-HB-04065a)

MEMBERSHIP DONATIONS

New members paid a joining fee and it varied according to their income. They paid 1 RM a month subscription; half a million members contributed six million RM annually. Starting in January 1931, members had to subscribe to a party-organised loan scheme and the interest generated another 800,000 RM, helping to finance the succession of political campaigns. Street collections and sponsored events also raised money.

Members paid entrance fees for meetings and the fee again depended on their income. Speakers constantly toured the country, fund raising, and a single meeting held in the 15,000-capacity Berlin Sports Palace stadium could raise over 15,000 RM. Members were also encouraged to buy newspapers, song sheets, flags, uniforms and signed photographs. The Brown Store sold all kinds of Nazi Party paraphernalia, including literature, clothing, flags and banners; the proceeds all went into the party coffers. The party was also supported by donations from newspapers.

Every month each member spent a little here and there. Voters also made contributions. The party would have been eighteen million RM richer if all the six million people who voted for the NSDAP in the September 1930 had contributed 3 RM in the month before.

Every pfennig counted towards the running of the party. (NARA-242-HB-03432)

A store selling clothing, mementos and Nazi Party paraphernalia. (NARA-242-HB-00830)

BUSINESS DONATIONS

Industrialists traditionally avoided supporting the Communists because of their trade union links. During the 1920s they also avoided the NSDAP, preferring to back to the Nationalist Party or the People's Party. A few exceptions included Hugo Stinnes, Kurt von Schroeder, Wilhelm Keppler and Fritz Thyssen. Others spread their donations across the parties and donated small amounts to the NSDAP as political insurance. The economic crisis of 1930 pushed more industrialists towards the NSDAP, including Emil Kirdorf and Friedrich Flick, just when it needed extra financial backing.

On 27 January 1932, Hitler was invited to Düsseldorf to address the Industry Club, a group of influential coal and steel barons from the Rhine and Westphalia. Hitler wanted their support and financial backing and he spent two hours explaining the party's policies on the economy, tailoring his views in an attempt win their trust. He told them Germany needed a powerful state and a thriving economy because unemployment was driving the people into the arms of the Communists. He also reminded them that thousands of SA and SS men were giving up their time and money to support the country. Hitler was given a standing ovation and some of the industrialists warmed to a party leader who opposed communism and the trade unions. The NSDAP soon had extra financial backing, helping it to continue political campaigning during the crucial year of 1932.

Once Hitler was appointed Chancellor and it was clear that the Nazis were going to gain power, industrialists queued up to offer their backing. Lucrative deals were on the table under the Nazis' 'cash for contracts' system as rearmament and full employment promised to bring huge profits. Gustav Krupp von Bohlen changed his views and in June 1933 he was appointed chairman of the Adolf Hitler Donation of the German Economy. The fund was set up to rationalise donations and businesses had to contribute if they wanted to benefit from Nazi policy decisions. It received 30 million RM in the first year. Martin Bormann administered the fund and he suggested contributions while controlling expenses. He also made sure that the Führer's favourite projects received plenty of money.

THE FINANCIAL BACKERS

HUGO STINNES (1870–1924)

Stinnes was a mining engineer who expanded his Ruhr business portfolio to coal mines, depots, barges and ships. He also acquired iron and steel factories and the company supplying gas and electricity to the Rhineland and Westphalia. The First World War substantially increased his fortune. Stinnes was a People's Party Reichstag delegate from 1920 to 1924 and he bought up newspapers so he could print his views. He also donated to the NSDAP, believing that it would help defeat the socialists and trade unionists. Stinnes died in April 1924 and his company was liquidated. His sons set up a new company and it became an important part of the Nazi rearmament programme.

KURT VON SCHROEDER (1889–1965)

Schroeder had amassed a huge fortune in banking after serving in the First World War and he supported the NSDAP in the hope of stopping the rise of communism. On 4 January 1933, Hitler and Papen secretly discussed plans for a new cabinet at Schroeder's Cologne house; there was a national scandal when news was leaked to the press. The Nazis appointed

Schroeder Head of the Trade Association of Private Bankers and President of the Rhineland Industrial Chamber in return for his help.

WILHELM KEPPLER (1882–1960)

Keppler was an early member of the NSDAP and the Keppler Circle, a group of businessmen and industrialists. He gave the party financial backing in the summer of 1931. Keppler was appointed Reich Commissioner of Economic Affairs in 1933 and three years later he became an adviser for the Four Year Plan. He went on to prepare for the Anschluss with Austria and he was appointed the country's Reich Commissioner based in Vienna in March 1938.

FRITZ THYSSEN (1873–1951)

Thyssen had financially supported nationalist patriots during the French occupation of the Ruhr in 1923. He became an early Nazi Party supporter after learning about Hitler's promise to break communism. By 1928 Thyssen was a chief shareholder of the United Steel Works and chairman of the International Steel Society. He joined the NSDAP in 1931 and urged other industrialists to support Hitler. The Nazis appointed Thyssen President of the National Employers' Association and the head of a new institute to research the effects of the corporate state in 1933. He quickly became alarmed by the Nazis' style of politics and disgusted by their persecution of Jewish communities. He resigned in protest from the Prussian Staatsrat in 1938 and spoke out against Germany's warlike attitude in the Reichstag the following year. He was eventually forced into exile in Switzerland.

EMIL KIRDORF (1847–1938)

Kirdorf was a ruthless businessman and employer who founded United Steel Works, Gelsenkircher Mine Works and the Rhine–Westphalian Coal Syndicate. He also controlled the

Hitler visits a factory belonging to one of the party fund contributors. (NARA-242-HB-04081)

Ruhr Treasury, a political fund set up to protect the interests of mining industries. He regularly contributed to the party after attending the 1929 Nuremberg rally. Kirdorf died in July 1938.

FRIEDRICH FLICK (1883–1972)

Flick had a long association with the iron and steel industry and by 1932 he was the head of United Steel, Daimler-Benz and Nobel Dynamite. Throughout the early 1930s he backed several nationalist parties and his donations reflected a party's share of the national vote; his donation to the NSDAP increased substantially once they were in power. Flick joined the NSDAP in 1937 and he became a member of Heinrich Himmler's Circle of Friends so he could benefit from SS contracts.

GUSTAV KRUPP VON BOHLEN UND HALBACH (1870–1950)

Krupp was born Gustav von Bohlen und Halbach, a diplomat who married into the Krupp family in 1906. Their armaments business became one of the leading German industries during the First World War. He was initially opposed to the NSDAP but he changed his mind after meeting Chancellor Hitler on 20 February 1933. As Chairman of the Association of German Industrialists, he promised the NSDAP sizable donations in exchange for armaments contracts. In May 1933 he was appointed chairman of the *Adolf Hitler-Spende*, the industrialists' cash for contracts fund.

THE PARTY MEMBERSHIP

The original members of the DAP and the NSDAP were mostly war veterans who longed for a return to the camaraderie of the trenches. They blamed Germany's economic and political difficulties on the Treaty of Versailles, on France, on the capitalists or the Jews; they frequently blamed all of them. The NSDAP's 25 Points represented their views.

The NSDAP was banned following the Munich Putsch in November 1923 and only 700 people renewed their membership when Hitler was released from prison in 1925. While Hitler's associates increased membership in Bavaria, Strasser and Goebbels did the same in northern Germany. Numbers increased steadily over the next five years, increasing dramatically when Germany's economic problems increased in 1930.

Date	Number of Members
December 1925	27,000
December 1926	49,000
December 1927	72,000
December 1928	108,000
December 1929	178,000
December 1930	389,000
December 1931	862,000
June 1932	1,200,000

Membership had reached eight million by the spring of 1933, one in ten of the German population. These latecomers were referred to as the 'Sweet Violets', the 'March Violets' or 'Those Who Joined in March'. Communists and socialists who had switched to the NSDAP were called 'Beefsteak Nazis'; brown on the outside and red on the inside.

THE SPECTRUM OF SUPPORT

While the working classes and the unemployed in the cities joined the Social Democrats or the Communists, the original NSDAP support was found amongst the lower middle classes and in rural areas. After the party's success in the September 1930 Reichstag election, support swelled as members of the civil service, graduate professions and aristocrats joined, people who were badly affected by the economic crisis. Goebbels referred to these new-comers as the *Septemberlings*. The range of membership of the NSDAP in 1930 is shown in the chart below

Occupation	Percentage
Labourers	26
White collar	24
Self-employed	19
Farmers	13
Civil service	8
Miscellaneous	10

Age Range	Percentage
18–20	1
21–30	36
31–40	31
41–50	18
51–60	10
60+	4

The NSDAP targeted specific social issues and the public responded, bringing support from a wide cross section of society. Location, religion, employment status and grievances were addressed to attract support from all ages, both sexes, and a wide range of social groups. Their initial support came from the lower middle class of Germany's Protestant towns rather than the Catholic Rhineland and Bavaria.

The NSDAP was unable to break the traditional communist strongholds in the cities but people in rural areas were susceptible to fresh propaganda where there was no organised political support. The NSDAP filled the vacuum and they gained support from local industries and in agricultural areas. They were also supported by small businessmen and the self-employed who were being squeezed by inflation and unemployment, while feeling threatened by big businesses and the trade unions. White-collar workers affected by the economic situation were also attracted to the NSDAP.

The female vote was significant. Traditionally women rarely voted, especially in rural areas, and those that did were usually influenced by their husbands or their church. By the spring of 1932 new propaganda campaigns targeted women's issues, drawing their attention to politics and many voted for the first time. The NSDAP won many votes from the female-dominated, non-union textile and domestic industries. In July 1932, over 6.5 million women chose to vote for the NSDAP.

NSDAP PARTY SCHOOL FOR ORATORS

Fritz Reinhardt (1895–1969), Gauleiter for Upper Bavaria-Swabia, established a school to train local party leaders how to speak effectively. After the NSDAP percentage of the vote increased significantly in his area, the party established a national school in 1928. Over the next five years, the school taught hundreds of Nazi leaders how to present effective speeches and field answers. The school also supplied speakers and prepared speeches.

Reinhardt was elected Reichstag delegate for Upper Bavaria-Swabia Constituency in 1930. He was appointed the State Secretary for the Reich Ministry of Finance in April 1933 and an SA-Gruppenführer in 1937.

PARTY AWARDS

Several awards were given to party members for exceptional achievements or long service. The Golden Badge of Honour was awarded for outstanding services for the NSDAP. Only a few hundred of the gold badges were issued and they were personally awarded by the Führer. The Blood Order was introduced in 1933 for the 1,500 party members who had taken part in the 1923 Munich Putsch. The silver medal was attached to a red band with a white enclosure.

PARTY DISCIPLINE

The NSDAP had to be above reproach if it was to appeal to voters. Judicial committees to deal with internal discipline and disobedience were established in 1921. The Investigation and Settlement Committee, the USCHLA, was set up in 1926 under Walter Buch (1883–1949). Buch had joined the SA in 1922, rising to command the Nuremberg area. The USCHLA also monitored problems arising from the NSDAP's confusing hierarchy. Its headquarters were in Munich and it had offices at Gau, Circle and Local Group level, to deal with local disciplinary issues.

Buch accompanied Hitler when Röhm was arrested in June 1934 and he supervised the executions in Stadelheim prison during the Night of the Long Knives. Six months later he was appointed Supreme Party Judge, the highest disciplinary authority after the Führer. He also controlled the Gau-based party courts. At first the USCHLA's harshest punishment was expulsion from the party. After 1933 the courts could recommend loss of employment or a prison sentence; anyone who broke the party rules after 1937 could be sent to a concentration camp.

Goebbels, Hitler and Hess are escorted through a crowd by their SS guards. (NARA-242-HB-03040)

GREETINGS AND SALUTES

The Nazis changed the German greeting 'good day', *Guten Tag*. The crowds shouted '*Heil Hitler*' when Hitler was released from Landsberg prison in January 1925 and Franz Pfeffer von Salomon formalised the greeting with the straight arm salute across the SA. Goebbels made it a regular greeting when he was Gauleiter of Berlin; all party members were soon using it. After July 1933 university lecturers, teachers, lawyers and state employees had to use it in court sessions, civil service meetings and lessons. It literally translates to 'Hail Hitler' or 'Salvation to Hitler'. Fellow Nazi supporters were often referred to as Comrades, or *Kameraden*. Anti-Nazis refused to use the greeting in defiance but they looked around first to make sure no one was watching. This look over the shoulder became known as the 'German Glance'.

Senior party members carry their standards at the Nuremburg Rally. (NARA-242-HB-2557)

Everyone wanted to touch the Führer's hand. (NARA-242-HB-2550)

CHAPTER FIVE

THE SEIZURE OF POWER

On 30 January 1933, Hitler was appointed Chancellor at the head of a new cabinet. Four weeks later the Reichstag burned down, and Article 48 of the constitution was implemented, suspending civil rights. On 5 March the NSDAP secured a majority in the chamber and at the first session at the Berlin Kroll Opera House, later in the month, the Enabling Act was voted in. The Act allowed the cabinet to pass laws and deviate from the constitution and the system of government. It also allowed the Nazis to alter government at Reich, state and local level to their own advantage.

HITLER'S FIRST CABINET

Hitler's new cabinet was a mixture of existing ministers and new ministers. While only two of the ten ministers were NSDAP members, they held posts which would turn out to be crucial in the first two months of the new administration. Hermann Göring was the President of the Reichstag with powers over the debating chamber; he was also a Minister without Portfolio. As Minister of the Interior, Wilhelm Frick had control of the police and the power to declare new security decrees, allowing the Nazis to manipulate law and order. Göring was also the Prussian Minister of the Interior, with control of half of Germany's police force.

Two members, Papen and Hugenberg, had supported Hitler as Chancellor in the misguided belief that they could control him and eventually replace him. Gürtner and Seldte had served in Papen's cabinet and they were both NSDAP sympathisers. Blomberg, Neurath, Krosigk and Eltz-Rühenach were also carried over from Papen's cabinet. Although none of the four had political affiliations, Neurath later joined the NSDAP.

The cabinet on 31 January 1934, the first anniversary of Hitler's appointment as Chancellor. (NARA-242-HB-03835)

Post	Name	Party
Chancellor	Adolf Hitler	NSDAP
Vice-Chancellor	Franz von Papen	Centre Party
Minister without Portfolio	Hermann Göring	NSDAP
Minister of the Interior	Wilhelm Frick	NSDAP
Minister of Justice	Franz Gürtner	Nationalist Party
Minister of Economics	Alfred Hugenberg	Nationalist Party
Minister of Finance	Lutz Graf Schwerin von Krosigk	no political party
Minister of Labour	Franz Seldte	Steel Helmet
Minister of Defence	Werner von Blomberg	no political party
Foreign Minister	Konstantin von Neurath	no political party
Minister of Communications	Paul von Eltz-Rühenach	no political party

While Seldte was appointed Minister of Labour, Hitler apologised to the other Steel Helmet leader, Theodor Duesterberg, about the Jewish 'slur' raised in the July 1932 presidential election. Duesterberg was offered a post in the cabinet but he refused and the Jewish 'slur' was revived. It split Duesterberg and Seldte, leaving the Steel Helmet organisation and its three million members ripe for takeover. In April, Franz Seldte joined the NSDAP.

THE NSDAP TAKES OVER THE CABINET

Six new ministers joined the cabinet over the next twelve months; all were NSDAP members.

March	Joseph Goebbels	Minister for Public Enlightenment and Propaganda
April	Hermann Göring	Minister of Aviation
June	Kurt Schmitt	replaces Hugenberg as Economics Minister
June	Richard Darré	replaces Hugenberg as Agricultural and Food Minister
December	Ernst Röhm	Minister without Portfolio
December	Rudolf Hess	Minister without Portfolio

SECURING A MAJORITY
30 JANUARY TO 21 MARCH 1933

60,000 SA and the SS celebrated Hitler's appointment with a huge torchlight procession through the streets of Berlin. The following day Hitler and Papen asked Hindenburg to dissolve the Reichstag to give the people the opportunity to ratify the new cabinet. The President agreed and the date for the election was set for 5 March, only 50 days away. Although there were widespread protests by Communists and Social Democrats across the country, they were uncoordinated and calls for strikes were ignored.

Over the next three weeks Hitler made it clear how he intended to improve the economy and reduce unemployment. He made his first radio broadcast to the people on 1 February, explaining how he wanted them to work together to help the NSDAP right the wrongs done to the country since the Treaty of Versailles. Two days later he told the Reichwehr's generals about his plans for conscription and rearmament. The NSDAP election campaign started on

10 February and thousands attended a huge meeting at the Berlin Sports Palace. The following day Hitler promised investment in the autobahn system and tax relief for the car industry. On 20 February he assured industrialists of his plan to oppose disarmament and democratic elections. Everyone was hearing what they wanted to hear.

At the same time, aggressive steps were been taken against the Communists. Five days after Hitler became Chancellor, Wilhelm Frick's Ministry of the Interior submitted a 'Decree for the Protection of the German People', extending the detention of anyone engaged in armed treasonable acts. It was used to ban left-wing meetings and newspapers, stifling the Communist Party's election campaign. However, it was the SA who was intensifying the violence.

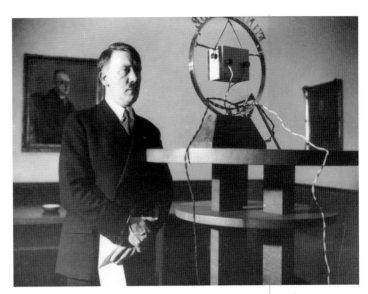

Hitler makes his first radio broadcast to the German people as Chancellor. (NARA-242-HB-00681)

Information collected by the Weimar Republic's Security Police over the previous fourteen years was checked against party records. While surveillance on NSDAP members was suspended, resources were diverted to arrest communists, including many of the Reichstag delegates. The Communist Party headquarters in Berlin were also raided and files detailing a possible attack on the government were allegedly discovered. On 22 February, 40,000 SA, SS and Steel Helmet members were sworn in as auxiliary policemen to counter the imaginary communist threat. They were immediately put to work, attacking party and union premises, newspapers offices, interrupting meetings and generally undermining the Communist Party's election campaign. The Communist hierarchy refused to react, in the belief that the Nazis would loose favour and Hitler would be forced to resign soon, as had his predecessors. It was a fatal mistake.

Firemen tackle the fire in the Reichstag. (NARA-242-HB-00186)

THE REICHSTAG FIRE
27 FEBRUARY 1933

Late on 27 February 1933, the Nazis' predictions about an attack on the government appeared to have come true when telephone calls were made to the Berlin Fire Department. The Reichstag building was on fire. Although fire engines raced to the scene, the fire took hold quickly and the building was extensively damaged before it was brought under control. The main

debating chamber was burnt out, leaving the dome in a dangerous condition, while the delegates' workroom and the restauarant had been badly affected; the reception area had also suffered considerable water damage.

The police discovered large amounts of incendiary material scattered around the building and they came to the immediate conclusion that a number of arsonists had entered the building via a tunnel leading from Hermann Göring's office. Göring was one of the first on the scene and he immediately accused the communists. The police had soon arrested Marius van der Lubbe, a known arsonist and communist sympathiser, inside the building and he was held as the main suspect. Many seriously doubted that he had acted alone.

CONSEQUENCES OF THE FIRE

Earlier on the same day as the Reichstag fire, Minister of Justice Franz Gürtner proposed a decree for the suppression of public order. On 28 February, Frick presented an amended version of the decree 'For the Protection of the People and State' before Hindenburg, asking him to bring Article 48 of the constitution into use. Frick's version allowed the government to take over states if public order was endangered. It also added a crucial point allowing the cabinet to implement it rather than the President.

The 84-year-old President agreed and the decree came into force. It suspended civil liberties, free speech and the right to assemble. It also introduced draconian penalties, including the death penalty for arson of public buildings; it also allowed the police to hold people indefinitely in protective custody without a court order. The decree stated that:

Hitler and Goebbels view the damage to the Reichstag. (NARA-242-HB-00188)

It is therefore permissible to restrict the rights of personal freedom, freedom of opinion, including the freedom of the press, the freedom to organise and assemble, the privacy of postal, telegraphic and telephonic communications, and warrants for house searches, orders for confiscations as well as restrictions on property, are also permissible beyond the legal limits otherwise prescribed.

The decree also allowed the cabinet to intervene, instead of the President, and it extended the powers of the Minister for the Interior over the states.

The Nazis could now arrest anyone they wanted without reason and hold them indefinitely, and they did so quickly. The SA went on the rampage and the communists were unprepared. Estimates vary widely but it is possible that over 10,000 'enemies of the state' were placed in protective custody over the next few days.

The SA, acting in their role as auxiliary policemen, set about raiding political party offices, breaking up political meetings and intimidating voters. They also arrested 100 Communist Reichstag delegates. The Communist Party was allowed to continue campaigning with new candidates so that voters did not shift to the Social Democrats.

THE REICHSTAG FIRE TRIAL

Speculation about the fire was rife across Germany. In response the authorities instigated legal proceedings in July 1933, making it an offence to spread rumours that the Nazis had been involved. The trial eventually started on 21 September 1933, seven months after the fire. It was held in Leipzig before the Fourth Penal Chamber of the Supreme Court of the German Reich and presided over by Judge Dr Wilhlem Bünger. There were five defendants, Marinus van der Lubbe, Georgi Dimitrov, Ernst Torgler, Blagoi Popov and Vassili Tanev; all five were accused of trying to provoke a rebellion.

MARINUS VAN DER LUBBE (1909–1934)
Van der Lubbe was born in Leiden in he province of Zuid-Holland. He had been partially blinded by lime while working as a builder's apprentice in 1925, and found himself without full time employment. He left the Netherlands in September 1931 to look for work. He was usually unsuccessful and drifted through Austria, Yugoslavia and Hungary before ending up in Germany. The young Dutchman was a sorry sight as he was cross-examined in chains and he often struggled to understand the questions while his answers were sometimes incoherent. During the cross-examination the court heard about three recent attempts he had made to set Berlin public buildings on fire. He was the ideal suspect for the Nazis.

GEORGI DIMITROV (1882–1949)
Dimitrov was the Bulgarian head of a secret communist network in Germany. He was an able defendant, challenging the prosecution and ridiculing the witnesses. He also made a mockery out of Göring's clumsy cross-examination.

ERNST TORGLER (1893–1963)
Torgler had been a Communist Party delegate in the Reichstag since 1924 and party chairman since 1929. He handed himself immediately after the fire.

BLAGOI POPOV (1902–1968)
Popov was a Bulgaria student and a communist activist.

VASSILI TANEV
Tanev was a Macedonian shoemaker and a communist activist.

The verdict was announced on 23 December 1933. Marinus Van der Lubbe was found guilty, but the other four defendants were released due to lack of evidence. The outcome greatly irritated the Nazi leadership.

Dimitrov remained in custody until February 1934 when he was freed following international pressure; he emigrated to Russia and became the Premier of Bulgaria after the Second World War. Torgler was rearrested and moved to a concentration camp. He was eventually released but in 1935 he was expelled from the Communist Party and joined the Social Democratic Party. Popov and Tanev were also acquitted.

Marinus Van der Lubbe was found guilty of high treason, insurrectionary arson and attempted common arson. He was sentenced to death and subjected to a perpetual loss of civil rights under a special retrospective law, the *Lex van der Lubbe*. He was executed by guillotine on 10 January 1934, three days before his 25th birthday, and buried in an unmarked grave on the Südfriedhof in Leipzig. .

The Nazis had made the Reichstag Fire Trial a public event and international observers had seen German justice in action. It would not happen again. After April 1934 cases of treason were handled by the new People's Court and held behind closed doors.

NAZI INVOLVEMENT IN THE FIRE

Over the months that followed, several attempts were made to place the blame for the fire on the Nazis. Dr Ernst Oberfohren of the Nationalist People's Party made the first attempt, blaming senior Nazis for planning and organising and fire, setting Lubbe up as the arsonist. A copy of his report found its way to the British newspaper, the *Manchester Guardian*, and it was published on 27 April 1933. Ten days later Oberfohren was found dead in Kiel, having allegedly committed suicide.

The Berlin Fire Department Chief, Walter Gempp, claimed that the call to the fire engines had been delayed by Göring and that his men had found a lorry stacked with incendiary material next to the Reichstag building. A few weeks later he was accused of being involved in communist activities but he persisted in repeating his findings during the trial. In September 1937, Gempp was arrested and convicted for malpractice; he was found strangled in his cell in May 1939.

The World Committee for the Victims of German Racism also published two books called *The Brown Book of the Reichstag Fire and the Hitler Terror* and *The Second Brown Book of the Riechstag Fire and the Hitler Terror*. The first covered the burning of the Reichstag while the second covered the trial. The United Scramblers smuggled copies of the books into Germany before the Gestapo arrested many of the group.

Historians continue to argue over who started the fire but one thing is certain; the timing of the Reichstag building suited the Nazi plans for the Third Reich and a police state. They also took immediate advantage of the situation in the aftermath of the fire to take control of Germany.

THE MARCH 1933 REICHSTAG ELECTION

A combination of fear and propaganda dominated the run up to the election on 5 March. The Police and the SA deployed on election day, intimidating voters as they headed to the polling booths. Only 17 million out of 45 million voters supported the NSDAP and it returned 288 out of 647 deputies. However, the Nazi-led coalition of Hitler, Papen and Hugenberg had a slim majority of 51.9 per cent.

Party	SPD	DNVP	DVP	Centre	DDPS	BVP	KPD	Others	Nazis
Delegates	120	52	2	74	–	18	81	–	288

Although the number of delegates was less than the Nazis had hoped for, it was enough to achieve what they wanted.

The opening ceremony was held on 21 March at the Garrison Church in Potsdam and two days later the first session of the Reichstag was held in the Berlin Kroll Opera House. Swastikas adorned the walls while SA and SS troops kept order. Goebbels ran a propaganda campaign over the next two months, arranging over 2,000 mass meetings across the country. He referred to dissenters as 'alarmists and critics' who would criticise anything new. The Nazis could now put into place their plans for their Third Reich.

Otto Dietrich, Hans Lammers, Goebbels, Wilhelm Frick, Hitler and Alfred Rosenberg study election results. (NARA-242-HB-07631a7)

Hindenburg reviews his troops. (NARA-242-HB-00267)

Hindenburg and
Hitler.

The ceremony
in Potsdam's
Garrison Church.
(NARA-242-HB-
00583)

VOTING UNDER THE NAZIS

There were no more Reichstag elections under the Third Reich but there were several plebiscites, or referendums, to confirm Hitler's actions. The first plebiscite followed Hitler's decision to walk out of the Geneva Disarmament Conference in October 1933. The Reichstag was dissolved and a plebiscite was held on 12 November. Although 95 per cent of the electorate approved, the SA used coercion, bullying and deception to persuade voters. Voters were escorted to polling stations and those who refused were beaten up or dragged around town with placards around their neck. Voting was held in public in some towns while mobile polling stations visited the sick.

A plebiscite in August 1934 confirmed Hitler's combined role as Chancellor and President. Another plebiscite followed the March 1938 Anschluss. It was claimed that over 99 per cent of Germans and Austrians voted yes. The public were also asked to approve a new list of NSDAP candidates for the Reichstag. Again over 99 per cent of Germans approved.

THE THIRD REICH AND THE FÜHRER

The Nazis adopted the title 'Third Reich' in the early 1920s and they planned to establish a regime which continued on from two previous German empires. The First Reich was the Holy Roman Empire which started in AD 962 and it lasted until Napoleon abolished it in 1806. The Second Reich was founded in 1871 by Otto von Bismarck following the Franco-Prussia War. It lasted until the Hohenzollern dynasty finished with the Armistice at the end of the First World War. The National Socialists also referred to the Third Reich as the 'Führer State' where the will of the Führer was the highest law of the land.

The *Führerlexikon* was a Who's Who of Nazi party leaders and hierarchy, published in 1934. It also included National Socialist martyrs, politicians, businessmen, civil servants, lawyers and technologists. The editor's research was faulty and while some senior party members were omitted, minor officials were included. No women or historical military leaders were included.

THE ENABLING ACT

The Reichstag opened for its first session in the Kroll Opera House on 21 March and the few Communist deputies who had not been arrested were forbidden to take their seats. Two days later SA storm troopers lined the walls of the debating chamber while Hitler proposed the Enabling Act. The Act would allow the cabinet to introduce laws without the consent of the Reichstag, even if they deviated from the constitution or altered it.

It was a simple piece of legislation designed to take advantage of Article 48 of the Weimar constitution. It would allow the cabinet, with the assent of the President, to rule without a Reichstag majority. It would also allow the cabinet to pass laws and rule by decree. The Act was a constitutional amendment and it required a two-thirds majority, with a two-thirds quorum, before it could be passed. Under normal circumstances the 81 Communist deputies and the 120 Social Democrat deputies could have been counted on to vote against the Act, but most of them were in prison or in exile.

Hitler had also already negotiated a deal with the Centre Party chairman, Ludwig Kaas, promising to retain civil servants affiliated with his party. He had also promised to protect

SA troopers line the walls of the Kroll Opera House as Goebbels speaks to the Reichstag. (NARA-242-HB-03957)

Catholics' civil and religious liberties. While Kaas had asked Hitler for written guarantees, he would never get them. The Nazis established a working committee with the Centre Party but it only met three times and achieved nothing. Former Chancellor Heinrich Brüning vigorously opposed the Enabling Act, but he eventually voted for it, in line with the rest of his party.

The Social Democrats planned to boycott the Reichstag session, leaving it short of the required quorum. The Reichstag President, Hermann Göring, countered the proposed veto by changing the chamber's procedural rules. He announced that any deputy who was 'absent without excuse' would be counted as present. The Social Democrat delegates had to attend to register their opposition and their chairman, Otto Wels, bravely spoke out against the Act, despite jeers and threats.

With 81 Communist and 26 Social Democrat deputies either in prison or in hiding, the result was a forgone conclusion. 441 delegates voted in favour of the Enabling Act and 94 voted against. The vote was approved by the Reichsrat and immediately countersigned by Hindenburg, Hitler, Minister of Interior Wilhelm Frick, Foreign Minister Konstantin von Neurath and Minister of Finance Lutz Schwerin von Krosigk. It was enacted the following day, bringing the end of democratic rule in Germany. In future the Nazis could use the Act to accomplish the 'legal seizure of power' Hitler had aspired to.

The formal name of the Enabling Act was the 'Law to Remedy the Distress of the People and the Nation'. It was a short piece of legislation which had far reaching consequences for the German people. The key parts of the five articles and their consequences are listed below:

Article 1: In addition to the procedure prescribed by the Constitution, laws of the Reich may also be enacted by the government of the Reich.

The government could pass legislation without the consent of the Reichstag.

A work detail at one of the new concentration camps.

Article 2:   Laws enacted by the government of the Reich may deviate from the Constitution as long as they do not affect the institutions of the Reichstag and the Reichsrat. The rights of the President remain undisturbed.

The government could pass legislation which altered the country's constitution.

Article 3:   Laws enacted by the Reich government shall be issued by the Chancellor and announced in the *Reich Gazette*. They shall take effect on the day following the announcement, unless they prescribe a different date.

Chancellor Hitler would sign legislation into law rather than President Hindenburg.

Article 4:   Treaties of the Reich with foreign states which affect matters of Reich legislation shall not require the approval of the bodies of the legislature. The government of the Reich shall issue the regulations required for the execution of such treaties.

The government would deal with foreign states without refering to the ministries.

Article 5:   This law takes effect with the day of its proclamation. It loses force on 1 April 1937 or if the present Reich government is replaced by another.

The Enabling Act was limited to four years or the lifetime of the government. It was renewed in 1937, 1939 and finally made permanent in 1943.

The cabinet now had the authority to pass laws without the consent of the Reichstag. Even so, the functions of the Reichstag dwindled as the Nazis increasingly relied on non-elected committees to decide policies and make decisions. The last cabinet meeting took place in February 1938. Initially the Reichstag, the Reichsrat and the office of the President were protected under the Act. They would be undermined and removed from the political process one by one over the next eighteen months.

Vote for Hitler and the NSDAP candidates – but was there a choice? (NARA-242-HB-1935a1)

A dejected Marinus van der Lubbe is led into court in chains to hear the guilty verdict. (NARA-242-2751a)

CHAPTER SIX

SECURING POWER

COORDINATION, *GLEICHSCHALTUNG*

'*Gleichschaltung*' has no direct translation into English, however, it can be described as synchronisation, coordination or bringing into line. It was the Nazis' term for coordinating the activities of the state and the activities of the party into one. A week after the March Reichstag elections, Hitler gave a speech explaining the need for *Gleichschaltung* and the 'coordination of the political will' in Germany. By the time the Reichstag opened two weeks later, the Nazis had already started implementing it. Over the next twelve months all areas of German life would be coordinated.

POLICE AND SECURITY

On 26 April, Göring merged the political and intelligence elements of the Prussian Police into the Gestapo. The SA had already been sworn in as auxiliary police and they held political prisoners in temporary camps. In Bavaria, Himmler was made commander of the Munich police and few days later Dachau concentration camp, one of many protective custody camps, was opened near Munich; it would become the model for camps across the country.

Aryanisation of the legal profession started in April 1933 as Nazi judges and lawyers replaced Jewish ones. Special Courts were established under the Malicious Practices Act to prosecute them outside the law. At the same time an amnesty was declared for Nazis who had committed offences 'for the good of the Reich' under the Weimar Republic. A People's Court was opened in Berlin at the end of March to deal with high treason.

Göring and Himmler merged their organisations and Himmler took control of the Gestapo in April 1934; in February 1936 Gestapo activities were placed above the law. Reinhard Heydrich was placed in control of the Security Police, combining the activities of the Criminal Police and the Gestapo in July 1936. In September

Party leaders study their agenda. (NARA-242-HB-18312a1)

Bormann and Hess address party leaders. (NARA-242-HB-18312)

1939 the Reich Main Security Office combined the activities of the Security Police, the Security Service and the SS intelligence service.

MEDIA AND CULTURE

On 13 March, Joseph Goebbels was appointed Reich Minister for Public Enlightenment and Propaganda, while Alfred Rosenberg was appointed head of the Reich Ministry of Culture. Between the two ministries, they aryanised visual art, music, the press, radio, literature, film and theatre, removing Jewish, anti–nationalistic and liberal employees while setting new Aryan standards.

TRADE UNIONS AND THE WORK FORCE

The traditional Labour Day on 1 May was renamed National Labour Day and Hitler spoke to half a million people on the Tempelhofer Field in Berlin. The following day the SA took over labour union offices across the country, arresting many union officials, while unions were disbanded and their funds seized. On 10 May the German Labour Front, a single unified workers' organisation, was formed. A week later workers were banned from striking while managements were prohibited from staging lock outs; compulsory taxes were added while wages were frozen. The Law for Reduction in Unemployment was introduced on 1 June,

Hitler and his deputy stand alongside cabinet members, Neurath, Frick, Blomberg and Krosigk. (NARA-242-HB-12360a1)

introducing work incentives. Cooperation between employers and employees was strengthened in January 1934 when Councils of Trust were set up to replace Works Councils. The 'Strength through Joy and Beauty of Labour' organisations worked to improve working conditions and provide recreational pursuits.

THE ECONOMY

In May the Nazis took many steps to kick start the economy, starting with Hitler's announcement that the road building programme would be extended. Soon afterwards Finance Ministry State Secretary Fritz Reinhardt presented the plan for economic recovery. Short-term credits, funded by exchange bills underwritten by the government, were introduced. With the help of the banks, civil service and industrialists – often under Nazi pressure – the economy received a boost. In February 1934 an economic law removed the powers of the Cartel Tribunal and handed them to a new Commercial Economy Organisation, working on behalf of the Minister of Economy.

Hitler appears at the window of the Chancellery. (NARA-242-HB-07644)

THE ELIMINATION OF OPPOSITION PARTIES

Communist deputies had been forbidden to take seats when the Reichstag opened on 21 March; most had already been imprisoned or escaped. After the unions had been closed down the Social Democrats were targeted and their leader, Otto Wels, fled to Prague. After 21 June deputies were refused entry to the Reichstag, meetings were banned and newspapers shut down. Two days later 3,000 members were arrested and tortured; some leaders were murdered. The Social Democrat Party was then dissolved.

Hugenberg reorganised the Nationalist Party as the German Nationalist Front to adapt to the Nazi regime but delegates were threatened or faced false accusations. Rumours also undermined Hugenberg's position and he was banned from speaking in the Reichstag and vilified in the press until he resigned on 26 June, fearing for his life. The Nationalist People's Party, German People's Party and the German Democratic Party folded over the next few days, followed by the Bavarian People's Party.

The Centre Party was supported by the Catholic Church but Kaas resigned and headed for Rome to work on the Concordat. Brüning had to deal with senior members being arrested and tortured while local parties were pressurised into closing and membership plummeted. It was agreed to close the party down on 5 July after the Concordat was signed and members were instructed to work with the Nazis; hardly any were welcomed. The Law concerning the Formation of the New Parties announced on 14 July made it illegal to form a new political party.

RELIGION

The Catholic Church had called for its members to support the new government on 28 March, and a Concordat between the Vatican and the Third Reich was signed on 20 July. Ludwig Müller had been appointed as the confidant and plenipotentiary for problems concerning the Protestant Church on 4 April. Friedrich von Bodelschwingh was elected Reich Bishop on 26 May but he resigned soon afterwards in protest at the Nazi plans for the Church. A written constitution for the new Reich Church was accepted by the Reichstag on 14 July. Ludwig Müller was eventually elected Reich Bishop on 27 September but a rival Confessional Church was formed in opposition to his appointment.

THE ARMED FORCES

By the start of 1934, the Nazis were ready to turn their attentions to the armed forces. On 1 February General von Hammerstein-Equord was forced to resign as Commander-in-Chief of the Reichswehr due to his anti-Nazi stance. He was replaced by General Werner von Blomberg, a Hitler supporter, and he dismissed 70 senior non-Aryan officers. Röhm's demand for the SA to form a national defence horrified the new commander and he incorporated the Nazi swastika into the armed forces' insignia.

Hitler made it clear at the end of the month that the SA would only deal with political matters. The new army had to be ready for defence in five years and ready to attack in eight. Until then the SA would supervise pre-military training and provide border protection. Röhm was unhappy about the news but dramatic events were soon to change the balance of power between the SA, the SS and the army.

THE NIGHT OF THE LONG KNIVES, THE BLOOD PURGE

After Hitler achieved power in 1933, there was anti-Hitler sentiment from several parts of the Nazi Party. Gregor Strasser's supporters were still looking to push their man forward. Some of the original working-class members of the party were angry about the takeover of the 'March Violets', middle-class members who had joined after March 1933. The SA were also feeling neglected. The Chief of Staff, Ernst Röhm, had increased membership to over four million in three years and they had fought street and beer hall battles for the past ten years. They were now forced to stand by and watch as the SS took over.

Röhm believed that the SA was the true army of the new Nazi Germany and he wanted to merge it with the Reichswehr, angering the generals. In the spring of 1934 he was also talking about removing Germany's traditional power groups, a Second Revolution supported by

Gregor Strasser. Victor Lutze, the Hanover SA leader reported this treasonous talk to Rudolf Hess, the Führer's deputy, and General Walther von Reichenau, Blomberg's chief of staff.

With President Hindenburg on his deathbed, Hitler was concerned that there could be a call for a return to monarchism and the Kaiser's second son, Augustus, a member of the SA, was the likely contender. While Hitler wanted to keep Röhm's friendship, he needed the support of the army generals and the industrialists; talk of a revolution was undermining their support.

Ernst Röhm stands at Hitler's shoulder during the 1933 Nuremberg Rally; nine months later he was murdered. (NARA-242-HB-02506)

In June 1934 events moved rapidly towards a bloody conclusion starting on the 4th when Hitler failed to reason with Röhm. Over the weeks that followed Heydrich's Security Service prepared names they believed were a threat to the party. The Nazi leadership also made suggestions. Victor Lutze used Röhm's own promotion list to identify SA commanders who were to be killed.

The Reich Deputy Chancellor, Franz von Papen, gave a public speech at Marburg University on 10 June 1934, calling for the return of civil rights while condemning the brutal implementation of *Gleichschaltung*. It had been largely

The new SA Chief of Staff, Victor Lutze, sits uncomfortably knowing that Himmler organised the murder of his predecessor. (NARA-242-HB-06980)

written by Edgar Jung and Erich Klausener and although it was discussed in higher circles, Goebbels suppressed its content.

On 20 June a shot fired at Hitler slightly wounded Himmler and it was blamed on the SA escort. Eight days later the army was mobilised while the Abwehr revealed that it had uncovered secret SA orders for a coup. The League of German Officers also expelled Röhm. Himmler gave the news of an impending revolt to senior SS and SD officers the following day and they prepared to counter it. The commander of the Berlin SS guard, Joseph Dietrich, was given extra weapons and transport by the army, ready to round up the accused.

On 29 June Hitler toured labour camps in the Rhineland before stopping for the night at Bad Godesberg near Bonn. He was joined by Goebbels, who had flown from Berlin with news that Karl Ernst, the Berlin SA commander had alerted his men. The report was a lie. It was Ernst's wedding day and he was driving to Bremen to start his honeymoon. The Bavarian Gauleiter, Adolf Wagner, also reported that around 3,000 Munich SA had been rampaging on the streets. They had been ordered out by anonymous notes designed to arouse suspicion. The traps were set.

Now that everyone was in place, Hitler summoned Victor Lutze, the Hanover SA commander, and gave him the surprise news that he was going to be the new Chief of Staff for the SA. Just after midnight on 30 June, Goebbels used the codeword 'Hummingbird' to alert the Prussian and Bavarian Ministers of the Interior. While Hermann Göring mobilised police units in Berlin, Adolf Wagner did the same in Munich. The SS–Leibstandarte Adolf Hitler was also alerted and two companies led by Joseph Dietrich headed south to Munich.

At first light on 30 June Hitler flew to Munich accompanied by Goebbels, Lutze and the NSDAP's Press Chief, Otto Dietrich. As soon as they arrived, the local SA commanders, Wilhelm Schmidt and August Schneidhuber, were ordered to Stadelheim jail where Hitler called them traitors before one of his bodyguards shot them. After the Bavarian Gauleiter was given lists of men to arrest across Bavaria, Hitler's party drove off to confront Röhm. Meanwhile, Rudolf Hess invited 150 SA leaders to the Brown House on the pretext that they were to attend a meeting. SS guards were waiting for them and they were held in the cellars of Lichterfelde Cadet School before many were shot four at a time in the courtyard.

Hitler had located the senior SA officers at the Hanselbauer Hotel in Bad Weissee. While Edmund Heines, the Silesia SA commander, was shot immediately after being found in bed with a young man, Röhm and the others were taken to Stadelheim prison where many were executed. Hitler ordered

Hitler visits the ailing President Hindenburg at his Neudeck Estate. (NARA-242-HB-06862a1)

Röhm to be held prisoner and he finished the day by preparing press statements in the Brown House before flying back to Berlin. He found that Göring had rounded up or tracked down hundreds of conservatives and many had been executed.

On 1 July, Hitler delayed making a decision over Röhm's fate until he had attended a public function. The SA Chief of Staff had to die but was he was going to be given the chance to take his own life. Although a revolver was left in his cell he refused, unable to come to terms with the Führer's decision. Eventually, two guards had to execute him in the cell.

At least 85 people died, including many SA commanders and twelve Reichstag deputies. Amongst them was Karl Ernst, the organiser of the 'Berlin plot'. He was arrested as he prepared to sail on his honeymoon and flown back to Berlin where he was executed. However, over 100 other men were killed for a variety of reasons. Some were political opponents such as Erich Klausener, the leader of Catholic Action. Some were dissidents in the party, like Gregor Strasser who was executed for having socialist views and for opposing Hitler on several occasions. One of the authors of the Marburg speech, Edgar Jung, was shot and while Vice-Chancellor von Papen escaped with his life, his secretary was shot at his desk as a warning.

Some were killed because of past grudges. 75-year-old Gustav Ritter von Kahr had interfered with the 1923 Munich uprising so he was beaten to death and his body was dumped in a swamp. A few senior Nazis also settled personal scores. Father Stempfle was killed for knowing too much about Hitler's relationship with Geli Raubal. Göring despised General Kurt von Schleicher, the political intriguer and he and his wife were shot at their home. A few mistakes were also made and Willi Schmid, a respected music critic, was killed instead of Willi Schmidt.

News of the killings was released in stages over the days that followed, accompanied by statements that they had been executions for traitorous conduct. On 1 July, Goebbels outlined the reasons for the murders during a national radio broadcast. Hitler explained them to the cabinet on 3 July, the same day that Wilhelm Frick, Minister of the Interior, drafted a law called 'Regarding Measures of State Self-Defence', legitimising the killings. Minister for Justice Franz Gürtner stated that it was just an extension of existing legislation. Ten days later Hitler appeared before the Reichstag to justify the killings, stating that he had had to act against four types of opponents to the state:

1) Communists supported by Jews
2) Political leaders of the old parties
3) A band of leftist revolutionaries headed by Röhm
4) Self-appointed critics and rumour mongers

Only the SA members who had been executed were mentioned in the speech and some deaths were attributed to suicides or accidents, while a few killings were justified because a prisoner had resisted arrest. He did not mention any of the others who were killed. Hitler concluded his speech with the words:

> In this hour I was responsible for the fate of the German people, and therefore I became the supreme Judge for the German people … Everyone must know that in all future time if he raises his hand to strike at the state, then certain death will be his lot.

A few months later, German refugees published the *White Book of the Purge* in Paris. It detailed the events and named 166 persons who had been killed; it was an incomplete list.

HINDENBURG'S DEATH

President Hindenburg had fallen ill in April and he retired from public life at the beginning of June. He died on the morning of 2 August 1934 at the age of 86. The Nazi cabinet had introduced a decree merging the Reich President's office with the Reich Chancellor's office a few hours before his death was announced. The Reich President's duties would also be transferred to the '*Führer und Reich Chancellor, Adolf Hitler*'. It gave Hitler total control over the Presidency, the Chancellery, the cabinet, the Reichstag and the Reichsrats. At the same time, General Werner von Blomberg ordered the armed forces to take a personal oath of loyalty to the Führer. A similar oath was introduced for civil servants later in the month. Nearly 90 per cent voted in favour of Hitler's new powers during a plebiscite held on 19 August.

CHAPTER SEVEN

THE NAZI STATE

The government was split into three levels, the National Authorities, the Reich Ministries and the Reich Offices.

NATIONAL AUTHORITIES

There were originally two Chancellery Offices, one for the Reich, acting on behalf of the Reich Ministries, and one for the President. They dealt with correspondence and acted as legal advisors. The role of the Presidential Chancellery diminished following Hindenburg's death and the establishment of a new Führer Chancellery in 1934.

OFFICE OF THE REICH CHANCELLERY

HANS LAMMER (1879–1962)

The office was the centre of communications and Lammers acted as the chief legal adviser for all ministries. Lammers was a county court judge before serving in the First World War. He joined the Ministry of the Interior as a jurist in 1921 and went on to serve as Reich Minister and State Secretary in the Reich Chancellery. When the Nazis seized power, he was appointed Chief of the Reich Chancellery because of his efficient administrative methods. He was also a member of the German Law Academy and the Prussian State Council.

Lammers was a member of Hitler's close circle and the Führer often consulted him on state matters. In 1937 he was appointed Minister without Portfolio allowing him to attend many meetings in the Führer's absence. Two years later he was appointed Ministerial Councillor for the Defence of the Reich making him one of Hitler's closest legal advisers.

OFFICE OF THE PRESIDENTIAL CHANCELLERY

OTTO MEISSNER (1880–1953)

After obtaining a law doctorate and serving in the First World War, Meissner became a civil servant. He was appointed Acting Advisor in the Bureau of the President, working for Friedrich Ebert in 1919 and Ministerial Director and Head of the Bureau of the President in 1920. Ebert appointed him State Secretary and he continued to serve as President

Hindenburg's legal advisor after his election in 1925. He helped convince the President to appoint Hitler Chancellor in 1933 and was retained as State Secretary under the Nazis. After Hindenburg's death in August 1934, the role of the President and the Chancellor were merged. Meissner's office was renamed the Office of the Presidential Chancellery but it only retained limited responsibilities for formal and representative matters. In 1937 his title was changed to State Minister of the Rank of a Federal Minister and Chief of the Presidential Chancellery of the Führer and Chancellor.

CHANCELLERY OF THE FÜHRER

PHILIP BOUHLER (1899–1945)
Bouhler was badly wounded in the First World War and, after dropping out of studies, he started writing for the Nazis' publishing house in Munich. By autumn 1922 he was second secretary of the NSDAP and he became the party's Reich Secretary after the 1923 Munich Putsch. He was elected Reichstag delegate for Westphalia in 1933; by the autumn of 1934 he was Chairman of the Munich Police.

Bouhler was appointed head of the Führer's Chancellery in 17 November 1934, preparing secret decrees and managing party business on behalf of Hitler. He also dealt with Hitler's private correspondence. The Führer's office was inundated with personal requests ranging from help finding work, to securing party membership, from asking Hitler to be a godfather to birthday wishes.

CHANGING THE CABINET

Salutes from the Nazi deputies in the Kroll House chamber. (NARA-242-HB-12360)

Hitler's original cabinet only had three NSDAP members, Hitler, Hermann Göring and Wilhelm Frick. The two NSDAP delegates remained in the cabinet; Hermann Göring was assigned to the new post of Minister of Air Traffic while Wilhelm Frick continued as Minister of the Interior. There were another three who were sympathisers; Franz Seldte, Minister of Labour, Franz Gürtner, Minister of Justice and Lutz Graf Schwerin von Krosigk, Minister of Finance.

Dr Joseph Goebbels was appointed Minister for Public Enlightenment and Propaganda on 13 March 1933. Alfred Hugenberg was forced to resign from the Ministry of Agriculture and Economics in June 1933. The Ministry was split into two with Nazis at their head; Kurt Schmitt as Minister for Economics and Richard Walther Darré as Minister for Nutrition and Agriculture. Bernhard Rust was appointed Minister for Science, Education and Culture in June 1934. Rudolf Hess and Ernst Röhm were appointed Ministers without Portfolio at the end of 1933.

The cabinet met every week until October 1933 but the Enabling Act allowed it to be bypassed and the number of meetings soon halved. By May 1934 the Nazis held the majority and before long it had stopped meeting.

Over the years that followed some members were forced to resign. Franz von Papen was removed from the post of Vice-Chancellor after his Marburg speech denounced Nazi policies in June 1934; he was fortunate not to be killed during the Night of the Long Knives. The Minister of Post and Transportation, Paul Freiherr von Eltz-Rübenach had refused to join the NSDAP, so his ministry was split and he was replaced by Julius Dorpmüller and Wilhelm Ohnesorge in February 1937.

Resistance to Hitler's plans to occupy Austria and Czechoslovakia in November 1937 resulted in the resignation of two ministers three months later. General Werner von Blomberg was forced to resign following a false personal scandal and his post of Minister of War was abolished as Hitler became the Supreme Commander of the Armed Forces. At the same time, Konstantin Freiherr von Neurath was replaced as Foreign Minister by Joachim von Ribbentrop.

One of the few times Hitler addressed the Reichstag delegates. (NARA-242-HB-06978a6)

REICH MINISTRIES

The Nazi government eventually had fourteen ministries controlling all aspects of German life. Each was led by a minister and by early 1934 the majority were dedicated Nazis. Another four Nazi delegates were appointed Ministers without Portfolio. The following ministers served between January 1933 and September 1939.

Ministry of Interior	Wilhelm Frick
Ministry of Justice	Franz Gürtner
Ministry of Finance	Lutz Schwerin von Krosigk
Ministry of Economics	Kurt Schmitt
	Hjalmar Schacht after July 1934
	Walther Funk after February 1938
Ministry of Labour	Franz Seldte
Ministry for Food and Agriculture	Richard Walther Darré after June 1934
Ministry of Defence, later Ministry of War	General Werner von Blombergy to 1938
Foreign Ministry	Konstantin Freiherr von Neurath
	Joachim von Ribbentrop, February 1938
Ministry for Enlightenment and Propaganda	Joseph Goebbels after March 1933
Ministry for Science, Education, and Instruction	Bernhard Rust after June 1934

Ministry for Ecclesiastical Affairs	Hanns Kerrl after July 1935
Ministry of Aviation	Hermann Göring after April 1933
Ministry of Communications	Paul Freiherr von Eltz-Rübenach
Ministry of Transport	Julius Dorpmüller after February 1937
Ministry of Post	Wilhelm Ohnesorge after February 1937
Ministers without Portfolio	Konstantin von Neurath, February 1938
	Rudolf Hess after December 1933
	Ernst Röhm after December 1933
	Hanns Kerrl after June 1934
	Hans Frank after December 1934
	Hjalmar Schacht after January 1939
	Arthur Seyss-Inquart after May 1939

In March 1935, Göring was appointed head of the Luftwaffe and in April 1936 General Werner von Fritsch, Commander-in-Chief of the Army, and Admiral Erich Raeder, Commander-in-Chief of the Navy joined the cabinet. The moves fused political and military decisions.

Nazi deputies listen intently to their Führer. (NARA-242-HB-06978a10)

THE REICH COMMITTEES

The committees decided policy on a diverse range of issues including law and order, the economy, health, education, diplomacy and transportation. Cabinet ministers were appointed to Reich Committees to present the views of their ministry. Ministers from different political parties were chosen under the Weimar Republic, representing a range of views of the government. The Nazi-controlled Reich Committees coordinated the state and the party into one, making the NSDAP 'the bearer of the concept of the German state'.

SECRET COUNCILS

The Nazis established five councils between 1933 and 1939, to work outside the official state channels. They were all committed to war planning and mobilising industry for rearmament.

April 1933	The Reich Defence Council
May 1935	The College of Three
September 1936	The Office of the Delegate of the Four Year Plan
February 1938	The Privy Cabinet Council
August 1939	Ministerial Council for the Defence of the Reich

Hitler leaves the Kroll Opera House, the temporary home of the Reichstag. (NARA-242-HB-06878a12)

THE REICH DEFENCE COUNCIL

The war-planning group was set up in April 1933 with Hitler in the chair, Göring as his alternate and Hans Lammers as secretary. General Wilhelm Keitel presided over the military representatives, General Fritsch for the army, Göring as Ministry of Aviation and Admiral Raeder for the navy. The party was represented by Rudolf Hess (Party Deputy) and the cabinet by Wilhelm Frick (Interior Ministry); Joseph Goebbels (Propaganda Ministry) and Hjalmar Schacht (Reichsbank) also attended. Walter Funk (Economics) and Joachim von Ribbentrop (Foreign Affairs) joined later. The council appointed a working committee of Reich defence officials to coordinate industries ready for rearmament.

THE COLLEGE OF THREE

The committee was established in May 1935 to draft rearmament and war strategy decrees. While Hjalmar Schacht represented the war economy and Field Marshal Wilhelm Keitel represented the armed forces; Wilhelm Frick coordinated the supporting activities of the Ministries of the Interior, Justice, Education, Church Affairs and Spatial Planning. Schacht was replaced by Funk in 1938.

Political decisions were often made by the Reich Leaders, bypassing the Reichstag. (NARA-242-HB-06302)

THE OFFICE OF THE DELEGATE OF THE FOUR YEAR PLAN

The office was announced at the September 1936 Nuremberg Rally with Hermann Göring as the Delegate and Paul Koerner as the State Secretary and Deputy. It was responsible for mobilising German industry in line with war planning. It had plenipotentiaries, or representatives, for the building industry, the chemical industry, metal ore mining, the armaments industry and the labour force.

THE PRIVY COUNCIL OR SECRET CABINET COUNCIL

The council was created after Commander-in-Chief von Blomberg and General of the Army Fritsch were removed in February 1938. Konstantin von Neurath, Head of the Privy Cabinet Council, was President and Hans Lammers, the Head of the Reich Chancellery, was secretary. The council members were Rudolf Hess, Joseph Goebbels and Joachim von Ribbentrop. They were joined by General Wilhelm Keitel, new head of the Wehrmacht, and the commanders of the other armed services.

MINISTERIAL COUNCIL FOR THE DEFENCE OF THE REICH

The members of the Reich Defence Council were appointed to the council in August 1939 with Hermann Göring as their chairman and Hans Lammers as their secretary. The Führer's Deputy sat with three representatives: Heinrich Himmler for the Reich Administration, Walter Funk for Economics and Wilhelm Keitel for the Wehrmacht's High Command. The council had authority over all areas of the government and it had broad powers to issue decrees with force of law. It also concealed some of the most important policies relating to preparation for war.

Reich Leaders salute the crowds as the state and the party merge into one. (NARA-242-HB-16935a11)

REICH OFFICES

The Reich had eight subordinate offices. Some were established to deal with specific Nazi projects:

Office of the Four Year Plan	Hermann Göring
Reich Youth Office	Baldur von Schirach
Office of the Reich Master Forester	Hermann Göring
Office of the Inspector for Highways	Dr Fritz Todt
Office of the President of the Reich Bank	Walther Funk
Reich Treasury Office	
General Inspector of the Reich Capital, Berlin	
Office of the Councillor for the Capital of the Movement, Munich	

OCCUPATION AUTHORITIES

Reich Protectorate of Bohemia and Moravia	Konstantin von Neurath
Deputy Reich Protector of Bohemia and Moravia	Reinhard Heydrich

THE GOVERNMENT

The Reichstag was the supreme law-making body of the Reich under the Weimar Republic. Its powers could be checked by initiatives raised by the President or the Council of the Reich, the Reichsrat. Referendums or plebiscites could also be held.

The Reichstag was based in Berlin and it was made up of 490–600 deputies in the 1930s. Each one represented a constituency, or *Wahlkreis,* covering a large rural area, a town or a city district. The Nazis only returned 12 out of 491 deputies during the May 1928 election, with less than three per cent of the vote. By July 1932 the number of Nazis had risen to 230 out of 599 deputies, having increased its percentage of the turnout to 37.

Germany was a federation of fifteen states, or *Lander*, of varying sizes, each headed by a governor. *Diets* or *Landtags* administered parliamentary duties in each state. Deputies again represented constituencies. The country had a population of 61.1 million in 1933 and over half lived in just two states: Prussia and Bavaria.

Lander	Population (million)
Prussia	38.2
Bavaria	7.4
Saxony	5.0
Wurttemberg	2.6
Baden	2.3
Thuringia	1.6
Hesse	1.4
Mecklenburg-Schwerin	0.7
Oldenburg	0.6
Brunswick	0.5
Anhalt	0.4
Lippe	0.2
Mecklenburg-Strelitz	0.1
Waldeck	0.06
Schaumburg-Lippe	0.05

Germany also had three independent cities, Lubeck, Bremen and Hamburg, known as *Hansa* towns dating from a medieval trade league.

IMPLEMENTING THE ENABLING ACT

The Enabling Act deprived the Reichstag of legislative powers, passing them to the cabinet. It only met a dozen times over the next six years and only NSDAP delegates were allowed to speak. Only four laws were passed, all without a vote.

The first use of the Enabling Act on 31 March 1933 stripped all the states, except Prussia, of power. *Landtags* were reconstituted on the basis of votes cast, excluding Communist and Social Democrat delegates who were in jail or in exile.

Under the second *Gleichschaltung* Law of 7 April 1933, Hitler appointed new state governors, *Reichsstatthalteren*. They were responsible for implementing the Nazi system of government at state level. They could appoint a new state minister, dissolve the state parliament, call elections, implement new laws, and appoint new civil servants and judges.

General Franz von Epp replaced the Bavarian prime minister on 7 April 1933 while Hermann Göring was appointed governer for Prussia on 25 April; between them they were responsible for 45 million people, over two-thirds of the country. The rest of the state governors had been appointed by June.

The governors in turn appointed government officials, choosing loyal Nazi Party members for senior posts. The only exception was Prussia; Hitler appointed his own government officials for the largest state in Germany. The two laws had replaced all the opponents in the Reichrats with party members.

REMOVING THE OPPOSITION

All the Communist Party delegates had been arrested the day after the Reichstag fire on 27 February 1933 and on 20 May the party assets were seized. On 22 June the Social Democrat party was banned and over the days that followed the Nationalist Party, the German People's Party, the Bavarian People's Party and the Centre Party dissolved in the hope of avoiding imprisonment of their members. The Law against the Establishment of Parties banned the creation of any new political parties after 14 July 1933.

THE CIVIL SERVICE

On 7 April the Law for the Restoration of the Civil Service was used to replace liberal and Jewish employees with Nazi supporters. It also removed the differences between the Reich, state and local government, allowing the Nazis to freely transfer loyal staff between the three.

The new Reich Civil Service League superseded all professional civil service organisations and over one million civil servants had to become members or lose their jobs. In July 1933 it became compulsory to use the greeting 'Heil Hitler' and give the Nazi salute. Members had to attend meetings outside office hours and pay substantial contributions to the NSDAP. In September 1937 they were ordered to boycott department stores to support the takeover of Jewish businesses.

Building work on the new Chancellery continued around the clock. (NARA-242-HB-16524)

MERGING PARTY AND STATE

On 1 December 1933 a new Law to Secure Unity of Party and Reich was introduced, cementing Hitler's role as Führer. The Nazis had achieved their dream of 'One Reich! One People! One Leader!' The final blow for democracy came into law on 30 January 1934, the first anniversary of Hitler's Chancellorship. The Law Concerning the Reconstruction of the Reich abandoned the concept of a federal republic. It handed the powers of the state Reichrats over to the Reich ministries, abolishing the federal states, or *Länder*, they represented. The party and the state had finally been fused into one under total Nazi control. It had taken twelve months.

LOCAL AUTHORITIES

Nazis seized control of many local authorities immediately after the March 1933 election, applying their policies across town and country communities. In many towns, the SA hounded local politicians, council officials and mayors out of office to make way for NSDAP members. At the same time civil servants joined the NSDAP to save their jobs; 1.6 million had joined by the summer of 1933.

The new German Association of Cities absorbed all municipal organisations in the summer of 1933, forming the German Local Authorities Association. Karl Fiehler was appointed chairman and he removed Jewish employees and political rivals while promoting party members. He also made sure that contracts were transferred from Jewish to Aryan businesses. Local authorities also had to cut their ties with the Jewish communities in their area, ranging from providing local amenities to maintaining graveyards.

KARL FIEHLER (1895–1969)

After serving in the First World War, Fiehler joined Munich city council in 1919. He was an early member of the NSDAP in 1920 and joined Hitler's bodyguard in 1923. He marched alongside Hitler during the Munich Putsch and was imprisoned in Landsberg. After his release, Fiehler was appointed honorary alderman in Munich council and he wrote the National Socialist policies for local councils and elections. He was Munich Ortsgruppenleiter by 1930.

Fiehler was elected to the Reichstag in March 1933 and called upon the SA to occupy Munich town hall. The Mayor resigned after an eleven-day siege of the city hall and two months later Fiehler was appointed Mayor. He was made honorary SS-Standartenführer in July 1933 and SS-Gruppenführer a year later.

As chairman of German Local Authorities Association, Fiehler became the Nazis' expert on local politics and he was appointed Secretary and then Head of the Main Office for Local Politics. He also continued to serve as the Mayor of Munich, overseeing the extensive building works for the NSDAP headquarters around Köenigsplatz.

Munich led the country in anti-Semitic actions, carrying out extensive boycotts of Jewish businesses and the main synagogue was destroyed by fire in June 1938. The public's indifferent response encouraged Goebbels to plan *Kristallnacht*, the widespread attacks on Jewish communities, in particular their businesses and synagogues.

Swastikas adorn Munich's town hall, making it clear who is in control of the local authority. (NARA-242-HB-12184)

CHAPTER EIGHT

THE NAZI CALENDAR

The NSDAP introduced several annual rituals to their calendar to rally support for the party during their rise to power. While some of the events were anniversaries of important events, others were political rallies. They were turned into national holidays after they took power. New pagan-style festivals were also introduced to replace Christian festivals.

30 JANUARY: THE DAY OF THE SEIZURE OF POWER
Celebrating Hitler's appointment as Chancellor in 1933.

24 FEBRUARY: THE FOUNDATION DAY OF THE NSDAP
Celebrating the anniversary of the announcement of the party's 25 Point Programme in Munich's Hofbrauhaus in 1920. The NSDAP was actually founded two months later but the anniversary was too close to Hitler's birthday.

16 MARCH: HEROES' REMEMBRANCE DAY
The fifth Sunday before Easter was the National Day of Mourning, a day dedicated to caring for German war cemeteries. The Nazis changed the day to 16 March and renamed it Heroes' Remembrance Day. The reintroduction of conscription in 1935 and the remilitarisation of the Rhineland in 1936 were also honoured on this day.

20 APRIL: ADOLF HITLER'S BIRTHDAY
The day was celebrated with public displays in honour of the Führer. Houses and streets were decorated with photographs, bunting and swastika flags. Towns and villages held carnivals and torchlight parades in his honour.

1 MAY: NATIONAL LABOUR DAY
Labour Day replaced the traditional spring festival day. The Nazis took the idea for May Day from the communists and they used it for their own workers' holiday. The first Labour Day in 1933 heralded the ban on trade unions and the foundation of the German Labour Front. While workers marched through city streets holding banners, there were celebrations including dancing around the Maypole, bonfires, and the proclamation of village kings and queens in rural areas. Dance and musical groups in regional costume also competed across the country.

SECOND SUNDAY IN MAY: MOTHERING SUNDAY

On Mothering Sunday 1939, three million mothers were awarded the Mother's Honour Cross by party leaders. It became an annual event.

Hundreds of swastikas flutter in the breeze across Luitpold Arena.

SUMMER: DAY OF THE SUMMER SOLSTICE

The summer solstice was celebrated with moonlit festivals and party dignitaries made 'fire speeches' around bonfires. After throwing wreaths dedicated to party martyrs or war heroes into the fire, the crowd leapt over the flames, lit torches and joined the procession home where they continued celebrating.

SEPTEMBER: REICH PARTY RALLY

The annual Party Day grew from its simple beginnings – the first was held in Munich in January 1923 – into a week-long festival of parades, war games and speeches in Nuremberg.

AUTUMN: HARVEST THANKSGIVING DAY

A Nazi version of the traditional harvest festival. Crowds gathered in rural communities to celebrate the gathering of the harvest and pay tribute to the farmer. Nazi leaders gave speeches during the festival.

9–10 NOVEMBER: THE DAY OF NATIONAL SOLIDARITY

The Old Guard of the November 1923 Putsch led a funeral-style march through the streets of Munich and lay wreaths at the Generals Hall, where the martyrs had been killed. A parade was then held at the nearby Temples of Honour, the site of the martyrs' tombs (see page 120).

WINTER: DAY OF THE WINTER SOLSTICE

A celebration designed to replace the Christian festival. The traditional Christmas festival season, with Saint Nicholas, Christmas trees, parties and gifts continued.

THE ANNUAL REICH PARTY DAY,
THE *REICHSPARTEITAG*

The annual Party Day grew from a small political rally into a week-long festival of processions, rallies, speeches, displays and war games. 20,000 spectators and party members gathered for the first rally in Munich in January 1923. Free Corps units were forced to parade without uniforms or weapons while the SA received its first standards. A second rally was held in Nuremberg in August 1923 on Julius Streicher's recommendation. The city had historical traditions, a suitable parade area and railway connections; it also had a sympathetic police force.

Hitler initiates new units by clasping their flag to the Blood Flag; Grimminger is to Hitler's right. (NARA-242-HB-22674)

80,000 Nazis paraded through the city before gathering in the Luitpold Arena for a memorial service honouring the fallen of the First World War. Hitler also spoke four times in the Exhibition Hall, speaking to 2,000 senior party members at a time. Three months later Hitler was arrested following the Munich Putsch and the NSDAP was banned.

Following Hitler's release from prison in December 1924, the next NSDAP rally was held in July 1926, in Weimar, Thuringia, one of the few states where he was allowed to speak. While trains draped with swastikas brought thousands of supporters to the city, the flag consecration ceremony had to be held in secret. Joseph Goebbels also spoke to the crowds for the first time.

The rally returned to Nuremberg in August 1927 as a three-day event. The flag consecration ceremony was held in public for the first time and the crowds silently watched while Jakob Grimminger mounted the platform with the Blood Flag to the sound of muffled drums. The battle-scarred flag had been carried during the 1923 Munich Putsch and Hitler held it in one hand as he walked through a forest of flags, touching each one in turn with his other hand. Heinrich Himmler also appeared on the podium for the first time.

A lack of funds prevented the NSDAP holding a rally in 1928 but 150,000 attended the next Party Day in August 1929 and they were entertained by speeches, Wagnerian music, parades, athletic displays and fireworks. The rally ended with a march through the city streets, past Hitler and his party comrades, in the main square. Money was again short in 1930 but organisers incorporated new ideas to increase the size and impact of the 1931 rally.

Once the Nazis were in power in 1933, the Nuremberg rally became an annual event and it was used to celebrate Germany's return to power and its growing strength. Journalists were invited from all over the world and given preferential treatment in the hope that they would give favourable reports about the new Third Reich. A new theme relating to the year's current events was chosen and each rally was more spectacular than the one before.

Hitler salutes Germany's war dead in front of silent crowds. (NARA-242-HB-22632a3)

The 1933 'Rally of Victory' celebrated the seizure of power and the victory over the Weimar Republic. Over half a million Nazi supporters travelled to Nuremberg for the four-day event and while some lodged in factories, churches and public buildings, many stayed on one of the huge camp sites; the Langerwasser Camp had tented accommodation for 200,000.

Hitler made his triumphant entrance to Nuremberg at the city railway station and SS guards kept the crowds at bay while he was driven to the nearby Deutscher Hof Hotel. He then emerged onto the balcony to greet the people and watch the opening parades.

A grandstand for 60,000 people had been prepared on the Luitpold Arena and the audience stood in silence as the long roll of the dead was read out by the SA commander Ernst Röhm. Two days were devoted to party parades and demonstrations by a variety of NSDAP organisations. Immense phalanxes of men marched through city streets decorated with swastika flags and banners while thousands of onlookers cheered them on. Hitler and the party leaders saluted them as they passed through the city's main square, which had been renamed Adolf-Hitler-Platz. Torchlight processions continued into the night while huge fireworks displays rounded off the celebrations. Public buildings were in constant use for meetings and Hitler's final address brought the rally to a close. The Nazi press published mementoes of the rally and various books and magazines were on offer for people to take home. The Nazi Party newspaper, the *People's Observer*, also printed special rally editions.

The 1934 rally lasted a week and although it did not have a theme to begin with, alternate titles were later attributed to it; the 'Rally of Unity and Strength', the 'Rally of Power', or the 'Rally of Will'. Each day was dedicated to a separate topic; 'Welcome Day', 'Congress of Labour', 'Fellowship', 'Politics', 'Youth', 'Storm Troopers' and 'the Armed Forces'.

For the first time Albert Speer stage-managed the rally. The architect was an expert at creating the maximum visual impact with the minimum effort and expense. Hitler's favourite filmmaker, Leni Riefenstahl, had produced a documentary film of the 1933 Rally entitled *Victory of the Faith*, but few people saw it. Ernst Röhm, leader of the SA, was murdered shortly after the film was released and his image was banned. Riefenstahl filmed the 1934 rally and *The Triumph of the Will* passed into cinematic history because of its portrayal of the hypnotic and overwhelming spectacle.

The 1935 rally was opened with a presentation of the *Meistersinger*, Richard Wagner's opera expressing Germany's 'world view'. The opera became an annual event. The theme was the 'Rally of Freedom' but it marked the start of oppression for the Jews when Herman Göring announced the Nuremberg Race Laws. The rally celebrated the recent introduction of conscription and while the Wehrmacht's new tanks and armoured cars paraded in the arenas, the Luftwaffe's new aircraft flew overhead.

The 1936 'Rally of Honour' celebrated the recent reoccupation of the Rhineland and thousands of spectators watched 250,000 party members parading through the streets.

Floodlights and burning torches had become an established part of the rally but 120 anti-aircraft searchlights were used for the first time, producing a fantastic night spectacle in the Zeppelin Arena. The British ambassador reported that their combined beams of light created 'a cathedral of ice'.

The 1937 rally was called the 'Rally of Labour', celebrating the fact that unemployment was only 1.8 million, a third of what it was when the Nazis came to power. Hitler also announced that the Third Reich would last 1,000 years; it lasted less than eight.

Over one million people attended the rally in September 1938 and it was called the 'Rally of Greater Germany' to celebrate the Anschluss with Austria in March. The imperial insignia was symbolically returned to Nuremberg during the rally. The 1939 rally was cancelled following Germany's invasion of Poland on 1 September and Britain and France's declaration of war; ironically it would have been titled the 'Rally of Peace'.

The party faithful gather inside the Luitpold Hall to hear their leaders speak. (NARA-242-HB-02466)

THE NUREMBURG RALLY GROUNDS

Luitpold Arena was used for the first two rallies in 1927 and 1929. A speaker's platform was built opposite a war memorial known as the Hall of Honour while grandstands were built around the open space. The arena was continually improved over the years under the direction of Albert Speer and its capacity had increased to 150,000 by 1937. The arena ceremony honoured Germany's war dead. Ranks of soldiers stood silently while Hitler and his leaders marched across the centre of the arena, from the podium to the Hall of Honour, saluted the 'Blood Flag', and laid a memorial wreath.

Senior party members gathered in Luitpold Hall to hear speeches and the building's interior was decorated with flags, coloured fabrics and lights to create a dramatic backdrop. Albert Speer redesigned the building between 1933 and 1935. The NSDAP outgrew the Luitpold Hall and in 1935 work started on a 50,000 capacity Congress Hall. There were plans for a new Culture Hall and an exhibition centre; neither were completed.

The SS listen to Hitler speak in the Luitpold Arena. (NARA-242-HB-15089a36)

The smaller Zeppelin Field was first used for parades in 1934 and a large colonnade, topped with a gilded swastika, was soon added to the grandstand. The arena area was improved for displays of military vehicles and war games. While flags fluttered around the arena by day, cauldrons of burning oil lit up the night sky. The nearby Municipal

Searchlights and torchlight illuminate the Zeppelin Field. (NARA-242-HB-22724)

Stadium was also upgraded so that the Hitler Youth could stage athletics displays.

Albert Speer planned the Mars Field, a huge open air arena with seating for 160,000 spectators and a huge statue of the goddess of victory taller than the Statue of Liberty. It was never completed. A wide avenue called the Great Road was built between Luitpold Arena and the Mars Field for the cancelled September 1939 rally. Two huge obelisks and a podium for Hitler to watch the passing parade were never built. The Great German Stadium for 400,000 would have been the largest stadium in the world, but it too was never built.

Temporary buildings depicting German lifestyle and interior design, prepared for the 1936 Berlin Olympics, were used during the 1937 rally. The Strength through Joy organisation turned them into a focal point for an exhibition centre complete with fairgrounds and attractions.

THE DAY OF NATIONAL SOLIDARITY

Julius Streicher leads the Nazi leaders on the route of the Munich Putsch. (NARA-242-HB-17035a2)

On 9 November 1924 Hitler and his fellow prisoners held a short memorial ceremony in his Landsberg prison cell to remember the men killed in the Putsch the year before. Twelve

months later the NSDAP leaders gathered in Munich and vowed to make the day a Nazi holiday. The SS was also formed on 9 November 1925.

The Nazi Old Guard paraded along the route of the original march every anniversary and in 1933 the day was declared a national holiday. The proceedings began on the evening of 8 November when Hitler spoke to senior party members in the Bürgerbräukeller, the scene of the abortive coup.

At midday on the 9th, Hitler and the Old Guard followed the original route, marching silently across Ludwig Bridge and under the Isar Tower into the city. The ceremony was styled like a funeral march and temporary obelisks topped with urns of burning oil lined the route. Buildings had also been swathed with black cloth, adding to the sombre tone. It was another case of maximum visual impact for minimum effort.

The town hall bells played the *Horst Wessel Lied* as the column passed through Marienplatz and it came to a halt at

the Generals Hall in Odeonplatz. The ceremony ended with a wreath laying ceremony at the memorial where the martyrs were killed.

Later that evening over 1,000 men of the SS-Leibstandarte Adolf Hitler gathered in Odeonplatz while Hitler addressed them from the steps of the Generals Hall and they in return swore their allegiance. This also became an annual event.

Two Temples of Honour were built next to the NSDAP's headquarters, the Brown House, and a huge ceremony was held when the bodies were re-interred there. The Parthenon-style structures formed the centre piece for many parades in Köenigsplatz.

While the 1938 anniversary event was being held, the diplomat, Ernst von Rath died in Paris, having being shot by Herschel Grynszpan. News of his death unleashed the nationwide attack on Jewish communities known as *Kristallnacht*, the night of glass. The 1939 parade was cancelled after an assassination attempt on Hitler's life in the Bürgerbräukeller.

THE OPEN AIR MEDLEY, *THINGSPIEL*

The NSDAP revived an ancient tradition called the '*Thing*', an old Teutonic tribal assembly, and the *Thingspiel*, an open air pagan spectacle. The outdoor gatherings were held in natural amphitheatres where Nazi leaders could speak to the crowds in a mystical setting. The first arena was built near Halle in 1934 and although over 1,000 were planned, fewer than 50 were built. They had a speaker podium and seating and, where possible, they were built in historical

Göring speaks at an open air gathering. (NARA-242-HB-13007)

or mythical settings, incorporating lakes, rocky outcrops or historic ruins. Theatrical presentations were also held in the arenas and they included military tattoos, mock battles by the Hitler Youth, acrobats and the inevitable speeches; the spectators were encouraged to dress in period costume. *Things* were eventually phased out in May 1936 as degenerate expressionist dramas and replaced by political rallies.

THE BAYREUTH FESTIVAL

Bayreuth was the home city of the Hitler's favourite composer, Richard Wagner. His operas had been performed at the Festival Hall since 1876 and he was also buried in the city. Hitler enjoyed attending the annual musical festival and he made sure that it received sponsorship money once the NSDAP was in power.

CHAPTER NINE

LAW AND ORDER

Germany's economic difficulties and the resulting unemployment and poverty had led to an increase in petty crime and black marketeering; organised crime had also profited handsomely. A series of weak governments had stopped the Weimar Republic reacting, undermining its reputation.

THE NAZI VIEW OF LAW AND ORDER

While Hitler had contempt for the traditional legal system, he believed that the law was a useful tool for achieving what the Nazis planned for Germany. While he preferred to be seen as a strong supporter of law and order in public, he privately believed that they should be used to control the people. Once in power, the Nazis wanted to have all the limits on their powers lifted, and they relied on lawyers to conceal their intentions behind legal jargon. Many senior NSDAP members were lawyers.

The Nazis wanted the public to accept and follow Nazi ideology. An individual who promoted it in their family life, social life and workplace was known as a 'self-coordinator'. The intelligence agencies would investigate anyone did not comply with the Nazi rules and the police had the powers to arrest them. The detention system then 'educated' perpetrators before they could return to society. The 'education' included hard labour and torture.

The legal system developed under the Third Reich matched the Führer's attitude to law. He had no interest in civil law, and laws relating to commercial contracts, torts and litigation over wills rarely changed under the Nazis. However, Hitler believed changes in criminal law were necessary to achieve what he wanted. Once the NSDAP had control of the government, criminal law underwent a major restructuring and the number of crimes dramatically increased as did the severity of penalties, in particular corporal and capital punishment. The number of offences subject to capital punishment rose and the axe or the guillotine were the preferred methods of execution.

Wilhelm Frick (centre) and Franz Gürtner (right). (NARA-242-HB-10140a1)

The Nazis introduced new laws to deal with 'enemies of the state', people engaged in political, religious or criminal activities which were harmful to the Reich. Additional racial laws were introduced against the Jewish community. Opposing National Socialism or its ideals were criminal actions and draconian laws were introduced to deal with anyone who opposed or conspired against the state. The legal principle of 'no punishment without crime' was rejected in favour of 'no crime without punishment'. Sentences were often applied retrospectively when a new law was introduced. An early example was the case of Marius van der Lubbe, the Reichstag arsonist. His offence did not carry the death sentence when it was carried out, but he was executed for breaking a new law, making arson of a public building a capital offense, which was applied retrospectively; it was known as the '*Lex van der Lubbe*'.

THE MINISTRY OF THE INTERIOR

WILHELM FRICK (1877–1946)

Frick was awarded a law doctorate at Heidelberg and he starting practising in Munich in 1912. A medical condition prevented him from serving in the First World War and by 1919 he was head of Munich's police department. He frequently encountered the NSDAP because of its meetings in the city, many of which ended in violent clashes. He supported the party's politics and helped to secure Hitler's release from custody several times. Frick organised the seizing of the city's police headquarters during the November 1923 Putsch. Although he was arrested and imprisoned, his sentence was suspended in 1924 and he returned to his police work.

Before 1933 each state had its own ministry of the interior to control police agencies in its area. Coordination between the state police forces was limited and their work often overlapped. Frick was returned as a Nazi delegate to the Reichstag in 1924, and in 1931 he was appointed Minister of the Interior for Thuringia, the first Nazi to hold a state office. He immediately removed police officers he considered unsuitable and rigged the selection process to favour Nazis. He also allowed National Socialist newspapers to resume publishing. When the Social Democratic Minister of the Interior, Carl Severing, complained, Frick threatened to dismiss the police force and deploy SA troopers on the streets to restore order; Severing backed down.

Frick was appointed Reich Minister of the Interior in Hitler's cabinet in January 1933 and he immediately set to work, replacing the local government in Bavaria with a Nazi regime. Once the Enabling Act had been passed he installed Nazi governors to run the new *Gaue*. He also implemented the aryanisation of the civil service. Although Frick was a tedious bureaucrat, he was a devoted civil servant who oversaw the Nazi laws, legalising Hitler's plans on the following premise: 'Right is what benefits the German people, wrong is what harms them.'

Hitler, Goebbels, Göring and Wilhelm Frick. (NARA-242-HB-23798a2)

He drafted and signed several hundred decrees and laws over the next six years, legalising the Nazi form of government. They abolished rival political parties, broke up trade unions and legalised the Gestapo's methods. His laws were responsible for sending 200,000 Germans to concentration camps by 1939. He also drafted, signed and activated dozens of laws designed to eliminate Jews from German life and the national economy, including the September 1935 Nuremberg Laws on citizenship and race.

THE MINISTRY OF JUSTICE

FRANZ GÜRTNER (1881–1941)

Gürtner pursued a legal career after serving in the First World War and was appointed Bavarian Minister of Justice in November 1922. As a right-wing sympathiser, he made sure that Hitler and the rest of the accused were treated leniently after the Munich Putsch. He became Minister of Justice in Papen's cabinet in 1932 and also served in Schleicher's and Hitler's cabinets. His protests against unlawful behaviour by the SA on the streets and in the concentration camps were ignored; he also complained about the Gestapo's unlawful methods. At the same time he legitimised many unsavoury aspects of the Nazi regime, starting with the Decree for Protection of the People and State, made at the time of the Reichstag fire.

Hans Frank speaks on law and order. (NARA-242-HB-20721a1)

HANS FRANK (1900–1946)

Frank briefly served in the trenches and then joined a Free Corps unit and the German Workers' Party. He also took part in the 1923 Munich Putsch. After passing the state bar examinations in 1926, he practised as an attorney in Munich, specialising in defending SA troopers arrested while fighting with political opponents. Frank became Hitler's personal lawyer, and he represented him in over 150 lawsuits; he eventually became head of the NSDAP's legal division in 1929. He was elected a delegate of the Reichstag in 1930.

Frank was appointed Bavarian Minister of Justice and Reich Minister of Justice in 1933. He also became the senior lawyer in the NSDAP as Head of the Party's Law Division, followed by presidencies of the German Law Front, the German Law Academy and the Chamber of International Law. He was also appointed Reich Minister without Portfolio in 1934, allowing him to work on a variety of legal issues.

THE LEGAL PROFESSION

The first stage of changing the legal profession to suit the Nazis was to remove the lawyers and judges they did not want and replace them with those they did. The aryanisation, or the removal of those with a Jewish background, of the legal profession started on 7 April 1933. Jewish judges were retired and the number of Jewish lawyers was limited; many were harassed into retirement. At the same time many judges and lawyers joined the NSDAP to save their jobs. Judges were appointed by the Minister of Justice, Franz Gürtner, a member of the Nationalist Party who had aligned himself with the NSDAP in 1933.

Many older institutionalised judges were retired if they opposed the Nazi plans to change the legal system. They were replaced by younger, often inexperienced judges who supported the NSDAP and enthusiastically promoted the party's views. There were few protests. At the same time, aryanisation of the education system excluded Jewish law students from their studies while the remaining students were subjected to careful supervision and indoctrination in the new style of law.

Judges had to make decisions in line with the NSDAP's nationalist and Aryan view of the state. While the powers of the prosecution were enhanced, those of the defence were reduced, leading to coercion and intimidation of defendants and witnesses. In criminal cases the defence counsel could only give evidence with the approval of the court. Local judicial procedures were influenced by the area Gauleiter or state governor and courts became known for giving arbitrary, and sometimes, bizarre decisions.

All legal organisations were merged with the National Socialist Lawyers' League into Hans Frank's German Law Front. Members' licenses were revoked if they failed to vote in elections or plebiscites, or refused to use the greeting 'Heil Hitler!' After September 1938, Jewish lawyers could only act as consultants for Jews and all their legal licences were cancelled two months later.

Judges salute the Führer. (NARA-242-HB-11583)

SPECIAL COURTS AND THE PEOPLE'S COURT

During the Reichstag Fire Trial, the defendants were allowed to question and ridicule Hermann Göring. Steps were immediately taken to make sure it would never happen again. A hierarchy of Special Courts was established to deal with a wide range of treasonable offences including black marketing, work slowdowns, industrial sabotage, making defeatist statements, political jokes or slanderous comments, distributing political material or painting anti-Nazi graffiti.

The People's Court was the senior Special Court and it opened in April 1934 ready to fast track trials for political prisoners outside the constitutional frame of law. The two judges were supported by three lay judges selected from party officials, the SS, SA and the armed forces, and the prosecution and defence lawyers usually sat in silence while the panel belittled the accused.

The courts tried around 3,400 people over the next five years and sentences were carried out immediately after the verdicts had been announced; appeals were not allowed. Punishments were severe, ranging from long sentences in concentration camps to the death penalty. To begin with the number of executions was low but they increased after 1936 under Judge Otto-Georg Thierack. The execution ceremony was banned and the guillotine replaced the axe in 1936; the age limit was lowered and women could also be executed.

THE POLICE

The police in Germany was state-run under the Weimar Republic and a lack of coordination led to an increase in organised crime across state boundaries. The Depression led to funding cuts at a time when unemployment, poverty and petty crime were rising, while the increase in political violence on the streets added to officers' workloads. The Weimar Republic's approach to criminality and civil liberties also made it harder to obtain convictions, leaving the police authorities open to criticism from the press and the public.

Many senior police officers were hounded out of office when the Nazis came to power, and replacements were appointed by the new party Gauleiters. In May and June 1933 the police were ordered to arrest known criminal bosses, seize their assets and close down their businesses. State and party police activities were merged in a series of changes under the Nazis. The Secret State Police, or Gestapo, was formed in April 1934 under Reinhard Heydrich to deal with political crimes against the state. In June 1936, Himmler was named head of all German police, to unify their duties across the Third Reich.

Hitler reviews a march past of the Order Police.

The Order Police had a range of departments for general policing matters and minor crimes. The Security Police was organised under Heydrich to combine the activities of the Criminal Police and the Gestapo. While the Criminal Police dealt with serious non-political crimes, the Gestapo continued to deal with political crimes. Heydrich also remained head of the Party Security Service, and the move consolidated the activities of the state and the party. In September 1939 the Reich Main Security Office brought together the activities of the Security Police, the Security Service and the SS intelligence service under Heydrich.

THE SECRET STATE POLICE,
GEHEIME STAATSPOLIZEI OR GESTAPO

The Gestapo was established to deal with political crimes across the Third Reich. The organisation had its roots in two rival organisations in Prussia and Bavaria. Hermann Göring took over Prussian Police Department 1A in April 1933, responsible for monitoring political activities and staffed it with Nazi sympathisers.

At the same time, Heinrich Himmler, the new Munich police president, established a Bavarian secret police staffed with Party Security Service officers and state civil servants. He extended his style of policing across several German states with the help of Heinrich Müller, a future head of the Gestapo.

The end of the line: the solitary confinement block.

By early 1934 enthusiasm for the new regime was waning and the number of anti-government rumours, complaints and jokes circulating was getting out of hand. Göring handed control of the Gestapo to Himmler in April 1934, to unify the political police forces across the Third Reich and take action. Columbia House in Berlin was an infamous Gestapo prison but activities moved to Sachsenhausen concentration camp in 1936.

The Gestapo was eventually removed from the Ministry of Interior's control. It was given formal national status in February 1936 and its activities were placed above the law, allowing its officers to arrest and interrogate political opponents, dissidents and complainers. The Gestapo became a shadowy security organ of the state, dreaded by the German people. Rumours of interrogation, torture in the cells, the threat of imprisonment in concentration camps or the death penalty, were effective at subduing resistance and complaints against the state. The Gestapo also kept Germany's borders secure. While Border Control Police units controlled immigration and emigration, Counterespionage Police units monitored anti-German activities in other European countries.

First-time offenders were usually questioned and given a verbal warning; it stopped many continuing their activities. Repeat offenders were taken into custody 'for the security of the state' and interrogated. Many Gestapo officers were experienced policemen who were allowed to torture suspects during interrogation. Physical and mental tortures were used to extract confessions, and techniques ranged from sleep deprivation and crude beatings to vicious medieval torture methods; some prisoners died during interrogation. Special Courts sentenced the 'guilty' as soon as the interrogation was over, sending many to concentration camps or to their deaths.

On 26 June 1936 the Gestapo came under Heinrich Heydrich's control when he was made joint Chief of the Security Police and the Security Service. In September 1936 the Berlin headquarters on Prinz Albrechtstrasse became the Gestapo's national headquarters. The Gestapo continued to work under Heydrich, forming Department IV of the new Reich Main Security Office in September 1939. The Central Intelligence Office, or Referat N, had the following departments:

Department A	Enemies of the State
Department B	Religious Sects and Churches
Department C	Administration and Party Affairs
Department D	Occupied Territories
Department E	Counterintelligence

Each city and town had a regional office and they reported the results of their findings to the area inspector; he in turn reported to both the Central Intelligence Office and the Security Service. The Gestapo also had an office in each concentration camp.

The Gestapo employed 20,000 officers but only 3,000 were members of the SS. The regional offices were small and large cities had fewer than 100 of them, towns fewer than 50. The Gestapo only employed a few agents, or V-men, and they were used to infiltrate underground political groups. Most officers were bureaucrats and clerical workers who recorded and indexed denunciations made by the public on colour-coded cards. Four out of five investigations started from a denunciation, and most of the officers' time was spent sorting the credible complaints from gossip and personal vendettas. The remaining complaints came from other departments' findings. As the departments came to work closer together it was often difficult to distinguish between a Gestapo investigation, a Security Service investigation and an SS investigation.

HEADS OF THE GESTAPO

RUDOLF DIELS (1900–1957)

Diels served briefly in the Germany Army during the First World War before enrolling to study law at Marburg University. in 1919. He entered the Prussian Ministry of the Interior in 1930 and became the senior police advisor under the Weimar Republic in 1932, working to arrest political activists. Diels offered his files to the NSDAP when it seized power and he persuaded Göring to establish a secret police. He was appointed the Chief of Department 1A in the Prussian State Police in April 1933 and he aryanised the police, replacing Jewish and liberal officers with Nazi supporters. He was the main interrogator of Marinus van der Lubbe following the Reichstag Fire.

Diels was supported by Göring but he was despised by Heinrich Himmler. and Reinhard Heydrich. His reputation was destroyed by political rivals and he was forced to leave his post for five weeks, avoiding execution during the Night of the Long Knives. After a brief spell of hiding in Czechoslovakia in September 1933, he returned to head the Gestapo. Himmler sacked Diels on 1 April 1934 and he was briefly made Deputy Police President of Berlin before being given a local government post in Cologne.

Berlin Gauleiter Joseph Goebbels and Berlin Police President Wolf-Heinrich von Graf Helldorf. (NARA-242-HB-04806)

HEINRICH MÜLLER (1901–1945)

Müller was Himmler's choice to head the Gestapo. After serving as a pilot for an artillery spotting unit on the Eastern Front during the First World War, and being decorated with the Iron Cross first and second class, Müller joined the Bavarian police in 1919, and was involved in the suppression of communist uprisings during the post-war years. He became an expert on communist activists, studying Soviet police methods to further his investigations. He He did not join the NSDAP, fearing it would compromise his job, but he was a loyal party supporter and helped to cover up the suicide of Hitler's niece, Geli Raubal on 17 September 1931.

Müller was appointed the Gestapo's second in command in February 1934 and he was promoted to head the service when Rudolf Diels was dismissed two months later. He relished in dealing with scandals, in particular the Blomberg-Fritsch affair in February 1938, and he carried out many difficult orders with professional ruthlessness. Müller became head of Department IV of the Reich Main Security Office when it opened in 1939; it was the bureaucratic name for the Gestapo headquarters.

THE ORDER POLICE, *ORDNUNGSPOLIZEI*, ORPO

The Order Police was organised in June 1936, unifying the state police forces into one dealing with general policing matters and minor crimes across the Third Reich. The Municipal Police covered urban areas, the County Police covered rural areas. Officers maintained a presence on the street and they supported crime prevention and prosecution, public safety and traffic control. OrPo officers were often the first to attend serious incidents, ranging from traffic accidents to murders. They would secure the scene and hand over the investigation to the Criminal Police.

The OrPo had a range of units covering all aspects of security. The Gendarmerie patrolled the border, villages, countryside and autobahns. The Traffic Police dealt with incidents on suburban roads. The Railway Police protected the railways while the Water Police patrolled the coast, ports, canals and rivers. The Radio Police protected broadcasting stations and monitored the airwaves for foreign broadcasts. The Postal Police guarded post offices and patrolled telephone and telegraph lines. Industrial premises were protected against sabotage by night watchmen known as Factory Protection Police. Air Protection Police units were organised in 1935 to aid the Fire Protection Police and they came under the Order Police in 1938. Technical Emergency units were also organised and engineering, technical and construction personnel were on call to deal with disasters and emergency situations.

The coordination of police activities begins; Heinrich Himmler and Kurt Daluege (right) sit side by side. (NARA-242-HB-06985a)

The coordination of police activities continues; Himmler and Daluege with Reinhard Heydrich third from right. (NARA-242-HB-08878a1)

THE HEAD OF THE ORDER POLICE

KURT DALUEGE (1897–1946)

Daluege fought with the German Army in the First World War and was decorated several times for bravery. After the war he served with the Rossbach group. He was an early member of the NSDAP, forming the first SA unit in Berlin. He also led an SS group between 1928 and 1933. He was elected to the Prussian Landtag in 1932 and he was the Reichstag delegate for East Berlin in March 1933. After aryanising the Prussian police force, Daluege was promoted to command the Order Police across Germany in June 1936. He also established the German Police Comradeship Organisation.

THE SECURITY POLICE, *SICHERHEITSPOLIZEI*, SIPO

The Security Police was formed in June 1936 to coordinate activities of the Criminal Police and the Gestapo under Reinhard Heydrich. While the Criminal Police continued to deal with non-political crimes, the Gestapo continued to investigate politically motivated crimes. Heydrich was also the head of the NSDAP's Security Service and the move merged the activities of the state and the party.

THE CRIMINAL POLICE, *KRIMINALPOLIZEI*, KRIPO

The Criminal Police was organised in June 1936, unifying the state police forces into one to deal with serious non-political crime investigations such as murder, rape and arson. Part of its duties was to collect intelligence on political activists and the Nazis used its files to round up political opponents after the Reichstag fire. Although many KriPo officers were offered an SS rank, some continued using their police titles. The Criminal Police came under the Security Police's control in 1936 and the organisation became a department of the Reich Main Security Office in September 1939.

HEAD OF THE CRIMINAL POLICE

ARTUR NEBE (1894–1945)

Nebe joined the Criminal Police after serving in the First World War and he rose to the rank of Police Commissionaire by 1924. In 1931, he secretly joined the NSDAP, the SA and the SS, while working for the Chief of Berlin's serious crimes unit, acting as the Nazis' inside man. He declared his membership when Hitler was appointed Chancellor and he was appointed head of the Criminal Police in April 1933. Although Nebe ignored Göring's order to kill Gregor Strasser in June 1934, he remained as head of the KriPo. His support for the regime continued to wane and he eventually passed on details of Gestapo activities to the Resistance.

THE SECURITY SERVICE, *SICHERHEITSDIENST*, SD

Heinrich Himmler opened a small SS intelligence agency in 1931 and it began collecting information on political opponents and troublemakers in the party. It was renamed the Security Service in 1932 and taken over by Reinhard Heydrich. The organisation's role increased when the Nazis seized power as 'enemies of the party' became 'enemies of the state'. On 9 June 1934, it became the sole Party Information Service and it was supported by Alfred Rosenberg's foreign intelligence service. It provided information on victims for the Blood Purge in June 1934.

Security Service officers worked undercover and were supported by a range of agents, confidants and informants; many were paid for their information. Those with selfish motives were known as 'secondary informants', while 'unreliables' had possible corrupt or ulterior motives. Security Service officers had powers to arrest suspects and information was usually forwarded to the Gestapo or the Criminal Police so they could act on it. Lawyers were on call to defend Security Service actions. The Security Police and Security Service frequently came into conflict during the course of their investigations and in the courts. While many of the Security Police were experienced officers, Security Service officers were often party supporters and enthusiastic amateurs; intense rivalries often developed between the two.

In June 1936, state and party intelligence activities were brought closer together when Reinhard Heydrich became combined head of the Security Police and the Security Service, in an attempt to combine their efforts. Offices were opened in Austria following the Anschluss in March 1938, and officers worked alongside the Gestapo and the General and Interior Administration to round up 'enemies of the state' listed by the Austrian Nazi Party. Over 67,000 people were arrested in Vienna alone by Security Service officers. Similar activities took place following the occupation of Czechoslovakia. The Security Service was finally merged with the Security Police under the Reich Main Security Office in September 1939.

THE REICH MAIN SECURITY OFFICE, RSHA

In September 1939, the RSHA merged state and party intelligence activities under one SS controlled office, headed by Reinhard Heydrich. It combined the activities of the Security Police, the Security Service and the SS intelligence service. The RSHA was split into seven sub-offices.

Office I	Personnel and Organisation
Office II	Administration, Law, and Finance
Office III	Security Service-Inland
Office IV	Gestapo
Office V	Criminal Police
Office VI	Security Service-Ausland
Office VII	Records, anti-Semitic propaganda

Otto Ohlendorf (1907–1951) headed the SD-Inland, covering internal matters and ethnic Germans in other countries. His office was split into five departments.

Department A	Law and Legal Structures
Department B	Race and Ethnic Matters
Department C	Cultural and Religious Matters
Department D	Industry and Commerce
Department E	High Society

Walter Schellenberg (1910–1952) headed SD-Ausland, carried out espionage outside German. His office was split into six departments.

Department A	Organisation and Administration
Department B	Western Europe
Department C	Soviet Union and Japan
Department D	United States
Department E	Eastern Europe
Department F	Technical Matters

REINHARD HEYDRICH (1904–1942)

Heydrich was born in Halle an der Saale and served as an officer in the German Navy

Reinhard Heydrich, as head of the Security Service.

in the 1920s but was court-martialled and dismissed in 1931 after an affair with a young lady. He joined the SS in 1932 and his wife introduced him to Himmler, who was immediately impressed by his organisational abilities and ruthlessness. The tall, blond, athletic man rose quickly through the ranks of the SS, due to Himmler's mentoring, and he played a leading role in the 1934 Blood Purge.

Fears about his possible Jewish ancestry drove Heydrich to be intensely anti-Semitic but it did not hinder his promotion prospects. On 26 June 1936 he was appointed combined chief of the Security Police and the Security Service. In September 1939 he was appointed head of the Reich Main Security Office.

STATE PRISONS

The Ministry of Justice continued to operate the state prison system. The 69,000-strong prison population increased 50 per cent in first year under the Nazis and it was eventually over 130,000. Many Nazi leaders, including Hitler, had experienced soft treatment in Germany's jails and they were determined to tighten up the system. Prison reformers were replaced by tough governors who eagerly imposed the new severe regulations introduced in May 1934. Education and rehabilitation came to an end, military drill replaced sport and a new system of penalties was introduced. Food and welfare facilities also deteriorated while overcrowding increased health problems, particularly for older prisoners.

The Nazis employed ex-SA troopers as extra prison guards and they meted out harsh and random punishments. The numbers engaged in hard labour also increased and by 1938 most prisoners were working in new labour camps run by ex-SA men. Conditions were often similar to the early concentration camps, or 'wild camps', set up in 1933.

The Nazis' attitude to crime was unpredictable and arbitrary; punishments frequently did not fit the crime. Habitual criminals could expect to receive harsh treatment and after November 1933 they could be held indefinitely after their third offence. Prison governors were allowed to recommend prisoners who should be held indefinitely.

The Nazis also resurrected some outdated or lapsed offences, including prostitution and homosexuality, increasing their severity. Laws could also be applied retrospectively. New political offences were emphasised while minor criminal offences were sometimes ignored. Penalties were often based on the political or propaganda slant of the crime. While people could be imprisoned for long periods or executed for distributing anti-Nazi pamphlets or making defamatory remarks about the regime, amnesties for minor crimes in August 1934 and April 1936 overturned 720,000 prosecutions.

There was often close cooperation between state prisons and the concentration camp system. Individual cases were assessed and prisoners could be transferred between the two, particularly if a crime was deemed to be both criminally and politically motivated. A prisoner could complete their prison sentence, be immediately rearrested on release by the Gestapo and then be held indefinitely in a concentration camp.

THE CONCENTRATION CAMP SYSTEM

The term 'concentration camp' was used for the first time by the British Army in South Africa. It used them between 1900 and 1902 to intern civilians, preventing them from providing support for the Boer guerrillas. Germany had also used them in south-west Africa. The Nazis planned to set up camps across Germany to hold 'enemies of the state' outside the jurisdiction of the existing state prison system. They also planned to use extreme measures to re-educate the prisoners.

Dachau's cynical motto 'work makes you free'.

The Reichstag Fire Decree on 28 February 1933 suspended civil liberties and outlined rules for protective custody in concentration camps. Temporary camps, known as 'wild camps', were established by the SA to hold thousands of political opponents, the Nazis' first target for arrests. Trade unionists, clergymen, the work-shy, criminals, pacifists, Jehovah's Witnesses, Jews and even errant Nazis were also rounded up over the years that followed.

CAMP LOCATIONS

In April 1933, space to hold 45,000 prisoners 'outside the jurisdiction of the law' was provided in 80 makeshift concentration camps. Most of them were disbanded over the months that followed as the numbers of prisoners dropped. 15,000 're-educated' prisoners were released on 31 July 1933 and the number had fallen to 22,000 by October 1933. There had, however, been 100,000 political arrests in twelve months and over 600 prisoners had died in custody.

Although the number of prisoners had fallen to 3,000 by the end of 1934, there were many more political prisoners in the state prisons. Permanent concentration camps were then established close to the following cities:

Berlin	Columbia-Haus
Bremen	Esterwegen
Chemnitz	Augustusberg
Dresden	Sachsenberg
Hamburg	Fuhlsbüttel
Kassel	Moringen
Leipzig	Bad Sulza
Munich	Dachau
Rhineland	Kislau
Torgau	Lictenburg
Ulm	Oberer Kuhberg

At first, women were held in state prisons. A women's camp guarded by members of the National Socialist Women's Front was opened in October 1933 at Moringen near Kassel. The inmates were moved to Lichtenburg in Saxony in March 1938.

In the early days the prisoners were kept busy building the new camps. Eventually they were trapped behind an electric fence, hidden behind concrete walls and kept under surveil-

A water-filled ditch, an electric fence and a high concrete wall secured each camp.

lance by armed guards in watchtowers. They then built workshops where they worked long hours as slave labour. New camps were opened at the following locations:

Ravensbruck	north of Berlin
Sachsenhausen	the Gestapo interrogation centre north of Berlin
Buchenwald	near Weimar
Flossenberg	north Bavaria
Mauthausen	near Linz, Austria, added in 1938 after the Anschluss with Austria
Theresienstadt	Czechoslovakia, added in 1939, following the occupation of Bohemia

Starting in 1936, criminals, asocials, the work-shy, prostitutes, homosexuals and other enemies of a 'socially and racially hygienic' state were imprisoned, increasing the camp population to 24,000. Another 36,000 prisoners were rounded up during *Kristallnacht* in November 1938, but most were released after a short period. The number of prisoners in the camp system had fallen to 21,400 when Germany invaded Poland in September 1939.

ORGANISING THE CAMP SYSTEM

The concentration camp system was administered by the SS. Theodor Eicke introduced training for guards and a new system of punishments across Germany. Oswald Pohl organised the hiring of prisoners for slave labour, raising large amounts of money for the SS.

THEODOR EICKE (1892–1943)

Theodor Eicke.

Eicke served in the First World War and then worked as a police officer until he was sacked for his anti-government attitude. He was then employed by I.G. Farben in 1923 as a commercial executive and counter-espionage officer. He joined the NSDAP and the SA in 1928, transferring to the SS in 1930; he was commanding a regiment in the Rhine-Palatinate region by November 1931.

In March 1932, Eicke was arrested and sentenced to two years in prison for carrying out bomb attacks on political enemies. He escaped to Italy and only returned when Hitler came to power a year later. Although Eicke's local Gaulieter dismissed him from the SS, believing he was deranged, he was readmitted and given command of the concentration camp at Dachau in June 1933. He quickly established a strict detention regime and a training programme for the guards.

His work brought Eicke to Himmler's attention and he was soon appointed Inspector of Concentration Camps across Germany and head of the Death's Head camp guards, the SS *Totenkopfverbände*. A few weeks later he was promoted to SS-Gruppenführer for his good work. The concentration camp system was run with brutal efficiency under his command and the guards were ordered to show no mercy for the prisoners, meting out corporal punishments, solitary confinement, torture and even murder.

Eicke shot Ernst Röhm in his cell after he refused to commit suicide following the Blood Purge in June 1934. Eicke took command of the SS-Totenkopf Division which was raised and trained at Dachau in November 1939, and he took command of the Death's Head units across Poland.

OSWALD POHL (1892–1951)

Pohl was serving as a naval officer when he joined the Nazi Party in 1922 and the SA four years later. His organisational abilities were spotted by Heinrich Himmler and in February 1934 he left the navy to become the chief administrative officer of the Reich Main Security Office. By June 1939 he had risen to the rank of SS-Obergruppenführer and was appointed ministerial director for the Ministry of the Interior. He controlled works projects for the concentration camp system, giving him access to thousands of slave labourers. As one of the Heinrich Himmler's 'Circle of Friends' he controlled business links between the camps and wealthy industrialists, making sure that the SS received huge amounts of money in exchange for lucrative contracts.

CONCENTRATION CAMP ADMINISTRATION

Konzentrations Lagers were commanded by an SS colonel, and an SS major headed the administration staff. SS-Totenkopf units provided the armed guards and they operated under existing prison regulations until new 'Disciplinary and Punishment Regulations for the Prisoner Camp' were introduced in October 1933. Guards could then execute any prisoner who resisted arrest or tried to escape. Death certificates were falsified to cover up murders. Serious rule infringements were dealt with in the solitary confinement block, a prison within a prison where torture was common. Minor infringements could result in punishment drills, reduced rations or a ban on mail. The indefinite length of sentence was one of the hardest things to accept. The camp administration was organised into five departments.

I Headquarters	Administration, disciplinary measures and mail censorship
II Political	Admitting and releasing inmates, prisoner records and interrogations
III Prisoner Camp	One guard section controlled the accommodation compound and the other guard section controlled the work details
IV Administration	Camp budget, purchasing and holding prisoners' possessions
V Medical	A doctor ran an infirmary but few prisoners received any medical care; he falsified the death certificates of murdered prisoners

THE PRISONERS

POLITICAL OPPONENTS

Members of rival political parties, Nazis who had broken party rules, foreign exchange violators, individuals who had spoke against the state or the Führer, and Jehovah's Witnesses.

CRIMINALS

'Security custody prisoners' were serving limited sentences while 'limited-term preventive custody prisoners' were habitual criminals. The guards bribed hardened criminals to keep the prisoners under control, threatening to punish them if their detail broke the rules; they ruthlessly exploited the inmates.

ANTI-SOCIALS

The work-shy, alcoholics, vagrants, beggars, prostitutes and homosexuals.

INFERIOR RACES

Jews were held in special barracks, given the worst jobs and subjected to cruel treatment. Gypsies were forced to live in special camps.

Inmates had their heads shaved and they wore distinctive striped clothing, with a serial number sewn on. A coloured triangle sewn onto their jacket denoted their crime.

Red	Political prisoners
Blue	Stateless prisoners
Violet	Religious prisoners
Pink	Homosexuals
Green	Criminals
Brown	Gypsies
Black	Homeless, alcoholics, work-shy, prostitutes and beggars

Jews also had to wear a yellow triangle over their crime triangle, forming a crude Star of David; a thick black border indicated if they had defied racial laws. Prisoners on labour discipline duties had the letter 'A' stitched to their tunic while the feeble minded had the word '*blod*' (stupid) sewn on theirs. Escapees had a red-and-white target sewn on their chest and back. A black strip under the triangle denoted a second offence, resulting in harsher punishment.

Over 200,000 inmates passed through the concentration camps between 1934 and 1939 and they were sent to a Workers' Educational Camp for training and indoctrination prior to release.

Thousands of prisoners mill around their dreary accommodation huts.

THE DAILY REGIME

Endless hard work, regular punishment and poor food broke the prisoners' spirits. They lived in cramped barracks which were run by *stubens*, hardened criminals who were rewarded if their block was clean and orderly and punished if it was not. Prisoners were woken from their narrow communal bed before dawn and made to stand in silence on the parade ground during the hour-long roll call; longer if someone was missing. Work details were also run by hardened criminals, called Capos, and they prisoners often forced to carry out pointless hard labour such as breaking rocks, shovelling gravel or carrying stone blocks. After evening roll call the prisoners returned to their barracks. Any free time was devoted to keeping the barracks clean.

Many punishments were carried out in front of the prisoners and they included whippings, beatings and hangings. Some were held in solitary confinement in the prison block, where they could be chained up in the dark with no food or water. Prisoners were often suspended with their hands tied behind their back, a torture known as pole hanging. The number of deaths in the concentration camps was relatively low until the start of the Second World War. Some committed suicide, encouraged to do so by the guards. Troublesome prisoners were often 'shot while trying to escape' or they 'died of natural causes'; in other words they were murdered.

A work detail stands in silence during their roll call.

CHAPTER TEN

THE ECONOMY AND LABOUR

HITLER'S EARLY VIEWS ON ECONOMY

Hitler had little interest in Germany's economics during the early days of the NSDAP; he preferred to concentrate on other aspects of politics. He originally followed 'interest slavery', Gottfried Feder's bizarre economy theory which blamed Germany's economic ruin on international financiers. He wanted to freeze interest and introduce interest-free loans to finance public works, eliminate finance capital and end international loans. He also wanted to seize Jewish properties and land estates.

Feder's radical economic theory was loosely represented in the party's 25 Points, and he was appointed chairman of the NSDAP's Economic Council. His theory soon proved to be unpopular with the voters. The NSDAP began promising assistance for small businesses to appeal to the middle-class vote. By the end of 1931 Hitler finally made a stand on economics to get the political and financial support he wanted from industrial and business magnates. Many of them were wary of Hitler's political posturing but a large number agreed to attend a private audience in January 1932. They continued to remain wary and although some donations followed, they were insignificant compared to what was being raised by the party members.

THE REICH MINISTRY OF FINANCE

LUTZ GRAF SCHWERIN VON KROSIGK (1887–1952)

Krosigk was a member of the German nobility who had studied law in England. He was wounded serving as an officer in the First World War and he became a government assessor in Hindenburg, Upper Silesia, following the Armistice. He entered the Ministry of Finance in 1921 and worked his way up through the organisation. Krosigk was appointed Finance Minister in

Minister of Finance Krosigk, Minister of Economics Schacht, unknown and Ernst Hülse from the Deutsche Bank. (NARA-242-HB-13782a4)

Chancellor Papen's coalition cabinet in 1932. He remained in this post in Hitler's cabinet. The Führer relied on the Ministry of Finance to fund rearmament and in February 1935 a law authorised the use of secret credit to rearm the country, a move opposed by Krosigk. However, he had no qualms about supporting the anti-Semitic pogroms or about making use of the large amount of money they generated.

THE REICH ECONOMY MINISTRY

ALFRED HUGENBERG (1865–1951)

Hugenberg was appointed Reich Minister of Economy and Agriculture in Hitler's first cabinet, in return for the Nationalist Party's support. The party gained only eight per cent in the March 1933 election and Hugenberg was intimidated into resigning by June 1933. His party folded soon afterwards. The Nazis split the ministry into the Economy Ministry and the Agriculture and Food Ministry and appointed two Nazis to head them.

KURT SCHMITT (1886–1950)

Schmitt studied for a law degree at Munich University before joining the Alliance Insurance Company. He was badly wounded in 1917 while serving as an officer, and eventually returned to work at his old company. By 1921 he was chairman and arranging loans for the NSDAP. Schmitt also became Director of the Stuttgart Social Insurance Corporation, and a leading expert on the insurance industry. Schmitt met the Circle of Friends of the Economy at the Berlin Kaiserhof in December 1932 and presented his anti-Semitic views. He joined the NSDAP when Hitler became Chancellor and was appointed Vice-President of the Berlin Chamber of Industry and of the Chamber of Commerce.

Schmitt replaced Hugenberg on 30 June 1933 and was made an honorary member of the SS. He became the Prussian representative in the Reich government in August and he was appointed to the Prussian State Council in October; he was also invited to join the Academy for German Law. His proposal to disband the Reich Federation of German Industry and place private industries under state control was resisted by business leaders. Schmitt had a heart attack in June 1934 and he became chairman of several companies after he recovered.

Reich Minister of Economics Hjalmar Schacht. (NARA-242-HB-01851)

HJALMAR SCHACHT (1877–1970)

Schacht had worked for the Dresdner Bank for over a decade before he became head of the National Bank for Germany in 1916, overseeing its merger with the Darmstadt Bank in 1922. He was appointed Reich Currency Commissioner in the Ministry of Finance in 1923 and he introduced the Rentenmark – a new currency backed by German land values and foreign loans – to halt inflation; it was soon known as the Reichsmark. Schacht was appointed President of the Reichsbank in December 1923. By 1930, Germany was facing economic disaster following the Wall Street collapse and he resigned in March 1930 in protest over the Young Plan.

Schacht supported the call for a strong state backed by a resilient economy after reading *Mein Kampf* and he introduced Hitler to industrialists. Schacht joined the Harzburg Front in October 1931, hoping it would bring down the government, but Hitler refused to join. Over the next twelve months Schacht was involved in the political negotiations which finally led to Hitler's appointment as Chancellor in January 1933.

Schacht was appointed President of the Reichsbank in March 1933 and Reich Minister of Economics in August 1934. He used his contacts to manipulate the economic system so that it could finance the Nazis' public works and rearmament programmes. Schacht was shocked by the brutality of Night of the Long Knives in June 1934 and he resigned in disgust at the anti-Semitic pogroms in November 1937. Hitler retained him as Minister without Portfolio but when it was clear that Hitler was preparing for war, Schacht joined the Resistance.

WALTHER FUNK (1890–1960)

Funk was drafted into the army but was discharged in 1916 due to ill health. He returned to journalism and became the editor of the Berlin Stock Exchange newspaper in 1922. Funk did not join the NSDAP until 1931, and despite having a reputation of being a notorious drunkard and a homosexual, he had many useful links with industrialists that the party exploited. He was appointed Chief of the Office for the Private Economy and he became Hitler's personal economics adviser, recommending investment in public works, the mechanisation of farms, road-building and the automobile industry.

Funk was appointed the Reich Government's Press Chief in January 1933 and the undersecretary of the Reich Ministry for Public Enlightenment and Propaganda in March 1933.

Joseph Goebbels, Walther Funk and Otto Dietrich prepare to speak about the economy. (NARA-242-HB-09205)

143

He was also appointed Chairman of the Reich Broadcasting Company. He was elected to the Reichstag in July 1933 and appointed Vice-President of the Reich Chamber of Culture.

By the time Funk became Minister of Economics in November 1937, following Schacht's resignation, the ministry's work was overshadowed by the Office of the Four Year Plan. A few months later he was appointed Plenipotentiary of the War Economy and in January 1939 he was appointed President of the Reichsbank, another of Schacht's offices.

THE MINISTRY OF AGRICULTURE

The farming industry was struggling when the Nazis took power in January 1933, as farm debts increased in the face of rising interest payments. Richard Darré was appointed head of the new Ministry of Agriculture in June 1933. He was instructed to safeguard farming and make Germany self-sufficient in agricultural products.

In September 1933, the Entailed Farm Law awarded small farms less than 125 hectares to the resident farmer, providing that he could prove his Aryan background to 1800. While these entailed estates would be inherited by a competent son, they could not be sold or mortgaged to raise cash. Plans were discussed to offer farms on the estates of bankrupt Junkers to disinherited farmers' children but they were unpopular and most moved into the cities to find work.

At the same time Jews were banned from farming. A law in June 1936 required the merging of many farms to increase efficiency and production. By 1939, many Aryan farmers had doubled their acreage by acquiring land confiscated from Jewish owners.

The National Socialist Farmers' Association represented farmers, while its officials mediated with regional agricultural experts working on behalf of the Office for Agriculture. Older farmers resented the changes but the younger generation were attracted to the ideas of the Nazis' 'Blood and Soil'. Most villagers adapted to Nazism providing their daily life did not change much; the majority were just content to be making a living after years of financial uncertainty.

The Reich Food Estate was established in September 1933 and it was organised to control every step of the food chain in Germany, with the aim of getting a fair price for all from the farmyard to the shop counter. It began by stabilising food prices at a profitable level for the farmer while fruit, grain and fishing associations were supported by import agencies. Agricultural prices rose 20 per cent over the next two years, but the pricing system once again turned against the farmer. By introducing a price freeze, rationing consumption and restricting imports, the organisation ended up once again reducing farmers' profits. The forced repatriation of immigrant workers also increased costs. Farm labourers' wages always remained lower than other industrial workers as money was directed to rearmament.

Germany was self sufficient in bread, meat, potatoes and sugar by 1939 but despite attempts to increase the volume of home produce, it always needed to import over fifteen per cent of its foodstuffs. It was also clear that the Reich Food Estate was riddled with corruption and many officials, including Darré, were involved. By 1939 it was apparent that the organisation had failed to improve farming or make Germany self-sufficient.

RICHARD WALTHER DARRÉ (1895–1953)

Darré was an artillery officer during the First World War and he briefly served with the Berlin Free Corps before returning to his agricultural studies. He was an early member of the NSDAP and Hitler was impressed by his theories on 'blood and soil' and his writings on race,

Marxism and agriculture. Darré organised the National Socialist Farmers' Association in 1931 and at the same time, Himmler also appointed him head of the SS Race and Resettlement Office in 1931. The office authenticated the Aryan background of intended SS brides; the office was soon checking all SS applicants.

Darré was appointed the German Farmers' Leader in April 1933 and Reich Food and Agriculture Minister responsible for all agriculture and farming matters in June 1933. He was elected to the Reichstag in November 1933. While his ministry duties waned, the Race and Resettlement Office expanded its duties to deal with the proposed resettlements in the East and he was promoted to SS-Gruppenführer.

Walther Darré prepares to speak. (NARA-242-HB-09175a2)

THE ECONOMY UNDER NAZI CONTROL

The Nazis expected full cooperation from industry and commerce in its drive to strengthen the German economy. It aimed to create full employment, accumulate foreign currency and expand the country's export markets. The state would control all aspects of the economy, ranging from prices and credit, the labour market, wages and production. Decisions would be driven by power-politics, and businessmen were expected to think in ideological terms rather than economic terms. They had to stop thinking about their personal profits and start thinking about a strong, independent national economy. Most businessmen welcomed the strict economic measures, but their early enthusiasm turned into frustration in the face of contradictory economic plans. Businessmen soon discovered that they had to suffer in silence or face losing their business.

The aryanisation of German businesses began in January 1937. It had a huge impact on the country's economy over the next two years, halving production in some industries and trades. The Nazis bought or confiscated all Jewish-owned businesses over the next two years, starting with large department stores, and owners were forced to sell at a fraction of the true value, usually to party members. Anyone who refused to sell could be imprisoned and have their business confiscated.

AUTARKY

Autarky is the concept of national self-sufficiency and the elimination of the need for imports. Hitler was determined that Germany had to produce everything it needed to succeed. In doing so, the country would not be vulnerable to naval blockades, such as those imposed during the First World War. Germany had to do two things to achieve autarky. It had to occupy areas with rich mineral deposits, beginning with the Saar, an area of Germany under French control. It also had to finance industry while it searched for synthetic substitutes. While Krupp was encouraged to finance the Buna project for synthetic rubber, I.G. Farben accelerated the research and development of synthetic fibres; it also set up the Brabag Company to produce petrol from lignite.

Schacht represented the Ministry of Economy's concerns over autarky, warning that it would limit Germany's exports and severely restrict its role in the international markets. Hitler responded by establishing an independent office to monitor imported raw materials. Göring's Office of the Four Year Plan opened in 1936 and it coordinated industrial output with rearmament. As the Third Reich expanded into Austria and Czechoslovakia, autarky could not keep pace with Germany's rearmament. By 1939 a third of raw materials were still being imported while annual exports had fallen from 13 to less than 5 billion RM.

THE DEFENCE ECONOMY

The term 'defence economy' was the Nazi euphemism for a war economy. It was introduced soon after the Nazis seized power, and the Reichsbank devised a new strategy to finance rearmament. The economy was controlled through the markets rather than through state takeover or nationalisation. However, the improvement in the world economy caused exports to fall while rearmament caused imports to rise. While other countries devalued their currencies to make imports cheaper, Germany did not, and its balance of payments was in deficit in 1934. In September, Schacht announced the imports would be switched to countries which accepted German exports.

Party leaders visit a new autobahn project. (NARA-242-HB-04989)

Expenditure was outstripping income, foreign debt was rising dramatically while reserves were falling; Germany was heading for bankruptcy. The Reichsbank had to issue special bank notes, starting in 1935, to continue payments to arms manufacturers. They were known as MEFO bills, an acronym for Metallurgical Research Incorporated. The bills were accepted by all German banks but they were not allowed to list them in their accounts, keeping rearmament and true inflation secret. Over the next four years over twelve billion marks worth of MEFO bills were issued. By June 1939 limits on printing Reichsmarks had also been lifted.

THE FOUR YEAR PLAN

In April 1935 Schacht was appointed Plenipotentiary-General for the War Economy. Cartels were strengthened and the country's industrial capacity increased under the Nazis but extensive development and expansion was needed if the projected requirements for rearmament were going to be met. Rearmament was depleting home resources and substitutes were still limited, but Schacht's repeated warnings were ignored.

On 9 September 1936 the Four Year Plan for economic development of the Reich was unveiled at the Nuremberg Rally with Hermann Göring as the Commissioner Plenipotentiary. It had six departments covering labour, agriculture, production, distribution, pricing and foreign exchange and they would be used to bypass the Ministry of Economics.

Even though Göring knew little about economic affairs, he was given complete control over the economy including the private and public sectors. The Four Year Plan would favour protection of agriculture and it aimed to make Germany industrially independent by 1940. The Plan would have four main effects on the German economy:

Hermann Göring with Paul (Pilli) Koerner, Chief of the Office of the Four Year Plan. (NARA-242-HB-05763)

A control of distribution by a monopoly industry
A reduction in the importance of banking capital
An increase in undistributed profits
Directors' interests put ahead of stockholders' interests

The Four Year Plan was just one of several economic regeneration plans around the world in the 1930s. While it outperformed President Roosevelt's New Deal in the US, both in size and scope, the Nazis borrowed several ideas from the Soviet's Second Five Year Plan, particularly the plans for militarisation.

New refineries, factories and aluminium plants were built, increasing the nation's output, particularly in synthetic fibre and automobile production. The quest for synthetic rubbers and fuels also proved to be successful. There were still shortages of rubber, oil and raw materials for steel and aluminium industries but Göring kept announcing expansion of the rearmament industries.

Numerous building and public works projects were started or expanded creating a shortage of building products; work on the autobahn system was also stepped up. Military defences along Germany's borders were extended and improved.

PREPARING FOR WAR

In October 1937, laws were introduced to eliminate small businesses from the economy. Small companies with capital less than 100,000 RM were forced to join new cartels organised by the Ministry of Economics or go out of business. It was also illegal to set up a new company with less than 500,000 RM capital. The combined effects of the two laws significantly reduced the number of businesses.

Göring was making a huge personal fortune out of mining and steel enterprises and he often came into conflict with Schacht over the handling of the nation's economy. By the end of 1937, Schacht had had enough and resigned from the Ministry of Economics and

A propaganda display comparing the increase in factory production with the reduction in unemployment. (NARA-242-HB-19322a2)

the Reichsbank, as the economy spiralled out of control. Walther Funk replaced him in both offices.

While government income had only increased from 10 to 15 billion RM between 1928 and 1939, expenditure had risen from 12 to 30 billion RM. By 1938, state spending was a massive 35 per cent of national income and taxes were only covering half of the 30,000 million RM being spent. Rearmament had risen fifteen-fold in six years until it was over 20 per cent of national income. The Nazis' attempts at running the economy had turned an annual surplus into an annual deficit of over 9 billion RM. By September 1939, Germany had a total debt of 38 billion RM but the plan was to pay for the debts by going to war.

PRIVATE INDUSTRY

Industrialists had been in a position to take advantage of the hyperinflation of 1922, and their huge loans were soon worthless. However, when the currency stabilised many found themselves overstretched and they went bankrupt. The survivors merged or set up cartels to cut costs, increase mechanisation and improve efficiency. A Cartel Tribunal had controlled relations between industrial cartels and consumers since November 1923.

Under a law declared on 27 February 1934, the Commercial Economy Organisation was established to control industry and consumer relations on behalf of the Ministry of Economy. A second law on 27 November completed the Nazis' economic plans for private industry and commerce.

Companies had to join two NSDAP-controlled economic organisations. The economic based Reich Groups and the regional based Economic Chambers encouraged links between the party and business, finance and industry. The Group and Chamber directors were tasked with implementing the government's directives and companies had to cooperate or go out of business.

Reich Groups encouraged companies to work together towards common goals. Industry, artisans, banks, commerce, insurance, power and transport companies were all expected to cooperate to maximise production. While Main Groups planned production, Economic Groups discussed financial needs and Professional Groups pooled technical expertise.

Economic Chambers covered one of the party *Gau* areas across Germany and they organised industrial, commercial and finance companies regionally for optimum production. The Chamber Director was a loyal Nazi businessman who advised the Gauleiter on local needs.

Companies had to follow government directives, invite senior Nazis onto their boards, and meet production targets, or go out of business. Those which cooperated profited and expanded while those that did not or could not were forced out of business. After 1937 connections between industry and the state increased, and it became increasingly important to have connections in government purchasing departments. Senior Nazi Party members were often awarded directorships to establish the contacts necessary to secure contracts. By September 1939, many members of the SS and party members were company directors.

I.G. Farben's success under the Weimar Republic and the Third Reich illustrates the close links between industry and politics; it was a classic example of how working with the state increased private profits. The Community of Interests of Dye Industries Incorporated specialised in producing gasoline, synthetic lubricating oils, synthetic rubber, poisonous gases, explosives, methanol, plasticisers, dyestuffs and nickel, making it Germany's largest company during the First World War. In the post-war years, it worked with other companies to oppose free trade. The cartel dictated procedures, set production quotas, exchanged patents and shared trademarks. The Weimar Republic introduced laws to control the cartels, but they failed to limit their monopoly and the companies continued to limit competition, regulate production and control trade. It allowed them to keep prices at inflated levels and the profits were split between the cartel members.

Nazi Party leaders and the I.G. Farben board initially distrusted each other. However, the NSDAP needed money for their election campaigns and Hitler promised to break the power of the unions in the hope of getting financial backing. The Nazis replaced the unions with the German Labour Front while the Industry Cartel was replaced by a new cartel working for the Nazi Party. I.G. Farben reorganised its factories for rearmament and it became a key component in Hitler's war plans, concentrating on producing strategic materials. Carl Krauch, the Four Year Plan's controller of chemical production, joined the I.G. Farben board in 1938. By working with the Nazis, the company became the largest in the Third Reich, making huge profits for the owners.

In retail, the Law for Protection of Individual Trade was introduced in May 1933. It banned chain stores from expanding and introducing discounts to protect small businesses. There was no protection for Jewish-owned businesses.

PUBLIC COMPANIES

When it became clear that private industry could not fulfil the Nazis' needs for rearmament, several new public companies were established to improve the economy. The Todt Organisation was established in 1938 under Dr Fritz Todt, a civil engineer and early member

of the NSDAP. It coordinated and administered the building of military installations, including the Siegfried Line, a series of fortifications along Germany's border with France. It also managed the expanding autobahn network.

The Four Year Plan needed steel production to increase but private manufacturers were reluctant to expand their factories until existing capacity was accounted for; they were also unwilling to use low quality domestic ore. The Hermann Göring National Works was established to break the monopoly and while private steel manufacturers were forced to buy 30 of the shares, the government claimed the rest of the company's capital and controlled the voting rights. The new company then produced the extra capacity set by the Four Year Plan.

Heinrich Himmler's contacts in business and its control of the concentration camp system also allowed the SS to build an extensive business empire. The German Excavation and Quarrying Company Limited was established in 1938 and it used slave labour in its quarries. The German Armament Works was set up the following year to take advantage of the rearmament programme; again slave labour was used to keep down costs and maximise profits.

THE TRANSPORTATION SYSTEM

THE NATIONAL HIGHWAYS: THE AUTOBAHNS

In 1928 the Weimar Republic announced a programme of public works, including plans for a network of new highways across Germany. Progress was slow due to the country's economic problems but the first section of autobahn, linking Cologne and Bonn, was opened in 1932.

Although the NSDAP campaigned against the new highways when they were opposition, Hitler supported an extensive road building programme when he became Chancellor.

The work reduced unemployment, benefited industries and the new roads allowed troops to move across the country without relying on the railway system. On 1 May 1933, Labour Day, Hitler announced a new autobahn system of 7,300 miles of four-lane highways. Despite opposition from the Minister for the Interior and the Minister for Transport, the Law on the Establishment of a Reichsautobahn Enterprise was announced in June and 30,000 workers started work in September 1933. The number would soon increase to 120,000. The roads were designed with four lanes and for vehicles travelling faster than 25mph.

Hitler tours a completed section of autobahn. (NARA-242-HB-12334a2)

The first section between Frankfurt and Darmstadt was opened in May 1935 and construction continued at a rapid pace; over 500 miles of autobahn was opened for traffic each year. Although a quarter of the network was complete by 1938, very few people could afford a car to drive on it. Although the number of cars on the roads had doubled to one million by 1936, ownership was still half that in France; only the military possessed large numbers of vehicles.

FRITZ TODT (1891–1942)

Todt served as a flying observer in the First World War until he wounded. He completed his studies and became a construction engineer, joining the NSDAP in 1922. He worked his way up through the ranks, becoming an SS-Standartenführer on Heinrich Himmler's staff in 1931, while it was still a small organisation.

Todt was appointed Inspector-General of the German Road and Highway System in 1933 and he took control of the large number of autobahn contracts across the country. He was also made a senior director of the Four Year Plan. His empire expanded to control the whole of the German construction industry, including roads, canals and power plants. In 1938 he was placed in charge of the line fortifications along Germany's border with France and Belgium, known as the West Wall or the Siegfried Line.

RAILWAYS

The Weimar Republic's constitution placed the responsibility for Germany's railways with the national government and the German Reich Railways was formed by merging the seven state railway companies in April 1920. The Dawes Plan demanded payments from the railways and the German Reich Railway Company was set up to operate them in August 1924. New streamlined steam engines and rolling stock were introduced over the years that followed, replacing the outdated stock inherited from the state railway companies. High speed trains, like the *Flying Hamburger*, appeared in the late 1930s while the Class 05 streamlined express engine could top 200km/hr.

Investment increased under Nazi control and the rail lines running from west to east had the highest priority, complementing troop movements associated with military planning. The

Party leaders turn out to see a new high speed train. (NARA-242-HB-17612)

rail network was returned to government control on 10 February 1937 and the swastika was added to the insignia. The Austrian Federal Railways were integrated into the German Reich Railways following the Anschluss in March 1938.

JULIUS DORPMÜLLER (1869–1945)

Dorpmüller left the Prussian state railway to work on the Chinese Imperial state railways in 1907. He was forced to leave when China declared war on Germany and he fled via Siberia and Russia. He reached Germany in 1918 and joined the German Reich Railway Company as an area manager. He became the temporary head of the organisation when the general manager fell ill in 1925 and he took over after he died the following year.

Dorpmüller held his position under the Nazis and was appointed Reich Minister of Communications when the rail system returned to government control in February 1937. He was confirmed as Transport Minister and General Manager of the German Reich Railway when the Law over the German Reich Railway was issued in July 1939.

AIRSHIPS

The prototype hydrogen airship, LZ-127, *Graf Zeppelin*, flew for the first time in July 1928, inspiring zeppelin fever across the world. The design of LZ-128 had to be changed following the crash of the British airship R-101 in October in which the passengers and crew perished in the hydrogen-fuelled fire. Changing to helium, a heavier but safer gas, resulted in a 50 per cent increase in size. Work on the LZ-129 started in autumn of 1931 but money was short and progress was slow.

When Hitler became Chancellor in 1933, the new Air Minister, Hermann Göring refused to sponsor airships, however, Propaganda Minister Joseph Goebbels believed they would showcase German technology and offered two million RM to Hugo Eckener's Zeppelin Company; Göring responded with another nine million RM.

The company was split into two in March 1935 and while the Zeppelin Airship Builders constructed the airships, the New German Zeppelin Shipping Company (DZR) controlled operations; the German national airline Lufthansa also owned half of the two companies. The move placed Ernst Lehmann, an NSDAP supporter, as head of operations.

After test flights at the beginning of March 1936, endurance trials were cancelled so that the *Hindenburg* could join the *Graf Zeppelin* on a three-day propaganda flight over the Rhineland. The airships broadcast announcements and dropped propaganda leaflets ahead of the referendum supporting the remilitarisation of the Rhineland. Although it was a success, the *Hindenburg* was damaged and engine troubles on the first transatlantic crossing tarnished its reputation.

The *Hindenburg* continued to be used as a propaganda tool, and the boxer Max Schmeling flew on it when he returned from the US to Germany after defeating Joe Louis in June 1936. Two months later it flew over the Berlin Olympic Games opening ceremony and over the

Tethering the
Graf Zeppelin.
(NARA-242-HB-
11492a1)

Nuremberg Rally in September. It was able to cross the Atlantic in under 48 hours, less than half the time of the fastest cruise ship, but at nearly twice the price. There was only room for 50 passengers and prices limited it to the rich and privileged. There were plans to use airships to transport mail but the early deliveries were mainly philately souvenirs.

The *Hindenburg* made 34 Atlantic crossings in 1936 and there were plans to increase the service in 1937 with the LZ–130. It was still, however, using hydrogen and on 6 May 1937 the *Hindenburg* crashed at Lakehurst, New Jersey. Only 36 people were killed but vivid newsreels showing people running for their lives from the huge flaming airship flashed around the world. They brought to an end 30 years of German airship flights.

ORGANISING THE LABOUR FORCE

NATIONAL SOCIALIST SHOP CELL ORGANISATION, NSBO

In 1928, Johannes Engel formed the National Socialist Constituency, the first NSDAP shop floor group, in the Berlin-based Knorr Brake factory; it soon changed its name to the National Socialist Workers' Combat Federation. Reinhard Muchow, the Berlin Gau Organisation Leader suggested forming NSDAP cells, or *Zellen*, in all workplaces to oppose communist workers' groups. Muchow and Engel set up the Secretariat for Workers' Affairs and the Gau Cell Organisation Department was formed in Berlin in May 1930. The Reich Cell Organisation Department took its place the following January and it was renamed the National Socialist Shop Cell Organisation on 8 March 1931. The NSBO campaigned for the NSDAP and organised workers to support party activities in factories across Germany over the next two years.

NSBO leaders expected to take over from labour unions when the Nazis came to power in January 1933 but the NSDAP did not want another factory floor-run organisation. The NSBO leadership was dominated by left-wingers who believed in fighting their capitalist employers on behalf of the workers, a view not shared by the party leadership. On 2 May 1933 Dr Robert Ley announced that the new German Labour Front would replace the NSBO.

Following a power struggle with Ley, the NSBO was banned from interfering in national or local labour affairs in December 1933. At the same time many NSBO leaders were accused of communist activities and held in concentration camps. The NSBO continued to function but it was a shadow of the original organisation, especially after Muchow was killed in a pub brawl. Gregor Strasser, one of the main supporters of the NSBO, was murdered during the Blood Purge in June 1934.

THE GERMAN LABOUR FRONT, DEUTSCHE ARBEITSFRONT, DAF

The NSDAP viewed the trade unions as relics of the Marxist class struggle and their offices were subjected to random attacks as soon as the Nazis came to power. The unions had hoped to work with the NSDAP, but plans were being laid replace them with a state-run workers' organisation. On 1 May 1933, labour rallies were held across the country under Nazi banners but many workers had been forced to attend and hear pledges to restore peace to the workplace.

The next day the Committee of Action for the Protection of German Labour took action, as SA troopers and NSBO representatives occupied union offices across the country. Over the week that followed, around 150 trade unions were disbanded and their assets were seized. The chairman of the council of unions, the General German Trade Union Federation, the ADGB, made a vain offer to assure union collaboration. His offer was rejected and many of his colleagues were imprisoned or went into hiding.

Crowds gather for the 1933 May Day celebration. (NARA-242-HB-05811)

The German Labour Front was established on 10 May with Robert Ley at its head. The state-controlled workers' union had over 20 million workers. Regional offices were split along party lines, into a hierarchy of *Gaue*, Circles, and Local Groups. Each Circle covered the workplaces in a city district, an entire town or a large rural area. A Local Group covered the workplaces in part of a city or a town or several villages. Factories and other workplaces were divided into Cells and Blocks. National Socialist Labour Offices were opened, offering better job opportunities for party members. It meant that the party was now running the shop floor on behalf of the state, not the employer.

The Front took control of the money and the property taken from the trade unions, giving it a huge budget. Money was used to assist workers, hold vocational courses and

run a workers' recreational organisation called Strength through Joy. Order Castle Schools were built to train future party leaders. A system of down payments for the new Volkswagen motor car was also started.

ROBERT LEY (1890–1945)

Ley had served as a pilot in the First World War and he joined the NSDAP in 1924 while working as a chemist. His crude and drunken behaviour made him unpopular with many Nazi leaders, particularly Goebbels, but his fierce anti-Semitism and loyalty to Hitler assured his rise through the party ranks. He was elected Rhineland delegate for the Prussian Landtag in 1928 and was elected to the Reichstag two years later. He replaced Gregor Strasser as Party Organisation Leader in 1932.

On 10 May 1933, Robert Ley was made head of the new German Labour Front and he claimed that Germany was the first European country to overcome the class struggle in 1935. He may have been right but it had been achieved at the expense of employees' rights. Ley was another corrupt party leader who received wages for different roles, royalties from publications and profits from newspapers.

Robert Ley. (NARA-242-HB-12989a1)

MOBILISING THE LABOUR FORCE

THE REICH LABOUR SERVICE, REICHSARBEITSDIENST, RAD

The Depression had doubled the unemployment level from 2.9 million in 1929 to 6 million by 1933; 30 per cent of the workforce. The Nazis pledged to reduce it to a minimal level. The Weimar government tried to reduce unemployment by employing 250,000 men on civic and agricultural construction projects under the Volunteer Labour Service.

The Nazis boycotted the Weimar Republic's volunteer organisations but they announced their first Law for Reduction of Unemployment, and 1,000 million RM, for their own Emergency Work Programmes, employing men on dam building, on farms and on the autobahn system in June 1933. Another 500 million RM was pledged under a second law in September. Labour-intensive environmental projects – including reforestation, land reclamation and river improvements – were also started. Unemployed men were offered places in labour battalions and it creating a cheap workforce for new public works projects while unemployment figures were reduced. All existing volunteer organisations were merged into the National Socialist Volunteer Labour Service and it was renamed the Reich Labour Service in 1934.

A law of June 1935 introduced obligatory service for all unemployed males between the ages of 19–25. 200,000 men at a time were summoned to work camps and assigned to farms

Reich Labour Service units march past Hitler at Nuremburg. (NARA-242-HB-22591a19)

or construction schemes for six months, with no regard for their previous occupation. They were counted as employed, even though they were unpaid. The Nazis saw the labour battalions as training units for the armed forces and it was a short step from carrying a shovel to shouldering a rifle. In May 1935 compulsory conscription of one year was introduced and it was increased to two years in August 1936; it again further reduced the number of unemployed. By September 1939, there were 750,000 men on active service and a million in reserve.

The Nazis kept their promise to reduce unemployment through compulsory employment and conscription rather than through effective economic policies. The recovery of the world markets from the effects of the Stock Market Crash had also worked in the Nazis' favour.

In September 1936, Hitler announced that unemployment had been reduced from over 6 million to 1.6 million out of a workforce of over 24 million. At the same time the number of young women or 'Labour Maids' for the Reich Labour Service was set at 25,000. Service was made compulsory for young females in 1939 increasing the number to 250,000; the majority worked in the service industry, allowing men to be redirected into rearmament industries.

The table charts annual changes in unemployment, January to December:

Date	Unemployed (million)
1933	6.0 to 4.0
1934	3.7 to 2.6
1935	3.0 to 2.5
1936	2.5 to 1.5
1937	1.8 to 1.0
1938	1.1 to 0.5
1939	0.3 to 0.1

Civil construction programs accounted for 500,000 jobs. Anti-Semitic pogroms and incentives to reduce the number of women in the labour market reduced the total by another million. People had to be actively seeking work not just signing on for benefits to count as unemployed, hiding 1.5 million from the figures, while occasional workers were now counted as full time employees. The rest were absorbed into the rearmament industry and the armed forces.

KONSTANTIN HIERL (1875–1955)

Hierl was serving as a major in the Reichswehr's Munich political department in September 1919 when he ordered Hitler to observe the German Workers' Party. The order led to Hitler joining the party and eventually becoming the leader of the NSDAP. Hierl also joined the NSDAP and he was appointed head of the Volunteer Labour Service in 1931. He became head of the National Socialist Labour Service in 1933 and the Reich Labour Service in 1934.

CONTROLLING THE LABOUR FORCE

A law of 19 May 1933 established twelve Trustees of Labour offices. Trustees were chosen by the government and they dealt with industrial relations, wages and negotiated contracts between employers and employees. In October the Law against Habitual and Dangerous Criminals was introduced, making it dangerous to remain out of work without good reason. The law gave the police powers to round up the work-shy, the homeless, the unemployed, beggars and alcoholics and send them to a concentration camp for re-education.

In January 1934, the Law for the Ordering of National Labour was announced to introduce harmony between the employer, known as the Plant Leader, and the employees, known as the Retinue. In reality the law favoured an employer who worked in the interest of the state.

The law was followed by the Labour Charter on 1 May 1934 which detailed the cooperation of capital and labour, encouraging management and workers to work together. Strikes and employers' lockouts were banned and although employees could be elected to arbitration Councils of Trust, wages were set and bargaining was forbidden. Redundancies were supposed to be reported to Courts of Honour but few cases were heard. Fixed taxation and charity donations were automatically deducted from pay packets.

A German Labour Front job centre. (NARA-242-HB-13228a13)

After June 1934 all artisans had to belong to a registered guild and after 1935 they had to pass an examination to be registered. However, standards were streamlined to such a level that professionalism was lost.

Laws in May 1934 and February 1935 introduced Work Books to record employees' employment, training, qualifications, experience and taxation; everyone had to possess one or they could not be employed. The books were handed in when starting a new job and returned at the end of employment. Labour Offices kept a registry of Work Books and anyone found misusing their book or making false entries were subject to severe penalties.

Work Books were used to draft employees to new industries if there was a shortage. Many were attracted to the high wages in the arms industries, forcing many small businesses to close. The decree on the Duty of Service in June 1938 allowed labour exchanges to temporarily redirect labour into rearmament industries and transfers were soon made indefinite.

The Labour Charter was heralded as successful because it ended industrial troubles. However, it was soon clear that it favoured the government and the employers rather than employees. Many workers were fed up with the new regime but they could only use passive resistance and disrupt production, working slowly or inefficiently. Employers sometimes called in the Gestapo to root out troublemakers on shop floors.

By 1937 the government had full control of wages, making sure that a national pay freeze was in effect. As the cost of living rose, workers' disposal income fell and unrest returned to the workplace. Wages fell by only ten per cent but the amount of deductions rose considerably. It meant that people had to work longer for less and they had to take overtime to make up their wages.

APPEASING THE LABOUR FORCE

THE STRENGTH THROUGH JOY MOVEMENT KRAFT DURCH FREUDE, KDF

Following the establishment of the German Labour Front in May 1933, the After Work Organisation was organised using money from trade union funds. The organisation aimed to make middle-class leisure activities available to the working classes. In raising their social standing and morale, it would increase their support for the government. The organisation's name was changed to 'Strength through Joy' in November 1933 and it spent 24 million RM in the first twelve months, subsidising leisure activities to organise leisure time. The organisation was grouped into offices for entertainments, travel, sports and education as well as workplace improvement competitions under the Beauty of Work scheme.

Factory workers gather to hear a speech supporting the 'Strength through Joy' movement. (NARA-242-HB-09536a2)

Workers could have subsidised membership of sports facilities and adult education courses and access to cheap theatre, exhibition and concert tickets. Hundreds of theatre and cabaret groups toured the country visiting factories. Eventually 35 million members attended concerts, operas, theatre performances and exhibitions although some were of a poor standard or undersubscribed.

Families were encouraged to take advantage of subsidised holidays, and five huge holiday complexes were planned along the north coast. Only one at Prora, a mile-long complex for 20,000 holidaymakers on the Baltic Sea island of Rügen was started in 1936; work was abandoned when war broke out. Foreign holidays to the Alps, Italy, Portugal and Norway were also encouraged and the organisation owned eight cruise ships, including two new ones, and rented four others; 180,000 Germans enjoyed cruises in 1938 but many were party officials. The holiday schemes proved popular, and German tourism doubled under the Nazis while the state railway and the tourist industry saw profits rise. However, many tourist facilities were poor and block booking undercut established tour companies. Hordes of working-class holidaymakers in rural areas often caused problems.

THE BEAUTY OF LABOUR SCHEME
SCHÖNHEIT DER ARBEIT

In January 1934, Robert Ley announced the Beauty of Labour scheme to improve working conditions in factories. Under the leadership of Albert Speer, government-led safety campaigns were instigated to improve productivity and gain the workers' support. Although the ideas helped production, employees had to carry them out in free time and pay for them. Studies of management practices, factory organisation and hygiene were carried out, while propaganda encouraged the workers to follow the Nazi way of life. Day trips, carnivals and folk dancing festivals were used to make political lectures more palatable.

THE NATIONAL VOCATIONS COMPETITION

In 1933 the annual National Vocations Competition was introduced to promote the Nazi way of life in industry and commerce. Competitions were designed to improve the employees' knowledge of their work and how it benefited the Nazi regime. Competitions were structured regionally and by profession, and competitors were tested on theory and practical work. Winners were treated like celebrities and they were escorted to Berlin where they were presented to Hitler and Ley. The competition was expanded in 1938 to include all types of workers including civil servants, managers and students. The number of competitors rose to 3.5 million.

THE PEOPLE'S CAR

DR FERDINAND PORSCHE (1875–1952)
Porsche had been associated with designing racing cars for Auto Union. Starting in 1933, he developed plans for a cheap car which could be mass produced. Hitler was immediately taken by the idea and he wanted the new car to be produced for the working classes. The car

The Strength through Joy village at the Nuremburg rally, the Nazis' 'ideal home' exhibition.

An advertisement for the People's Car.

was originally called the KdF Wagen, the *Kraft durch Freude* or 'Strength through Joy' car, but the name People's Car was soon adopted. The project was unveiled in 1935 with promises for cars for all and over 330,000 workers subscribed 100 million RM. However, the Fallersleben factory near Brunswick did not open until the autumn of 1938 and production turned to an all-purpose military vehicle after Germany invaded Poland in September 1939. Nobody received a People's Car and no subscriptions were returned.

CHAPTER ELEVEN

RELIGION AND SCIENCE

RELIGION UNDER THE NAZIS

Although Hitler was born a Catholic, he rejected Christianity because of its Jewish and Oriental origins. It also promoted mercy, love and salvation as well as the protection of the sick and the poor. All of these were alien to his beliefs for a strong state. The 25 Point Programme was announced in February 1920, and promised freedom for religions, unless they endangered the German race. While the party did not promote any particular faith, it vowed to attack the Jewish faith. Although Hitler ignored religion, the NSDAP's head of ideology, Alfred Rosenberg, promoted Positive Christianity, emphasising old Nordic values, the spirit of the hero and racialism. In 1934, Professor Ernst Bergmann of Leipzig University (1881–1945) issued the 25 Points of the German Religion; the five main points were:

1) The Jewish Old Testament and parts of the New Testament were not suitable
2) Christ was a Nordic martyr put to death by the Jews
3) Adolf Hitler was the new messiah sent to earth to save the world from the Jews
4) The swastika was the symbol of German Christianity
5) Land, blood, soul and art were the basis of German Christianity

Bergmann also stated that God had to be German.

Before seizing power in 1933, Hitler repeatedly stated that the NSDAP would allow the Catholic and Protestant churches religious freedom and that he was looking for friendly relations. Some believed that the NSDAP would rescue Christianity from the communist threat. However, Hitler believed that National Socialism was a religion and the Führer Principle promoted him as a God-like figure.

THE PROTESTANT CHURCH AND THE GERMAN FAITH MOVEMENT

Positive Christianity was advocated by Alfred Rosenberg, the intellectual head of the Third Reich. He reasoned that Christianity was a transitional stage towards the rejection of Protestantism and Catholicism and it would be replaced by a German Nordic race. The spirit of the hero would take the place of the crucifixion while the symbol of the cross would be replaced by the orb of the sun. As the Nazis synchronised Christianity with Nordic paganism, he aimed to harmonise the belief in Christ with the Laws of Blood and Soil. While Hitler was opposed to traditional Christian ethics, he did not actively support Positive Christianity.

The Protestant Church had 40 million members but the Nazis believed that it was weaker than the Catholic Church. They wanted to abolish the 28 regional church bodies and merge their 600,000 members under a new Reich Bishop. Fritz von Bodelschwingh was voted Reich Bishop of the Protestant Reich Church but he was not the Nazis' choice and was removed after a few weeks.

LUDWIG MÜLLER (1883–1945)

Müller was an early supporter of the NSDAP who had served as a chaplain and church leader in East Prussia, and was Hitler's choice for Reich Bishop. He was duly elected by a national synod in July 1933. He was also appointed State Bishop for Prussia, a largely Protestant area.

Reich Bishop Ludwig Müller salutes the crowds. (NARA-242-HB-08287)

The Association of German Christians formed the Protestant Reich Church in July 1933 after gaining a large majority in the church elections and the constitution was then recognised by the Reichstag. The new church united 28 regional churches and it introduced Positive Christianity, aryanising Christianity, ignoring the Old Testament and other Jewish references. Members were called 'Believers in God' and government employees, including civil servants and teachers, were expected to join. In September 1933 there was a call to ban all Jewish employees of the church. The Church saw baptised Jews as Christians but the Nazis did not.

PASTOR MARTIN NIEMÖLLER (1892–1984)

Pastor Niemöller set up the 6,000-strong Emergency Pastors League with Dietrich Bonhoeffer in September 1933 to oppose the Protestant Reich Church; it was later named the Confessional Church. Niemöller had served as a submarine commander in the First World War before studying theology and working for the Westphalia Inner Mission during the economic crisis. He was appointed pastor of the Berlin-Dahlem Church in 1931 and although he initially supported the Nazis and joined the NSDAP, he soon realised what the Nazi regime had in store for Germany. Ludwig Müller banned any mention of the League's revolt and he merged all the Protestant youth organisations and their one million members into the Hitler Youth.

The Confessional Synod of the German Evangelical Church met in Barmen in May 1934 and Professor Karl Barth's declaration called for a rejection of the Nazis' 'world view' because it was incompatible with Christianity.

Nearly a third of the 18,000 Protestant pastors had joined the League by the end of the 1934. Anti-regime sermons attracted quiet resistance from all quarters and bishops

An open air church service for a Berlin SA unit. (NARA-242-HB-00993)

An SA standard bearer by the altar and swastika armbands around the church. (NARA-242-HB-00688)

were reinstated. A Ministry of Church Affairs was set up in July 1935 to curb unruly pastors. The Gestapo also started banning services, closing church schools and confiscating church property. Over 700 pastors were arrested over the next two years and sent to concentration camps. Many Christians simply stayed away from their church, saddened by the political interference in their religion.

Niemöller was finally arrested in July 1937 and tried before a Special Court eight months later. He was imprisoned to Sachsenhausen and Dachau concentration camps and held prisoner until the end of the war. Niemöller summed up the situation he faced in Nazi Germany as follows:

First they took the Communists …
… but I was not a Communist so I said nothing.
Then they took the Socialist Democrats…
… but I was not a Socialist Democrat so I did nothing.
Then it was trade unionists turn …
… but I was not a trade unionist.
And then they took the Jews …
… but I was not a Jew, so I did little.
Then when they came and took me …
… there was no one left who could have stood up for me.

Followers of the new German Faith Movement wanted to convert Christmas into a pagan solstice festivals, banning nativity plays and carols. They also wanted to remove the Christian element of the birth, marriage and death rituals. Reich Youth Dedication Ceremonies were introduced to welcome children into the Movement while steps were taken to stop daily prayers in the classroom. The Nazis lost interest in Positive Christianity when it was clear that it had failed to replace or absorb traditional religions. By 1937 government relations with the Reich Church were limited.

MINISTRY OF ECCLESIASTICAL AFFAIRS

HANNS KERRL (1887–1941)

Kerrl was a lawyer and a decorated First World War officer. He joined the NSDAP in 1923 and soon became involved in regional politics. Although he supported the Strasser brothers during the 1920s, he remained a close friend of Goebbels. He became President of the Prussia Landtag in 1932 and a Reich Minister without Portfolio and Reich Commissioner for Justice in March 1933. His first move was to retire Jewish judges and introduce the limit on Jewish lawyers. Kerrl was appointed the Reich Minister of Ecclesiastical Affairs in July 1935 and he worked hard to strike a delicate balance between the Nazi leaders and the Catholic and Protestant churches. His Ministry showed no mercy for the Jewish communities.

THE CATHOLIC CHURCH

The takeover is complete; swastika flags dominate the church. (NARA-242-HB-18503a1)

Hitler's upbringing had taught him to respect the power of the Catholic Church and the Nazis took steps to make peace with the Vatican in 1933. Vice-Chancellor Franz von Papen worked with Cardinal Pacelli to determine the future role of the Catholic Church in the Third Reich. The Concordat was announced during an elaborate ceremony in the Vatican on 20 July 1933.

The Church legal status, its property and its role in education were guaranteed
The Church would administer its affairs without interference from the government
The Church would keep out of politics
German citizens had the freedom to practise religion

The Church hoped it would be allowed to continue unmolested if it gave a degree of support to the regime. In reality, Hitler had no intention of allowing the Church to continue freely and the terms of the Concordat was soon ignored. Bishops tried to remain on good terms with the Nazi government but it had soon banned religious processions, censored the Catholic press and forbidden pastoral letters. The Security Service also spied and reported on sermons.

Attacks on Catholicism in Rosenberg's book, *The Myth of the Twentieth Century,* and false accusations by the Propaganda Ministry undermined the Church. Priests and monks were arrested on faked charges of immorality while monasteries and convents were closed down.

Rome granted Cardinal Michael von Faulhaber, Archbishop of Munich-Freising, a papal legate and diplomatic immunity, allowing him to make statements against the regime. In March 1937, Pope Pius XI wrote a protest letter which began with the words, 'with burning concern', complaining about the breaches of the

A mass marriage ceremony. (NARA-242-HB-02997a11)

Concordat, the violation of human rights and the persecution of Catholics. The letter was distributed secretly around the country and read from every pulpit as a form of national protest. In response Goebbels intensified scandals and over 1,000 priests were held on false charges of homosexuality and child abuse while claims were made that the Church supported them.

Catholic Youth organisations numbered 1.5 million members and the majority attended faith schools. Hitler Youth groups were encouraged to start fights with their local rival, and one by one the organisations were forced to close. The faith schools had been turned into community schools by the summer of 1939. The control of boys and girls by the Hitler Youth undermined future support for both the Protestant and Catholic Churches.

POPE PIUS XI, ACHILLE RATTI (1857–1939)

Ratti gained a triple doctorate in philosophy, theology, and law at Lombard College in Rome before teaching theology and serving as director of the Milan Library. He transferred to the Vatican Library in 1912 and after briefly serving as the Apostolic Nuncio to Poland, was appointed Archbishop of Lepanto in 1919. After serving as Archbishop and then Cardinal of Milan he was elected Pope Pius XI in 1922.

The Pope's initial concerns were with the state of Italy. By 1929 he had finalised the Lateran Treaty and agreed a concordat with Mussolini, restoring the temporal power of the papacy. Two years later he felt the need to issue a protest letter titled 'We Do Not Have Need', complaining about pagan worship by Italian Fascists.

When the Nazis came to power in 1933, Pius turned his attentions to Germany and Austria, agreeing a host of concordats and treaties. For the second time the Catholic Church found itself in conflict with a dictatorship and it was forced to complain about the persecution of Catholics. Pope Pius XI died in Rome on 10 February 1939.

POPE PIUS XII, EUGENIO PACELLI (1876–1958)

Pacelli had served as a professor of ecclesiastical diplomacy in Rome before he was appointed the Archbishop of Sardis in 1917. He also served as the Nuncio to Bavaria and then for the whole of Germany. He was appointed cardinal in 1929 and the Vatican Secretary of State in 1930. He became an experienced diplomat who concluded the concordats and treaties with Germany. Pacelli was elected Pope Pius XII in March 1939.

GERMANY'S PAPAL REPRESENTATIVE

MICHAEL FAULHABER (1869–1952)

Faulhaber was born in Klosterheidenfeld and served as a priest in Würzburg from 1892 to 1910. He was the first German chaplain to be awarded the Iron Cross for his service on the Western Front in 1916. He was the Bishop of Speyer from 1911 and the Archbishop of Munich-Freising from 1917. He was appointed cardinal in 1921 and promoted Bavarian Catholicism. Following the March 1933 elections, he reported the German situation to Rome emphasising how the Nazis were different from the Italian fascists. He did, however, believe that the Nazis would protect the church against communism and he urged the Pope to work with them.

The promises made under the July 1933 Concordat were soon broken and in November 1933, Faulhaber protested that the German people were being forced into a form of paganism. On 4 November 1936, Hitler personally assured him that the Nazis wanted to defend Christianity and defeat Bolshevism, but Faulhaber did not believe him. He helped to draft the papal encyclical, *In Deep Concern*, in 1937; the Nazis responded by stepping up their harassment of the Church.

Faulhaber asked Catholics to pray for the peaceful cooperation of the Church and the state during the Anschluss with Austria in 1938. He also asked bishops to congratulate Hitler following the September 1938 Czech crisis.

The Cardinal's faith was severely tested during the attacks on the Jewish community in Munich during *Kristallnacht*. He provided a lorry so that the city's Chief Rabbi could rescue religious objects from his burning synagogue. A few months later Carl Friedrich Goerdeler tried to get Faulhaber's support for a plot against Hitler's life; the Cardinal refused to commit himself.

SCIENCE UNDER THE NAZIS

The universities were an early target of the Nazis and aryanisation removed many prominent scientists from their academic posts, adversely affecting research. Teaching standards generally declined under the Nazis, due to the exodus of Jewish scientists and the increasing isolation from international academia. Attempts to eliminate 'degenerate science' – any scientific research or paper which was based on abstract theories and formalism – proved to be difficult.

The Nazis established the Emergency Association of German Science and the government awarded large budgets for Aryan-based research; it was later renamed the German Research Community. Physics was particularly troubled because of the discovery of new scientific theories including relativity and quantum mechanics by the Jewish scientist, Albert Einstein. While chemistry hardly changed, biology was redirected towards racial experiments; attempts to change the emphasis in mathematics failed.

While academia suffered, research and development in industry prospered as huge budgets for military projects – ranging from synthetic fuels to new weapons – were made available. Money was also provided for research into synthetic fibres and agricultural fertilisers. Discoveries included nuclear fusion, aerial infrared photography and electron microscopes, while inventions included the jet propulsion engine, the diesel motor and the intercontinental ballistic missile.

Hitler takes interest in a model of a new chemical plant. (NARA-242-HB-06448a6)

SCIENTISTS

Two leading German scientists who had recently been awarded Nobel Prizes were treated completely differently under the Nazis' Aryan Clause.

JOHANNES STARK (1874–1951)

Stark was a physicist who was awarded a Nobel Prize in 1919 for his work on electromagnetism. Three years later he was forced to leave Wurzburg University due to his attacks on Albert Einstein and the theory of relativity. Over the next ten years he promoted factual German science and opposed research by Jewish scientists, making him a favourite of the NSDAP; he also emphasised racial doctrine. When the Nazis came to power he was made President of the Emergency Association of German Science, later the German Research Community.

Hitler and his adjutant Julius Schaub study a display on new metallurgical technology. (NARA-242-6448a2)

Lufthansa displays the advances in German aeronautical technology. (NARA-242-6412)

ALBERT EINSTEIN (1879–1955)

Einstein was born in Germany but took Swiss citizenship after attending a Swiss university. He was appointed Professor at the University of Berlin in 1913 and his publication on the Special and General Theory of Relativity three years later changed the world of physics. He was awarded a Nobel Prize for his work in 1921.

Einstein was visiting California when the Nazis came to power in January 1933. His property was seized and his books were burned in front of his university in May the same year. He decided never to return to Germany and continued his work in the US.

In August 1939, Einstein wrote to President Roosevelt about the possibility of developing an atomic bomb. His suggestion ultimately led to the Manhattan Project and the atomic bombs which brought the Second World War to an end; two were dropped on Hiroshima and Nagasaki in Japan six years later.

CHAPTER TWELVE

THE PRESS, RADIO AND PROPAGANDA

The Ministry for Public Enlightenment and Propaganda opened on 13 March 1933, staffed with young, educated party members rather than experienced civil servants. It was headed by Dr Joseph Goebbels, and he was given responsibility for propaganda, the press and the radio. Three state secretaries eventually worked for Goebbels:

Newspapers, German and foreign press	Walther Funk to 1937 and then Otto Dietrich
Tourism	Hermann Esser after 1935
Culture, propaganda, the arts, radio	Karl Hanke after 1937

DR JOSEPH GOEBBELS (1897–1945)

Goebbels was was born in Rheydt in the Ruhr district. He was rejected for army service in the First World War because of a crippled foot, caused by a bout of osteomyelitis in childhood. He turned to education, completing a doctorate in philology at Heidelberg University by 1921. He joined the NSDAP in 1922 and after failing to get his poetry and plays published, he moved to the Ruhr district to work as editor of the *People's Freedom* newspaper. He also became business manager for the North Rhineland *Gau*, editing Gregor Strasser's publications.

Goebbels switched his allegiance to Hitler after the Bamberg Party Conference in February 1926. He was appointed Gauleiter for Berlin-Brandenburg and tasked with increasing the support across the capital, using his newspaper *The Assault* to raise the party's profile and attack political opponents.

Goebbels was a talented speaker and a propaganda expert who adapted American advertising techniques for the NSDAP. He also introduced the 'Heil Hitler!' greeting between party members and turned the murdered SA trooper, Horst Wessel, into a martyr promoting his song, '*Horst Wessel Lied*'. It eventually became the official party anthem.

In May 1928, Goebbels was elected to the Reichstag, representing the Berlin Constituency, and the following year

Dr Joseph Goebbels, the master of Nazi propaganda. (NARA-242-HB-05901)

Goebbels studies new pamphlets. (NARA-242-HB-16956)

he was appointed the NSDAP's Head of Propaganda. He played a vital part in revitalising campaigns for Reichstag delegates over the next five years, helping to increase the NSDAP's share of the vote until it was largest political party. He also promoted Hitler and organised his two presidency campaigns in 1932, which brought him national recognition. During this period Goebbels became one of Hitler's most intimate and influential advisers. This notwithstanding, he was an unpopular member of the NSDAP's hierarchy and he frequently came into conflict with other leading Nazis, particularly Hermann Göring and Joachim von Ribbentrop.

Goebbels' role in the party increased following Hitler's appointment as Chancellor in January 1933. Two months later he was appointed Reich Minister for Public Enlightenment and Propaganda, giving him huge influence over all aspects of German life, in particular literature, music, theatre, dance, art, newspapers, film and radio. After banning Jewish and liberal intellectuals under the Aryan Clause his ministry coordinated all areas of culture to confirm with the NSDAP's ideology.

As well as a close interest in Germany's film industry, Goebbels promoted radio and television as propaganda tools. He encouraged the manufacture of an affordable radio set in 1933, which could only receive German stations, and two years later a limited television service was launched in Berlin.

Goebbels was supported by his wife, Magda Quant, who had married him after divorcing a Jewish businessman. The couple had six children who were favourites of Hitler. Goebbels enjoyed a luxurious lifestyle, hosting lavish parties and entertaining celebrities, particularly from the film industry. He used his influence to gain access to young stage and film actresses and he had several liaisons which became public knowledge. His wife nearly ended their marriage following an affair with the Czech actress Lida Barova 1938; Hitler had to intervene to prevent them divorcing.

THE PRESS

Newspapers were the main way of distributing news after the First World War. Germany did not have national newspapers under the Weimar Republic and people relied on regional newspapers like the *Munich Observer* and the *Berlin Daily* for information. Many of the smaller publishing houses printed politically biased journals and Bavarian nationalists favoured the *People's Observer* and the *Miesbach Advertiser*. Social Democrats read *Forwards* while communist supporters bought the *Red Flag*.

Media magnates started to buy up the small publishing houses, producing larger circulation newspapers and Alfred Hugenberg eventually dominated the nationalist press. Political parties continued to use the small regional newspapers to spread their news and propaganda and many were sponsored by or bought by political parties. The NSDAP newspapers specialised in sensationalism to promote their views, fabricating scandals and false rumours to undermine their political opponents. Editors devoted a lot of time and money to libel cases.

The political newspapers were eventually undermined by a new style of cheap, popular illustrated newspapers. They were dominated by non-political local news and scandal, sport and crime.

THE NAZI NEWSPAPERS

The bi-weekly *Munich Observer* changed its name to the *People's Observer* after the First World War. Although it printed pro-nationalist and anti-Semitic articles, personal differences meant that it did not favour the German Workers' Party. When it was in financial difficulties, Dietrich Eckart and Ernst Röhm asked General Franz von Epp to raise money to buy it for the party. Epp borrowed some money from wealthy friends and some from army funds.

The *People's Observer* became the NSDAP's official newspaper with Alfred Rosenberg as editor and Max Amann as business manager. Extra funding from Munich businessmen allowed it to appear as a large format daily newspaper in February 1923, increasing the circulation. As inflation soared the price increased to eight billion marks a copy, a sign of Germany's economic difficulties.

Rosenberg wanted the newspaper to represent party politics while Amann preferred sensational articles, believing that gossip sold newspapers. Amann usually got his way and in September 1923 the newspaper was in trouble for slandering General von Seeckt, the chief of staff of the German armed forces. Seeckt tried to ban the newspaper but the Bavarian Premier and the Munich area army commander refused, fearing riots. The newspaper called the November 1923 Putsch 'Hitler's

Hitler keeps up to date with events with the *People's Observer*. (NARA-242-HB-18156a1)

171

Triumph', but it was banned while he was imprisoned. It reappeared on Bavaria's news stands in February 1925, headed by Hitler's editorial titled 'A New Beginning'.

In November 1926 the monthly *Illustrated Observer,* a pictorial magazine, was published, and fortnightly editions soon appeared. The *National Socialist Monthly* was also edited by Alfred Rosenberg and printed by the Eher Publishing House.

The *People's Observer* remained a Munich paper and circulation never exceeded 130,000. General Kurt von Schleicher used Reichswehr money to cover the newspaper's debts at the end of the 1932. It spearheaded Amann's growing press empire under the Nazi regime, and simultaneous Berlin and Munich editions made it Germany's first national newspaper; a Vienna edition was printed after the Anschluss in 1938.

THE ATTACK, DER ANGRIFF

Goebbels published *The Attack* in 1927 to attract north Germans to the NSDAP. He often published sensational articles to gain publicity. He also controlled *Das Reich*, a higher quality weekly newspaper.

THE STORMER, DER STÜRMER

After serving as a junior officer in the First World War, Julius Streicher (1885–1946) returned to teaching and formed his own political party in Nuremberg. He offered his membership to the NSDAP in 1921. Two years later he established *Der Stürmer*, a notorious newspaper filled with false scandals about the Jewish community, vulgar anti-Semitic cartoons and outrageous articles supporting Hitler and the NSDAP. Although Streicher claimed it was the only newspaper Hitler read, many considered it to be gutter press.

Streicher took part in the 1923 Munich Putsch and he was appointed Gauleiter for Franconia when the NSDAP reformed. Although he was dismissed from his teaching post, his newspaper increased its circulation as the NSDAP grew. As self-proclaimed 'Number One Jew Baiter', he advocated anti-Semitism, urging violent action against the Jews.

Streicher was elected as the Franconia delegate to the Bavarian Landtag in 1929. He was elected the Reichstag delegate for Thuringia in January 1933. As head of the Central Committee for Counteracting Jewish Atrocity Tales and Boycotts, he organised anti-Semitic propaganda. He was promoted to SS-Gruppenführer the following year.

Streicher amassed a huge fortune, dishonestly acquiring Jewish property while revelling in administering the increasing number of pogroms. His behaviour became increasingly eccentric while his obnoxious manners and sadistic deeds drew unwelcome attention from other Nazi leaders. By 1939 Hitler had tired of Streicher's

Julius Streicher rallies the crowds. (NARA-242-HB-16350)

behaviour and after reprimanding him for libellous conduct on several occasions, he finally placed a speaking ban on the Gauleiter.

OTHER NAZI NEWSPAPERS

The Black Corps, '*Das Schwarze Korps*' reflected SS-Reichsleiter Heinrich Himmler's opinions. *The Stinging Nettle* was a newsletter used to publish scandal, rumour and humour which could have exposed the larger newspapers to expensive libel cases.

THE PRESS UNDER THE NAZIS

When Goebbels was appointed head of the Propaganda Ministry in March 1933, he became responsible for controlling over 3,600 newspapers and hundreds of magazines. Opposition newspapers were immediately banned while the Reich Press Chamber monitored the remaining publications. The Reich Press Law of October 1933 forced editors to sack Jewish and liberal staff, in pursuit of a 'racially clean journalism'. Pressure was also put on Jewish publishing houses to sell out; those that did not were banned from publishing until they were bankrupt. In December 1933 the Propaganda Ministry took over Hugenberg's Telegraph Union and Wolff's Telegraph Office press agencies to regulate what was printed. Goebbels detailed daily instructions containing as much about what not to publish as what was allowed; it left editors little leeway. Temporary closures and the threat of bankruptcy eventually brought them all into line.

Subscriptions for opposition newspapers fell dramatically as people feared being targeted and nearly 1,000 newspapers had been forced out of business by 1937. The Nazis added over 25 new papers in 1933 and quadrupled the circulation of their funded newspapers to three million making it a highly profitable business. The *People's Observer* alone increased its circulation ten-fold to over a million a day. *Der Stormer* sold 500,000 and copies were ordered en masse to sell on the streets. By 1939 the Nazi-owned Eher Publishing House owned two out of three newspapers and magazines.

Every morning, Goebbels briefed the editors of the Berlin daily newspapers and news correspondents representing publications in other cities and towns. He dictated what had to appear in the news that day, severely limiting what could or could not be published. Similar directives were issued to smaller newspapers by telegram or mail.

Newspapers had to conform to Nazi policies or close down. Editors of good quality newspapers only kept their job if they toed the party line, while journalists had to praise Nazi leaders and their policies if they wanted to continue working. In 1937 Otto Dietrich became the Reich Press Chief and he took over responsibility for delivering the daily briefings. The following year he introduced the Editors Law, making each editor personally responsible for any statements in their newspaper. Anti-government remarks would result in the editor's prosecution.

One of the few newspapers to maintain a degree of independence under the Nazis was the *Frankfurt Times*. Goebbels wanted to make the most of its good international reputation and present it as a good example of German journalism.

Goebbels was anxious to get support from foreign publications and he provided luxurious apartments for their journalists, treating them to lavish entertainment. Only a few were deceived by his charisma. All foreign papers were banned when the war started in September 1939.

Der Stürmer contained a mixture of anti-Semitism and outrageous rumours.

HANS FRITZSCHE (1900–1953)

After serving in the ranks in the First World War, Fritzsche edited a monthly journal. He joined the Hugenberg press empire in 1924 and was an editor with the *Telegraph Union* and chief editor with the International News Service. He was appointed head of *Broadcast*, *Rundfunk*, the German wireless news service in 1932. In May 1933, he became Head of the Press Section's News Service, and he circulated Goebbels's instructions to hundreds of editors, newspaper representatives and journalists. Fritzsche was also appointed Head of the Press Section's Wireless Service and his staff monitored radio programmes, including those broadcast to other countries.

OTTO DIETRICH (1897–1952)

After serving in the First World War, Dietrich studied economics, philosophy and political science, gaining a doctorate in political science in 1921. He soon joined the NSDAP, becoming a confidant of Hitler. As business manager of the *Augsburg Newspaper* and son-in-law of the owner of the *Westphalia-Rhine* newspaper, he was the ideal mediator between Hitler and the Rhineland industrialists. His contacts donated a lot of sponsorship money to the NSDAP. He was appointed the Party Press Chief in August 1931 and he joined the SS in December 1932.

Otto Dietrich and Max Amman. (NARA-242-HB-03401)

Dietrich was given the task of coordinating the German press in 1933 but his work overlapped with Goebbels's Reich Press Chamber and there were disputes between the two. He accompanied Hitler to Bad Wiessee at the end of June 1934 and witnessed the murders of Röhm and his subordinates. He then briefed the press on the Nazi Party's view of the Night of the Long Knives and how the murders had been carried out in the interests of the state.

Dietrich was appointed Reich Press Chief and State Secretary to the Propaganda Ministry in 1937 and he was given the task of presenting the Nazi 'world view' to the German people. The importance of his role increased following the invasion of Poland in September 1939 and the newspapers had to adhere to his Daily Directive when they reported news from the front.

MAX AMANN (1891–1957)

Amann was Hitler's company sergeant during the First World War. He joined the NSDAP and the SA in 1921, becoming the party's first business manager. He became director of the Eher Publishing House, the Nazis' official publishing house, and controlled the NSDAP's Munich newspapers. Eher Publishing House printed early editions of Hitler's *Mein Kampf* after Amann had shortened the title from *Four and a Half Years of Struggle against Lies, Stupidity, and Cowardice*. He dealt with the book's royalty payments and became a wealthy man as sales increased. He also worked in the SA central office after 1925, meeting many influential Nazis.

In November 1933, Amann was appointed President of the Reich Association of Newspaper Publishers and President of the Reich Press Chamber. Publishing houses were aryanised and monitored under his control. The Chamber had the power to close down any which did not follow the party line.

RADIO UNDER THE NAZIS

State-controlled radio stations were established after the First World War and they were operated by the Postmaster General's office. Goebbels knew that spoken propaganda was more powerful than the written version and that many German families relied on their radio for news. The Nazis subsidised cheap People's Receivers with a limited range so that families

Goebbels was fascinated with the propaganda value of the radio. (NARA-242-HB-14253a1)

could receive home broadcasts. By 1939 70 per cent of households had one and it allowed the government to keep in contact with rural areas.

In March 1933 the state radio was transferred to the Ministry of Propaganda under Eugen Hadamowsky's Reich Radio Chamber, and it was soon broadcasting a mixture of heavily censored news, National Socialist propaganda and classical music. Listeners could also tune into regional stations. The Chamber was instructed to purge radio stations of Jewish and liberal staff in July 1933.

Regular political radio broadcasts were made by party leaders and sirens sounded in factories across Germany when the Führer spoke so that workers could listen to him. The amount of propaganda reduced over time in favour of music programmes, to maximise the impact of subtle messages.

Radio stations were established on Germany's borders to broadcast into adjacent countries. A transmitter in Cologne covered Belgium while another in Frankfurt-am-Main covered the French border area; Hamburg and Bremen covered Denmark to the north. Transmitters in Gleiwitz and Breslau broadcast to German-speaking people in Czechoslovakia while a Munich transmitter covered Austria. A high powered transmitter in Seesen, Berlin, covered the rest of the world with 24-hour broadcasts in several languages.

NAZI PROPAGANDA

The Nazis' skilful use of propaganda was a major factor in increasing their share of the vote. Dr Paul Joseph Goebbels studied American promotion and advertising methods, adapting them to promote the Nazi Party. He realised that people were more receptive to simple and insistent forms of propaganda and they were subjected to a barrage of messages in the press and on the radio. Under Goebbels' control, political rallies were transformed into stirring pageants with music, lighting and flags forming backdrops to the speeches and parades. Many of Hitler's successes and the Nazi Party's triumphs were due to Goebbels.

The Reich Propaganda Office had a national leadership office coordinating propaganda across the Reich. While over 300 officials and 500 employees worked around the clock, monitoring events around the world, special propaganda agents were on standby to attend events or incidents.

NAZI PROPAGANDA SLOGANS

Nazi slogans were short and direct making them memorable and repeatable. One of Hitler's favourite slogans was 'Germany Awake', *Deutschland Erwache*, evoking a feeling of nationalism and desire to join in; it was used on Nazi standards. The idea that the Führer and the country were one was expressed in the slogan 'Germany is Hitler, Hitler is Germany'. The Führer's deputy, Rudolf Hess, would encourage disciplined chanting by calling out the slogan after Hitler had finished speaking at party meetings.

The concept that the people and the country were one was suggested in the slogan 'Blood and Soil'. The Nazi Party's desire for extra living space for the German people was demanded in the slogan 'People without Space'. Many slogans were anti-Semitic, blaming Germany's problems on the Jews with slogans such as 'The Jews are our Misfortune' and 'Perish Judah'. Anti-Semitic slogans were often chanted during attacks on Jewish businesses or as general harassment.

Many Nazi leaders used slogans to support their calls for a community spirit, full employment and rearmament. While Goebbels called for a 'Community of Need, Bread, and Fate' Göring explained that if the German people had to choose between making 'Butter or Guns', they would have to choose guns.

'Germany Awake', a Nazi rally call. (NARA-242-HB-02559)

Posters for a Hitler Youth rally. (NARA-242-HB-10467, 10468)

Floodlit parades
encouraged
voters to support
the NSDAP.
(NARA-242-HB-
2263)

Goebbels, the
master of Nazi
propaganda,
tours the country
during an election
campaign.
(NARA-242-HB-
1654a)

CHAPTER THIRTEEN

CULTURE

Hitler's ambition to be an artist was dashed when he was repeatedly refused admission to the Vienna Fine Arts Academy. He made a meagre living out of painting landscape postcards for several years before the First World War, but he never forgave those who had rejected him.

Hitler outlined his preferences for culture in his book, *Mein Kampf*. He believed that race was the foundation of all culture and he promoted Aryan idealism while rejecting Jewish materialism. Alfred Rosenberg established the Fighting League for German Culture in 1929 to promote Hitler's views. The lifting of post-war censorship had resulted in a wave of radical and modernist literature, literature, music, art and cinema across Germany. The older generations reacted against it, believing that morals were being undermined as younger people turned away from old values. The Nazis were determined to implement their own values.

The Aryan Clause was introduced in June 1933 and it excluded Jews from taking part in all cultural activities and the League started to aryanise fine art, cinema, music, literature and theatre. Hundreds of directors, producers, actors, actresses, writers, artists and technicians were forced to leave their jobs and many went into exile where some worked on anti-Nazi projects. The press and the radio were also affected.

THE REICH CHAMBER OF CULTURE

The Reich Chamber of Culture replaced the Fighting League on 22 September 1933 and it was headed by Joseph Goebbels. It had seven chambers devoted to promoting Nazi culture in all forms of artistic creation. Many of the original heads were replaced because they did not apply aryanisation vigorously enough.

Reich Visual Arts Chamber	Eugen Hönig, Adolf Ziegler in 1936
Reich Film Chamber	Fritz Scheuermann, Oswald Lehnich in 1935
	Carl Froelich in 1939
Reich Music Chamber	Richard Strauss, Peter Raabe in 1935
Reich Theatre Chamber	Otto Laubinger, Rainer Schlosser in 1935
	Ludwig Korner in 1938
Reich Press Chamber	Max Amann
Reich Radio Chamber	Horst Dressler-Andress (closed in October 1939)
Reich Literature Chamber	Hans Blunck, Hanns Johst in 1935

Membership of the chambers was compulsory. Jewish, anti-nationalistic and liberal artists and performers were excluded from their profession and put out of work, imprisoned or forced into exile. The work of the Reich Chamber of Culture was closely linked to Goebbels' Ministry for Public Enlightenment and Propaganda, and there were clashes between the two ministries.

HEAD OF IDEOLOGY

ALFRED ROSENBERG (1893–1946)

Rosenberg was born in Estonia and after studying engineering and architecture, he fled to Paris following the Russian revolution. After moving to Munich and obtaining German citizenship, Rosenberg joined the NSDAP in 1919. Although he was a moody and reserved man, his persuasive and ambitious nature kept him inside Hitler's inner circle as advisor on foreign affairs. He became editor of the *People's Observer* in 1921 and he used it to voice his anti-Semitic views.

Rosenberg became the spiritual leader of National Socialism, publishing his own pamphlet 'The Trace of Jews in the History of the World' and he reissued the fake 'Protocols of the Elders of Zion'. Although he fled during the 1923 Munich Putsch, he was appointed Party Leader while Hitler was in prison. He was unable to keep the NSDAP together.

After Hitler was released, Rosenberg returned to writing, founding the German People's Publishing House in 1926 which published a monthly magazine called *The World Struggle*. He published his first book *The Myth of the Twentieth Century* in 1930. It explained his theory on how liberalism had disrupted the ascendancy of the Nordic people, allowing other races to seize power. It became a Nazi bestseller, second only to Hitler's *Mein Kampf*.

The Party head of ideology, Alfred Rosenberg. (NARA-242-HB-05107)

Rosenberg went on to fulfil two roles for the NSDAP. In 1929, he headed the Fighting League for German Culture, promoting the National Socialist view of German life, and by 1933 it had 38,000 members. The establishment of the Propaganda and Enlightenment Ministry in March 1933 caused rivalries, which Goebbels' state department usually won.

The League went on to train party members in National Socialist ideology. After 1933 it was known as the National Socialist Cultural Community. Rosenberg was also head of the Party Foreign Affairs Department, controlling spies in many countries. The office administered the German Academic Exchange Service. Rosenberg was sent to London in May 1933 in an attempt to appease the British government; the visit was a complete failure.

VISUAL ARTS

Although German artists had worldwide recognition, Hitler criticised the trend towards modern art in *Mein Kampf*, ridiculing expressionism, impressionism and surrealism as stupid and immoral. He preferred realistic and heroic paintings and he vowed to cleanse the German art world of degenerate art. He supported Rosenberg's Fighting League for German Culture when it campaigned against decadent art.

The Reich Visual Arts Chamber had to approve the work of over 42,000 artists before they could continue painting, drawing or sculpting. Jewish artists were banned from exhibiting their work after September 1933. The Chamber was also responsible for a wide range of visual art encompassing the work of architects, garden and interior designers, antique dealers and craft shops.

The Nazis wanted landscape paintings, architectural studies and scenes of warlike or gallant acts. Sculptures had to be heroic, pure and monumental in style and Arno Breker and Josef Thorek were Hitler's favourite sculptors. The Führer sponsored art competitions, encouraging artists to follow his own tastes. An artist's standing would be judged by the importance of the subject he was commissioned to produce.

Hitler, the failed artist, studies one of his favourite painting styles, the landscape. (NARA-242-HB-13439a3)

The works of Chamber members were monitored on a regular basis. The Gestapo could raid artists' studios and implement a range of bans, stopping artists from painting, exhibiting or teaching. Serious breaches could result in expulsion from the Chamber and art stores were forbidden from selling supplies to banned artists. Many prominent artists chose to emigrate so they could continue to work.

Art galleries and museums organised degenerate art exhibitions. Goebbels sponsored two state-organised art exhibitions, contrasting degenerate modern art with Nazi preferred art, to get Hitler's approval. Professor Adolf Ziegler led a panel of four artists on a tour of dozens of galleries and museums across Germany looking for examples of unacceptable art. They identified and confiscated 12,800 items, including paintings, drawings and sculptures. 700 important items were sold to other countries and the foreign currency that was raised was used to import

A sculpture depicting the perfect human physique being prepared for the Olympic Games. (NARA-242-HB-19721)

armaments. The Munich Degenerate Art Exhibition opened in March 1936 and thousands of people viewed 6,500 unframed paintings propped against walls, complete with derogatory titles.

At the same period, Ziegler's panel chose 15,000 items for the Greater Germany Art Exhibition, an exhibition of Nazi-approved art. Paul Troost designed the House of German Art in Munich to exhibit them and Hitler selected 900 works; paintings of Storm Troopers, rustic family scenes and Amazonian-style scenes were favourites. It opened in July 1937.

Many more German people attended the Degenerate Art Exhibition than the Greater Germany Art Exhibition. In 1939 over 4,800 of the modern art paintings were taken to the Berlin fire department headquarters and burnt.

FILM

The golden days of silent German cinema came to an end in the 1920s, as actors and directors left for the US. The American film industry was booming in Hollywood, where the good weather and light favoured filming. Only a small number of German films with sound were still being produced by UFA, a company run by Nazi sympathisers. Although Nazi leaders were merely interested in the propaganda potential of the cinema, Goebbels was obsessed by it. He wanted the German film industry to counter Hollywood with Aryan-orientated films.

In April 1933, American film companies were instructed to sack Jewish employees and two months later the Aryan Clause banned Jews from working in the film industry. The Directors' and Actors' Association, DACHO, was closed down when it challenged Goebbels' decision. The industry was thrown into chaos as many talented German directors, producers, cameramen, musical composers, actors and actresses emigrated, many of them to Hollywood. Many non-Jewish employees also left in protest, including singer and actress Marlene Dietrich who had appeared in the 1930 film *The Blue Angel*. She settled in the US in 1937 and continued her work, including recording the famous song, 'Lili Marlene'.

Victor Lutze, the new head of the SA looks on as Leni Riefenstahl discusses the filming of the 1934 Nuremberg Rally with Hitler. (NARA-242-HB-7675)

The Nazis produced three major propaganda films in 1933; *SA Mann Brand* was a tribute to Nazi storm troopers; *Hitlerjunge Quex* was the story of a young man murdered by communists; *Hans Westmar* was a biography of Horst Wessel. All three were box-office failures. The Chamber started censoring imported films in January 1934. It banned any which included Jewish actors or actresses and any with an unsuitable attitude or an immoral outlook. The film world reacted strongly and the number of German film exports fell sharply. Taxation quadrupled on imported films in November 1934 but exchanges were introduced in February 1935 to boost German exports.

Filmmaking continued but scripts were censored before filming began and control over production increased. The industry also produced hundreds of propaganda shorts, documentaries and newsreels. Goebbels became increasingly involved and eventually personally responsible for approving every film. In April 1935 he was delighted to welcome 2,000 delegates from 40 nations to the International Film Congress, held in the Berlin Kroll Opera House.

Leni Riefenstahl (1902–2003) became the Nazis' favourite film maker. She

Film crews captured Hitler's every move for the film, *Triumph of the Will*. (NARA-242-HB-22633a13)

changed her career from ballet dancer to set up her own film company in 1931. She had already produced *The Holy Mountain* and *The Blue Light* when Hitler appointed her director and producer of films for the Nazi Party. Her first short film, *Victory of Faith*, covered the 1933 Nuremberg Rally, but the murder of Ernst Röhm and the banning of his image meant that few saw it. Her masterpiece was the *Triumph of the Will* a record of the 1934 Nuremberg Rally. Riefenstahl used elevators, camera tracks and film pits to get important filming angles. She was supported by 30 cameramen and a large staff of technical workers. The film was a masterpiece of film direction and production and it appeared in 1936, winning several awards. She also filmed *Olympia*, covering the 1936 Berlin Olympic Games. It was released in April 1938 in two parts, *The Festival of the Nations* and *The Festival of Beauty*.

By 1937 the German film industry was in serious financial difficulties but Goebbels continued to subsidise films which he believed were politically and artistically valuable. He nationalised UFA, Tobis and Bavaria Company, the last three independent film companies, when they ran into trouble. By 1939 the state was financing two out of every three films made and the ministry turned its attentions to a series of anti-Semitic films.

The number of cinemagoers doubled under the Nazis and when the Chamber took over, over half of films shown were comedies, one in four were politically based; a similar number were dramas. The number of political films declined.

Goebbels was also attracted to established film actresses and ambitious starlets. He entertained them either in the privacy of his ministry office or on his Schwanenwerder estate, near Berlin. Some succumbed to his attentions to further their career.

MUSIC

Germany was steeped in the classical music tradition ranging back to the eighteenth-century composer Ludwig van Beethoven. While Felix Mendelssohn, Robert Schumann and Richard Wagner dominated the early nineteenth century, Johann Brahms did the same at the end. The Bayreuth Wagner Festival and the Salzburg Mozart Festival continued the classical tradition.

The Reich Music Chamber was headed by Germany's leading classical composer, Richard Strauss (1864–1949). The Aryan Clause forced Jewish composers, musicians and musicians to leave their orchestras and many went into exile. Music by the Jewish composers Giacomo Meyerbeer and Mendelssohn was also banned.

Contemporary active musical experiment and performance had become fashionable under the Weimar Republic and Germany's principal contemporary composer, Paul Hindemith (1895–1963), was a world leader in a new style of music called atonality. Goebbels supported Hindemith because of his important status, but Rosenberg was adamant that he had to go and the Nazis banned atonal music as decadent.

The world of music was restricted under the Nazis but it did not suffer as much as other cultural activities. It was also difficult to ban individuals listening to music in private. A Degenerate Music Exhibition was held in Munich in May 1938, but again it was more popular than the Nazis hoped it would be. Concerts were well attended but the choice was limited and many audiences had to be content with Wagner performances. Two new young composers, Werner Egk and Carl Orfl, were commissioned to write music for the 1936 Olympic Games.

Strauss was eventually forced to resign in 1935 because of his continued collaboration with Stefan Zweig, a Jewish opera librettist. The composer and conductor, Wilhelm Furtwängler (1886–1954), also stepped down to support Paul Hindemith.

American jazz and swing were also driven underground because of their American-Caribbean background. Jazz music was banned from the radio, while clubs were raided or shut down because they attracted non-conforming youngsters. The saxophone was banned as a symbol of decadence.

RICHARD WAGNER (1813–1883)

Wagner was Hitler's favourite composer. After studying at Dresden and Leipzig he became the conductor of the Magdeburg Opera. While living in Paris in poverty, he perfected his unique operatic style combining poetry, music and dance to tell stories of Teutonic legend, heroism and nationalism. The annual Bayreuth Wagner Festival became an important event in the Nazi calendar and the party gave it subsidies and tax exemptions.

THEATRE

Theatre had thrived under the Weimar Republic but it suffered after the Aryan Clause forced Jewish producers, playwrights, directors and actors to leave their jobs in 1933; many emigrated. Standards fell and the Nazis favoured historically-based, propaganda-driven or racially-orientated plays. The public rejected them. Discount tickets offered by the 'Strength through Joy' movement artificially increased audiences.

The Nazis introduced a theatrical experience known as the *Thingspiel*, based on Teutonic tribal assemblies. A mixture of tattoo and pageantry were suppported by parading SA and Hitler Youth formations. The spectacles were held in amphitheatres known as *Thingspielplatten* and although they were popular in the early days, they were replaced by Nazi Party rallies.

LITERATURE

The world of literature was seriously affected when the Nazis came to power. A list of Jewish, liberal and anti-Nazi authors was drawn up and students were encouraged to remove their books from university libraries. On the night of 10 May 1933, thousands of young Nazis paraded in front of the University of Berlin, throwing books onto a huge burning pyre. It was just one of many demonstrations around the country

Hitler and Goebbels are the star guests at the opera. (NARA-242-HB-06318)

and it was just the start of the Nazis' censorship. Bookshops and libraries continued to be raided as hundreds of new titles were added to the list of banned books.

While Jewish authors and liberal writers left Germany fearing for their lives, others emigrated because they did not want to continue writing under Nazi rule. Over 2,500 writers left Germany, including several Nobel Prize winners. Some of those who left were Thomas Mann, Heinrich Mann, Erich Maria Remarque, Emil Ludwig, Lion Feuchtwanger, Albert Einstein, Arnold Zweig, Stefan Zweig, Ernst Toller, Franz Werfel, Jakob Wassermann, Bruno Frank and Bertolt Brecht. Many authors who stayed behind in Germany were forbidden to publish while a few were arrested and held in concentration camps.

Non-German Jewish authors, both living and dead, were also banned by the Nazis, including Emile Zola, Marcel Proust, Jack London, Maxim Gorky, Arthur Schnitzler, Helen Keller, H.G. Wells, Sigmund Freud, Henri Barbusse, Margaret Sanger and Upton Sinclair.

Phillip Bouhler, Head of the Chancellery of the Führer, was also appointed Chairman of the Official Party Inspection Commission for the Protection of National Socialist Literature. After 1933, writers had to produce approved works in one of four categories:

Promoting the front line camaraderie of the trenches
Supporting the Nazi 'world view'
Celebrating the mysticism of being German
Upholding the racial prowess of the German Nordic

Hitler's *Mein Kampf* was presented as the highest form of literary art and over six million copies had been sold by 1940. Goebbels worked hard to support the German literary scene. The Reich Chamber of Literature had to approve every book manuscript before it was published and every script before a play was performed.

Many new bookshops and libraries were opened under the Nazis and by 1939 the Chamber controlled over 3,000 authors, 2,500 publishing houses and 23,000 bookshops. It monitored the annual sales of over one million books and controlled the publication of 20,000 new books every year. Over 50 national literary prizes were introduced to encourage new authors. However, the approved writing styles attracted mediocre writers, many of them ardent Nazi supporters. The German public turned their back on most and only a few were translated into other languages.

ARCHITECTURE

Architecture was a lifelong passion of Hitler's and his preference was for huge seventeenth-century Baroque-style buildings. His favourite architect was Paul Troost and in 1930 he was commissioned to redesign the Barlow Palace in Munich to serve as the NSDAP headquarters; it was renamed the Brown House.

Once the Nazis were in power, the Reich Chamber of Architects closed down Jewish-owned practices, but it took time to stop modernist architects from practising. Many schemes were drawn up to build and redesign new state and municipal administration offices in a style combining neo-Baroque and neo-Classic. In the autumn of 1933 Troost was commissioned to redesign the Berlin Chancellery residence. He also designed a range of Nazi Party buildings around Hitler's Munich offices. While the arena for the 1936 Berlin Olympics could hold 100,000, new arenas and buildings were added to the Nuremburg rally grounds.

Hitler had plans to completely rebuild Berlin as the centre of Germany's political, economic and military power. The new metropolis would have two wide avenues,

Albert Speer and Hitler study a model of the 'Strength through Joy' holiday complex to be built at Prora, on the Baltic Sea island. (NARA-242-HB-22204)

running north–south and west–east and they would be lined by huge public buildings. They would intersect at a massive Triumphal Arch in the centre of the main plaza. Hitler and Speer worked on a series of models which were displayed in the Fine Arts Academy, but construction stopped at the outbreak of war in 1939 and their plans to rebuild Germany's capital remained a dream.

The Nazis also influenced town planning and town centres were often redesigned as small-scale versions of the Berlin blueprint. Central urban communities were built around a square adorned with sculptures, while avenues were lined with public buildings. The housing shortage across Germany was met by public works programmes, but while the rich lived in huge apartments and houses, the working classes were crammed into People's Apartments, cheap, cell-like apartment blocks favoured by the Nazis.

Construction work on the NSDAP headquarters in Munich, the Capital of the Movement. (NARA-242-HB-14952)

THE NAZI ARCHITECTS

PAUL TROOST (1878–1934)

Troost began his career designing luxurious interiors of transatlantic liners. His first architectural schemes were the spartan, Classical designs popular in 1920s Germany. He was commissioned to redesign the Nazi Party headquarters in Munich and Hitler was delighted with his plans. The Führer often visited Troost's studio and they spent hours discussing grandiose building plans, including Munich's House of German Art. As Hitler's favourite, Troost had free rein while his critics were banned from working on public projects. He died on 21 March 1934.

Albert Speer displays one of his simple, yet effective, designs for a backdrop of flags at a rally.

ALBERT SPEER (1905–1981)

Speer took Troost's place as Hitler's favourite architect. He had studied architecture before working at Berlin Technical College. He joined the NSDAP in 1931 and the SS the following year, completing several minor interior architectural design projects for Joseph Goebbels, in the latter's capacity as Berlin Gauleiter.

He was commissioned to arrange the stage effects for the 1933 May Day rally on Berlin's Tempelhof Field and his cheap

Albert Speer's model for the new 50,000-seater Congress Hall in Nuremburg. (NARA-242-HB-9171)

Martin Bormann and Albert Speer escort Hitler around the work being carried out on Luitpold Arena in Nuremburg. (NARA-242-HB-14275a)

solution used huge flags and lighting effects to create a spectacular visual backdrop. The following year he was employed to do the same for the 1934 Nuremburg Rally, and the appointment brought him to Hitler's notice. Hitler and Speer spent hours designing cities, palaces, state offices, stadia and monuments.

Speer was appointed section leader of the German Labour Front and he joined the Deputy Führer's staff; his next appointment was General Architectural Inspector of the Reich in 1937. He went on to design the German exhibit at the Party Exhibition, the Party Palace in Nuremberg and the Reich Chancellory in Berlin.

CHAPTER FOURTEEN

THE FAMILY, WELFARE AND HEALTH

The heart of National Socialist ideology started with the family. The man was expected to work for the state or serve in the armed forces while his wife supported him at home. Parents were expected to raise a large number of children and support them in their Hitler Youth activities. Boys would be encouraged to aspire to join the armed forces while girls would be encouraged to want to raise families of their own.

THE FAMILY

Women's emancipation introduced millions of new voters to the world of German politics. Over eleven million women were working after the First World War, many of them in traditional male occupations. They were also allowed to enter higher professions.

Hitler opposed feminism and women's liberation. The original party programme defined the woman's role as supporting her husband and raising her children. The Nazis excluded women from taking part in politics and their slogans, 'Children, Church, Kitchen' and 'the women's place is in the home' summarised their view. While party leaders criticised feminists, unmarried women and lesbians, they worked hard to secure the support and the vote of married women at a time when they were coming to terms with politics.

The NSDAP also realised that the large numbers of women working in domestic duties and the textile industries were not unionised; they exploited the fact and targeted their votes. Their ideas on the woman's role as wife and mother proved to be more popular that the communist calls for equal pay and equal opportunities. Nazi views on women's fashion – which involved demure clothing, hair tied up, no lipstick and a ban on smoking – generally failed.

The Nazis organised a small girls' section in the Hitler Youth in 1927 but it was relatively unpopular until membership was made compulsory in 1936. In 1938 there were still only 25,000 women employed by the Reich Labour Service and compulsory service was introduced for single women under 25. Most of them spent their six months service working on farms or in domestic service.

Single women initially profited under the Nazis due to the temporary increase in university admissions and employment opportunities offered during the economic boom. However, the Nazis had soon implemented policies to limit young women's options, encouraging them to marry and raise families. The number of places for female students was limited and the number of young women in university fell from 18,300 to 5,400 between 1933 and 1939.

Young children
and old war
veterans alike give
the Nazi salute.
(NARA-242-HB-
12697)

Many women were forced to marry due to the increasing discrimination in education and the employment market. By 1937, 800,000 women had been forced out of employment, encouraged to marry and have children by financial incentives. They were replaced by men, and the overall effect of supporting sexism in the workplace was to reduce unemployment.

Marriage loans and vouchers for household goods were offered to young men and women and nearly 700,000 couples benefited between August 1933 and December 1936; married men were also taxed at a lower rate than bachelors. The Nazis expected a wife to support her husband, look after the home and raise their children to have National Socialist ideals, encouraging them to take an active role in one of the youth organisations. They were also persuaded to be frugal. The National Socialist People's Welfare Organisation established the Mother and Child Welfare Fund to support families who had fallen on hard times.

Even though Germany was allegedly short of living space, Hitler made repeated calls to families to have more children to increase the population. The Nazis limited the term 'family' to households with four children or more. While allowances and gifts were presented to parents of newborn infants, large families were awarded tax incentives and child subsidies. They made little difference and most marriages were due to the improved economic conditions. The Reich Mother's Service made collections on Mother's Day and used the money to fund classes where experienced mothers could teach new ones.

The term 'Blessed with Children' was often used by Nazi leaders. On Mothering Sunday 1939 over three million mothers were awarded the Honour Cross of the German Mother. Annual presentations were made on the second Sunday in May and recipients wore miniature replicas of the cross as a badge of honour. The awards came in three classes; bronze for four or five children, silver for six or seven and gold for eight or more. Hitler was appointed godfather of a tenth child. Members of the Hitler Youth and the German Girls' League had to salute any woman wearing a cross.

Childless couples were denounced as worse than 'deserters on the battlefield' and they were subjected to a higher tax rate. After 1938, a man could apply for a divorce under the Marriage Law if his wife could not or would not have children. Unmarried couples who had illegitimate children were given no financial benefits.

WOMEN'S ORGANISATIONS

Isbeth Zander founded the German Women's Order and members helped with propaganda, hiding and carrying weapons, and ran nursing services and soup kitchens for the SA. Zander was replaced in 1931 after the organisation ran into debt and she was implicated in a scandal. Gertrud Baumer was the head of the new National Socialist Women's Organisation and it began coordinating women's clubs and societies into one organisation after January 1933. The term 'bringing-in-line' was used and takeovers were kept low key with the minimum of interference and confrontation. The preferred method was to infiltrate the society and denounce executives as anti-family, communist, unpatriotic or abortion supporters. The aim was to get Nazi supporters voted onto the executive where they could dominate meetings and persuade the members to join the Women's Order. Committee members who refused to cooperate were removed with support from the Berlin head office. Religious groups were frequently uncooperative. Women's professional associations were affiliated to equivalent men's associations but they ranked below them as auxiliaries.

Gertrud Scholtz-Klink addresses a meeting of the National Socialist Women's League. (NARA-242-HB-23786)

All women's organisations had been coordinated by 1934 and Gertrud Scholtz-Klink (1902–1999) was appointed Reich Woman's Leader at the head of all the National Socialist women's organisations including the Frauenwerk, the federal organisation of women, the German Women's Bureau (part of the German Labour Front), the Woman's Labour Service and the Women's Order of the Red Cross. She promoted the following ideals for German women:

Woman is entrusted in the life of the nation with a great task, the care of man, soul, body, and mind. It is the mission of the woman to minister in the home and in her profession to the needs of life from the first to the last moment of man's existence. Her mission in marriage is ... comrade, helper and womanly complement of man. This is the right of woman in the New Germany.

Scholtz-Klink was a petite, feminine woman whose first husband had died, leaving her with six children. Two of the children had also died and she struggled to raise the others before she married for a second time and had another five. She had been a Nazi associate member since the early days and was the women's leader in Baden from 1929. Although Scholtz-Klink was an energetic worker and an effective organiser, she was expected to be a role model for German women, supporting party policies while avoiding controversy. She also made it clear that politics was not for women.

WOMEN'S CONCENTRATION CAMPS

The first concentration camp for women was opened at Moringen in October 1933 and to begin with communists, socialists and members of rival youth organisations were held there. Criminals, prostitutes, Jehovah's Witnesses and Jews were imprisoned next. A second women's camp was opened at Lichtenburg in Saxony in 1938 followed by a third at Ravensbruck, Mecklenburg, in 1939.

WELFARE ORGANISATIONS

The Weimar Republic had introduced a free and wide-reaching welfare state but the cost of administering it grew rapidly. Unemployment insurances were introduced for those who were employed, and while the system worked when unemployment was low, it came under immense pressure when unemployment rose quickly. Promises were not met and intense means testing made it unpopular.

What the system promised and what people got were different and it was weighed down by bureaucracy. While the system had been embraced by modern industries, traditional industries distrusted the Weimar Republic's handling of it. The Nazis organised two huge welfare organisations to control the lives of everyone who was not working under the German Labour Front or serving in the armed forces.

Goebbels launches the second annual Winter Relief Fund. (NARA-242-HB-08564a2)

NATIONAL SOCIALIST PEOPLE'S WELFARE ORGANISATION

The Nazis did not like social welfare but they did not want to alienate the unemployed. The People's Welfare Organisation dealt with those who had fallen on hard times, particularly during the winter. Over 1.5 million volunteers would organise soup kitchens, dish out food and clothes parcels and collect money. By 1939 its membership was second only in size to the German Labour Front with 17 million recipients.

Erich Hilgenfeldt was appointed Reich Commissioner for the Nazis' main charity relief scheme, the Winter Support Programme in September 1933. It organised the Winter Relief fund, the *Winterhilfe*, a government charity to help those who had fallen on hard times. Nazi leaders appeared alongside movie and theatre stars during the launch of the annual Winter Relief Day. In November 1934 competing charities had to suspend winter collections under the Collection Law.

During the winter, a mandatory ten per cent tax was deduced from workers' wages for Winter Relief. Families were also encouraged to participate in weekly One Pot meal days, making cheap stews and donating the savings to the fund. Storm Troopers would visit homes to collect the money saved. Jewish department stores were expected to make large contributions to the Winter Relief fund until they were closed down or bought out.

Party members held street collections and the public were pressurised into making contributions. A lapel badge worn on the coat or a plaque nailed to the door was the only way to stop further harassment from collectors. Villages displayed Boards of Shame, listing those who refused to make donations; the press printed similar lists.

By 1939 550 million RM were being raised every winter, reducing the state liability. The amount of aid available was increased by exempting criminals, alcoholics, the work-shy, homosexuals and prostitutes; Jews were also banned from receiving aid in the winter of 1935–36. The Nazis were more concerned with helping the thousands of disabled war veterans.

Severe means testing meant that those fit to work were employed under the Reich Labour Service. This forced voluntary work reduced unemployment and the burden on the welfare system at the same time. The Nazis would eventually halve the number of recipients. This style of welfare meant that the state was no longer responsible for those who could not help themselves.

ERICH HILGENFELDT (1897–1945)

Hilgenfeldt served as a pilot in the First World War before working as a building salesman. He joined the Reich Statistical Office in 1928 and three years later he was a Berlin city councillor. Hilgenfeldt had also joined the NSDAP and after organising a successful charity collection for Hitler's birthday in 1931, Goebbels made him head of the National Socialist People's Welfare Organisation. He expanded it into a huge nationwide scheme after 1933, absorbing all non-Nazi charity organisations; he became an honorary member of the SS in 1937.

WAR VETERANS' AID ORGANISATION

The NSDAP held the hundreds of thousands of wounded First World War veterans in high esteem. The organisation held veterans' meetings, provided welfare for invalids, organised suitable work and provided food and shelter for those who had fallen on hard times.

Hitler discusses the National Socialist People's Welfare Organisation with Erich Hilgenfeldt. (NARA-242-HB-7651a4)

War veterans march through Berlin's Brandenburg Gate. (NARA-242-HB-7648)

The organisation expanded to cover the Reich after the Nazis came to power and it helped to organise parades and charity collections. Hanns Oberlindober acted as financial settlement advisor for the Reich Employment Minister. To begin with, Jewish war veterans were given special exemptions from anti-Semitic laws. This did not last long.

HANNS OBERLINDOBER (1896–1949)

Oberlindober was a decorated war veteran who lost his arm in the First World War. He joined the NSDAP in 1922 and worked as a journalist for the party. He was a Nazi town councillor from 1924 to 1929 and at the same time he rose to the rank of brigade commander in the SA. He was elected to the Reichstag for the Breslau Constituency in 1930, switching to the Hessen Nassau Constituency in 1932. Oberlindober travelled extensively to contact similar organisations and used his travels as a cover for international espionage.

HEALTH UNDER THE NAZIS

The Nazis wanted a pure and healthy Aryan race and their crude investigations into genealogy led to forced sterilisations and a secretive state-run euthanasia programme.

THE REICH DOCTORS' LEAGUE

The National Socialist Doctors' League was established for doctors who were members of the NSDAP. It became the Reich Doctors' League when the Nazis came to power and it absorbed all other doctor associations. Doctors had to join the League or lose their medical licenses. The number of Jewish doctors was limited in April 1933 and they were banned from public clinics and health institutions in March 1936, limiting them to private practice; they had been forced to stop practising by the end of 1938. Aryan practices benefited from the increase in patients and so did doctors' wages. They did, however, have to accept a lot of government interference and come to terms with non-professional healers being granted practising status.

The Reich Physicians' Chamber set standards for doctors and medical practices, making sure that doctors adhered to Nazi policies on all aspects of health. Health Offices were established across the Reich to administer government health programmes, covering sexual health, sterilisation and euthanasia.

The state forced doctors to breach patient confidentiality on mental issues, alcoholism and sexual diseases. They also had to participate in the assessment of disabled patients for euthanasia, the selection of mental patients and the administering of lethal drugs.

Although the Nazis allowed contraception, they closed down birth control clinics. Abortions were stopped, unless they were on medical grounds, and the number carried out dropped by 90 per cent. They were, however, allowed on racial grounds after 1935.

Goebbels introduces the arrival of mobile health check units. (NARA-242-HB-05883)

HEADS OF THE DOCTORS' LEAGUE

GERHARD WAGNER (1888–1939)

Wagner was awarded the Iron Cross whilst serving as a doctor in the trenches in the First World War. He ran his own Munich practice whilst serving in the Free Corps and he became the leader of the Upper Silesia German Community Association. He joined the NSDAP in 1929, becoming co-founder of the National Socialist Doctor's League, and he became the head of the League in 1932. Wagner was appointed leader of the National Health Main Office in 1933 and he was also elected member of the Palatinate Landtag. He was appointed head of the Reich Doctors' League and the Commissioner for National Health in 1934. He was made leader of the Reich Physicians' Chamber in 1935 and two years later he was promoted to SA-Obergruppenführer. Wagner died suddenly of natural causes in March 1939.

LEONARDO CONTI (1900–1945)

Conti was practising medicine when he joined the NSDAP in 1923 and he became the first SA doctor in Berlin. He organised the SA Sanitation Corps and the National Socialist Doctors League in the Berlin Gau. He was elected to the Prussian Landtag in 1932. Conti was appointed Reich Health Leader and State Secretary for Health in the Ministry of the Interior following Wagner's death in March 1939. The T-4 Euthanasia programme came under his department.

THE STERILISATION PROGRAM

The Law for the Prevention of Hereditarily Diseased Offspring was introduced in July 1933, and it was the start of a compulsory sterilisation programme. A media campaign was launched and propaganda films were shown before forced sterilisations began in January 1934. Doctors had to register every known case of hereditary illness with one of the 200 Hereditary Health Courts. The decision to sterilise was made by two physicians and a district judge. Sterilisation was not directed at those who could not reproduce, such as the insane and seriously ill, but at those who could reproduce and did not fit the regime's standards. Prostitutes, the work-shy, beggars and vagrants were also included.

Over 350,000 men and women were sterilised by 1939, and the majority of them were in institutions. While men had vasectomies, women had their ovarian tubes ligated. Irradiation using x-rays and radium was also tried.

Marriage loans and child benefits were stopped for couples with hereditary diseases. In October 1935, the Law for the Protection for Hereditary Health of the German People required couples to prove that they had no family history of disabling hereditary diseases before they were allowed to marry.

THE T-4 PROGRAMME

Hitler, Göring, Dr Karl Brandt and Joseph Dietrich. (NARA-242-HB-05066)

The National Coordinating Agency for Therapeutic and Medical Establishments was run by Philip Bouhler, the Chief of the Chancellery of the Führer, and Dr Karl Brandt, the Führer's personal physician. It was code named T-4, which referred to the address of the head office, Tiergartenstrasse 4, in Berlin.

In August 1939, the Reich Committee for the Scientific Registration of Serious Hereditary and Congenitally Based Diseases was established and it was made compulsory for parents to register malformed children. The following month the programme was extended to include mentally ill adults living in asylums. Clinics also had to register patients they had been treating for more than five years. Reports were assessed by three independent medical referees and the majority vote decided the patients' fate; the referees did not meet the patients.

A euthanasia programme was started and several asylums were equipped with gas chambers which used carbon monoxide gas to asphyxiate the patients. Others were killed by lethal injection. Over the next two years more than 50,000 people were killed under the T-4 programme. There were no post mortems and fake death certificates and letters of condolence were posted to the families to maintain the secrecy of the programme. The programme also began research into three areas:

1) Experiments in mass sterilisation
2) Euthanasia for incurables
3) Direct extermination by special treatment, *Sonderbehandlung*

This research would lead to the Final Solution, the Holocaust, and the murder of over six million Jews and other enemies of the Third Reich.

CHAPTER FIFTEEN

EDUCATION, YOUTH AND SPORT

Germany's youth had not lived through the First World War but grew up with the spectre of its horrors. They experienced the results the Treaty of Versailles and economic hardship, including hyperinflation and the Depression. Many became politicised as they grew older, preferring to support the extreme ends of the political spectrum. They would soon come under the influence of the Nazis.

EDUCATION

Germany had a model education system under the Weimar Republic but Hitler was hostile to the education authorities and to intellectuals. All levels of teaching, from kindergarten to university, were changed under Nazi rule, while chosen teachers were forced to teach the new National Socialist curriculum. The result was a catastrophic decline in education standards under the Third Reich.

BERNHARD RUST (1883–1945)

Rust was the minister responsible for the Nazi education system. After passing his teaching examination in 1908 and extensive service in the First World War, Rust joined the NSDAP in 1922, becoming the Gauleiter for Hanover-Brunswick by 1925. Despite his support for the Strasser brothers, he remained a favourite of Hitler's and he was elected to the Reichstag in September 1930. In February 1933, Rust was appointed Prussian Minister of Science, Art and Education and he joined the cabinet as Reich Minister for Science, Education and Culture in April 1934. In both posts he implemented pogroms on Jewish lecturers and teachers and organised the increasing

Reich Minister Bernhard Rust.

segregation and ultimate expulsion of students and children from the education system. Rust also administered the Nazi changes in the school curricula.

SCHOOLS

Indoctrination started with pre-school children in nursery schools. Primary and secondary schools already supported nationalist views under the Weimar Republic and the transformation of the German educational system to National Socialist ideals was smooth. After January 1934 teachers had to educate pupils in the spirit of National Socialism and children were expected to listen to speeches on the radio, watch propaganda films and attend Nazi festivals. While new course books were introduced, many existing ones were banned as unsuitable.

In April 1933, the Law for Preventing Overcrowding in German Schools and Colleges set quotas in schools according to the ratio of Aryans and non-Aryans in the local population. It forced many children to leave school. In November 1935 segregation was introduced into schools for the first time; Jewish children were forced to use separate playgrounds and locker rooms. They were expelled from German schools following *Kristallnacht* in November 1938.

Teachers were state employees and subject to the April 1933 Law for the Reestablishment of a Professional Civil Service. Jewish and liberal teachers were forced to leave their jobs and their places were taken by Nazi supporters.

Hans Schemm had formed the National Socialist Teachers' League in April 1927 and many teachers welcomed the changes; membership increased from 12,000 to 220,000 in 1933. Other teachers' associations closed down or merged into the League and it was renamed the Reich Teachers' League in 1935 and by 1936 virtually every teacher was a member; those who did not join were hounded from their jobs.

After May 1936, teachers were taught about the new curriculum on compulsory teacher training courses held at special educational camps. By 1938 two-thirds of elementary school teachers had attended the compulsory one-month National Socialist teaching course. School assistants joined many classes and they were usually untrained, poorly educated political

Lessons started with the obligatory salute.

activists. Many teachers lived in fear of denunciations from their pupils or other teachers and those who did not like the situation retired, resulting in larger classes. The Youth Protection Chamber adjudicated over children's rights and it usually supported teachers who used corporal punishment.

The National Socialist School Children's League was merged with the Hitler Youth in May 1933 and the school curriculum was quickly changed to reflect National Socialist ideals. History, biology and Germanics courses were increased while two new courses on German culture and the Nazi 'world view' emphasised Teutonic greatness, Nordic sagas and the Nazi struggle for power. The new biology course focused on race research, while the mathematics course was focused on solving military questions and tactical problems.

The German Society for Military Policy and Science was tasked with preparing children for military service. A mixture of Reichswehr, SA and Steel Helmet officers and professors of military science attended a secret meeting in Berlin in October 1933. They concluded that boys needed a sport-based curriculum. While physical training and sports were increased, religious instruction was reduced; it was eventually removed from the curriculum. The society also intensified the military-based training for the Hitler Youth.

Girls studied domestic science and hygiene which led to a valueless qualification known as the Pudding Matric. The number of girls attending grammar school fell dramatically, and after 1937 they were barred entry.

Childen spent a large amount of their time devoted to their Hitler Youth organisation. After complaints from the school authorities, they were eventually instructed to grant pupils leave to attend Hitler Youth functions. Special courses were also arranged to help Hitler Youth members through their exams.

The curriculum changes and the race laws had a catastrophic effect on the German education system and standards fell rapidly. The school-leaving examination was completely abandoned in 1935.

UNIVERSITIES

Students had grown up under the Treaty of Versailles and they had seen their country ruined by the Depression. It turned many into supporting the right-wing, nationalist views of the NSDAP. Lecturers and students at German universities promoted the Nazis' rise to power and there were anti-Semitic riots at many major universities throughout 1931 and 1932. The majority of Prussian students demanded the total exclusion of Jewish students from their establishments.

University staff also welcomed the Third Reich and in March 1933, 300 professors addressed a manifesto supporting Hitler to voters. Two months later students emptied libraries of Jewish and anti-nationalist publications, burning them on pyres while their literature professors gave supporting speeches.

While Alfred Rosenberg's department dealt with the ideological education of the Nazi Party, Alfred Baeumler, a leading philosopher professor at Berlin University, headed the liaison between the universities and the National Socialists. Walther Schultze was the head of the physical education department in the Bavarian State Ministry and president of the State Academy of Medicine in Munich. He was appointed head of the National Socialist Lecturers' Alliance in 1935. Membership was compulsory and lecturers were closely monitored. The organisation was renamed the Reich Lecturers' Alliance in 1935.

University students vote while a SA trooper looks on. (NARA-242-HB-00073)

Starting in 1933, academia was aryanised and over 1,200 Jewish and liberal academics were forced to leave their posts over the next two years. Teaching standards declined following their dismissal while course standards deteriorated due to a rigid adherence to Nazi Party policies. In April 1933, the Law for Preventing Overcrowding in German Schools and Colleges set quotas for Jewish university students and it forced many students to leave their studies.

There was a struggle for control in the universities between the ministry, party leaders, lecturers and students. While students denounced their lecturers and influenced appointments, party members were banned from joining fraternities resulting in fighting on campuses. The National Socialist German Students' League eventually replaced the fraternal organisations and their Working Group Leaders monitored students and dealt with complaints. Although the Student League opened work camps and comradeship houses, it did not introduce the same level of indoctrination as schools did.

The Reich Student Council was devoted to maintaining student standards and in March 1934 a law was announced stating that its four goals were to promote the physical, moral, intellectual and eugenic standards of youth. Military training had also been made compulsory for students, reducing teaching time, and standards fell. Conscription encouraged many prospective students to join the army officer corps.

In January 1934, the quota of female entrants was limited to ten per cent and the number attending fell from 17,000 to 6,000. They also had to have a year of domestic training before starting their studies. Overall student numbers more than halved from 104,000 in 1931 to 41,000 in 1939 and law and humanities departments were particularly affected.

GUSTAV SCHEEL (1907–1979)

Scheel became involved in right-wing youth movements at school and while studying law, politics and theology at Heidelberg, he became the chairman of the German Students Club in 1928. He transferred to the National Socialist German Students League in 1929 and joined both the NSDAP and the SA while studying medicine.

As Heidelberg College Group Leader, Scheel led the student protests in 1932 to remove Emil Gumbel, the statistician who had compiled a study of Nazi murders. He became chairman of the Heidelberg General Students' Board and set the standard for influencing university appointments. After sitting his medical examination in 1934, he was appointed Leader of the National Socialist German Students' League. At the same time he became a senior member of the Security Service, and he encouraged many students to work for the SS Reich Main Security Office.

POLITICAL AND MILITARY SCHOOLS

The Nazis established three types of schools devoted to political and military training outside the normal education system.

NAPOLAS

Bernard Rust opened three Napolas in April 1933 under the control of August Heissmeyer, to prepare students for posts in the government or in the armed forces. They were run by SS and SA offices along the style of the Imperial Germany military cadet institutes. Candidates were nominated by an SS-Obergruppenführer and priority was given to the sons of officers and loyal Nazis. Applicants had to pass the strict selection criteria, which focused on racial background and physical fitness, and membership of the Hitler Youth was obligatory. Only 20 per cent of applicants were accepted and only one in three of the students finished the rigorous training program.

21 schools had been established by 1939, including four in Austria and one in the Sudeten area of Czechoslovakia. The SS had also taken control of the Napola school system. The National Socialist German High School based in Feldafing competed with the Napolas to train future Nazi leaders.

ADOLF HITLER SCHOOLS

Nine boarding schools for boys aged 12–18 were announced by Baldur von Schirach and Robert Ley in April 1937, as competition for the Napolas. During their second year in the *Jungvolk*, candidates' racial backgrounds were checked before they were sent on a two-month selection camp; Aryan physical appearance was preferable. Successful applicants embarked on a six-year study programme and their progress was closely monitored. However, educational standards were low, teachers were poor and some pupils could not grasp the concepts. Their training included many competitive games and they were encouraged to work together during military-style exercises. Graduates were expected to graduate to the Ordensburgen (see below). The buildings were never completed and only a few hundred students attended before the war stopped progress.

ORDER CASTLES, ORDENSBURGEN

The Order Castles were elite youth academies which trained students for high office in the party. The three schools, Falkenburg in Pomerania, Vogelsang in the Rhineland and Sonthofen in Bavaria, were named after medieval fortresses built by the Teutonic Knights and other orders. They were built between 1934 and 1936 in isolated rural settings, designed to give the students a feeling of medieval spiritualism. An intended fourth school at Marienburg and a teacher training establishment at Chiem were never built.

The castles were run by Robert Ley, leader of the German Labour Front. While physical entry requirements were high, educational requirements were not; only 1 in 100 candidates had graduated from university. Candidates were usually in their mid-twenties, and they had usually already spent six years at one the Adolf Hitler Schools, two years employed by the Reich Labour Service and another four years working for the Nazi Party. It was considered a great honour to be accepted.

Each school housed 1,000 students, or '*Junkers*', and they were closely supervised by 500 instructors, administrative staff and grooms. Students spent one year at each school and all four had specialised courses:

Sonthofen
Order Castle.
(NARA-242-HB-
19460)

Falkenburg	athletics, boxing, riding, and gliding
Vogelsang	physical training
Sonthofen	mountain climbing and skiing
Marienburg	Eastern European instruction

During their stay, students were subjected to a harsh training regime and rigorous discipline. They had to be obedient and respectful at all times and punishments were severe. Graduates were expected to enter the higher echelons of the Nazi party.

YOUTH MOVEMENTS

POST-FIRST WORLD WAR YOUTH MOVEMENTS

There were many German youth organisations before the First World War including the Birds of Passage and the German Rambler's League. Members usually sought to reject the social and materialistic trappings of Germany's industrial revolution, wishing to return to a basic way of living, if only at the weekend. Boys and girls wore simple dress and they spent their free time hiking, cycling, camping and singing old German folksongs around a camp fire. Although some members promoted Teutonic idealism, nationalism and anti-Semitism, the groups were generally apolitical. Many German boys and girls joined one of the church-sponsored youth organisations.

By 1914 there were 25,000 members in youth organisations but the catastrophic effects of the First World War decimated their membership and destroyed their ideals. Two new types of group emerged in the chaotic years following the Armistice as Germany's youth became politically active. While left-wing politicians formed communist youth movements, right-wing politicians formed nationalist ones. To begin with these groups were disorganised and members changed their affiliations freely.

COORDINATION OF GERMAN YOUTH

The NSDAP's own youth organisations – the Hitler Youth and the German Girls' League – grew in proportion to the size of the membership. Once the Nazis were in power they applied *Gleichschaltung* to Germany's youth organisations, coordinating them all into their own two organisations. While they closed down left-wing organisations, large right-wing organisations like the Young Steel Helmet were incorporated into the Hitler Youth in July 1933. Small nationalistic groups like the Greater German League were also shut down after the police and SS raided their annual camp in June 1933.

THE HITLER YOUTH, HITLERJUGEND

The Hitler Youth was the male youth organisation of the NSDAP and it grew from a small bands of teenage boys into a huge mandatory youth organisation. The organisation aimed to replace the family as the boy's mentor, indoctrinating him in Nazi ideals. Members were engaged in a wide range of activities and military-style training, increasing their fitness and awareness.

At first the German Workers' Party did not have an affiliated youth organisation. Teenage NSDAP members joined the SA, but Gustav (Adolf) Lenk started forming Youth League units for youths aged 14–18 around the Munich area in March 1922. Boys aged 14–16 were organised into Young Men's Groups while boys aged 16–18 joined Adolf Hitler's Young Storm Troops.

Youth League units were placed under the control of the SA and members had six main goals; to increase membership, support Völkisch ideals, educate people about the love of their homeland and the German people, have a high regard for moral and civilised values but have contempt for Jewish ideals.

Hitler announced the organisation of the Youth League in May 1922 and the *People's Observer* started printing a weekly youth supplement in August 1922. 900 members attended the Remembrance Day parade in Nuremberg in September 1922. A month later, Hitler presented the Youth League with their first flag when they paraded at the NSDAP rally in Coburg.

Although the Youth League participated in the January 1923 party rally in Munich, members were forbidden to take part in the

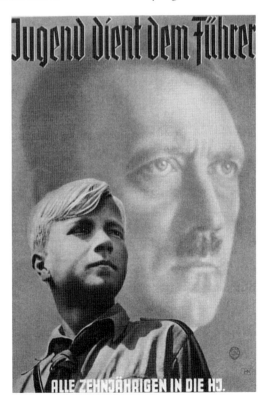

'The Youth Works for the Führer.' A poster encourages all ten-year-olds to join the Hitler Youth.

203

Beer Hall Putsch in November 1923. Even so, the organisation was banned and Lenk was jailed for taking part. After his release in April 1924 he started a new organisation called the Great German Youth Movement; he was briefly held in custody for starting an illegal organisation. Lenk organised the German Military Youth on his release but soon went bankrupt and he retired due to ill health.

The Youth League reformed when the NSDAP did, at the start of 1925. Edmund Heines was the first commander but he was soon replaced by Kurt Gruber, an effective organiser, who separated the organisation from the SA. He introduced a new uniform, using a brown shirt and black shorts, and an armband with a new diamond pattern symbol. Gruber also copied the NSDAP's organisational structure.

1st Department	Administration and Treasury
2nd Department	Education and Organisation
3rd Department	Welfare
4th Department	Racial Questions
5th Department	Film and Photography
6th Department	Politics and Trade Unions
7th Department	Propaganda
8th Department	Art and Culture
9th Department	Young Boys' Section
10th Department	Girls' Section
11th Department	Sport
12th Department	Press
13th Department	Excursions and Travel
14th Department	Military Sports

The name 'Hitler Youth', 'Association of German Workers' Youth' or *Hitlerjugend*, was used after the summer of 1925 and the name was adopted at the party day in Weimar in July 1926. Membership fees, sponsored marches and two monthly newspapers brought in extra income. Gruber added the 'Young Folk', *Jungvolk*, for boys aged 10–14 in 1928 but membership was only 18,000 by 1930.

Hitler Youth sing the '*Horst Wessel Lied*' during their Home Evening. (NARA-242-HB-09643)

A power struggle between Baldur von Schirach and Kurt Gruber resulted in Gruber's resignation. Schirach had a reputation for motivating youngsters and he saw to it that the Hitler Youth came under the SA once more in April 1931. He was soon raising the organisation's profile and reorganised it with the *Hitlerjugend* taking young people aged 15–18 and the *Jungvolk* taking boys aged 7–15; youth leaders were organised into Rings.

At the same time, Adrian Theodor von Renteln, head of the National Socialist Schoolchildren's League, was working to improve the leadership of the movement by removing incompetent youth leaders. After

Renteln resigned to take up his post in the Reichstag, Baldur von Schirach was named as the new Reich Youth Leader on 16 June 1932. Membership increased under his leadership, but while over 70,000 boys and girls attended the Reich Youth Day in Potsdam in October, the Hitler Youth was still only 20,000-strong in January 1933.

The Reich Council of Youth Organisations had over five million members belonging to over 70 organisations when the Nazis seized power. Its offices were closed down and its records were confiscated in April 1933. While Jewish and Marxist youth organisations were closed down, organisations like the Young Steel Helmet were absorbed into the Hitler Youth, increasing membership to four million by 1935. Religious-based youth groups were allowed to continue until action had been taken against their parent church.

The Hitler Youth was intended to be a vehicle for accelerating the indoctrination of boys and girls outside of school. Schirach adopted a theme starting in 1933, the Year of Organisation, and leaders spent the next twelve months focused on administration and organisation. In June, Baldur von Schirach was appointed head of the Hitler Youth, reporting directly to the Führer.

In the meantime, nationwide schemes were established to stimulate the youth into joining the NSDAP youth organisations. Hiking was promoted and youth hostels and Hitler Youth rest camps were established across the country. Reading was also encouraged and the Reich Youth Library held approved books and papers. Many activities had military overtones; younger boys practised with air guns and older boys practised with small-calibre rifles, and everyone participated in roll calls, war games, parades and map reading.

1934 was the Year of Schooling and youth leaders attended three-week training sessions at Reich leadership schools to improve their skills. A National Vocational Competition, with area and national rounds, was also introduced to encourage boys and girls to take part. By September 1934 fourteen-year-old boys and girls were working on farms for the Agricultural Auxiliary Service, part of the Reich's Land Service. 1934 was also the year the Hitler Youth created its own disciplinary organisation, the Hitler Youth Patrol Force. Members kept control at meetings and denounced disloyal members; they were also encouraged to report on enemies of the state, including their own parents. It was particularly hard for Communist and Social Democrat supporters to see their children indoctrinated by the Nazis.

1935 was the Year of Bodily Strengthening and physical training was increased from two hours a week to two hours a day in the national curriculum. Sports competitions were held regularly and medals were awarded for outstanding performances. The Day of the State Youth also became a huge annual summer athletics events. By now, over 60 per cent of German youngsters had joined the Hitler Youth and 54,000 boys paraded at the September Nuremberg Rally and heard Hitler tell them to be 'as swift as a greyhound, as tough as leather and as hard as Krupp steel'.

Schirach's objective for 1936 – the Year of Young People – was to get every German boy and girl aged 10–14 join the Hitler Youth. The *Jungvolk* swore an oath of allegiance to Germany and to Adolf Hitler in a huge ceremony at Marienburg Castle in East Prussia on the Führer's 47th birthday: 'In the presence of this blood banner which represents our Führer, I swear to devote all my energies and my strength to the saviour of our country, Adolf Hitler. I am willing and ready to give up my life for him, so help me God.' In December 1936, the Hitler Youth was made an official educational establishment and membership for boys over fifteen was made obligatory. All youths from the age of ten had to be educated according to Nationalist Socialist ideals.

Hitler Youth salute the Reich Youth Leader in Munich's Odeonplatz. (NARA-242-HB-14242)

1937 was the Year of the Home and Schirach added a number of military-style organisations to the Hitler Youth. While the Hitler Youth Flier Corps held courses on model-plane construction, glider and flying lessons for over 120,000 boys, the 55,000 members of the Hitler Youth Marine Corps had sailing lessons on the Baltic coast. The Hitler Youth Motor Corps trained 60,000 boys how to drive cars and fix engines while the Hitler Communications Youth Corps trained others in the art of signalling. A musical division enrolled talented musicians and the Hitler Youth Equestrian Corps enrolled expert horse riders. A separate organisation trained recruits for the SS, with a special emphasis on producing concentration camp guards for the future.

1938 was the Year of Understanding and the Austrian Hitler Youth were added to the German organisation in March. Sudeten region youth groups followed when German troops crossed the border in September.

By now, the Hitler Youth leadership claimed that over 75 per cent of all German youths were members and that they were being taught by 8,000 full-time leaders and 720,000 part-time leaders; many of them were schoolteachers. Over 80,000 members converged on Nuremberg in September, taking part in military manoeuvres in front of Nazi leaders. The Führer told them that: 'You, my youth, are our nation's most precious guarantee for a great future, and you are destined to be the leaders of a glorious new order under the supremacy of National Socialism. Never forget that one day you will rule the world!'

Some members took part in the attacks on Jewish synagogues and businesses in November 1939, even though Schirach had given strict instructions not to do so; he was forced to ban any further participation in anti-Semitic actions.

1939 was the Year of Health and the legal obligation for German children to join one of the youth organisations was announced in March; only Jewish children would not be members. It allowed the state to place children in orphanages if their parents would not allow them to enrol. Catholic-based youth organisations were the last to be merged with the Hitler Youth.

HITLER YOUTH ORGANISATION

Hitler Youth units were organised along the same lines as the army. Departments dealt with hygiene, labour service, sanitation, propaganda, youths abroad, aviation training and leadership. The boys wore military-style uniforms and their black armband had a single runic S and each unit had a triangular patch; specialist units had their own badges and insignia. The Hitler Youth was organised nationally as follows:

Obergebiete	5 *Gebiete* or 375,000 boys	
Gebiete	5 *Oberbanne* or 75,000 boys	
Oberbanne	5 *Banne* or 15,000 boys	
Banne	5 *Unterbanne* or 3,000 boys	similar to a regiment
Unterbanne	4 *Gefolgschaften* or 600 boys	similar to a battalion
Gefolgschaften	3 *Scharen* or 150 boys	similar to a company
Scharen	3 *Kameradschaften* or 50 boys	similar to a platoon
Kameradschaften	15 boys	similar to a squad

Members of a Young Men's Group question a machine-gun team. (NARA-242-HB-13844a3)

Sounding the reveille at a Hitler Youth rally. (NARA-242-HB-19751)

HITLER YOUTH ACTIVITIES

The organisation's political agenda and training was outlined by the national headquarters and organised by the local headquarters. A busy schedule of indoor and outdoor activities during the weekly 'home evenings' kept the boys entertained and each task was turned into a team or individual-based competition. Boys also planned local propaganda activities, including parades, recruitment drives and sponsored events. Many events were held in conjunction with the SA.

Every boy had a Performance Booklet to record his progress, and they were encouraged to improve through peer approval. The Hitler Youth wanted to turn the boy's unit into his home away from home, weaning him away from his parents' control.

Outdoor games involved war games or hide and seek games with names like 'trapper and Indian'. The highlight of the schedule was camping trips. They involved hiking, camping games and singing Hitler Youth songs around the camp fire.

The boys were subjected to tough drilling, known as 'grinding', and brawling was encouraged to toughen them up. While many boys excelled in the rough and tumble of training, weaker boys were bullied. Hitler Youth units were often aggressive towards non-members. Cases of excessive bullying and sexual abuse by youth leaders and older boys were covered up by the authorities.

THE YOUNG PEOPLE, JUNGVOLK

The junior division of the Hitler Youth catered for boys from 10-14 and they were known as *pimpfs*. Boys shadowed members of their local unit until they were deemed

fit to join. The initiation test included learning Nazi ideology through 'sword words', short memorable phrases, and the words of the anthem, '*Horst Wessel Lied*'. Physical tests involved running 60 metres in twelve seconds and a cross-country hike of a day and a half. Boys were also tested on semaphore signalling, laying telephone wires, and small arms drill for the Boys' Examination. Members were eligible for the Hitler Youth on their fourteenth birthday and they were proud to wear the uniform and carry the Hitler Youth's special dagger inscribed 'blood and honour'. The *Jungfolk* was organised as follows:

Jungbanne	5 *Stämme* or 3,000 boys	similar to a regiment
Stämme	4 *Fähnlien* or 600 boys	similar to a battalion
Fähnlien	3 *Jungzüge* or 150 boys	similar to a company
Jungzüge	3 *Jungenschaften* or 50 boys	similar to a platoon
Jungenschaften	15 boys	similar to a squad

YOUNG WOMEN'S ORGANISATIONS

The NSDAP formed a youth group for girls in 1923, but only a small number of girls joined. The Hitler Youth Sisterhood was organised for girls over the age of fourteen in 1928 and it became the party's girls' youth organisation the following year. It was renamed the German Girls League, the *Bund Deutscher Mädel*, in July 1930; the uniform was a long navy blue skirt, a white blouse, a brown jacket and long hair was worn in twin pigtails. The Young Girls Group was founded in April 1931 for girls aged 10–14. The organisation began with the male-orientated activities undertaken by the boys, but these proved unpopular, so new tasks encouraging

Members of a Young Girls Group practise needlework during their Home Evening. (NARA-242-HB-9645a1)

comradeship, physical fitness and female-orientated activities were introduced. The girls gathered regularly to play music, sing songs and practise arts and crafts.

In 1937, the Faith and Beauty organisation was established for young women aged 17–21. It taught them how to be ideal National Socialist wives and mothers who would raise healthy and racially pure children. They trained for marriage, attending courses in household activities, domestic science and fashion design; many tasks were turned into competitions. Physical education and sporting events also played an important part in the curriculum.

Membership of the German Girls League was made compulsory in 1936 for girls aged fifteen and over, and more than two million girls were being organised by 125,000 part-time leaders in local and regional units.

Boredom is etched across the faces of these girls as they listen to endless speeches. (NARA-242-HB-14126a4)

Gauverbände	5 Obergaue or 375,000 girls	
Obergaue	5 Gaue or 75,000 girls	
Gaue	5 Untergaue or 15,000 girls	
Untergaue	5 Mädelringe or 3,000 girls	similar to a regiment
Mädelringe	4 Gruppen or 600 girls	similar to a battalion
Gruppen	3 Scharen or 150 girls	similar to a company
Scharen	3 Mädelschaften or 50 girls	similar to a platoon
Mädelschaften	15 girls	similar to a squad

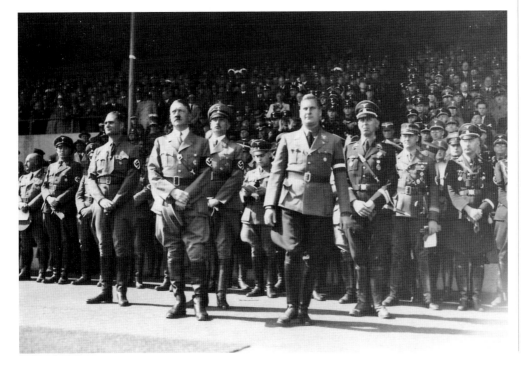

The Führer addresses the Hitler Youth in Nuremburg's Municipal Stadium; Bernard Rust is behind Hitler, Schirach is to his left. (NARA-242-HB-22628a13)

THE REICH YOUTH LEADER

BALDUR VON SCHIRACH (1907–1974)

Schirach was forced to leave the Young German League due to his anti-Christian and anti-Semitic views, and in 1925 he joined the NSDAP and the Munich SA. He came into contact with many leading Nazis after marrying Henny Hoffmann, the daughter of the party photographer, Heinrich Hoffmann. Although he was often ridiculed for his effeminate and sentimental behaviour, complimentary poetry about Hitler made sure he remained part of the Führer's circle of friends.

Schirach joined the National Socialist Students' League and the National Socialist Pupils' League in 1928, and became leader of the Students' League in 1929. The League targeted student issues and it was soon more popular than fraternities in many universities. Schirach's organisational skills did not go unnoticed, and in October 1931 he was appointed the Reich Youth Leader with Karl Nadensberg as his assistant. His Reich Youth Office was responsible for the administration and training of the youth organisations and one of his first tasks was to bring together 100,000 children for a rally in Potsdam in 1932.

In June 1933 Schirach was appointed Hitler Youth Leader; he was 26. He left the Hitler Youth in December 1939 following rumours about his effeminate behaviour; he joined a Wehrmacht unit shortly afterwards. Artur Axmann took his place.

SPORT

All kinds of sporting activities, individual and team, indoor and outdoor, were popular across Germany during the Weimar Republic years. This interest was promoted and supported by the Nazis during the Third Reich years.

Hitler himself was reluctant to indulge in any kind of exercise, except for a short daily walk. However, he believed that sport was essential for strengthening Germany's youth and

Sport was used to encourage competiveness, enthusiasm and physical fitness. (NARA-242-HB-07888)

he listed it as one of the seven requirements of 'the business of the state' in *Mein Kampf*. Sport encouraged individuals to become physically fit and competitive and their collective enthusiasm could be used to promote national enthusiasm.

The National Socialist Sports League promoted sport among Nazi party members under the Weimar Republic. The head of the German Reich Committee for Sports, Theodor Lewald, was forced to resign by the Nazis in May 1933 because his grandmother was Jewish, and the organisation was closed down a month later. It was replaced by the German Reich League for Sports headed by Hans von Tschammer und Osten. Promoting physical exercise and sport became a state issue and propaganda was used to advertise all kinds of events ranging from soccer matches to indoor athletics.

Sport was aryanised under *Gleichschaltung* and Hitler was adamant that German Aryans had to triumph. Boys and girls were encouraged to participate in sports and in 1938 the amount of physical training in schools was increased; boxing became compulsory for students in the upper classes. Sporting prowess became an essential attribute for students and while successful athletes excelled in the Nazi education system, poor ones could be expelled. The political schools, the Napolas, emphasised rowing, sailing, gliding, shooting and boxing.

The German football squad give the salute. (NARA-242-HB-12176)

The Nazi attitude to sport was reflected in the sports imagery of the time, which promoted racial superiority and physical power. Artists idealised athletes' heroic strength, muscle tone and Aryan features. The German Reich League for Sports controlled all sports facilities, clubs and bodies including the German Olympic Committee. Jewish athletes were barred from general sports clubs and they had to train at Jewish-owned facilities, which suffered from a lack of funding; they were eventually closed down.

Austrian and Czechoslovakian sporting associations were absorbed into the German Reich League for Sports in 1938 and at the end of the year the organisation was renamed the National Socialist Reich League for Sports. Adult men and women were also encouraged to take up exercise, and sports were officially promoted in factories. Workers were given time off during the day for exercise classes.

The treatment of the top German sportsman and sportswoman epitomises the attitudes of the Nazi regime.

Max Schmeling won the German heavyweight championship in 1928 and he went on to become the first (and only) German heavyweight champion of the world when he beat Jack Sharkey in June 1930. Two years later he lost it to Sharkey in a rematch. He went on to beat the American Joe Louis, nicknamed the Brown Bomber, in New York in June 1936, and he received a hero's welcome when he returned to Germany. As the underdog in the fight, the Nazis used

Max Schmeling on his triumphant return to Germany. (NARA-242-HB-21301)

Schmeling's victory for propaganda, hailing it as a victory of an Aryan German over an African-American athlete. The rematch in June 1938 was a short-lived affair in which Louis easily beat Schmeling. Germany's number one boxer regained his European heavyweight champion title in 1939.

In 1925, Helene Mayer became women's fencing champion of the Weimar Republic at the age of fifteen. Three years later she won a gold medal in the Amsterdam Olympic Games and went on to win the national championship in Italy. The tall, athletic blond woman was portrayed as

an example of Aryan superiority by the Nazis until they discovered that her mother and maternal grandparents were Jewish. All media references to Mayer were suddenly, but quietly, dropped and she had to emigrate to the US to continue training. Although she participated in the 1936 Berlin Olympic Games, and gave the Nazi salute when she was awarded the silver medal, she immediately returned to the US.

HANS VON TSCHAMMER UND OSTEN (1887–1943)

After serving in the First World War, Tschammer und Osten joined the NSDAP in 1929, becoming an SA-Gruppenführer two years later. He was elected Reichstag member for

Hans von Tschammer und Osten at the Winter Olympics in Garmisch-Partenkirchen. (NARA-242-HB-17914a3)

Magdeburg in March 1933 and four months later he was appointed Reich Sports Leader.

Although Tschammer und Osten did not have a sporting background, he was an able and active sports promoter. The German Reich League for Sports became the only sporting body in Germany, absorbing and disbanding all other organisations. While sporting events and training were modernised for Aryan athletes, Jews were banned from using state-run sporting facilities.

Tschammer und Osten played a major role in the organisation of the Berlin Olympic Games together with Dr Carl Diem, the former secretary of the German Sports Office, the pre-Nazi sporting organisation. He also appointed Karl Ritter von Halt to preside over the Committee of the 4th Winter Olympics held at Garmisch-Partenkirchen. The ban on non-Aryans in the German Olympic team was severely criticised and he was not elected to the International Olympic Committee.

THE XITH BERLIN OLYMPIAD

In May 1931, the International Olympic Committee awarded the XIth Olympiad to Berlin, a sign that Germany had been accepted back into the world community after the First World War. When the Nazis came to power in January 1933, the press initially denounced the forthcoming games as a festival dominated by Jews. Goebbels quickly convinced Hitler that the games would be a tremendous propaganda opportunity to showcase the Third Reich's achievements.

While Nazi propaganda portrayed Germany as the perfect host for the games, the International Olympic Committee rules forbade discrimination based on race or religion. Many countries had taken note of the anti-Semitic campaigns across Germany and considered boycotting the games. Large demonstrations were held across the US and there were smaller rallies elsewhere. Inspections of German sports facilities in 1934 gave the false impression that Jewish athletes were being treated fairly.

The Nazis soon embraced the idea of using the Olympics to showcase the Third Reich. (NARA-242-HB-11234a1)

There was also the question of black athletes competing, but the discrimination against African-American athletes in the US meant that it was hypocritical to complain about the Nazi attitude to race. Eighteen African-Americans eventually attended the games.

The US agreed to participate in the XIth Olympiad in December 1935 and Jewish athletes were allowed to decide if they wanted to attend. Other countries soon followed and 49 teams eventually competed, far more than the 1932 Los Angeles Olympics. In the meantime, the construction of nine arenas, including a huge stadium in Berlin, progressed rapidly with the help of a 20 million RM subsidy from the government.

The new Olympic complex: the track and field stadium is at the top and the swimming pool at the bottom. (NARA-242-HB-22041)

The Winter Olympics were held in Garmisch-Partenkirchen in the Bavarian Alps in February 1936. Anti-Jewish signs were removed from public view and Rudi Ball, a half-Jewish member of the German ice hockey team, was allowed to compete. The games were a success and attention quickly turned to the summer event.

Work progressed on the stadia and propaganda advertising the games increased. As the opening day drew near, artists were commissioned to create huge paintings and statues to adorn the sports arenas. Once again anti-Jewish signs were temporarily removed and the anti-Semitic newspaper *Der Stürmer* disappeared from newsstands. The Berlin Police had also been ordered to round up over 800 Gypsies around Berlin and they were held in a camp until

The lavish opening ceremony. (NARA-242-HB-22234a7)

Hitler meets the German Olympic team. (NARA-242-HB-22280a2)

the games were over. Anti-homosexual laws were also relaxed for foreign visitors.

Goebbels wanted the Games to be a showcase of choreographed pageantry, record-breaking athletic feats and warm German hospitality, making it memorable for both the athletes and spectators. His ministry issued a number of directives concerning press coverage and there was strict censorship over the press, radio, film and publishing.

On 1 August 1936, the cheers of 110,000 spectators drowned out the sounds of Richard Strauss's musical fanfares as Hitler opened the XIth Olympiad. A parade of 40,000 SA men was followed by the National Anthem, *Deutschland*, and the NSDAP anthem, sung by a 3,000-strong choir.

Dr Carl Diem had introduced two new rituals to the opening ceremony. The 5,000 athletes marched into the stadium, team by team in alphabetical order. While Germany had the largest team with 348 athletes, the US had 312 members (the Soviet Union was not participating in the 1930s). They were followed by a torch bearer who lit the Olympic flame above the arena. A relay of runners had carried the torch from Greece, passing through the Balkans and Austria into Germany.

The stadium erupted when the German shot-putter, Hans Woellke, won the first gold medal on opening day; he was the first German in history to win an Olympic track-and-field event. Another German, Gerhard Stock, finished third while Tilly Fleischer won the women's javelin competition later in the day. The Führer congratulated the three athletes but he left the stadium when two African-American athletes won medals. He did not congratulate any more athletes.

The star of the games was Jesse Owens, an African-American sprinter. He won four gold medals in the long jump, the 100-metre, the 200-metre and the 400-metre relay. The eighteen African-American athletes dominated the track and field events, winning fourteen medals, including eight gold medals, for the US team.

The German team won the highest number of medals, leaving Hitler in a buoyant mood, and he wanted the event to return indefinitely to Berlin after the 1940 Tokyo Olympics. Thirteen Jewish athletes, or athletes of Jewish descent, won medals. Although Helene Mayer, the half-Jewish fencer, was allowed to compete, other Jewish athletes were not. Gretel Bergmann, a high jump athlete, was banned just before the opening ceremony. Bergmann and Mayer later emigrated.

Two days after the Olympics finished Captain Wolfgang Fürstner, the head of the Olympic village, committed suicide; he had been dismissed from active military service because of his Jewish ancestry. Although German hospitality and organisation had been second to none during the games, the anti-Semitic restrictions resumed as soon as they had finished. The film *Olympia*, Leni Riefenstahl's documentary of the Games, was a lasting reminder of the event; it was released in 1938.

MOTOR RACING

Adolf Hitler was disgusted to learn that Germany motor companies did not enter cars in the European Grand Prix races. After watching an Italian car win the Berlin Grand Prix at Avus in 1933 he gave instructions to direct funds to two companies. The Mercedes Benz team was managed by Alfred Neubauer, while their engineering team was led by Rudolf Uhlenhaut. Rudolf Carraciola and Manfred von Brauchitsch were the Mercedes Benz drivers. Dr Ferdinand Porsche was the engineer for the smaller Auto Union team and its driver was Hans Stuck.

Motor sports became popular across Germany under the Nazis but meetings were dominated by military parades and officialdom. Adolf Huhnlein was appointed Corps Leader of National Socialist Motor Corps in 1934 and he attended many races on behalf of the party.

Mercedes Benz entered their W25 racing car and the Auto Union entered their A Type in the French Grand Prix in July 1934. Although both suffered from mechanical problems during their first race, the German teams were dominating the track by the end of the season; Stuck won the German Grand Prix. German drivers won the European Championships for the next four years, with Rudolf Carraciola winning in 1935, 1937 and 1938 for Mercedes

Adolf Hühnlein, National Socialist Motor Corps leader, in the pits during a motor race. (NARA-242-HB-06263)

Benz while Bernd Rosemeyer won it for Auto Union in 1936. Rosenbeyer was killed in a motoring accident in 1938. An Auto Union car won the Yugoslavian Grand Prix at Belgrade on 3 September 1939, the day that Great Britain, France and Poland declared war on Germany; it was the last race for six years.

Athletes practise forming the Olympic symbol for the opening ceremony. (NARA-242-HB-21047a)

The Olympic flame crosses Germany. (NARA-242-HB-22184)

CHAPTER SIXTEEN

RECLAIMING GERMANY'S BORDERS

THE LEAGUE OF NATIONS AND THE LOCARNO TREATY

The League of Nations was established on 28 June 1919 as part of the Treaty of Versailles. 42 countries agreed to arbitrate in national disputes, in the hope of securing long-term peace across Europe. President Woodrow Wilson of the US conceived the idea but his country did not become a member and it opted to take an isolationist approach to European diplomacy. The first meeting was held in Paris on 16 January 1920.

In February 1925, the German Foreign Minister, Gustav Stresemann, offered France a pact of mutual guarantee and non-aggression, and Britain promoted it over the summer. France and Germany agreed the Rhineland Pact in the town of Locarno, Switzerland, on 16 October, easing tension on their mutual border. Although six other treaties were agreed, the border between Germany and Poland was not discussed. The Locarno Treaty allowed Germany to join the League of Nations in September 1926.

The trust established with the Weimar government was quickly broken when the Nazis came to power. Hitler believed that the League of Nations was an Allied agency standing in the way of his plans, and he treated it as such. Alfred Rosenberg's visit to London on 1 May 1933, failed to reassure Britain of Germany's peaceful motives. Hitler's speech calling for peace on 17 May also failed. Germany withdrew from the League in September 1933 and disarmament talks in Geneva a month later. A plebiscite across Germany ratified Hitler's decision. Germany undermined the League of Nations by signing a separate treaty with Poland on 26 January 1934, securing its eastern border.

The Soviet Union joined the League of Nations in 1934, but it was soon clear that the League had little influence over European diplomacy. It failed to stop Italy's invasion of Ethiopia or the Spanish Civil War. It also failed to intervene in Germany rearmament or act following its reoccupation of the Rhineland in March 1936. European diplomacy would, once again, become a matter of individual countries making their own pacts and alliances.

THE EXPERIENCED DIPLOMAT

KONSTANTIN FREIHERR VON NEURATH (1873–1956)

Neurath joined the Foreign Office in 1901. He held many diplomatic posts over the next 30

Ulrich von Hassel, the German ambassador for Italy, Hitler and Konstantin von Neurath. (NARA-242-HB-06560)

years, including German Consul General in London, the Embassy Counsellor in Constantinople and the German envoy in Copenhagen. After serving as Ambassador to Italy and Great Britain, he was appointed Foreign Minister in both Papen's and Schleicher's cabinets in 1932. He continued to serve in Hitler's cabinet.

Neurath served the Nazis for five years as the acceptable face of Germany diplomacy. He had to join the NSDAP and the SS, with the rank of SS-Obergruppenführer. However, Hitler became increasingly dissatisfied by Neurath's tentative diplomacy and he preferred to work with the Ribbentrop Bureau and Rosenberg's Party Foreign Affairs Department, two new Nazi diplomatic offices.

Neurath advised Hitler to withdraw from the Geneva Disarmament Conference in October 1933, and three years later he denounced the Locarno Treaty on the Führer's behalf. His career ended after he objected to Hitler's plans for aggressive expansion at the Hossbach Conference in November 1937. He was replaced by Joachim von Ribbentrop on 4 February 1938.

Neurath was kept on as Minister without Portfolio. He was also appointed head of the new Secret Cabinet Council presiding over the chief of staff and the heads of the three armed services. The new cabinet was never used.

Neurath was appointed Reich Protector of Bohemia and Moravia in March 1939. He had to oversee the implementation of Nazi policies in the two regions, including the destruction of rival political parties, the disbandment of the trade unions, the censoring of the press and the implementation of anti-Semitic pogroms.

The signs declare that 'The Saar is German; Return it to the Reich.' (NARA-242-HB-07735)

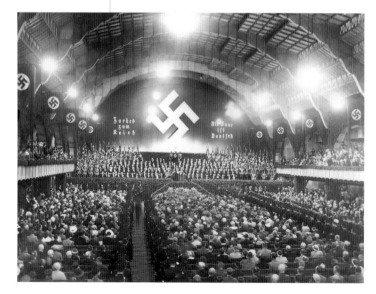

RECLAIMING GERMANY'S BORDERS

The majority of Germany's coal, iron and steel production came from the Ruhr area in north-west Germany. French and Belgian troops occupied the area in January 1923, when it was clear that Germany could not pay its war reparations. After two years of resistance and sabotage, the payments were restored and the troops withdrew.

Two areas of Germany were still affected by the Treaty of Versailles when the Nazis came to power. Over 440,000 people lived in the Saar area east of the Rhine, and the Treaty of Versailles had placed its coal, iron and steel production under the control of the League of Nations in 1919. France was allowed to mine the coal as repayment for the damage done to its own coalfields during the First World War. The people of the Saar felt that they were under foreign rule and, following a violent political campaign in January 1935, 90 per cent voted for a reunion with Germany. The League of Nations approved the decision and the return of the area to German control was celebrated as a break from the Treaty of Versailles. Third Reich laws were quickly implemented.

Germany's border area with Belgium and France had been demilitarised under the Treaty of Versailles. German troops were not allowed to enter the territory west of

Crowds gather as German troops march across the Rhine in Cologne. (NARA-242-HB-19028)

the Rhine nor a narrow strip east of the river, including the cities of Cologne, Düsseldorf and Bonn. Hitler gave orders to occupy the area at the start of 1936. He used the excuse that the recent Franco-Soviet Pact had broken the Treaty of Locarno to justify the occupation. He also hoped that the move would strain diplomatic ties between France and Britain; he was right.

On 7 March, 3,000 German troops entered the area as part of Operation *Winter Exercise* while another 30,000 waited on the east bank of the Rhine. It was risky to send such a small force and they had orders to withdraw if French troops opposed the occupation, but they did not. France believed there were far more and did not want to risk a major confrontation. Germany now had possession of all her industry and a referendum on 29 March 1936 returned 99 per cent of the votes in favour of Hitler's decision.

MUSSOLINI AND THE RISE OF THE ITALIAN FASCISTS

The word 'fascism' comes from the Latin word '*fasces*', a Roman symbol of authority depicting bundles of rods circling an axe. Following the Armistice, violent nationalism was promoted in Italy to counter communism and the poor economic situation. Benito Mussolini (1883–1945), an elementary school teacher and war veteran, formed the Union of Combat political party, and called for the state to set high standards for the people.

Intellectuals, the middle classes, farmers, ex-soldiers and youths joined Mussolini's party and they became known as the Blackshirts. They attacked communist meetings and broke up industrial disputes, forcing strikers to go back to work; the police supported their actions and stood by and watched.

By 1921, Mussolini's party had 30 seats in the Italian parliament and on 22 October 1922 over 50,000 Blackshirts marched on Rome. While the crowds gathered outside, Mussolini intimidated the Chamber of Deputies and forced Premier Luigi Facta to resign. A few days

A strutting Mussolini overshadows a subdued Hitler. (NARA-242-HB-07069)

later, King Victor Emmanuel III appointed Mussolini as Italy's new prime minister.

The new administration quickly replaced Italy's democracy with a ruthless dictatorship. They dismissed ministers and arrested political opponents. The Socialist Party finally withdrew from parliament after their leader, Giacomo Matteotti, was murdered in 1924. Mussolini headed the National Directory to control the armed services and foreign affairs. While Italy agreed non-aggression pacts and treaties across the Mediterranean, troops secured new colonies to acquire raw materials.

The Grand Council controlled internal affairs and legislated by decree, suspending civil rights, censoring the media and banning political meetings. Party supporters replaced professionals in the civil service to make sure that government policies were implemented. Regular military parades, a new anthem, '*Giovinezza*', and the revival of the Roman salute celebrated the accomplishments of the Italian Fascist State.

A restructured financial system and revised taxation stabilised the troubled economy, and Italy had soon paid off overseas debts. The country then started to encourage foreign investment and negotiate new trade pacts. By 1926 Italy had been turned into a corporate state, dominated by government-controlled syndicates. An extensive public works programme was used to lower unemployment. Working hours, wages and holidays were fixed by a Charter of Labour, while strikes and management lockouts were banned.

Discipline and obedience was taught from an early age and young boys joined the *Balilla*, graduating to the *Avanguardia* when they became teenagers. They joined the Union of Combat and served in the military at 21. Girls were taught to run the family home and raise children. Bonuses and tax exemptions encouraged couples to marry and even family life was affected by the banning of birth control, divorce and emigration.

A Concordat with the Catholic Church was agreed in February 1929; Pope Pius XI recognised the Kingdom of Italy and the Fascists recognised papal authority in the Vatican city-state. It was the longed-for settlement of the Roman question.

The NSDAP looked up to the Italian example in the 1930s, but after Hitler's appointment as Chancellor in 1933 the roles were quickly reversed. Germany's attempt to form a union with Austria in 1934 was thwarted when Italian troops assembled at the Brenner Pass; the two dictators smoothed over their differences in Venice the following June.

In April 1935, representatives from Britain and France met Mussolini in the town of Stresa in Italy. They reaffirmed their commitment to Austria's independence, isolating Germany in European diplomacy. The situation quickly changed after Italian troops invaded Abyssinia in

Mussolini and Hitler disagreed over Austria. (NARA-242-HB-07093)

October. Britain and France turned against Mussolini while Hitler obligingly took a neutral stand and refused to impose sanctions. In return, Mussolini made it clear that he would not interfere if Germany moved again against Austria.

Hitler and Mussolini both sent troops to Spain to support General Franco's army in 1936. Many lessons were learnt during the Civil War. An alliance between their two countries, known as the Rome–Berlin Axis, was agreed in October 1936, countering the alliance between Britain, France and the Netherlands. It was followed by a joint Anti-Comintern Pact in 1937. As Mussolini's power waned, Hitler's increased, and the German armed forces demonstrated their new weapons when the Italian dictator visited in September 1937.

Italy stood by when German troops crossed the Austrian border on 12 March 1938. The formal alliance between Germany and Italy – known as the Pact of Steel – was signed on 22 May 1939. Mussolini stood by his promise and Italy aligned itself with the Third Reich when Germany invaded Poland four months later.

FRANCO AND THE SPANISH CIVIL WAR

In July 1936 General Franco led an uprising against the Popular Front government of Spain. It quickly degenerated into a bloody civil war between the Republicans and the Nationalists. Hitler and Mussolini viewed the war as a conflict between communism and fascism and both countries promised support for the fascists, anxious to stop the Communist Party allying with France.

German planes immediately flew to Spain and began ferrying Franco's troops to key places on the front. An 11,000-strong German force led by General Hugo Sperrle, called the Condor Legion, armed with infantry, tanks, anti-aircraft and anti-tank units, reached Cadiz in November 1936. While the German Mediterranean Fleet bombarded the port

Troops from the Condor Legion prepare to leave Spain.

of Almeria, several squadrons of Junker-52 bombers and Heinkel-51 fighters bombed and strafed towns across Spain. The Luftwaffe experimented with urban bombing and it carried out a sustained air raid against the small towns of Durango and Guernica in northern Spain in the spring of 1937; 1,600 were killed and another 800 injured. A larger raid followed on Barcelona the following year.

Hitler purposely kept the Legion small to prevent the civil war escalating, but over 16,000 German troops had experienced combat by the time the Legion withdrew in May 1939. Their commanders had learnt many valuable lessons about tactics and weapons. The Italian contribution to the Spanish Civil War was much larger and Mussolini directed an entire division to support Franco's Nationalist troops. Over 50,000 Italian troops had experienced combat by the end of the war.

JAPAN

German admirals meet their Japanese counterparts in the Chancellery. (NARA-242-HB-5933)

In November 1936, Hitler arranged for Ribbentrop to sign an Anti-Comintern Pact with Japan. Germany and Japan also agreed on a defensive alliance against the Soviet Union, secretly pledging economic and diplomatic assistance to each other. The significance of the Berlin-Rome-Tokyo Axis would not become apparent until the Second World War had begun.

CHAPTER SEVENTEEN

CREATING A GREATER GERMANY

After German troops had secured the country's borders, Hitler could turn his attentions to creating a greater Germany, through the invasion of Austria and Czechoslovakia. The alteration of Germany's borders following the First World War meant that many German speaking people were under, what they considered to be, a foreign government. The Nazis sought to take advantage of this, helping to stir up anti-government support by financing local Nazi groups.

HITLER'S PLANS FOR WAR

Field Marshal Werner von Blomberg and Admiral Erich Raeder, the commander of the German Navy, requested an audience with Hitler in the autumn of 1937. They wanted to discuss rearmament, in particular the sharing of resources. Hitler invited three others to join the meeting on 5 November; General Werner von Fritsch, commander-in-chief of the Army, Hermann Göring, commander-in-chief of the Luftwaffe, and Konstantin von Neurath, the Foreign Minister. Hitler's military adjutant, Colonel Friedrich Hossbach, took notes.

After making it clear that the meeting should be kept secret, Hitler spoke for over two hours, but he did not talk about sharing resources. He outlined his plan for the future, calling it his 'last will and testament'. Hitler also predicted the immediate future of Europe. He believed that France was Germany's greatest threat, rather than Russia. Currently France had its own internal difficulties to deal with, while Britain was occupied with prob-

Admiral Raeder, General Blomberg and General Fritsch. (NARA-242-HB-15097a1)

lems across the Empire. While France would not consider war with Germany without British support, it was in Germany's interests if they both became involved in the Spanish Civil War.

Hitler also reminded the small group that he wanted the Third Reich to be self-sufficient, but it was still short of food and metal ores, and shortages would rise as living standards rose. He wanted Germany to complete rearmament by 1943 but if it delayed beyond 1945, it would be overtaken in the arms race. The Third Reich needed resources quickly to achieve his plans.

Hitler also reminded the group that Germany needed extra living space. He planned to obtain it by occupying Austria and Czechoslovakia. The two countries could provide food for another five or six million people if three million non-Germans were forced into exile. The occupation would also provide enough soldiers for twelve more divisions.

Hitler then predicted three possible scenarios to achieve his expansion plan:

Occupy Czechoslovakia if France's army became involved in internal problems
Occupy Czechoslovakia and Austria if France used its army in an external situation
Occupy Czechoslovakia and Austria if Italy went to war with a Franco-British alliance

Hitler and Joachim von Ribbentrop, his favourite diplomat. (NARA-242-HB-13279)

Hitler stressed the need for a *Blitzkrieg* – his name for a lightning invasion by mechanised troops – of both countries. He believed that while Mussolini would not object to the invasion of Czechoslovakia, he might object to German troops occupying Austria because of their mutual border.

Blomberg, Fritsch and Neurath were shocked by Hitler's plan and they were critical of him for contemplating a war with France and Britain. All three would be sacked three months later. The notes from the meeting became known as the Hossbach Memorandum because Hitler's military adjutant, Colonel Hossbach took the minutes of the meeting.

In May 1939 Hitler told senior officers at a conference at the Reich Chancellery that war was an essential part of his plans. He also stated his desire for war during a meeting at his Berchtesgaden home in August. Two weeks later German troops invaded Poland.

JOACHIM VON RIBBENTROP (1893–1946)

Ribbentrop was a commercial representative in Canada when the First World War forced him to return to Germany where he served in the trenches. He then worked as a wine salesman and his marriage to the daughter of a wealthy champagne producer in 1920 brought him into contact with many influential people. A change in the law also allowed him to add the prefix 'von' to his name.

Ribbentrop met Hitler in 1928 but he did not join the NSDAP until May 1932, becoming an SS colonel. His ambition, vanity and domineering presence allowed him to prise his way into Hitler's circle of friends. He learned what the Führer wanted and then worked to make it happen. This subservience was scorned by many Old Guard party members.

Hitler negotiated his first cabinet in Ribbentrop's house in Berlin-Dahlem in January 1933. A few weeks later Ribbentrop was appointed head of the Ribbentrop

Ribbentrop shows off his new SS uniform. (NARA-242-HB-23637)

Bureau, a new diplomatic office set up to bypass the Foreign Office and report directly to the Deputy Leader, Rudolf Hess. The Bureau soon had over 300 staff, employing journalists and careerists rather than diplomats.

Ribbentrop was appointed Ambassador-Plenipotentiary-at-Large in 1935 and he toured countries looking for ways to undermine European diplomacy. Although he discussed disarmament with foreign diplomats, he was always looking for ways to assist German rearmament. On several occasions he negotiated agreements without informing the Foreign Office, including the June 1935 Anglo-German Naval Agreement and the 1936 Anti-Comintern Pact with Japan.

Ribbentrop's career took an uncomfortable turn in August 1936 when he was appointed ambassador to Britain. His attempts to encourage understanding between the two countries failed due to his awkward behaviour. Greeting King George V with the Nazi salute during a visit to London was just one of several embarrassing moments. The experience turned Ribbentrop into a convinced Anglophobe and it encouraged him to support the Berlin-Rome-Tokyo Axis.

On 4 February 1938, Konstantin von Neurath was sacked for criticising Hitler's plans for war and Ribbentrop replaced him as Foreign Minister. Over the next twelve months he was involved in the Austria and Czechoslovakia crises, repeatedly giving Hitler incorrect or misleading information. Ribbentrop's blundering continued during the negotiations with Poland and Russia in the summer of 1939. He also convinced the Führer that the British would not be able to provide support for Poland.

On 23 August 1939, Ribbentrop and Soviet Foreign Minister Vyacheslav M. Molotov signed a non-aggression agreement in Moscow. It was presented as a peaceful move to the world press but a secret clause provided for the partition of Poland. The return of the Baltic Corridor, joining the city port of Danzig to the rest of the Third Reich was the reason given for the dispute with Poland, but it just paved the way for Germany's invasion of Poland on 1 September 1939. Two days later Britain and France declared war on Germany. Ribbentrop signed a second German-Soviet treaty at the end of the Polish campaign on 28 September 1939, readjusting the partition of Poland.

AUSTRIA

The Austro-Hungarian Empire had been dissolved by the Treaty of Saint Germann-en-Laye in September 1919 and any reunion with Germany was banned under the Treaty of Versailles. During the economic difficulties in the 1920s, the German-speaking people called for a union, or *Anschluss*, with Germany. The first steps were taken after the Austrian economy was severely weakened in the wake of the world financial crisis. The Weimar government considered a customs union with Austria in March 1931, but France, Czechoslovakia, Yugoslavia and Romania raised objections and the International Court of Justice in The Hague rejected it. As unemployment and poverty rose, so did anti-Semitism and discontent with the government.

AUSTRIAN UPRISINGS

Engelbert Dollfuss (1892–1934) had been the Austrian Chancellor and Foreign Minister since May 1932. Hitler was Austrian by birth and he turned his attentions to a union of Germany and Austria as soon as the Nazis had secured their position in Germany. There had been tension and fighting between the Socialists and the Christian Social Party and Dollfuss refused to assemble the parliament in 1933, in order to remain in control. A Socialist rebellion in February 1934 was stopped by government troops assisted by fascist militia; hundreds were killed and thousands were arrested in the street battles.

Ernst Starhemberg (1899–1956) had taken part in the 1923 Munich Putsch and then returned to Austria, becoming the head of the Homeland Protection Party and Minister of the Interior by 1930. Dollfuss appointed him Vice-Chancellor in 1932 and tasked him with bringing the right-wing parties together as the Austrian Fatherland Front.

The Front was soon dominated by Austrian Nazis and Austrian Legion SS and SA paramilitaries who attacked railways, power stations and government buildings with German support to undermine the government. By the summer, the time was ripe for a coup. On 25 July 1934, 150 Austrian SS, who had trained in Germany, dressed in Austrian Army uniforms and seized the Federal Chancellery. They shot Dollfuss and took control of the Vienna radio station, broadcasting the news that the government had resigned. Uprisings across the country were put down by the Austrian Army and within a short time they had regained control of the capital, ending the coup.

The German Army had assembled along the Austrian border ready to cross when news of a successful coup was received; it never came. Mussolini had also mobilised four divisions at the Brenner Pass. Fearing a confrontation with Italy, Hitler was forced to call off the occupation, allowing the Austrian government to sort out its internal problems. He did, however, appoint Vice-Chancellor Papen (who was still in shock after the Blood Purge) as ambassador to Vienna.

Dr Kurt von Schuschnigg (1897–1977) was a member of the Christian Social Party and had worked in several ministries before joining the Ministry of Justice in 1932. He refused to bow to Hitler's demands and he took steps to limit the strength of the Home Guard and other paramilitary formations after replacing Dollfuss. Schuschnigg failed to rally the Fatherland Front and in 1936 he was forced to ban the paramilitary Home Defence League for anti-government activities.

Schuschnigg secured an Austro-German agreement in July 1936, recognising Austria's sovereignty, but his position was undermined by the signing of the Rome-Berlin Axis in October 1936. Austria no longer had Mussolini's support against Hitler's attentions.

The Committee of Seven was set up in Vienna at the beginning of 1938 to mediate between the government and the Austrian Nazis. There were suspicions that it was supported by Germany and they were realised when the police discovered documents calling for a revolt by Austrian Nazis. The documents were signed by Hitler's Deputy Führer, Rudolf Hess.

THE UNION, DIE ANSCHLUSS

Dr Kurt von Schuschnigg was bullied into working with Germany on 12 February 1938 at the Berghof in Berchtesgaden, and Hitler's argument was that the majority of Austrians favoured the Anschluss. The agreement legalised the Austrian Nazi Party, released convicted Nazis while assuring economic and military collaboration between the two countries. Arthur Seyss-Inquart, who had been working with the Nazis, was appointed Minister of the Interior, and over the days that followed the army and police stood by as the Nazis demonstrated against the government.

On 9 March, Schuschnigg tried to get his revenge by announcing a referendum on Austrian independence to be held four days later. On 11 March 1938, the German border with Austria was closed as the 8th Army assembled at the crossing points. Hitler made a series of demands which had to be met to avoid an invasion. He demanded a postponement to the referendum. Schuschnigg had to resign and the new Chancellor was to be Arthur Seyss-Inquart. Schuschnigg agreed but as soon as the Austrian President appointed Seyss-Inquart, Hitler changed his terms. That evening, Seyss-Inquart was ordered to send a telegram asking

German troops were met by jubilant crowds in every town and village.

Hitler declares the Anschluss in the Square of Heroes.

Jews are taunted and humiliated as they are forced to scrub the streets.

for help from German troops 'to restore order'. Hitler's desire for a bloodless coup of Austria had been realised. At the same time, Mussolini gave assurances that he would not interfere.

On the morning of 12 March, General Fedor von Bock's 8th Army crossed the Austrian border and headed south for Vienna. Although the advance was badly organised, the Austrian Army did not resist and Bock's troops were greeted by cheering Austrians with salutes, flags and flowers. Hitler's car crossed the border in the afternoon at Braunau, his birthplace, and in the evening he was given an enthusiastic welcome in Linz where he had spent time as a teenager. The drive across Austria turned into a triumphal tour and Goebbels called the occupation the 'Flower Wars'. Hitler's tour ended in Vienna where over 200,000 Austrians heard him proclaim the Anschluss in the Square of Heroes.

Schuschnigg resigned and he was held in a concentration camp; he was not the only one. The Austrian Nazis immediately started rounding up political opponents, trade unionists, army officers and over 30,000 Jews. Germany had had five years to come to terms with the series of changes the Nazis made to law and order; Austria got them all at once.

The train system, the postal system and banking were immediately merged with Germany's,

while Germans took over companies; gold and foreign currency reserves were also taken. Austrians were quickly employed as the German Labour Front moved in, and they were soon working long hours for the Four Year Plan. Hundreds of army officers were retired and German police and Gestapo officers were drafted in. Over 21,000 'enemies of the state' were arrested in one night and held in Dachau concentration camp, and a new camp opened at Mauthausen.

There were 200,000 Jews in Austria, the majority living in Vienna, and they were immediately subjected to the full might of the Nazi pogroms. While Austrian Nazis went on the rampage, attacking and humiliating any Jewish person they could find, aryanisation was implemented in every walk of life. Virtually all Jewish businesses had been closed or bought out in six months, while thousands were thrown out onto the streets when their apartments were confiscated. Many looked to emigrate and the Central Agency for Jewish Emigration was set up under Adolph Eichmann. The Agency specialised in systematically robbing Jews wishing to leave; it became a model for the future.

Over the next four weeks, the Austrian Nazis prepared for the referendum, tailoring their actions to get support. On 10 April 1938, voters were asked 'do you agree to the reunion of Austria with the German Reich carried out on March 13 and do you vote for Adolf Hitler?' The Anschluss was accepted by an affirmative vote of 99 per cent in a total vote of 99.59 per cent of the qualified electorate of Germany. Yet again the Nazis had used coercion to get the result they wanted.

AUSTRIAN NAZIS

ARTHUR SEYSS-INQUART (1892–1946)

Seyss-Inquart recovered from wounds received in the First World War to become a lawyer in Vienna. He did not join the Austrian National Socialist Party but he secretly cooperated with the Germans to undermine the government. His dealings increased after he was appointed State Councillor in 1937. In February 1938, he was appointed Minister of the Interior at Hitler's insistence, allowing him to take control of the Austrian police. He was also able to give the German Army permission to cross the border unopposed. Seyss-Inquart was appointed Chancellor at Hitler's insistence on 11 March and he was known as Reich Governor of the Eastern March, the Eastmark, or 'Ostmark' as Germany called Austria. He held the position until 30 April 1939.

Arthur Seyss-Inquart undermined the Austrian government. (NARA-242-HB-32992a1)

ODILO GLOBOCNIK (1904–1945)

Globocnik was a builder who joined the Austrian National Socialist Party in 1930. He was admitted to the SS in 1933 and was a deputy district leader for the NSDAP until he was arrested for political crimes. Following his release, he mediated between Hitler's contacts and the Austrian Nazis and by 1936 he had been appointed the party leader for Carinthia, a state in the south of the country. Following the Anschluss, Globocnik was appointed Vienna's Gauleiter in May 1938. He was sacked the following January for scandalous behaviour.

JOSEPH BURCKEL (1895–1944)

Burckel started teaching after serving in the First World War. He resigned in 1925 after joining the NSDAP to run *The Iron Hammer* newspaper; he was soon the Gauleiter for the Rhineland-Palatinate area. He was elected to the Reichstag as the Saar delegate in 1930 and he succeeded Papen as the Saar Plenipotentiary in 1934. Burckel was named the area's Reich Commissioner when it returned to German control the following year.

Burckel was tasked with organising the referendum following the Anschluss, and in April he was appointed Reich Governor of Austria, applying *Gleichschaltung* and German-style laws across the country. He also acted as the Gauleiter for Vienna in January 1939, after Globocnik was sacked.

ERNST KALTENBRUNNER (1903–1946)

Kaltenbrunner was a tall man, with piercing eyes and distinctive scars on his cheek. The Linz lawyer joined the Austrian National Socialist Party in 1932 and he was imprisoned after the 1934 Putsch and again for taking part in the murder of Dollfuss. Following his release, he took command of the Austrian SS in 1935 and helped German troops after they crossed the border in March 1938. The SS was turned into an auxiliary police force following the Anschluss and it arrested many prominent Austrians including Chancellor Schuschnigg. They also attacked political opponents, trade unions and Jewish communities as *Gleichschaltung* and German laws were applied. He was appointed State Secretary for Internal Security in Vienna.

CZECHOSLOVAKIA

The Republic of Czechoslovakia was created in 1919 from Bohemia, Moravia, Austrian Silesia and the former Hungarian areas of Slovakia and Ruthenia. The country had a population of fourteen million; over three million German-speaking people lived in the mountainous border area of Bohemia known as the Sudetenland.

While central Czechoslovakia became prosperous from rich mineral resources, the German-speaking people in the Sudetenland borderlands experienced high unemployment; many claimed the government was discriminating against them. Hitler was aware of these inequalities and he intended to take advantage of them. Many looked enviously to the revitalised German economy, but the rest of Czechoslovakia was opposed to Hitler and Germany. The pro-Nazi Sudeten German Party was formed in 1935 by Konrad Henlein and it started causing civil unrest, with financial help from the German Foreign Office. It had a sizeable number of votes.

Hitler started his campaign against Czechoslovakia in February 1938, reminding the Reichstag about the plight of the Sudeten Germans while the Nazi press denounced Czech atrocities. Hitler was aware that the Sudetenland was a well fortified mountainous area and the large and well-equipped Czechoslovakian Army was ready to defend it. He was also aware that Britain and France would become involved. Hitler wanted the Czech raw materials and armament industries for the Four Year Plan and he instructed the Wehrmacht to prepare two invasion plans. 'Case Red' assumed that the French Army would react to an attack on the Sudetenland and troops had to be deployed to counter them. 'Case Green' assumed that they would not.

The Chief of the General Staff, General Ludwig Beck, canvassed against attacking Czechoslovakia but he was outnumbered and resigned. He gathered a circle of military and civilian conspirators and planned to overthrow Hitler, but attempts to get help from Britain failed, as did the plot.

With the help of Goebbels' propaganda, the Sudeten German Party increased its anti-government activities as soon as the Austrian Anschluss had been settled in March 1938. Tension grew and both armies mobilised troops along the border after several Germans were killed in a frontier

A Hitler Youth rally calling for the unification of German-speaking people. (NARA-242-HB-12736a3)

incident. While France and the Soviet Union pledged their support for Czechoslovakia, Britain refused to support France. It was the news that Hitler wanted to hear; he had split the Allies.

With Hitler's support, Henlein declared an autonomous German province on 24 April 1938 to stir up more trouble across Czechoslovakia. To their surprise the government agreed to his demand in the hope of restoring order; it also promised equal employment opportunities and economic relief. With Germany's support, the Sudeten German Party continued to cause trouble until President Eduard Beneš was forced to proclaim martial law. The party responded by forming the Sudeten Free Corps paramilitary units which spent the summer causing disruption.

THE MUNICH AGREEMENT

Hitler called a secret meeting of generals on 30 May and he ordered them to prepare for Case Green, concentrating their full forces on the Czech border. They had to be ready to cross the Czech border on 1 October 1938.

Matters eventually came to a head between Germany and Czechoslovakia in September 1938 after a difficult summer for Eduard Beneš. His attempts to reach a settlement with the Sudeten German Party had failed, and on the 12th, Hitler announced at Nuremberg that he would send troops into the Sudetenland to support the Sudeten

Prime Minister Chamberlain arrives at the Berghof.

Germans. The news prompted the British Prime Minister, Neville Chamberlain, to fly to Berchtesgaden to negotiate on behalf of the Czechoslovakian government. The Führer was adamant that the Sudetenland must become part of the Third Reich.

Chamberlain returned to London to consult with his cabinet and the French Premier, Edouard Daladier. On 20 September they declared that the Sudetenland would be handed over to Germany to avoid plunging Europe into war. The Czechoslovakian cabinet had not been consulted but they agreed to the declaration before resigning. The new cabinet under General Jan Syrovy ordered a general mobilisation while the army prepared to counter the impending German invasion; the Soviet Union pledged support for Czechoslovakia. President Eduard Beneš, however, wanted support from Britain and France.

Mussolini did not interfere in Hitler's expansion plans.

Chamberlain returned to Germany on 22 September to give Hitler the news at Bad Godesberg in the Rhineland. He was stunned when the Führer demanded control of a larger area of the Sudetenland. He also set an ultimatum for the decision for 28 September, otherwise troops would cross the border on 1 October. Poland and Hungary had also put in similar claims to Czechoslovakian territory. Göring and Mussolini managed to convince Hitler to postpone the invasion and they arranged a conference at Hitler's Munich headquarters to settle the issue.

The third meeting between Chamberlain, Daladier, Mussolini and Hitler took place on 29 September; the Soviet Union and Czechoslovakia were excluded. The Führer had reduced his demands and while the British and French premiers agreed to accept them, the Czechoslovakian representatives had to be pressurised into agreeing. The agreement was drawn up on 29 September and signed early the next day; it would be known as Black Wednesday.

Although the Munich Agreement took the Wehrmacht by surprise, Hitler was delighted. Yet again he had outwitted the European heads of state and proved his generals wrong. As far as Chamberlain was concerned he had avoided a European war and he arrived back in London declaring that he had obtained 'peace for our time'. The peace would last less than twelve months.

THE OCCUPATION OF THE SUDETENLAND

The Sudetenland was divided into four zones and they were occupied in turn between 1 and 7 October. A fifth zone, setting the new Czechoslovakian frontier, was decided by an international mission; it was occupied on 10 October. The occupation left Germany in control of the fortified mountainous border area, leaving the rest of Czechoslovakia defenceless. It also left numerous important industries – in particular armaments industries – in Germany's hands.

The Germans again implemented *Gleichschaltung* across the region, arresting political opponents, disbanding trade unions and subjecting the Jewish communities to pogroms. Over 10,000 were arrested with the help of lists prepared by the German Sudeten Party and held in the new Theresienstadt concentration camp in Bohemia. President Beneš resigned on 5 October and he went on to head a government in exile in England.

200,000 people fled the German-occupied area and became refugees in the Czechoslovakian-controlled area. 90 per cent of Jews left, knowing what to expect. Sudeten Germans were given jobs during the aryanisation process, Czechs lost theirs. The Czech language was banned, their organisations were closed down and its people were turned into second-class citizens.

German troops drive into Prague.

On 30 September Poland demanded an area of territory and moved in on 2 October. After Czechoslovakia failed to reach a compromise with Hungary, southern Slovakia and one million people were ceded to Hungary on 2 November. On 4 December over 97 per cent of the remaining population in the Sudetenland area voted for the NSDAP, while half a million joined the Nazi Party. Again coercion was used.

THE OCCUPATION OF THE REST OF CZECHOSLOVAKIA

The Slovak People's Party, the right-wing nationalist party, formed a government under Jozef Tiso on 7 October and a month later Emil Hácha was elected president of a country in turmoil. After negotiations between Germany and Poland broke down in January 1939, Hitler turned his attentions to occupying the rest of the Czechoslovakian territory where the industries and military dumps were located.

Czechs and Slovaks were in dispute and Czech troops occupied Bratislava on 10 March 1939; four days later the Slovak parliament declared independence. Hitler had prepared to take advantage of the troubles and the invasion of Bohemia and Moravia was ordered for 15 March. After negotiations between Hitler and Tiso on 13 March, the Slovak government declared independence. Carpatho-Ukraine also declared independence and President Hácha met Hitler in Berlin on the night of 14/15 March, and learned that German troops were

Hitler proudly supports his troops. (NARA-242-HB-13288a1)

preparing to invade. The Führer ignored Hácha's pleas to spare his country and he stormed out after making him clear that he had ordered an invasion. Göring and Ribbentrop went on to threaten to bomb Prague if German troops were turned back at the border; the Czechoslovakian president collapsed in shock.

Hácha was revived and he quickly agreed to the German threats. Hours later, German troop were marching towards Prague. German troops moved quickly into Bohemia and Moravia; yet again there was no opposition but this time there were no

flowers, only sullen faces. Hungarian troops entered Carpatho-Ukraine on the same day and quickly overran Czechoslovakian resistance. On 16 March, Hitler flew to Czechoslovakia and proclaimed Bohemia and Moravia a German protectorate at Prague Castle. The same day Hungary seized more Slovak territory.

The Wehrmacht welcomed the addition of 800 tanks and 2,000 artillery pieces to its arsenal while the Luftwaffe took possession of 1,000 planes. The area was then subjected to *Gleichschaltung* and while Slovakian people were conscripted into working for the German rearmaments industry, the Jewish communities were subjected to the wide range of pogroms.

CZECHOSLOVAKIAN PRESIDENTS

EDUARD BENEŠ (1884–1948)

Beneš was a peasant who worked his way up to be a university lecturer. During the First World War he went into exile in Paris and established the Czechoslovak National Council with Tomas Masaryk. Following the Armistice, the two returned to the new state of Czechoslovakia and while Masaryk was appointed President, Beneš became the Foreign Minister.

Beneš was voted President in 1935, as the troubles with the Sudeten German Party were beginning, and he managed to form an entente with Yugoslavia and Romania. By 1938 he was dealing with Konrad Henlein's threats while Hitler denounced him as a warmonger and German troops massed along the border. Beneš was virtually excluded from the meetings over the Sudetenland in September 1938 and he was forced to agree to hand it over to Germany. He resigned from the presidency after the Munich Agreement had been signed.

EMIL HÁCHA (1872–1945)

Hácha was a lawyer who became the first President of the Czechoslovakia Supreme Administration Court in 1925. He succeeded Eduard Beneš in November 1938 and he tried to maintain his country's independence. Slovakia and Ruthenia made increasing demands for independence in March 1939, again made with German assistance. On the night of 14/15 March Hitler bullied the ill Hácha to allow troops to occupy Bohemia and Moravia.

Hácha continued to serve as State President of the Reich Protectorate of Bohemia and Moravia, the puppet leader working for Reich Protector Konstantin von Neurath and Reich Governor Konrad Henlein. Most Czechoslovakians ignored Hácha's calls to support the new regime, preferring to continue supporting the exiled Eduard Beneš.

THE SUDETEN-GERMAN HOMELAND FRONT

KONRAD HENLEIN (1898–1945)

Henlein served in the Austrian Army during the First World War. He became a gymnastics teacher and by 1931 he was the head of the German Gymnastics Association of Czechoslovakia. He founded the Sudeten-German Homeland Front in October 1933 with Karl Frank (1898–1945), a book store owner specialising in right-wing literature, using a subsidy from the Berlin Foreign Office, and it began calling for Sudetenland's independence. The party organised the Sport Abteilung along similar lines to the German SA and over 20,000 members attended the first mass meeting in October 1934. By 1935 44 deputies had been elected to the Czechoslovakian parliament and the party was starting to influence the country's politics.

Following the Anschluss, Hitler promised Henlein support and he worked closely with the German Foreign Office during visits to Germany. In April 1938, Henlein announced eight demands for autonomy of the Sudeten Germans and the Czech government agreed. Henlein broke off negotiations, blaming a minor technicality, because he wanted to undermine the government. Civil unrest increased over the summer until the people of Sudetenland rose against the Czech government, forcing Henlein to flee to Germany fearing arrest. Henlein returned to Czechoslovakia in May 1939, after German troops had occupied Bohemia and Moravia and he was appointed Gauleiter of the Sudetenland. Karl Frank was appointed Gauleiter of Bohemia and Moravia.

THE BALTIC COAST

The Treaty of Versailles ceded control of two Baltic seaports in East Prussia from Germany. Memel was transferred to the new state of Lithuania, while Danzig (Gdansk) was made a demilitarised free city. Both cities were separated from Germany by a strip of coastline, given to Poland as access to the Baltic Sea. The Nazis wanted this Polish Corridor returned to re-link East Prussia to the Fatherland.

Memel had a large German-speaking population and the city's Nazi Party demanded a reunion with Germany. After Czechoslovakia was occupied in March 1939, Hitler turned his attentions to the Baltic. He threatened to start bombing Lithuania on 20 March and three days later German troops were allowed to take over Memel. Calls for Danzig's return were refused. Danzig and the Polish Corridor would have to be taken by force during the September 1939 invasion of Poland.

A political rally calling for the return of Danzig to Germany. (NARA-242-HB-11527b)

THE NON-AGGRESSION PACT WITH THE SOVIET UNION

The Communist Soviet Union and National Socialist Germany were ideological enemies. Stalin viewed Hitler with deepening suspicion when the Nazis came to power, but he underestimated the determination and resourcefulness of the German people. Hitler's support of General Franco's cause against the Soviet-backed Republicans in the Spanish Civil War illustrated the extent of Germany's rearmament. The Soviet Union's own armed forces were in a poor state following the communist purges. Senior officers and technical experts had been imprisoned or executed, leaving political officers in control. A lack of funding and industry had also paralysed rearmament and military training.

Stalin was becoming increasingly isolated from European affairs and he was infuriated by his exclusion from the Munich Crisis meetings in September 1938. Britain and France opened negotiations with Russia at the beginning of 1939, asking it to guarantee assistance for its neighbouring states. Stalin preferred to establish a defensive buffer against Germany, and he wanted to occupy the countries stretching from the Baltic to the Black Sea. The proposal to occupy so many free countries with Soviet troops concerned Prime Minister Chamberlain and Premier Daladier. It would also allow Hitler to concentrate on France and Great Britain.

After the two leaders left empty handed, Stalin expressed his disappointment with the Western democracies for rejecting his plans for collective security during the Communist Party Congress in March 1939. It opened the way for discussions between Germany and the Soviet Union. On 29 March Chamberlain guaranteed to step in for Poland's independence, but how could Britain help when it was so far away?

Hitler drew a line under the negotiations for Danzig and the Polish Corridor and on 3 April he ordered the Wehrmacht to prepare to invade Poland, setting 1 September as the date for the invasion. On 22 May the alliance with Italy was stepped up to become a Pact of Steel. Hitler and Stalin also prepared to negotiate. While Hitler stopped publicly criticising communism, Stalin sacked the hard line Soviet Foreign Commissar, Maxim Litvinov, and replaced him with the moderate Vyacheslav M. Molotov.

Stalin had purged his generals and industrialists, therefore while his armies were unprepared for war with Germany, his industries were not in a position to rectify the matter. He knew that Hitler intended to attack Poland and he was looking for a way to protect his own country. The Western powers refused to intervene and he was forced to negotiate and consider carving up Poland.

German and Russian relations improved dramatically over the summer while the rest of Europe looked on. Ribbentrop started to negotiate an economic deal with Molotov at the beginning of August. When it was clear that the Russian diplomats were stalling, Hitler inter-

Ribbentrop looks smug, Stalin looks pleased, Molotov is sat with his head bowed.

vened and asked Stalin to meet Ribbentrop, assuring him that Germany's intentions was serious. The pact was signed on 24 August. Both countries agreed not to attack the other, or support a third county if the other was attacked. Additionally, neither country would join an alliance intending to attack the other.

London and Paris were dismayed by the news, even though they did not know the most sinister clause of the pact. A secret protocol was attached, dividing Poland in two. Germany would occupy the area west of the rivers Narew, Vistula and San, while the Soviets would occupy the lands to the east, Latvia, Lithuania and Estonia. Hitler and Stalin had sealed Poland's fate and Germany was about to plunge Europe into war.

POLAND

Germany and Poland had signed a ten-year non aggression pact on 26 January 1934, the Nazis' first diplomatic move after they seized power. Although the pact relieved tensions across Europe, particularly in the Soviet Union, Hitler had no intention of keeping it. Poland obstructed Germany's expansion in the east and he believed that the Poles were a sub-human Slavic race who had to be removed to make living space for Aryan Germans. The Polish Corridor had been taken from Germany under the Treaty of Versailles and separated East Prussia from the rest of Germany. It continued to be a controversial area which was treated like a lost territory.

Great Britain and France guaranteed Poland's independence following the occupation of Czechoslovakia in March 1939, but Hitler ignored their offer of assistance; they were too far away to intervene. He insisted on the annexation of Danzig and the return of the Polish Corridor.

On 3 April 1939, Field Marshal Wilhelm Keitel, chief of the High Command of the armed forces, was given a directive to prepare for Case White, the invasion of Poland. After a summer of diplomacy, the signing of the Ribbentrop-Molotov Pact on 23 August 1939 sealed Poland's fate. Hitler and Stalin had divided the country in two and all that was needed was an excuse to cross the border.

The excuse was Operation Himmler, a plan of subterfuge devised by Reinhard Heydrich and approved by Hitler. German soldiers staged a number of incidents along the Polish border, indicating attacks by Poles. The main one was carried out on 31 August 1939 at the radio station near the border town of Gleiwitz. Soldiers dressed in Polish Army uniforms captured the radio station and broadcast an anti-German message. Three men, prisoners of the Gestapo, were dressed as Poles, killed with a fatal injection and then shot. Their bodies were left as evidence at the radio station of a Polish attack. It became the justification for the invasion of Poland on 1 September 1939. Several prisoners were held at the concentration camp of Dachau for such subterfuge purposes and they were referred to as 'canned goods'.

In the early hours of 1 September 1939, the German battleship *Schleswig-Holstein* opened fire on installations at Danzig while Stuka bombers flew overhead. All along the Polish border German troops crossed over as Case White began. Chamberlain's attempts to contact Hitler failed and at 11am on 3 September he was forced to declare that Great Britain was 'now at war with Germany.'

Ribbentrop and Himmler discuss plans for a Greater Germany. (NARA-242-HB 22246a17)

Edward, who abdicated from the throne of Great Britain in 1936, and his wife Wallis Simpson, visit Hitler's Berghof in the Alps.

CHAPTER EIGHTEEN

GERMANY'S ARMED FORCES

THE REICH DEFENSIVE FORCES, *REICHSWEHR*

Germany's armed forces were severely restricted under articles 160 to 210 of the 1919 Treaty of Versailles. The Reichswehr came into existence in January 1921 under General Hans von Seeckt (1866–1936), a veteran of the Eastern Front who had served as Chief of Staff with the XIth Army and the Turkish Army.

The Reichswehr was limited to 100,000 troops (13.4 million served in the First World War), allowing Germany to only protect its borders and deal with internal unrest. Conscription was banned while associations and clubs were banned from military training and possessing weapons. The General Staff was also dissolved and troops were withdrawn from the Rhineland area along the French border; fortifications along the French border were demolished. While hundreds of thousands of men were demobilised, vast stocks of heavy artillery and surplus ammunition were handed over to the Allies. An Allied Control Commission supervised the reductions in manpower, weapons and equipment and then monitored the Reichswehr's activities.

The heads of the three armed forces. General Mackensen, a First World War veteran and Nazi supporter, and General Blomberg march alongside Hitler. (NARA-242-HB-11161a3)

THE ARMY, HEER

The Reichswehr Army was organised into two group commands, seven infantry divisions and three cavalry divisions. Seeckt introduced a new training programme for the army and in 1920 labour commando units were already being organised to get around the manpower limit. Veterans were also being secretly recruited into paramilitary units called Free Corps. Some of these units were deployed along the Polish border while others were used to deal with communist uprisings.

The mass confiscation of old weapons at the end of the First World War gave the army the opportunity to experiment

with new weapon designs. After 1923 weapons were secretly bought from Russia, allowing troops to train with modern rapid-firing assault rifles while the Allies were still using obsolete weapons. German police were also allowed to be issued with machine pistols because they were not covered by the treaty and they often became involved in internal security matters.

Germany's tank development in the First World War had been very limited and the treaty banned them altogether. However, experimental models were passed off as tractors while crews trained in secret in the Soviet Union. Seeckt was dismissed in October 1926 after making a number of controversial decisions.

THE NAVY, KRIEGSMARINE

The treaty limited Germany's powerful navy to six small battleships under 10,000 tonnes, six cruisers and twelve destroyers. All its U-boats had been scuttled while new ones were banned. Manpower was also reduced to 15,000 men. All the Naval Command could do was to prepare a naval strategy and discuss designs for surface ships and submarines.

THE AIR FORCE, LUFTWAFFE

Germany was banned from possessing military aircraft but General Seeckt secretly authorised a new German Air Force in 1923. While the government-backed commercial airline Lufthansa kept Germany's aircraft industry busy, it was also training pilots. Pilots and aircrew practised with gliding clubs across the country and they had 50,000 members by 1932. Designers worked on new monoplane designs and prototypes were tested in secret in the Soviet Union.

Swearing allegiance to the Führer. (NARA-242-HB-17003a2)

FUSING THE PARTY AND THE MILITARY

General Werner von Blomberg was appointed Minister of Defence on 1 January 1933 and he played an important part in helping the Nazis secure control over the armed forces. The relationship between the armed forces and Hitler changed significantly between 1933 and 1939. To begin with the generals tolerated the new Chancellor, believing that he was a political upstart who would soon resign as his predecessors had done. They were also concerned about the rise of the paramilitary SA.

After the SA leadership was decimated during the June 1934 Blood Purge, the organisation's influence waned and many generals started to accept Hitler. When President Hindenburg died in August 1934, Hitler became the self-appointed Supreme Commander of the Armed Forces. Blomberg ordered all members of the military to take an oath of personal loyalty to their Führer.

> I swear by God this sacred oath that I shall render unconditional obedience to Adolf Hitler, the Führer of the German Reich, supreme commander of the armed forces, and that I shall at all times be prepared, as a brave soldier, to give my life for this oath.

While some generals were unhappy with the new oath, the majority acquiesced. Hitler believed that it was treasonable to deviate from it. The generals were pleased to accept the reintroduction of conscription in March 1935, while the rapid expansion and rearmament of the armed forces meant that many senior officers were promoted.

THE WEHRMACHT, ARMED FORCES

In 1935 the Ministry of Defence was renamed the Ministry of War and Blomberg's title changed accordingly; he was also appointed Commander-in-Chief of the Armed Forces. Under the Defence Law decreed on 21 May 1935 the name 'Reichswehr' was replaced by 'Wehrmacht' for the combined armed forces of the Third Reich. Its rapid expansion created a shortage of experienced officers, and after exhausting the supply of retired and reserve officers, SA officers were recruited to make up the shortfall. NSDAP members were favoured and senior officers watched with dismay while these People's Officers exerted their influence over the rank and file. The result was a lowering of educational and military standards for the sake of increased political motivation.

Plans were also afoot to undermine the influence of senior officers over the German armed forces. In 1937 Colonel Walther Warlimont's report for the War Ministry suggested the reorganisation of the armed forces. It proposed there be one supreme commander supported by a high command to coordinate the three branches. It also recommended increasing the Führer's influence over military planning and strategic decisions at the expense of senior generals.

SUPREME COMMANDER OF THE ARMED FORCES

Following the Hossbach Conference in November 1937, when Hitler privately declared his plans for war, the Security Service fabricated scandals about General Blomberg and General Fritsch. Both were forced to resign. The post of Minister of War was abolished and Hitler became the Supreme Commander and Minister of War. Wilhelm Keitel, a general who carried out the Führer's wishes without question, was appointed Chief of Staff to head the new High Command of the Armed Forces. Fourteen generals and over 40 senior officers who were likely to oppose Hitler's plans were retired and replaced with Nazi sympathisers. At the same time Neurath was replaced as Foreign Minister by Joachim von Ribbentrop and Funk replaced Schacht at the Ministry of Economics. Hitler explained his reasons to the Reichstag on 20 February. Two weeks later the negotiations for the Austrian Anschluss began.

THE ARMED FORCES HIGH COMMAND: OKW

The German High Command was divided into four departments:

General Office — personnel and training
Operations Staff — operational planning
Foreign intelligence — collecting information on allies and enemies
Economic and Armament Office — supplies and logistics

COMMANDERS OF THE ARMED SERVICES

WERNER VON BLOMBERG (1878–1946)

Blomberg became adjutant general of the Reichswehr in 1927 and commander of the Konigsberg Defence District in 1929. He met Hitler in August 1930 and became a loyal supporter. On 1 January 1933, he was appointed Minister of Defence and head of the armed forces and he retained the post when the Nazis came to power at the end of the month.

Blomberg was dismayed by the SA's attempts to usurp the army and he was quietly relieved when the organisation's hierarchy was executed in June 1934. Following the death of President Hindenburg two months later, Blomberg called upon officers to make a personal oath of loyalty to the Führer. He was appointed supreme commander of the new Wehrmacht in May 1935 and headed the armed forces during the rearmament over the next three years. He was promoted to Field Marshal in 1936.

General Werner von Blomberg, Chief of the German Armed Forces. (NARA-242-HB-16330)

Blomberg was appalled by Hitler's plans for war which were announced at the Hossbach Conference, and relations between them deteriorated rapidly. Blomberg was a 59-year-old widower when he married 26-year-old secretary, Erna (or Margarete) Gruhn, on 12 January 1938; Hitler was their best man and Göring acted as a witness. Their new married life was marred by exaggerated rumours about Gruhn's past, originating from a dossier held by the chief of the Berlin Police. General Wilhelm Keitel had refused to tell Hitler but Göring made sure he found out. Gruhn's crime was to have appeared in pornographic photographs many years before. Hitler was furious and Blomberg resigned on 4 February 1938 and left for Capri with his wife, after refusing to annul his marriage.

WILHELM KEITEL (1882–1946)

Keitel was severely wounded serving as an officer in the First World War. He rose through the ranks and between 1929 and 1934 he was active in the organisation of the Reichswehr and the Wehrmacht. He started working for the Ministry of War at the end of 1935. Keitel was appointed Chief of the High Command of the Armed Forces, following the Blomberg-Fritsch affair and was promoted to full general in November 1938. General Alfred Jodl was his Chief of Operations Staff. Their roles were strictly controlled by Hitler and they became increasingly subservient to the Führer's wishes.

THE ARMED SERVICES HIGH COMMANDS

Each of the three armed services had its own high command, 'Oberkommando' (Oberkommando Heer was known as OKH), and they reported to OKW's planning staff.

Army High Command OKH	Colonel General Werner von Fritsch (1935–1938)
	Field Marshal Walther von Brauchitsch (1938–1941)
Navy High Command OKM	Grand Admiral Erich Raeder (1928–1943)
Air Force High Command OKL	Reich Marshall Hermann Göring (1935–1945)

THE FOREIGN INTELLIGENCE OFFICE, AUSLAND ABWEHR

The Office of Foreign Intelligence collected and analysed information on other countries. It was renamed the Foreign Intelligence Office of the Wehrmacht in February 1938.

WILHELM CANARIS (1887–1945)

Canaris was born in Aplerbeck in Westphalia. He served in the navy during the First World War, and was serving on the cruiser SMS *Dresden* when it was scuttled after the Battle of Falklands in 1914. He escaped through Argentina back to Germany and was then employed on secret missions in Spain. After the war, he organised Free Corps units before he was appointed as a staff officer in the Baltic fleets, rising to command the battleship *Schliesen*.

Canaris was a Nazi supporter to begin with, and in January 1935 he was appointed head of the Abwehr (the OKW's counterintelligence department) in the Ministry of War. Canaris was a complex character who wavered between supporting and opposing Hitler's policies and while he joined the Resistance, he continued working diligently for his own department. He also often drew the incorrect conclusions from foreign intelligence.

HANS OSTER (1888–1945)

Oster served in the army on the Western Front during the First World War, and in the Reichswehr until his dismissal following an affair in 1932. He was reemployed in the Foreign Intelligence Office. He opposed the Nazis after his superior officer, General von Bredow, was murdered in June 1934. Oster was appointed Canaris's chief of staff in 1935. They worked closely with General Halder's resistance group in September 1938. The proposed coup never materialised due to the ceding of the Sudetenland. The pair also sent a prominent officer, Fabian von Schlabrendorff, to London to warn the British government of Hitler's plans to invade Poland.

Armoured cars drive through Berlin's Brandenburg Gate. (NARA-242-HB-19790a4)

THE ARMY, *HEER*

KURT VON HAMMERSTEIN EQUORD (1878–1943)

Hammerstein Equord was a veteran who was promoted to command the army in 1930. He lobbied Hindenburg on behalf of the army generals against appointing Hitler as Chancellor. The Nazis forced him to resign in January 1934. He joined the senior army officers preparing to confront Hitler in 1938, but they backed down when British appeasement policies over the Sudetenland undermined their position. Hammerstein Equord was recalled to duty in September 1939 but he was retired in 1940 due to doubts about his loyalty.

WERNER VON FRITSCH (1880–1939)

Fritsch was a First World War veteran who was promoted to divisional commander in 1930 and lieutenant-general in July 1932. He was a reserved man who was shocked by the Nazis' approach to civil liberties, but he chose to stay silent. He replaced Hammerstein Equord in 1934 and his title changed to commander-in-chief in October 1935; he supervised the expansion and rearmament of the army. He protested against Hitler's plans to wage war during the Hossbach Conference in November 1937, believing that the army was not ready. At the start of 1938, he was accused of a homosexual offence dating back to November 1934. An unreliable witness had allegedly seen the general with a youth at Potsdam railroad station. Fritsch vehemently denied the charge but, as a lifelong bachelor, he was vulnerable to the accusation. Although an army court of honour acquitted him 'for proven innocence', his career was over and he resigned on 4 February 1938. He was later recalled by his old artillery regiment and he commanded it during the invasion of Poland. He was killed in action on 22 September 1939; several witnesses believed that he deliberately walked to his death.

WALTHER VON BRAUCHITSCH (1881–1948)

Brauchitsch served in the First World War and was a divisional commander by 1933. He became commander-in-chief of the army following Fritsch's resignation in February 1938. Although Brauchitsch disagreed with Hitler's plans, he felt bound by his oath of loyalty. His wife, a fanatical National Socialist, also urged him to support the Führer. When General Ludwig Beck asked for his cooperation during the general's conspiracy, he neither joined nor reported the plot. Brauchitsch was the senior ranking army officer at the outbreak of the Second World War.

LUDWIG BECK (1880–1944)

Beck served on the general staff in the First World War and was appointed adjutant general in October 1933. He became the Chief of the Army General Staff and played a major role in the military decisions concerning rearmament and expansion of the army, and the plans for the Anschluss. He objected to the plans to occupy the Sudetenland, believing that the army was unprepared. He gathered generals to oppose it but failed to get Britain's backing. He resigned on 18 August 1938.

DEFENCE DISTRICTS, WEHRKREIS

The army was split into administrative Defence Districts or *Wehrkreis*, numbered with a Roman numeral. During peacetime each one had a headquarters and one active infantry corps; the *Wehrkreis* commander was the corps commander.

ARMOURED DIVISION

1 *Schützen* brigade, 1 regiment with 2 battalions
1 panzer brigade with 2 panzer regiments each with 2 battalions
1 anti-tank battalion
1 artillery regiment with 2 battalions
1 motorcycle battalion
1 panzer signals battalion
1 pioneer battalion
1 reconnaissance battalion

The *Schützen* brigade had infantry mounted in halftracks; they were renamed *Panzergrenadiers* after 1942.

Hitler reviews the Wehrmacht's new armoured formations at Nuremberg. (NARA-242-HB-22665a5)

INFANTRY DIVISION

3 infantry regiments each with 3 battalions
1 light artillery regiment with 3 detachments
1 heavy artillery detachment
1 pioneer battalion
1 anti-tank detachment
1 observation detachment
1 propaganda detachment
1 news agency detachment
1 medical detachment
1 replacement battalion

The backbone of
the Wehrmacht,
the infantry.
(NARA-242-HB-
19796a8)

Brandenburgers were elite units trained along the same lines to British commandos or US Rangers. They were taught to capture and hold important structures or buildings, demolishing them if necessary; many soldiers were multi-lingual. Training was carried out at a secret location near Brandenburg. The Abwehr sent teams into Poland to capture key installations prior to the invasion in September 1939.

BORDER DEFENCES

France started building an elaborate defensive line, named after the French Minister of War Andre Maginot (1877–1932), along its eastern border in 1929. The Maginot Line stretched from the Swiss border to the town of Montmedy on the Belgian border. Fortifications could not be extended any further due to Belgian objections and rising costs. An elaborate system of forts and bunkers faced the German frontier by 1934 and while the French public were assured that they gave them protection, the military experts assumed that the Germans would move troops through the Ardennes and outflank them.

Hitler was convinced that France was committed to a defensive strategy and although he advocated a *Blitzkrieg* strategy, he wanted a similar line of fortifications opposite the Maginot Line in case Germany became involved in a two-front war. Work started on the West Wall in 1938 and a thin line of bunkers, trenches, barbed wire and tank obstacles was soon ready after a drafted labour force worked around the clock in dangerous conditions.

THE LIGHTNING WAR, BLITZKRIEG

The need for rapid movement on the battlefield, spearheaded by well trained and
armed troops supported by mobile artillery
units, had been identified in the First World
War. Shock tactics had been used to break
through the Allied lines during the final
German offensives of spring 1918 but they
were limited to the speed of the infantry
advance. Improved engines, suspensions and
weapons made it possible to build reliable
tanks, armoured cars and halftracks which
could drive deep into enemy territory. Dive
bombers could give close support while the
addition of a well-planned logistics system
made fast advances possible. The Reichswehr

General Werner
von Fritsch (second
from left) and other
generals discuss
military manoeuvres
with Hitler.
(NARA-242-HB-
23633a1)

developed the strategy of the lightning war, or *Blitzkrieg*, to take advantage of the developments.

The first German campaign Case White, *Fall Weiss*, was directed at Poland and over 60
infantry, armoured and mechanised divisions were divided into two army groups.

ARMY GROUP NORTH: COLONEL GENERAL FEDOR VON BOCK

Army Group Reserves	10th Panzer Division
	73rd Infantry Division
	206th Infantry Division
	208th Infantry Division

4TH ARMY: GENERAL OF ARTILLERY GÜNTHER VON KLUGE

Frontier Guard	207th Infantry Division
XIX Corps	3rd Panzer Division
	2nd Motorised Division
	20th Motorised Division
II Corps	3rd Infantry Division
	32nd Infantry Division
III Corps	50th Infantry Division
	'Netze' Infantry Brigade
Reserves	23rd Infantry Division
	218th Infantry Division

3RD ARMY: GENERAL OF ARTILLERY GEORG VON KÜCHLER

XXVI Corps	1st Motorised Division
XXI Corps	21st Infantry Division
	228th Infantry Division
I Corps	Panzer-Division *Kempf*
	11th Infantry Division
	61st Infantry Division

Wodrig Corps	1st Infantry Division
	12th Infantry Division (later XXVI Corps)
Brand Corps	Lötzen and Goldap Infantry Brigades
Reserves	217th Infantry Division
	1st Cavalry Brigade

ARMY GROUP SOUTH: COLONEL GENERAL GERD VON RUNDSTEDT

VII Corps	27th Infantry Division
	68th Infantry Division
	1st Mountain Division
Reserves	62nd Infantry Division
	213th Infantry Division
	221st Infantry Division

8TH ARMY: GENERAL OF INFANTRY JOHANNES BLASKOWITZ

X Corps	24th Infantry Division
	30th Infantry Division
XIII Corps	10th Infantry Division
	17th Infantry Division
	SS-Division (motorised)

10TH ARMY: GENERAL OF ARTILLERY WALTER VON REICHENAU

XI Corps	18th Infantry Division
	19th Infantry Division
XVI Corps	1st Panzer-Division
	14th Infantry Division
	31st Infantry Division
IV Corps	4th Infantry Division
	46th Infantry Division
XV Corps	2nd Light Division
XIV Corps	4th Panzer Division
	13th Motorised Division
	29th Motorised Division
Reserves	1st Light Division
	3rd Light Division

14TH ARMY: COLONEL GENERAL WILHELM LIST

XXII Corps	2nd Mountain Division
VIII Corps	5th Panzer-Division
	8th Infantry Division
	28th Infantry Division
	239th Infantry Division
XVII Corps	7th Infantry Division
	44th Infantry Division
	45th Infantry Division

XVIII Corps	2nd Panzer-Division
	4th Light Division
	3rd Mountain Division

SLOVAKIAN ARMY BERNOLAK: GENERAL FERDINAND ČATLOŠ
1st Infantry Division Janošík
2nd Infantry Division Škultéty
20th Infantry Division Razus
Fast Troops Group Kaličniak

THE NAVY, *KRIEGSMARINE*

NAVAL STRATEGY

The Versailles Treaty limited the German Navy to six small battleships, six cruisers and twelve destroyers; submarines were not allowed. Germany did not want to engage in naval rivalry with Britain and in May 1935 it set out to secure a naval agreement which would assist Hitler's plans for an Anschluss with Austria. The Kriegsmarine suggested limiting its fleet to 35 per cent of the tonnage of the Royal Navy with five battleships, 21 cruisers and 64 destroyers. It would, however, remove the ban on submarines. The British government agreed to Germany's request, without consulting the League of Nations or referring to France or Italy. While the agreement secured British domination of the high seas, it weakened the diplomatic ties between Britain and France, strengthening Germany's position on mainland Europe.

Hitler meets his admirals. (NARA-242-HB-20971)

249

Memorial for the Battle of Skagerrak – the German name for the largest naval battle of the First World War, the Battle of Jutland – which took place on 31 May 1916. (NARA-242-HB-20685a10)

Launching the hull of the pocket battleship, *Admiral Graf Spee*. (NARA-242-HB-06823)

The Kriegsmarine high command immediately discussed future naval strategy and there were two schools of thought. While some wanted a small surface fleet and a large submarine fleet for coastal protection, others called for a large surface fleet and a small submarine fleet. The Wehrmacht's military strategists believed that the next war would start against Poland or France, and Britain would not become a threat until mainland Europe had been conquered. Orders for a large surface fleet with a small number of U-boats were placed and the shipyards began work immediately.

The plan was codenamed Z-Plan and the Kriegsmarine planned to expand to 800 ships and 201,000 men by 1945 at a cost of 33 billion RM. The final fleet would have 13 battleships and battle cruisers, 15 pocket battleships, 4 aircraft carriers, 23 cruisers, 22 large destroyers called *Spähkreuzer* and over 700 smaller support vessels.

Whether the German shipyards could have built the ships or if the rest of Europe would have accepted the expansion are matters for speculation. Germany broke the naval treaty with Britain in April 1939, expecting that they would be at war sooner than originally planned. The shipyards were ordered to increase production, but by September 1939 only eleven ships of light cruiser class or larger were ready, while another seven were under construction. Only 21 destroyers and 57 U-boats were ready for coastal protection.

The outbreak of war diverted resources from naval production to the army and the Luftwaffe. Z-Plan was stopped and incomplete ships were scrapped. The shipyards had to switch to building submarines; there was no time to complete a surface fleet.

THE NAVAL COMMANDERS

HANS VON FRIEDEBURG (1895-1945)

Friedeburg served on surface ships and U-boats in the First World War. He was promoted to lieutenant commander in 1933 and he was appointed to the Naval High Command in 1934 with Heinrich Himmler's help.

Hitler reviews the growing German fleet. (NARA-242-HB-34972a18)

ERICH RAEDER (1876–1960)

Raeder was a chief of staff during the First World War and served in the Battle of Jutland on 31 May 1916. He was appointed chief of the Naval High Command in 1928. Although he was not a dedicated Nazi, he was impressed by Hitler and he accepted the post of Commander-in-Chief of the Navy in 1935. Raeder proposed the Z-Plan and he directed the rearmament of the Kriegsmarine. After declining the honour several times, he accepted the rank of Grand Admiral in 1939.

KARL DÖNITZ (1891–1980)

Dönitz served in the Naval Air Arm in the First World War and was captured on a U-boat at the end of the war. After the Armistice, he was an inspector of torpedo boats until he transferred to cruisers; he eventually captained the *Emden*. Dönitz was a dedicated Nazi and was appointed to head the new U-boat Command in September 1935.

THE LUFTWAFFE

Military aviation was prohibited under the terms of the Treaty of Versailles so civil aviation was placed under military control, allowing a new air force to be developed. The construction of civil aircraft was forbidden until 1922 and designers spent the time experimenting with metal monoplane prototypes, with variable-pitch propellers, cantilevered wings and retractable undercarriages. Manufacturers included Messerschmitt, Junkers, Heinkel, Dornier and Focke Wulf and the new designs made Lufthansa the most technically advanced commercial airline in the world. While military pilots trained with Lufthansa, aircrew trained in secret in Russia. Many pilots also obtained flying experience with private gliding and flying clubs across Germany.

Luftwaffe anti-aircraft guns and planes battle it out over Nuremberg's Zeppelin Field. (NARA-242-HB-22660a2)

Reich Air Commissioner Hermann Göring became head of the Reich Air Travel Ministry in March 1933; it was a cover for military activities. The German Air Sports Association absorbed private and national organisations on 15 May 1933, taking responsibility for recruitment and training of pilots and aircrews. The date would later become the Luftwaffe's official birthday. Many members of the National Socialist Flyers Corps transferred to the Association, giving it a strong Nazi base.

In March 1935, Göring unveiled the new Luftwaffe with himself as the new Commander-in-Chief. At the same time the Luftwaffe absorbed members of gliding and flying clubs and took command of army flak units. Germany's new military air force had 1,900 planes and over 20,000 officers and men, facts that surprised and concerned the world. The Luftwaffe split Germany into six air circuits, or *luftkreise*, which were organised as follows:

Group (*Geschwader*)	120 planes organised into three wings
Wing (*Gruppen*)	40 planes organised into three squadrons
Squadron (*Staffeln*)	12–16 planes

Some bomber groups had double the number of wings and planes.

The Luftwaffe was held on standby during the Anschluss with Austria, and Göring threatened to bomb Czechoslovakia ahead of the occupation of the Sudetenland in September 1938. Although aircraft production slowed down in 1938, Germany had over 4,000 military planes by the summer of 1939, organised as follows:

9 hunting groups	1,100 Messerschmitt Bf 109E single-engine fighters
4 destroyer groups	1,100 Messerschmitt Bf 110 twin-engine heavy fighters
4 dive fighting groups	290 Junkers Ju 87 Stuka dive bombers
11 fighting groups	1,100 Heinkel He 111 and Dornier Do 17Z bombers
500 Ju 52 transport planes	
300 reconnaissance planes	

Only twelve Junkers Ju 88 had been completed due to design difficulties.

In September 1939, over 1,600 combat aircraft of Air Fleet (*Luftflotten*) I and IV attacked Poland. They quickly destroyed the Polish Air Force, leaving squadrons free to support ground attacks. Another 2,600 aircraft of Luftflotten II and III faced France and Britain in the west.

LUFTWAFFE STRATEGY

Walther Wever, Chief of the Luftwaffe General Staff, held war games in December 1934 and he concluded that Germany needed long-range bombers capable of striking at French and Russian industries. The long-range Ural Bomber was developed to support the strategy.

Wever died in an air crash on 3 June 1936 and Luftwaffe planning changed under Ernst Udet and Albert Kesselring. They wanted a short-range tactical air force capable of destroying the enemy's air force and their support ground troops. Production was switched to fast medium bombers and dive-bombers, a move which pleased Hitler; he was only interested in the quantity rather than the quality of bombers built.

In August 1936, 20 German Ju-52 transport planes ferried 10,000 of General Franco's Nationalist troops from Morocco to Spain at the beginning of the Civil War; it was the first large airlift in history. By November over 200 German aircraft had been deployed to Spain and they flew with the Condor Legion. Pilots spent the next two years developing new flying tactics and urban bombing techniques, raiding many places such as Guernica and Barcelona.

COMMANDER OF THE LUFTWAFFE

HERMANN GÖRING (1893–1946)

Göring served as an infantry officer in the First World War before transferring to the German Air Force; he became commander of Baron Manfred von Richthofen's Flying Circus in 1918. Following the Armistice he worked at the Fokker Aircraft Works as an advisor for the Danish government, as a stunt pilot and as a commercial pilot. He met Carin von Kantzow in Sweden and she divorced her aristocratic husband to marry the glamorous, yet impoverished, German pilot. She introduced him to Hitler in the autumn of 1922 and he was appointed commander of the SA in December. Göring was wounded during the 1923 Munich Putsch but he escaped to Austria and Italy before returning to Sweden. He became addicted to morphine as he recovered from his wound and he was jailed for possession of drugs. Göring returned to Germany in 1926 following an amnesty for political activists and he became one of the first NSDAP Reichstag delegates in 1928.

Field Marshall Hermann Göring. (NARA-242-HB-32811)

By 1932 he was the President of the Chamber and he abused his position on several occasions to help the NSDAP secure power. He was then appointed Reich Minister without Portfolio, Reich Commissioner for Air and Prussian Minister President. He was also appointed Prussian Minister of the Interior, aryanising Germany's largest police force. Although he was implicated in the Reichstag fire in February 1933, he organised the arrest of 4,000 Communist and Social Democrat supporters immediately afterwards. He was a key organiser for the Berlin operations during the Blood Purge in June 1934 and he was rewarded by being appointed Hitler's deputy in December.

Göring relaxing at his hunting lodge. (NARA-242-HB-16021a4)

The Luftwaffe flies overhead. (NARA-242-HB-15079a57)

Göring used his position to acquire a small palace in Berlin, a large house at Berchtesgaden near Hitler's Berghof, and a large estate north of the capital where he pursued his passion for hunting. His estate house was built in the style of a hunting lodge and it was maintained by servants dressed in period costume. He also enjoyed fine art and he abused his position to enlarge his personal collection. His first wife had died in 1931 and Göring had her remains interred on the estate, naming it Karinhall in her memory.

By this time Göring was an overweight egotist with a love of uniforms, and his elaborate manners and childish behaviour irritated many other Nazi leaders. He married actress Emmy Sonnemann in April 1935 in a lavish affair and she often took on the role of unofficial first lady of the Third Reich. Her flamboyant character made her unpopular with many Nazi leaders.

Göring was appointed commander of the Luftwaffe when it was unveiled on 1 March 1935 but he left the administration to his able assistants, Erhard Milch and Ernst Udet. He was promoted to full general in 1936.

Due to Hjalmar Schacht's cautious approach in the Reich Ministry of Economics, Hitler appointed Göring Commissioner Plenipotentiary for the Four Year Plan, giving him powers to prepare industry for rearmament. He founded the state-sponsored Hermann Göring Reich Works steel manufacturing company when the private sector refused to fulfil his orders. It was yet another way to increase his personal fortune.

Göring plotted the Blomberg-Fritsch crisis in February 1938 and was rewarded with the rank of Field Marshal. He also played a central role in the Austrian Anschluss and threatened to bomb Prague if the Czechoslovakians refused to let German troops enter the Sudetenland. He believed that his Luftwaffe was invincible and on 9 August 1939 he bragged that 'not a single bomb will fall on the Ruhr. If an enemy plane reaches the Ruhr, my name is not Hermann Göring, you can call me Meier!' He would rue his words over the next six years.

However, Göring disagreed with Hitler's plans to invade Poland and he used a Swedish intermediary to negotiate with Prime Minister Chamberlain; the attempt failed. Just before the invasion, Hitler appointed Göring Chairman of the Reich Council for National Defence and made him his successor in the event of his death. He also bestowed a new title on his favourite lieutenant – Reich Marshal (*Reichsmarschall*).

THE LUFTWAFFE FOUNDERS

ERHARD MILCH (1892–1972)

Milch served as an airman in the First World War and he continued to work in civil aviation, joining Junkers in 1923. Three years later he was appointed director of Lufthansa's finance division. He was also closely connected with the Nazis and in 1933 Göring appointed him State Secretary in the Air Ministry and the Luftwaffe's armament chief. When the Nazis discovered that his mother was Jewish, Göring forced her to sign a legal affidavit stating that Milch had been fathered out of wedlock with another woman. Milch solved many of the Luftwaffe's early technical problems and he had been promoted to general by 1938; he commanded the Fifth Air Fleet in September 1939.

Göring and the heads of the Luftwaffe. (NARA-242-HB-05639)

ERNST UDET (1896–1941)

Udet served as a fighter-pilot in the First World War and then became a professional flyer and stunt pilot. He was appointed Inspector of Fighters in 1935 and Chief in the Reich Air Ministry's technical office the following year. Udet was a technical genius who drew on experience to advocate speed and manoeuvrability in the skies; he was a supporter of fighter and fighter bomber production.

Shadows of military planes flying over Nuremburg's Zeppelin Field during a military parade. (NARA-242-HB-15079a22)

WALTHER WEVER (1887–1936)

Wever was director of infantry training for the Reichswehr and he was appointed chief of the Luftwaffe's Air Command Office in September 1933. He was a strong advocate of strategic bombing; he was killed in an air crash in June 1936.

ALBERT KESSELRING (1885–1960)

Kesselring served in the First World War and rose through the ranks following the Armistice until he was discharged in 1933. He joined the Reich Commissariat for Aviation and became Chief General Staff of the Luftwaffe following Wever's death in 1936. He advocated tactical bombers and worked on combined ground and air tactics for the planned Blitzkriegs. Kesselring was the head of Air Force I, Luftflotte I during the invasion of Poland in September 1939.

Saluting a
naval regatta.
(NARA-242-HB-
20655a2)

Panzers drive
past the Führer.
(NARA-242-HB-
19777)

CHAPTER NINETEEN

MILITARY HARDWARE

At the end of the First World War, the German armed forces were stripped of many of their heavy weapons. Tanks and military planes were banned and only a small number of old warships were allowed. The secret development of new weapons and secret training of crews progressed slowly under the Weimar Republic but they were accelerated under the Nazis. By the 1935 Nuremberg Rally, Germany was ready to show the world that it had a strong army and air force, while the navy was preparing to build new ships.

THE TANKS, *PANZERS*

The Treaty of Versailles had banned the design, manufacture and deployment of tanks but a secret study of First World War tactics concluded that the German army needed a range of tanks for different roles. The first tank prototype, called the 'Large Tractor', was tested in 1926 and it was armed with a 75mm gun. Two years later the 'Light Tractor' prototype appeared armed with a 37mm gun.

General Oswald Lutz and his chief of staff, Lieutenant-Colonel Heinz Guderian, developed the theory of mechanised warfare. Guderian was a First World War veteran who thought that radio communications were essential to control the fast moving armoured battles proposed by 'lightning war', *Blitzkrieg*.

Guderian wanted a mixture of tank designs supported by armoured halftracks carrying infantry and armoured cars carrying out reconnaissance. He initially wanted two designs. A slow moving tank, armed with a 37mm cannon and machine guns, would support the infantry. A fast tank, armed with a 75mm cannon and thick armour, would break through enemy lines. He later asked for a main combat tank combining the best features of the two designs. The breakthrough tank would be the Panzer IV while the main combat tank would be the Panzer III. He also asked for a heavy tank armed with a 150mm cannon, but the specifications were impractical.

A small training tank was produced while the prototypes were being designed and built; it was designated the Panzer I. Further delays in production of the Panzer III and IV required a second interim design, the Panzer II. After seeing Guderian's early manoeuvres in 1934, Hitler sanctioned the formation of the first tank battalion. The number of panzer division formations grew rapidly and by September 1939 the Wehrmacht had seven Panzer divisions. Many were equipped with LT-35 tanks captured in Czechoslovakia; an improved LT-38 was also being manufactured.

Guderian was promoted to General of Armoured Troops in 1938 and he saw the Blitzkrieg in action in September 1939 when he served as commander of XIX Army Corps in Poland.

TANK SPECIFICATIONS

Army vehicles were known as Special Purpose Vehicles, or SDKfz and each one had a number; the Panzer I was the SDKfz 101. Tanks were called armoured fighting vehicles, or *Panzerkampfwagen*, shortened to Panzer. Each model had a numbered mark and a letter marking the variation, the *Ausführung*; for example the Panzer Kpfw II, Ausf F was the Mark II tank, variation F.

PANZER I, SDKFZ 101

Designs for a training tank were drawn up in 1932, but production did not get underway until 1934. The small hull and turret were only big enough for two crew men, while its thin armour, a lack of anti-tank armament and short range severely limited its use. Over 120 of them saw combat during the Spanish Civil War and experiments were carried out with heavier armament. By September 1939 nearly 1,900 Panzer Is had been produced and despite the tank's limitations, they allowed the Wehrmacht to practise armoured warfare.

PANZER KPFW I AUSF A

Manufacturers	Krupp, Henschel, MAN, Krupp-Gruson, Daimler-Benz	
Size	weight	5.88 tonnes
	length	4.02m
	width	2.06m
	height	1.72m
Armament	primary	2 x 7.92mm MG 13 machine guns with 2250 rounds
Hull Armour	front	13mm
	side	15mm
	rear	13mm
	top	6mm
	bottom	6mm
Turret Armour	front	15mm
	side	13mm
	rear	13mm
	top	8mm
	bottom	8mm
Engine	100 hp Maybach NL38TR six-cylinder engine	
Speed	37km/h on road	
Range	Up to 145km on road, 97km off road	

PANZER II, SDKFZ 121

Following delays in the design of the Panzer III and Panzer IV, several manufacturers were called upon to start building an interim tank. It was to have a 20mm cannon and a three-man crew. Work started in 1935 and first one rolled off the production line eighteen months later.

PANZER KPFW II AUSF F

Manufacturers	MAN, Daimler–Benz, Henschel, Wegmann, Alkett, MIAG, FAMO	
Size	weight	11.5 tonnes
	length	4.81m
	width	2.22m
	height	1.99m
Armament	primary	20-mm KwK 30 cannon with 180 rounds
	secondary	7.92-mm MG 34 machine gun with 2250 rounds
Hull Armour	front	35mm
	side	20mm
	rear	15mm
	top	15mm
	bottom	5mm
Turret Armour	front	35mm
	side	15mm
	rear	15mm
	top	10mm
	bottom	10mm
Engine	140 hp Maybach 6-cylinder in-line engine	
Speed	maximum 40km/h on and off road	
Range	up to 200km on and off road.	

PANZER III, SDKFZ 141

Design of the Panzer III started in January 1934, and Variation A tanks, armed with 37mm cannons, were delivered in 1937. However, mass production of the Variation F, armed with 50mm cannons, did not start until 1939 and only 98 were ready for the invasion of Poland. It had a five-man crew, a driver, radio operator/bow machine-gunner, gunner, loader and commander.

PANZER III, AUSF F

Size	weight	23.0 tonnes
	length	6.41m
	width	2.90m
	height	2.5m
Armament	primar	1 × 37mm KwK 36 L/46.5, Ausf A–F
	secondary	2 x coaxial and 1 x hull 7.92 machine guns
Hull Armour	front	30mm
	side	30mm
	rear	30mm
	top	10mm
	bottom	5mm
Turret Armour	front	30mm
	side	30mm
	rear	30mm
	top	10mm
	bottom	5mm
Engine		12-cylinder Maybach HL 120 TRM 300 PS
Speed		40km/h road, 20km/h off road
Range		155km

A Panzer IV tracks through deep mud. (NARA-242-HB-39552)

PANZER IV, SDKFZ 161

Designs for a medium tractor, or 'accompanying vehicle' – armed with a short-barrelled 75mm gun to destroy anti-tank guns and pillboxes in support of infantry attacks – were requested in January 1934. Production of the five-man tank started in 1936 but the armour of the Variation A was too thin and only 35 were built. The Variation B had thicker armour, a stronger engine and an improved transmission but only 44 were built before the Variation C appeared in 1938 with a stronger turret. Production ceased after only 140 had been made. The Variation D appeared in August 1939 with a higher velocity gun and thicker armour. The upgrades stalled production and only 211 had been produced by September 1939, leaving the Panzer III as the main battle tank in Poland and France.

PANZER IV AUSF D

Size	weight	18.1 tonnes
	length	7.02m
	width	2.88m
	height	2.68m
Armament	primary	75mm KwK 37 L/24 main gun with 87 rounds
	secondary	2 or 3 x 7.92-mm machine guns
Hull Armour	front	30mm
	side	20mm
	rear	20mm
	top	10mm
	bottom	5mm
Turret Armour	front	30mm
	side	20mm
	rear	20mm
	top	10mm
	bottom	5mm
Engine	12-cylinder Maybach HL 120 TRM 300 PS	
Speed	42km/h road, 16km/h off road	
Range	200km	

PANZER 35(T)

The Czech Army chose Škoda's prototypes in 1934; the first deliveries of the Light Tank Model 35 (*Lehký Tank vzor 35*) were made in December 1936. Over 430 were built over the next three years and organised into four mobile divisions, used to suppress rioting in the Sudetenland and to stop Hungarian and Polish troops crossing the border. Over 240 tanks were seized by the Germans when they occupied Czechoslovakia and they renamed it the LTM 35 tank. Production of the four-man tank continued and many were deployed in the Polish campaign. The tank was renamed the Panzer 35(t) in January 1940 (the (t) designation stood for *Tschechisch* or 'Czech').

Manufacturer	Škoda, Českomoravská-Kolben-Daněk's	
Size	weight	10.5 tonnes
	length	4.90m
	width	2.06m
	height	2.37m
Armament	primary	37mm KwK 34(t) gun with 72 rounds
	secondary	2 x 7.92mm machine guns with 1,800 rounds
Turret Armour	front	25mm
	side	15mm
	rear	15mm
	top	8mm
	bottom	8mm
Hull Armour	front	25mm
	side	16mm
	rear	19mm

	top	8mm
	bottom	8mm
Engine		4-cylinder, water-cooled Škoda T11/0 120 horsepower
Range		120km or 190km
Speed		34km/h

PANZER 38(T), SDKFZ 140

An improved version of the LT 35 was ordered by the Czech Army in July 1938 but none had been made by the time the Germans occupied the country. The Wehrmacht ordered production to begin under the name LTM 38, and 78 were ready for the invasion of Poland. The driver and bow machine gunner/radio operator sat in the hull while the commander, gunner and loader sat in the turret. It was renamed the Panzer 38(t) in January 1940.

Manufacturer	ČKD	
Size	weight	9.85 tonnes
	length	4.61m
	width	2.14m
	height	2.25m
Hull Armour	front	25mm
	side	25mm
	rear	25mm
	top	10mm
	bottom	10mm
Turret Armour	front	25mm
	side	25mm
	rear	25mm
	top	10mm
	bottom	10mm
Armament	primary	1 x 37mm KwK 38(t) L/47.8 with 90 rounds
	secondary	2 x 7.92mm ZB53 machine gun with 2,250 rounds
Engine		Praga Type TNHPS/II water-cooled, 6-cylinder 125 PS
Speed		42km/h on road and 15km/h off road
Range		250km on road and 100km cross-country

ARMOURED CARS, LEICHTER PANZERSPÄHWAGEN

The Light Armoured Reconnaissance Vehicle was a four-wheel drive armoured car; it had an Auto Union chassis with an angled armoured body and turret. The open turret was protected by a wire-mesh anti-grenade screen while the two-man crew used vision ports cut into the armour. The armoured cars were organised into reconnaissance battalions, *Aufklärungs-Abteilungs*, and although they were useful where there were good road networks, Sdkfz 250 halftracks had to carry out reconnaissance across rough terrain. Several models were manufactured; the Sakfz 222 had an extra crew member.

SdKfz 221	The basic model armed with a single machine gun
SdKfz 221	Armed with 28mm sPzB41 gun in a modified turret
SdKfz 222	Armed with a 20mm KwK 30 L/55 auto cannon and a machinegun
SdKfz 223	Radio equipped version with 'bed-frame' antenna over the body

SDKFZ 221

Manufacturer	Schicau and Maschinenfabrik Niedersachsen	
Hull Armour	front	8mm
	side	8mm
	rear	5mm
	top	5mm
	bottom	5mm
Turret Armour	front	8mm
	side	8mm
	rear	5mm
	top	5mm
	bottom	5mm
Armament	primary	1 x machine gun
Engine	Horch 3.5 67 kW (90 hp)	
Range	300km	
Speed	80km/hr on road and 40km/h cross-country	

ANTI-TANK AND ANTI-AIRCRAFT GUNS

The prototype 88mm anti-aircraft gun (*Flugabwehr-Kanone* 18 or FlaK 18) appeared in 1928 mounted on a cruciform gun carriage and it needed a SdKfz 7 halftrack to tow it. The gun had a 360° arc and could fire over fifteen rounds a minute. Production increased under Nazi rule and after it proved to be an all round anti-aircraft and anti-tank weapon in the Spanish Civil War, the modified FlaK 36 was introduced with an armoured shield.

The 88mm FlaK gun could be used in an anti-tank or anti-aircraft role. (NARA-242-HB-23639)

The Pak 36 (*Panzerabwehrkanone* 36) was a small anti-tank gun which could be man-handled. It fired a 37mm calibre shell and had an effective range of 300m.

The 75mm FK16nA (75mm *Feld Kanone 16 neuer Art*, or new artillery field gun) was a re-barrelled version of the First World War era 77mm FK16. It had a centre trail, wooden spoked wheels and had to be horse-drawn. The redesigned 75mm FK18 was lighter and had a split trail but it was not used until 1938; the FK38 had a longer barrel for a higher velocity.

A camouflaged Pak36 anti-aircraft gun. (NARA-242-HB-14738)

SHIPS AND U-BOATS OF THE *KREIGSMARINE*

BATTLESHIPS, SCHLACHTSCHIFF

Germany was allowed to keep six active pre-Dreadnought battleships from the Braunschweig and Deutschland classes under the terms of the Versailles Treaty, and another two on reserve. These 14,200 tonne ships had been built in 1904 and 1905 and they were very outdated. The Braunschweig class had been decommissioned by 1917 but two had been kept at sea for coastal defence and training purposes. They were armed with four 28mm (10-inch) guns, had a range of 7,725km and a maximum speed of 18.5 knots.

The original design for a new 35,000 tonne Class F battleship complied with the Versailles Treaty. The *Gneisenau* and *Scharnhorst* were laid down in 1935 and they were armed with eight 33mm (13-inch) guns. It was soon clear that the new French battleships were larger and Germany responded. The *Bismarck* and *Tirpitz* were laid down in 1936 and although they were officially classed at 35,000 tonnes, they had secretly been upgraded to 50,000.

BISMARK CLASS

	displacement 50,956 tonnes	
	2,092 crew	
	4 aircraft	
Dimensions	length	251m
	beam	36m
	draft	9.9m
Armament	primary	8 x 15-inch
		12 x 6-inch
		16 x 4-inch
	secondary	16 x 37mm
		20 x 20mm
Armour Deck		80–120mm
		belt up to 320mm
		turrets up to 360mm

Performance speed 30.1 knots

      range 10,035km at 16 knots, 6,020km at 30 knots

AIRCRAFT CARRIER, FLUGZEUGTRÄGER

The Class A Aircraft Carrier, the *Graf Zeppelin*, was laid down in December 1936. Although the hull was launched two years later, Germanys only aircraft carrier was never completed and it was scrapped.

HEAVY CRUISERS, SCHWERE KREUZER

Five were ordered but only *Admiral Hipper* and *Blucher* were ready by September 1939. The *Prinz Eugen* was commissioned a year later; the *Seydlitz* and the *Lutzow* were scrapped. They had a 10,000 tonnes displacement and a crew of 1,340. Their main armament were 8 x 203mm guns; they also had 12 x 100mm, 12 x 37mm and 8 x 20mm guns as secondary armament.

 The three Deutschland Class heavy cruisers, *Deutschland, Admiral Scheer* and *Admiral Graf Spee*, were launched between 1931 and 1934. They were referred to as 'pocket battleships' because of the amount of firepower they had. They had a 16,200 tonnes displacement and a crew of 1,150. Their main armaments were 6 x 280mm guns and 8 x 150mm guns; they had 6 x 105mm, 8 x 37mm and 10 x 20mm guns as secondary armament. They also had eight torpedo tubes.

CRUISERS, KREUZER

Hundreds turn out to view a naval regatta led by a cruiser. (NARA-242-HB-07780)

The German Navy kept four obsolete pre-Dreadnought Deutschland Class cruisers, *Schlesien, Schleswig-Holstein, Hannover* and *Hessen* under the Treaty of Versailles. The first three new 'K' Class cruisers, *Konigsberg, Karlsruhe* and *Koln*, adhered to the 6,000 tonnes unloaded displacement limit set under the Treaty of Versailles; they had a crew of 610. It was soon discovered that they suffered from structural and stability problems, limiting them to coastal waters. Their main armaments were 3 x 150mm guns; they had 6 x 88mm, 8 x 37mm and 8 x 20mm guns as secondary armament. They also had eight torpedo tubes. Two redesigned Leipzig Class cruisers ignored the Treaty of Versailles and they rectified the problems of the K Class; the *Leipzig* was commissioned in 1931 and *Nürnberg* in 1934. They had a displacement of 8,380 tonness and a crew of 850. They had the same armament as the K Class cruisers.

AUXILIARY CRUISERS, HILFSKREUZER

On the outbreak of war, the German Navy commissioned eleven auxiliary cruisers ranging from 9,400 tonnes down to 3,900 tonnes. They were merchantmen usually armed with 6 x 150mm guns and a range of smaller secondary guns, torpedoes and mines. All the guns were hidden behind fake superstructure and the ships sailed under neutral flags. The first one was launched in March 1940.

DESTROYERS, ZERSTÖRER

The first four 1934 destroyers were equipped for mine laying but they had many serious design faults. The forward turrets could not be used in heavy seas and the turbine engines were underpowered. Modifications to the next twelve 1934A destroyers resolved some of the problems while the larger 1936 destroyers solved more. Only six had been completed when a 1936A destroyer was introduced with a new 150mm gun.

1924 Model Torpedo Boats. (NARA-242-HB-07781)

ESCORT VESSELS, FLOTTENBEGLEITERS

The original escort vessels had unreliable engines and suffered from poor seaworthiness. Few were used and while a fast escort vessel (*Schnelle Flottenbegleiter*) was planned, none were built.

MINE LAYING AND SWEEPING

The German Navy had no specific mine laying vessels at the start of the war and mining operations were carried out by cruisers, destroyers, torpedo boats and submarines. The Versailles Treaty allowed the navy to have 34 coal-fired steam driven minesweepers but they were converted into submarine tenders, training ships and escorts when the new *Minensuchboot 1935* appeared. These heavily armed vessels were manoeuvrable and seaworthy but they were also expensive to build; they were quickly replaced by a simpler design.

The smaller R-Boat, *Räumboote*, was designed to operate in shallow waters and often escorted larger ships and

U-boats to and from their bases. Pathmarker boats (*Sperrbrecher*) were built to withstand mine explosions and they were used to lead convoys through mined areas. They were soon equipped with the VES-System, a magnetic field generator designed to detonate magnetic mines.

TORPEDO BOATS, TORPEDOBOOT

The original 1923 and 1924 model torpedo boats were small destroyers armed with torpedoes. The new 1935 and 1937 torpedo boats were smaller and faster, having been designed for torpedo attacks, escort duty, mine laying and coastal patrolling. The 1939 model Naval Torpedo Boat (*Flottentorpedoboot*) was larger and similar to destroyer escorts in other navies.

FAST ATTACK BOATS, SCHNELLBOOTEN

Only 18 S-Boats were in service in September 1939 but they soon took over coastal duties even though they could only carry six mines. Many more were made and the Allies eventually called them E-Boats.

SUBMARINES, U-BOATS

The Type I U-boat prototype was launched in 1935 and while Type IIAs were manoeuvrable and fast, they had a limited range and a limited number of torpedoes. The Type IIB, IIC and IID U-boats were longer and they could travel further. Around 45 had been built by September 1939.

Moored
Type I U-boats.
(NARA-242-HB-
16066)

TYPE IIB

Dimensions	length	42.7m
	beam	4.1m
	diving depth	150m
Displacement	279 tonnes surface	
	414 tonnes submerged	
Speed	13 knots surface	
	7 knots submerged	
Range	4,985km at 8 knots surface	
	70km at 4 knots submerged	
Armament	3 x bow torpedo tubes	
	5 torpedoes or 18 mines; 1 x 20mm	

The Type VIIB and VIIC U-boats were longer still and they had a stronger hull to increase their diving depth.

TYPE VIIB

Dimensions	length	66,60m
	beam	6.20m
	diving depth	280 m
Displacement	769 tonnes surface	
	871 tonnes submerged	
Performance	speed	17.7 knots
	7.6 knots submerged	
Range	13,675km at 10 knots surface	
	209km at 2 knots submerged	
Armament	4 x bow torpedo tubes	
	1 x stern torpedo tube	
	14 torpedoes or 39 mines	
	1 x 88mm deck gun	
	1 x 37mm deck gun	
	2 x 20mm deck guns	

PLANES OF THE LUFTWAFFE

MESSERSCHMITT BF 109: SHORT RANGE FIGHTER

The prototype of Willy Messerschmitt's Bf 109 was tested on 28 May 1935 and the first production model, the Bf 109B-1, was delivered at the beginning of 1937. The new fighters performed well in the Spanish Civil War later that year and the Bf 109C-1 appeared in the autumn of 1937 with an improved engine. Arado, Erla, Focke-Wolf and Fieseler built them under licence, and by September 1939 over 1,000 were in service.

MESSERSCHMITT BF-109G-6

Dimensions	length	9.02m
	width	9.92m
	height	3.41m
Performance	speed	620km/h
	ceiling	11,735m
	range	724km
Weight	empty	2,673kg
	loaded	3,150kg
Engine	1800-hp Daimler-Benz DB-605 inverted V-12 piston engine	
Armaments	2x 13mm MG131 machine guns	
	3x 20mm MG151 cannon	

MESSERSCHMITT BF 110: LONG RANGE FIGHTER

Willy Messerschmitt started designing the Bf110 at the end of 1934, as a long range fighter to protect bombers, but it was soon clear that it needed two engines to carry the necessary fuel. The original prototype was sluggish and a stronger engine had to be developed before the first test flights took place in May 1936. The Bf 110C entered service in 1939 and over 500 were ready by the end of the year. Ten Bf 110 *Groups* acted in a ground-support role during the invasion of Poland but only a few more were built after the campaign.

MESSERSCHMITT BF 110G-4

Dimensions	length	12.67m
	width	16.27m
	height	4.0m
Weight	empty	4,975kg
	loaded	9,888kg
Performance	speed	550km/h
	ceiling	7,924m
	range	2,100km
Engines	2 x Daimler–Benz DB605B twelve cylinder inverted-V liquid-cooled	
Armaments	2 x 30mm MK 108 cannon	
	2 x 20mm MG 151 cannon in nose	
	2 x flexible 7.9mm MG 81 machine-guns in rear cockpit	

JUNKERS JU 87 STUKA: DIVE BOMBER

A swept wing design and non-retractable undercarriage gave the two-seater Ju87 a distinctive silhouette as it dived towards a target, while sirens fitted on the wings emitted a screeching wail. It was capable of delivering precision bombing attacks and was used to devastating effect during the Spanish Civil War.

Ju 87 fighter bombers prepare for takeoff. (NARA-242-HB-38912a1)

JUNKERS JU 87D-1

Dimensions	length	11.50m
	width	13.80m
	height	3.90m
Performance	speed	410km/hr
	ceiling	7,290m
	range	1,535km
Weight	empty	3,900kg
	loaded	6,600kg
	ordnance	1,803kg
Engine	One Jumo 211J-1 inverted-V piston engine generating 1,400hp	
Armaments	2 x 7.92mm forward machine guns	
	2 x 7.92mm rear-facing machine guns	
	2 x 37mm under wing anti-tank cannons and anti-personnel munitions	

JUNKERS JU 88: MEDIUM BOMBER

This twin-engine monoplane, with its thin fuselage and single vertical tail, was the fastest Luftwaffe bomber. It had a four-man crew and bomb racks were added to the wings to compliment the internal bomb load.

JU 88A-4

Dimensions	length	14.40m
	width	20.0m
	height	4.85m
Performance	speed	450km/hr
	ceiling	8,200m
	range	2,730km
Weight	empty	9,860kg
	loaded	14,000kg
	ordnance	3,600kg
Engine	2 x Jumo 211J-1 or 211J-2 series V12 engines generating 1,340hp	
Armaments	7 x 7.92mm MG15 or MG81 machine guns; nose, dorsal and ventral	

HEINKEL HE 111: MEDIUM BOMBER

Siegfried and Walter Günter developed the Heinkel He 111 as a passenger transport aircraft but the twin-engine monoplane was easily converted to carry 4,000kg of bombs. The low wing-mounted engines and the glass nose gave the plane a distinctive profile and the five-man crew had six machine guns for protection; the He 111 H-16 had a 20mm cannon mounted in the nose. The first prototype flew in 1935 and a year later a number of He 111B-1 aircraft flew with the Condor Legion in Spain.

HEINKEL HE 111H-16

Dimensions	length	16.4m
	width	22.6m
	height	3.4m
Performance	speed	436km/hr
	ceiling	6,700m
	range	1,950km
Weight	empty	8,680kg
	loaded	14,000kg
Engines	2 x Junkers Jumo 211F inverted V-12 piston engines	
Armaments	1 x 20mm MG FF cannon in nose position	
	1 x 13mm MG 131 machine gun in dorsal position	
	2 x 7.92mm MG 15 machine guns in rear of ventral gondola position	
	2 x 7.92mm MG 81 machine guns in two beam positions	
Bomb load	2,000kg internal and 2,000kg external	

The He 111 bomber. (NARA-242-HB-40969a3)

DORNIER DO 17: MEDIUM BOMBER

This high-speed plane was developed to deliver mail and production started in 1934. The addition of eight machine guns and the conversion of the fuselage to accommodate bombs turned it into a bomber with a five-man crew. The twin-engine aircraft had a long thin fuselage and it could carry up to 1,000kg of ordnance.

DORNIER DO 17Z

Dimensions	length	15.80m
	width	18.00m
	height	4.55m
Performance	speed	310km/hr
	ceiling	8,200m
	range	740km
Weight	empty	5,210kg
	loaded	8,590kg
Engines	2 x BMW Bramo 323P Fafnir air-cooled engines	
Armaments	8 x 7.9mm machine guns; nose, dorsal turret, ventral turret and waist	

JUNKERS JU 52: TRANSPORT PLANE

Ernst Zindel had designed a single engine transport plane which Junkers developed into a three-engine aircraft with a distinctive nose engine; the corrugated skinned fuselage gave it extra strength. Production began in 1932 and over 100 flew with the Condor Legion in

The three-engined Ju 52 transport plane. (NARA-242-HB-13823)

Spain. The plane was designed to carry eighteen troops or supplies but a few were converted into bombers. The Ju 52 had a three-man crew and it became the backbone of the Luftwaffe's transport fleet.

JUNKERS JU 52/3M G7E

Dimensions	length	18.9m
	width	29.25m
	height	4.5m
Performance	speed	265km/h
	ceiling	5,490m
	range	870km
Weight	loaded	10,990kg
Engines	3 x BMW 132T radial engines	
Armament	1 x 13mm MG 131 machine gun	
	2 x 7.92mm MG 15 machine guns	

CHAPTER TWENTY

THE STORM DIVISION
STURM ABTEILUNG, SA

HISTORY

The Germany Workers' Party formed the Raiding Group (*Rollkommando*), to protect meetings in 1920 and it changed its name to the Timed Volunteers, (*Zeitfreiwilligen*), and then the Order Troop (*Ordnertruppe*). The Order Troop was banned after only a few weeks but Emil Maurice reformed it as the Gymnastic and Sports Detachment (*Turn und Sportabteilung*). Hans Klintzsch took command in the summer of 1921 and the name, Storm Division (*Sturm Abteilung* or SA) was adopted in November after a particularly fierce fight in the Hofbräuhaus in Munich.

Membership increased following a demonstration in Munich in August 1922 and two months later 800 members fought communists during a German Day parade. Standards were presented at the first party day in Munich in January 1923.

Hermann Göring took command in May 1923 and he organised the SA into regiments, battalions and companies (*Standarten*, *Sturmbannen* and *Hundertschaften*). While mechanics joined the Transport Division, (*Vehrkehrsabteilung*), the Field Jäger Corps (*Feldjägerkorps*) guarded meetings while the Staff Guard, (*Stabswache*) protected leaders.

Storm troopers salute their standards during a parade on waste ground. (NARA-242-HB-00988)

The SA was banned following the Munich Putsch in November 1923 and while Hitler and other Nazi leaders were in prison, Röhm formed the Frontbann and members used sports as a cover for their activities.

The SA was reformed in February 1925 by Heinrich von Helldorf while Röhm recruited for the Combat Policy League, a private officers' club. In November Franz Pfeffer von Salomon took command and membership increased slowly as men joined looking for food and comradeship.

Salomon left in August 1930 when Hitler refused to allow SA members to stand as Reichstag delegates, and he was temporarily replaced by Dr Otto Wagener. A lack of payments also led to a revolt in eastern Germany. After one SA unit attacked Goebbels' Berlin office and beat up his guards, Hitler sacked their leader, Walther Stennes, and took over the SA until Ernst Röhm returned from Bolivia in January 1931.

Röhm was unpopular with many senior Nazis – in particular Göring and Himmler – but he brought order to the SA by introducing military training. The SA increased from 100,000 to 400,000 during his first twelve months and the organisation played an important role in raising the party's popularity. The large numbers of SA men on the streets forced Chancellor Brüning's cabinet to ban the organisation in April 1932. The ban was lifted two months later when Franz von Papen became Chancellor; the violence continued in the run-up to the July election.

Hitler was appointed Chancellor in January 1933 and two months later the NSDAP secured a working majority in the Reichstag. The SA were sworn in as auxiliary police and in Berlin alone, Göring called up 24,000 SA men. Across Germany, the SA was used to help round up political opponents following the Reichstag fire, holding them in makeshift Wild Camps, the precursor to concentration camps. They also occupied union offices and arrested union leaders in May.

The SA was involved in boycotting Jewish businesses, but they were starting to get out of hand and in August Göring removed their auxiliary police powers. It was clear that their role was diminishing and members were getting bored because there was no electioneering or fighting with political opponents. By October 1933, Göring was concerned that the organisation was getting out of control and he founded the SA-Feldjägerkorps to restore order. Membership increased dramatically to 4.5 million when it absorbed the Steel Helmet ex-serviceman's organisation in December, making it many times the size of the Reichswehr.

SA leaders were also disillusioned by the Nazi regime and it was feared that there could be a civil war if their powers were not checked. Local attacks on army supplies and arms dumps raised suspicions but Röhm's calls to merge the SA and the Reichswehr into a national militia, or People's Army, infuriated senior Nazis and the army generals. His talk of a Second Revolution against the establishment threatened to undermine Hitler's position; he was even rude about Hitler. By the spring of 1934 the Führer believed that the time had come to curb the organisation.

On 10 June 1934, Hitler ordered Röhm to stand the SA down in July, but rumours of an SA revolt continued and the Nazi leadership demanded action. The Security

Hitler reviews an SA unit. (NARA-242-HB-001701a)

Service was given instructions to present information that Röhm was planning a revolution. On 30 June Hitler travelled to Bad Wiesee in Bavaria to arrest Röhm and his companions, while squads from the SS-Leibstandarte Adolf Hitler rounded up dozens of senior SA officers across the country. Munich's SA commanders were ordered to attend a meeting in the NSDAP headquarters, and were surprised to find themselves under arrest. Dozens were murdered in the Blood Purge, or the Night of the Long Knives.

Viktor Lutze was appointed Chief of Staff and the SA became a shadow of its former self while the SS was made a separate organisation. Actions against unruly elements of the SA were stepped up and membership fell rapidly to 1.6 million by October 1935. Rigid entrance requirements and conscription stopped it rising again.

The NSK (Motor Corps) was also separated from the SA. The SA took over responsibility for training before and after military service, while SA Defence Teams, (SA-Wehrmannschaften) provided personnel for non-military security forces. In 1939 the elite SA Commander's Hall Regiment (SA-Standarte Feldherrnhalle) provided personnel for infantry and parachute units.

An SA music section arrives at Nuremberg station, ready for the rally. (NARA-242-HB-14971a1)

ORGANISATION

The SA changed from a simple structure based on groups of 100 men to an army-style structure with hundreds of thousands of men organised into brigades, regiments, battalions and companies.

ORIGINAL ORGANISATION

Hundertschaft	100 men in 4 *Zug* of 25 men
Zug	organised into three *Gruppe* each with 9 men

ORGANISATION AFTER HERMANN GÖRING'S REORGANISATION

Gausturm for each Gau	split into *Brigades*
Brigade	2–5 *Standarten*
Standarte	2–5 *Stürme*
Sturm	2–4 *Truppen*
Trupp	5–8 *Gruppen* of 10 men

ORGANISATION UNDER THE COMMAND OF ERNST RÖHM

Six *Obergruppen*	corresponding to an army corps area
Gruppen (division)	Several *Gausturm* according to geography and recruitment
Gausturm (brigade)	3 *Standarten* of 50,000 men
Standarte (regiment)	5–6 *Sturmbann* of 5,500 men
Sturmbann (battalion)	6–10 *Sturm* of 1,000 men
Sturm (company)	2–3 *Truppen* of 150 men
Truppe (platoon)	5–6 *Scharen* of 50 men
Schar (squad)	10 men

STURM ABTEILUNG COMMANDERS

FRANZ PFEFFER VON SALOMON (1888–1968)

Salomon joined Röhm's Frontbann in 1924 and transferred to the SA when it reformed in 1925. He served as Gauleiter for Thuringia and Westphalia until he was promoted to command the SA in 1926. While he wanted the organisation to concentrate on protecting meetings, they were often called upon to attack opponents. Salomon had to deal with poverty amongst his membership and the situation came to a head when his deputy, Walter Stennes, led a mutiny in Berlin in August 1930. Salomon was relieved after Hitler refused to let SA members stand for the imminent Reichstag elections.

ERNST RÖHM (1887–1934)

Röhm served as an officer in the First World War and he joined the Free Corps following the Armistice before serving as a captain in the Reichswehr. The short, fat man with a scarred face was fanatical and unsophisticated but his hidden cache of weapons helped General Epp's plot against the Communist government in Munich. Röhm was drawn to Hitler's leadership and the NSDAP overlooked his homosexuality in the hope of attracting his followers.

Röhm's group failed to capture the Munich army commander during the 1923 Munich Putsch and he was arrested. After he was released on probation, he emigrated to Bolivia to work as a military instructor.

Röhm returned to Germany when Hitler asked him to command the SA and membership increased dramatically under his command. In return for his service, Röhm was appointed to the cabinet in December 1933, as Minister without Portfolio. By 1934 the SA had 4,500,000 members but Hitler's distrust was growing. He correctly believed that Röhm wanted to replace the Reichswehr and create a socialist state. As Röhm's disobedience increased, so did the rumours, and Lutze brought the matter to a head when he exposed Röhm's plans.

On 30 June 1934 Hitler went to Bad Wiessee to confront the SA leaders. Röhm was arrested and two days later a gun was placed in his cell so he could commit

Chief of Staff Ernst Röhm in light-coloured uniform in the centre and Gruppenführer Karl Ernst, leader of the Berlin SA on the left; both were murdered during the Blood Purge. (NARA-242-HB-03058a)

suicide. He refused and Theodor Eicke's SS squad killed him.

The press reported that Röhm had been killed to prevent a rebellion and Hitler repeated the accusation before the Reichstag on 11 July 1934. While the SA leadership had been purged of Röhm supporters, there were rumours that a group, known as Röhm's Avengers, murdered several SS leaders over the next two years.

VIKTOR LUTZE (1890–1943)

After serving in the First World War, Lutze joined the NSDAP in 1922. He became deputy Gauleiter for the Ruhr area in 1925 and an active leader of the local SA; he was voted Reichstag deputy for Hanover-Braunschweig in the September 1930 election. Once the Nazis came to power he was promoted to SA-Obergruppenführer and was appointed police president of Hanover and a member of the Prussian State Council.

Lutze reported Röhm's plans to turn the SA into a National Socialist army to Hitler, prompting him to take action. He then accompanied Hitler to Bad Wiessee to confront the SA leaders. Hitler appointed Lutze as Röhm's replacement with orders to stop excessive activities, including drinking, lewdness and parties. The SA was quickly reduced to training duties under his command.

Chief of Staff Victor Lutze. (NARA-242-HB-07727a1)

NATIONAL SOCIALIST FLYERS' CORPS, NSFK

The National Socialist Flyers' Corps was formed in January 1932 under Korpsführer Friedrich Christiansen to promote interest in aviation in the German youth. It was divided into three sections: powered flight, gliders and ballooning; it later established a ski school at Zell-am-See in Austria.

It was closely associated with the Hitler Youth and younger members participated in aeronautics classes and model flying competitions. Members progressed to ballooning, gliders and powered flight at the age of fourteen. The NSFK owned sixteen gliding and aviation schools and it used hundreds of other glider sites across Germany. Sporting events and competitions were encouraged at all levels.

After the Nazis seized power, a decree incorporated the NSFK into the Reich as a legal corporation and the organisation continued to grow. At the same time the German Air Sports Federation was disbanded while the NSFK absorbed all flying organisations. Many NSFK members transferred to the Luftwaffe when it was unveiled in March 1935, giving it a strong Nazi base. The role of the NSFK then diminished rapidly.

NATIONAL SOCIALIST MOTOR CORPS, NSKK

The SA formed Motor Driver Squads in 1928 but they were badly organised. The National Socialist Automobile Corps was formed in April 1930 under Korpsführer Adolf Hühnlein and it organised mechanically-minded NSDAP members into groups. While boys were taught about cars, engines and driving in the Motorist–Hitler Youth, adults were encouraged to learn the same skills and join one of the National Socialist Motor Corps units.

Membership numbered over 30,000 by January 1933 and the NSKK took over control of all motor clubs in September, increasing its numbers to over 350,000. By 1939 the Motor Sports Schools across Germany were training drivers for the army.

A mass SA rally. (NARA-242-HB-2875)

SA units parade past their leader, Ernst Röhm. (NARA-242-HB 2884)

CHAPTER TWENTY-ONE

THE PROTECTION ECHELON, THE *SCHUTZSTAFFEL*, SS

The SS started in 1925 with a few dozen hand-picked bodyguards chosen to protect party leaders. Heinrich Himmler took over the small organisation in January 1929 and over the next ten years it expanded to include thousands of men responsible for all aspects the internal security of the Third Reich. By 1939 it had grown into a huge organisation encompassing the state police, the party police, armed units, a network of concentration camps and a large business empire employing camp labour.

THE SS UNDER THE WEIMAR REPUBLIC

The term '*Schutzstaffel*' translates as 'defence echelon'; the first eight-man bodyguard was formed by Julius Schreck to protect Hitler at the beginning of 1925, after he was released from Landsberg prison. The group was part of the SA and additional bodyguard details were formed at district NSDAP headquarters in September to protect local leaders. Six Gaue were organised the following year with district headquarters at Berlin-Brandenburg, Franken, Niederbayern, South Rhineland and Sachsen. They reported to Joseph Berchtold's headquarters office, the SS-Oberleitung.

A young Himmler acts as a bodyguard for Franz Schwarz, the NSDAP treasurer.

Erhard Heiden was appointed Reichsführer-SS in 1927 but membership declined and he was forced to resign after allegations that he used a Jewish tailor were released (he would be murdered on Himmler's orders in April 1933). Heiden was replaced in January 1929 by his deputy, Heinrich Himmler. The SS was only 280-strong and he reorganised the SS-Oberleitung into the SS-Oberstab with five departments:

Abteilung I	Administration
Abteilung II	Personnel
Abteilung III	Finance
Abteilung IV	Security
Abteilung V	Race

Three area offices, SS-Oberführerbereiche, covering west, east and south Germany were formed. Membership had increased to 1,000 by the end of the year and each area controlled several brigades, SS-Brigaden, each divided into regiment-sized SS-Standarten.

The SS eventually became independent of the SA in November 1930 and it continued to expand rapidly in size until a second reorganisation was required in 1931. The headquarters was renamed the SS-Amt, or SS Office, and it had five departments:

Section I	Headquarters Staff
Section II	Personnel Office
Section III	Administration Office
Section IV	SS Reserves
Section V	SS Medical Corps

The country was also split into five SS-Gruppen, north, west, east, south and south-west. In August 1931 the Security Service Office was organised under Reinhard Heydrich to control the party police as they collected information on political opponents; it also rooted out infiltrators in the SS. The Race and Resettlement Office was organised under Richard Darré to ensure the racial purity of the SS.

THE SS UNDER THE THIRD REICH

The SS numbered nearly 50,000 when Hitler was made Chancellor. Following the Reichstag fire in February 1933, SS units were authorised to act as auxiliary police units and they were used to round up enemies of the state. Although prisoners were handed over to the SA, plans to make the SS responsible for the Third Reich's internal security began in March 1933. At the same time the SS-Leibstandarte Adolf Hitler was organised under Joseph Dietrich,

Himmler squares up to Göring at Hitler's Berghof. (NARA-242-HB-24102a6)

as the core of the Armed Troops SS, the *Verfügungstruppe-SS*, separating it from the General SS, the *Allgemeine-SS*. It would expand to battalion size over the next twelve months.

Himmler was also appointed police president of Munich in March 1933 and a month later he became commander of the Bavarian political police, merging state and party activities. A new concentration camp at Dachau became a model camp and over the months that followed the SS took control of all the concentration camps across Germany from the SA.

The SA leadership was getting restless by the spring of 1934 and calls for a Second Revolution concerned the Nazi hierarchy. Himmler already had control of police across parts of Germany and in April 1934 he increased his empire when he was appointed head of all the police outside Prussia. At the same time Heydrich was appointed head of the Gestapo and in June 1934 the Security Service became the sole intelligence service of the party. At the end of June the SS-Leibstandarte Adolf Hitler rounded up victims during the Night of the Long Knives, carrying out many of the executions. A month later the SS was formally separated from the SA.

1936 was the next year of change and while the Gestapo was given national status in February, 3,000 concentration camp guards were organised into three Death's Head Regiments or *Totenkopfstandarten* in March.

SS PERSONNEL

Reichsführer-SS and Chief of the German Police	Heinrich Himmler
Chief of Himmler's Personal Staff	Karl Wolff
Head of the Reich Main Security Office	Reinhard Heydrich after September 1939
Chief Administrative Officer in the Reich Main Security Office	Oswald Pohl
Race and Resettlement Department	Richard Walther Darré

An SS security cordon around the Führer. (NARA-242-HB-05356)

The SS was organised as follows:

Senior Groups	*Obergruppen*
Groups	*Gruppen*
Sections	*Abschnitte*
Regiments	*Standarten*
Battalions	*Stürmbanne*
Storm Troops	*Stürme*
Troops	*Truppen*
Bands	*Scharen*

The SS divided Germany in 'higher sections', '*oberabschnitten*', military districts equivalent to an army '*wehrkreis*'; each one was split into 'sections', '*abschnitten*'.

HEINRICH HIMMLER (1900–1945)

After gaining an agriculture diploma at Munich Technical College, Himmler became a laboratory technician. The mild-mannered man with glasses, moustache and the look of a schoolteacher, joined Ernst Röhm's Reich War Flag Free Corps unit and he carried their flag during the 1923 Munich Putsch.

After the Putsch, Himmler returned to Landshut to run a chicken farm and sell advertising space for the *People's Observer*. He worked as Gregor Strasser's secretary while he was acting Gauleiter for Bavaria. He was appointed Party

Hitler reviews an SS unit. (NARA-242-HB-14568a3)

Propaganda Leader in 1925 and deputy leader of the *Schutzstaffel* in 1926. It was the start of his lifelong association with the SS.

Himmler became Reichsführer-SS in January 1929 when it only numbered 280 and he began expanding its membership and responsibilities. Reinhard Heydrich was appointed head of the Security Service in 1931 and the two men were masters of accumulating information on other party members. They often used it to further the role of the SS. They also aimed to introduce racial purity into the organisation, improving its elite status ahead of the SA. By the time the Nazis controlled Germany, the SS had over 50,000 members.

Himmler was appointed the Munich police chief in March 1933 and he established Dachau concentration camp to hold enemies of the state. With the help of Reinhard Heydrich, Kurt Daluege and Walter Schellenberg, the SS expanded control across the German police. Himmler was given control of the Gestapo in April 1934 and appointed Reinhard Heydrich as its head. At the same time he was handed control of all police activities outside Prussia. The SS played a large part in identifying victims and then murdering them in the Blood Purge in June 1934. Himmler was finally handed control of all police activities across Germany in June 1936. The merging of state and party police activities under Heydrich's Reich Main Security Office in September 1939 completed Himmler's empire of political oppression in the Third Reich.

SS UNIFORMS AND RITUALS

To begin with the SS wore the same brown shirts and breeches as the SA. A black ski-cap, a black tie and the SS insignia marked the difference. The SS symbol was portrayed as two lightning flashes, imitating runic characters. A black uniform was introduced when the SS was made independent from the SA in November 1930; a swastika band was also worn on the arm. Their well-groomed black shirts, greatcoats and breeches stood out against the SA's crumpled brown shirts. Black boots, belts, caps, helmets and tie completed the uniform of

Standard bearer of the SS-Leibstandarte Adolf Hitler. (NARA-242-HB-21562a13)

the party's elite. Honorary SS officers also wore a ceremonial version of the uniform.

The SS prided itself on its elite status and applicants had to be age 17½ to 22, have no criminal record or record of mental illness. While physical standards were high, intellectual standards were not. Applicants had their racial purity checked back to the eighteenth century. After 1932 members carried a Clan Book detailing their family history and records were maintained by the Race and Resettlement Office.

Applicants were accepted during a mass parade in Munich on the November anniversary of the Beer Hall Putsch. After completing basic training they took an oath of allegiance to the Führer on Hitler's birthday. Training continued, emphasising sport and political indoctrination. They finally entered the SS at a ceremonial parade in October at which they were awarded their engraved SS dagger. Members would swear by their motto, 'Believe! Obey! Fight!' and they kept up with the news with *The Black Corps*, a weekly newspaper controlled by Himmler. Future brides also had their racial purity checked and traditional weddings were replaced by pagan-style rituals.

An SS ritual ceremony. (NARA-242-HB-12963)

ADMINISTRATION OFFICES

PERSONAL STAFF FOR THE REICH LEADER SS

After serving in the First World War, Karl Wolff (1900–1984) worked in banking until the recession forced him to start his own public relations company in 1925. He joined the NSDAP and the SS in 1931 and was elected to the Reichstag in March 1933. Wolff became Himmler's adjutant in June 1933 and he dealt with Himmler's schedule, conveying Himmler's orders to the other SS offices. He was eventually promoted to SS-Obergruppenführer.

SS MAIN ADMINISTRATIVE OFFICE

An SS Office for the headquarters staff was formed in 1931 and it was renamed the SS-Oberführerbereichen when the Nazis came to power. The office was again reorganised to deal with recruitment in January 1935 and it was called the SS Main Administrative Office. It organised ideological, physical and vocational training, Germanic education, medical records and requisitioning. The office was headed by Gottlob Berger who had been wounded serving as an officer in the First World War. He joined the NSDAP and the SA in 1922. He did not join the SS until 1936 but his organisational abilities made him ideal to head the highly influential office.

SS recruits prepare for physical exercise; the motto reads 'My Honour is my Loyalty'. (NARA-242-HB-21562a20)

SS MAIN PERSONNEL OFFICE

The office was opened under SS-Gruppenführer Walter Schmitt in September 1939 to maintain records of officers and potential officers for the expanding General SS and Armed Troops SS. It also recorded awards, training, honours and disciplinary action. Records for the rank and file were limited.

LEGAL OFFICES

WERNER BEST (1903–1989)

Best completed his law doctorate at Heidelberg in 1927 but he was soon imprisoned for his nationalist views by the French authorities in the Ruhr. He joined the Hesse justice department in 1929 and became the NSDAP's legal advisor in 1930. He drafted the Boxheim Papers, the Nazi plan for seizing power following a communist revolution, and he had to resign from his job when they were discovered.

Best was appointed police commissioner of Hesse in March 1933 and the state governor four months later. By 1935 he was Reinhard Heydrich's deputy and legal adviser for the SS. He worked on the premise that 'as long as the police carries out the will of the leadership, it is acting legally'. He worked to expand the Gestapo and the Security Service and he was appointed head of Section I of the Race and Resettlement Office in September 1939.

THE MAIN OFFICE OF SS LEGAL MATTERS

The office was established under SS-Obergruppenführer Paul Scarfe (1879–1945) in 1934 after SS concentration guards were charged for unlawfully killing prisoners in Dachau concentration camp. It developed new laws and codes for the SS, placing members above regular German law. The office also dealt with disciplinary matters, including sentencing, pardons and reprieves.

SECURITY OFFICES

MAIN OFFICE OF THE ORDER POLICE

Himmler was named head of the Order Police, the ORPO (see chapter nine), in June 1936 combining the offices of the Chief of German police and the Reichsführer-SS. The move removed all uniformed law enforcement agencies from state control, merging police duties with the SS.

THE REICH MAIN SECURITY OFFICE: RSHA

The office merged all state and party intelligence activities under one SS controlled office headed by Reinhard Heydrich in September 1939. It combined the activities of the Security Police, the Criminal Police, the Security Service and the SS intelligence service (see chapter nine).

RACE AND EXPANSION OFFICES

THE RACE AND RESETTLEMENT OFFICE: RuSHA

The office was originally organised in 1931 under Richard Darré to authenticate the Aryan ancestry of the fiancées of SS soldiers, but few marriages were banned. The office expanded its duties to cover all SS members, dealing with administration, race, education, marriage and family. Officers had to trace their ancestry back to 1750 while the ranks had to trace it back to 1800. The office became known as the guardian of the ideological and racial purity of the SS. The office also provided speakers to lecture SS members on Aryan history.

Himmler and Dárre listen intently. (NARA-242-HB-10593)

The office established SS entrance requirements and potential members had to be in good physical condition, have a general bearing and Nordic appearance. Intellectual achievements were not considered. However, many members were found to be unsuitable and between 1933 and 1935 hundreds were sacked, particularly homosexuals and alcoholics, to make the organisation superior to the SA.

Race experts had plans on how to populate the 'Living Space', '*lebensraum*', after the army had occupied the lands to the east of Germany. Slavs and Jews would be moved (most would be were killed), making space for racially–approved families. The office had departments covering population policy and settlement. It planned to initially settle 840,000 people with another 1,100,000 a few months later; there would be an annual resettlement of 200,000 people over the next ten years.

In December 1935 the Race and Resettlement Office established the Well of Life Registered Society to promote the Nazi view on human evolution and counter the falling birth rate. Himmler wanted the *Lebensborn* programme to aid 'racially valuable' married and unmarried mothers and their children, providing accommodation for them in maternity homes. Illegitimacy was acceptable if child was healthy and racially pure. The programme later expanded to include orphanages and adoption programmes. Himmler showed a great deal of personal interest in the programme and control transferred to his personal staff in 1938. There were only 8,000 members by 1939.

WELFARE OFFICE FOR ETHNIC GERMANS

The office of SS-Obergruppenführer Werner Lorenz planned for the welfare of Germans emigrating to the Living Space. It checked candidates for settlement for racial purity, skills and politics. It would then locate families and organise agricultural and construction projects. It would also provide cultural, educational and financial support.

MAIN OFFICE OF THE REICH COMMISSIONER FOR THE CONSOLIDATION OF GERMAN NATIONHOOD

In 1939 the Race and Resettlement Office and the Welfare Office for Ethnic Germans combined their roles to organise emigration and resettlement in the new Living Space. The office also made arrangements to clear the areas, preparing to move the Slavs into concentration camps for forced labour. In wartime it would organise Sonderkommandos, or killing units, to exterminate Jews and other undesirables.

BUSINESS ENTERPRISES

ECONOMIC AND ADMINISTRATIVE MAIN OFFICE

After serving in the navy in the First World War, Oswald Pohl (1892–1951) dropped out of university and joined the Free Corps, transferring to the Reichsmarine in 1920. He joined the SA in 1925 and the NSDAP in 1926. After meeting Heinrich Himmler in 1933, Pohl was appointed as deputy to the chief of the SS Administrative Office on the Reichführer's staff. He became chief when his superior died and his role expanded to Reich Treasurer for the SS in June 1935. He was responsible for making money from the concentration camp system and he set up the Concentration Camps Inspectorate to maintain standards and maximise profits.

In April 1939 the SS Administrative Office was reorganised as the separate SS Economic and Administrative Main Office, responsible for deploying the slave labour from the 20 concentration camps to dozens of satellite work camps. It became a highly lucrative business as industries paid the SS to employ the prison inmates. The office also looked after companies and business enterprises owned by the SS, either directly or indirectly. German Economic Enterprises was the holding company for all businesses and industries controlled of the SS. Pohl also ran the SS Budget and Construction Office.

Hitler and Himmler visit an SS-run construction contract. (NARA-242-HB-05043)

By 1939 the SS controlled several major businesses. The German Excavation and Quarrying Company Limited produced building materials while the German Armament Works produced a large range of military products. Another company was involved in food-stuffs, estates, forestry and fishery while a textile company and leatherworks in Ravensbruck women's concentration camp produced SS uniforms. The SS business empire also profited from the aryanisation of Jewish businesses. Following the annexation of the Sudetenland, the SS seized many businesses including furniture manufacturing, soft-drink suppliers and mineral water plants.

HEINRICH HIMMLER'S 'CIRCLE OF FRIENDS'

Industry had contributed large amounts to the NSDAP election campaigns of 1932 and 1933 and the connections continued after the Nazis took power. Chief executives from indus-try, banking and insurance regularly met Heinrich Himmler to arrange new contracts in exchange for cash handouts exceeding one million RM a year. They were often rewarded with an honorary senior rank in the SS to increase their political influence in the world of business. Small businessmen could become a Patron Member of the SS, making contributions in return for favours. Industries were sometimes offered cheap labour supplied by concentra-tion camps. As profits rose, companies were expected to make further donations to the SS. Himmler used the money to fund SS companies and projects.

MUTUAL SPONSORSHIP

Himmler wanted to enhance the elite nature of the SS by offering honorary ranks to party leaders, titled men, businessmen and select societies. The title Honorary Leader was granted to many senior NSDAP officials and they were promoted to a high SS rank. By 1938 around one in five SS-Obergruppenführers and one in ten SS-Standartenführers came from titled families. Although these honorary commanders had no duties or powers, the rank and the uniform enhanced reputations and opened doors in business.

SS MILITARY ORGANISATIONS

SS COMBAT TROOPS, SS VERFÜGUNGSTRUPPE

Armed bodyguards were part of the General-SS (Allgemeine-SS), until the Nazis seized power. Armed units were formed in March 1933 and they paraded as the SS-Leibstandarte Adolf Hitler at the September Nuremburg rally under the command of Joseph Sepp Dietrich. The unit carried out many of the executions during the Blood Purge in June 1934, prompting Hitler to propose eventually expanding them into three divisions. The army gen-erals supported the idea because they preferred the military bearing of the SS compared to the unruliness of the SA. Two more regiments had been formed by 1937, Deutschland and Germania. In August 1938, a decree added a clear military role to the SS and the Combat Troops and Death's Head Troops merged into the Armed SS, (Waffen-SS), in May 1939.

Himmler watches over his subordinates during a military exercise. (NARA-242-HB-20563a6)

Joseph Dietrich reviews the SS-Leibstandarte Adolf Hitler. (NARA-242-HB-04617)

SS DEATH'S HEAD TROOPS, SS TOTENKOPFVERBÄNDE

Guard units, known as '*Wachtruppen*', were formed to control the new concentration camps in March 1933. They wore brown uniforms and had a skull and crossbones, or 'Death's Head' badge on their caps. Following early disciplinary and organisational problems, Theodor Eicke was appointed Inspector of Concentration Camps in April 1934. He quickly introduced strict regulations and discipline for the 3,500 camp guards across Germany.

In March 1936 the units were named the SS Death's Head, the *SS-Totenkopfverbände*. A number of units carried out 'special political duties', arresting political activists, during the occupation of Austria and Czechoslovakia.

The Death's Head units became part of the Waffen-SS in March 1939. On the outbreak of war in September 1939, the *Totenkopfverbände* increased in strength to 6,500 and guard units formed the cadre of the SS Death's Head tank division, the *SS-Panzerdivision-Totenkopf*.

The SS crew of a 75mm le.IG 18 infantry support gun. (NARA-242-HB-18427a21)

ARMED SS, WAFFEN SS

The SS Combat Troops and the SS Death's Head units merged as the Waffen-SS in March 1939. Hitler correctly had doubts about the loyalty of the Wehrmacht's leadership and he wanted an elite armed force with chosen commanders. He planned to create a special army of highly trained men indoctrinated with Nazi ideals. The strength of the Waffen SS rose from 9,000 in September to over 150,000 by the start of 1941.

JOSEF 'SEPP' DIETRICH (1892–1966)

Dietrich was a butcher by trade who had to take on many jobs to make ends meet after serving in the First World War. He was an early member of the NSDAP and his willingness to engage hecklers during political meetings brought him to Hitler's attention. He was appointed commander of Hitler's personal bodyguard in 1928 and he accompanied him during his election campaigns. Dietrich was also elected to the Reichstag in 1930, as the delegate for Lower Bavaria's *Wahlkreis*. By 1931 he was SS-Gruppenführer.

Dietrich was promoted to SS-Oberstgruppenführer and appointed commander of Hitler's bodyguard regiment, SS-Leibstandarte Adolf Hitler, when

Dietrich studies his operation map during a training exercise. (NARA-242-HB-13675)

it formed in September 1933. He played a prominent part in the Blood Purge in June 1934, shooting several senior SA men. He was promoted to General of the Waffen-SS and appointed a member of the Prussian State Council soon afterwards.

TRAINING SCHOOLS

Officer training schools for SS armed troops was established in 1936, offering a high standard of training in tactics, mapping, combat and weapon training. One school was based in Brunswick Castle while a new establishment was opened in Bad Tölz, south of Munich, in 1937. They accepted capable recruits from any social background, in contrast to the army.

ARCHAEOLOGY AND MYSTICISM

SOCIETY FOR RESEARCH AND TEACHING OF ANCESTRAL HERITAGE

The SS founded the *Ahnenerbe* in 1935 to prove their Aryan theories through academic study and archaeological investigations. Staff members studied the spread of racial doctrine around the world and they mixed science, mythology and romanticism to prove their research.

The *Ahnenerbe* was integrated into the SS in 1937 under the same administrative branch as the concentration camps. Himmler took a personal interest in their investigations and by 1938 all German funded archaeological excavations were under the organisation. Archaeologists were involved in a diverse range of investigations ranging from expeditions to Tibet and the Near East to the excavation of Viking fortresses.

MYSTICISM

Oswald Pohl established the Society for the Preservation and Fostering of German Cultural Monuments and the chief project was the restoration of Wewelsburg Castle using concentration camp labour. Himmler was fascinated with mysticism and wanted the castle as a base for the Holy Order of the SS. The twelve senior members of the SS met there several times a year after 1934, gathering around a circular Arthurian table, beneath runic coats-of-arms. While scientists studied racial applied research, historians and archaeologists studied Nordic history and folklore in the SS sponsored library.

SS standard bearers. (NARA-242-HB-2554)

CHAPTER TWENTY-TWO

ENEMIES OF THE STATE

The Germany Workers' Party stated their views on race in their 25 Point Programme announced in February 1920. It stated that 'citizenship to be determined by race; no Jew to be a German' and while the party did not bind itself exclusively to any religion, it would 'fight against Jewish materialism'. The NSDAP adopted the programme.

Random acts of violence against Jewish communities throughout the 1920s were replaced by government policy in 1933. Wide ranging anti-Semitic legislation over the next six years segregated Jews in German society and excluded them from the economy. By January 1939 Hitler made it clear that a war would result in the 'extermination of the Jewish race in Europe', and he made the statement knowing full well that Germany was planning for war. The plans for a Final Solution to the Jewish Question were finally coordinated by Reinhard Heydrich at the Wannasse Conference in January 1942.

Approximately six million Jews perished over the next three years, as well as millions of other 'enemies', including Romani, Poles, Soviet prisoners of war, the disabled, homosexuals, political opponents and Jehovah's Witnesses. This is the narrative of the events which laid the foundations for the Holocaust.

THE PROTOCOLS OF THE ELDERS OF ZION

Many anti-Semitic arguments stemmed from the controversial publication *The Protocols of the Elders of Zion*. The text claimed to be the minutes of a secret Zionist congress held in Switzerland in 1897. The congress had allegedly outlined the establishment of a Jewish world-state, declared an undermining of the Aryan peoples and detailed plots to carry out terrorist attacks on European capitals.

The Russian secret police had actually written the *Protocols* and they had based their text on a French pamphlet satirising Napoleon III. The police then used the book to justify Russian anti-Semitic pogroms. Despite its shady background, the book was translated into many languages and circulated around the world after the First World War.

The Times exposed the *Protocols* as a forgery in 1921. More denunciations followed but it was still distributed and a German version was edited by Alfred Rosenberg for the NSDAP to use. Hitler referred to the *Protocols* in *Mein Kampf* and it became a standard school textbook under the Nazi regime.

THE EARLY POGROMS
MARCH 1933 TO SEPTEMBER 1935

The Nazi majority was endorsed in the election on 5 March 1933 and four days later SA and Stahlhelm units went on the rampage against Jewish communities. For the first time the police did not stop them; the attacks had been condoned by the government. The NSDAP leaders were concerned that random acts of violence against Jewish communities would undermine the government's authority and they started to look for ways to eliminate Jews from economic life without adversely affecting the economy.

NSDAP Action Committees held a peaceful boycott outside Jewish shops on 1 April, insisting on 'Quiet, Discipline and No Violence!' Members of the SA and the SS put up notices and handed out leaflets, advising the public not to enter the stores. Similar actions were carried out by the Combat League of Middle Class Retailers, an organisation devoted to boycotting Jewish stores. Government loans were non-redeemable in Jewish stores and state or party contracts could not be made with them; Aryan suppliers also stopped dealing with them. Shops continued to be boycotted at Christmas, while random and organised acts of violence against property and employees forced many to close down.

The Action Committees also demanded limits on the number of Jews in all professions, determined by the ratio of Aryans and non-Aryans in the population. The limits would be applied to the medical and legal professions to begin with; university lecturers and high schools teachers would follow.

On 7 April, the new Law for the Re-creation of Civil Service Professionalism forced many Jewish civil service employees to resign. While First World War veterans were exempt, they could not be promoted. The law also allowed for the promotion of Nazi sympathisers to new posts. In doing so the government was ensuring that their new laws and policies would be implemented

Goebbels announces the one-day boycott of Jewish businesses to a Berlin crowd. (NARA-242-HB-00748)

without question. It took until the end of the year to apply the law but the Nazis knew that the civil service would implement their laws and decrees with enthusiasm in the future. Jewish communities set up organisations to help the unemployed find jobs, retrain and receive welfare.

On 11 April the first attempt at defining a non-Aryan was made in the Aryan Clause. They were described as 'anyone descended from non-Aryan, especially Jewish, parents or grandparents. One parent or grandparent classifies the descendant as non-Aryan … especially if one parent or grandparent was of the Jewish faith.' Later definitions would go into more detail, particularly regarding those of mixed parentage. Every German citizen would eventually have to obtain an ancestry passport which detailed their family background. A new business of ancestry charts flourished and black marketeers profited from providing fake information.

SA troopers stick posters to the windows of a Jewish shop. (NARA-242-HB-00739)

Members of the Protestant Church also had to prove their Aryan ancestry for two or three generations. Those who failed to do so were called Jew-Christians, '*Juden-Christen*', and they were excluded from their church. The move split the Protestant faith and while the new NSDAP-sponsored church, the German Faith Movement, welcomed the Aryan Clause, the Confessional Church rejected it.

The Aryan Clause would eventually ban Jews from all cultural activities including the film industry, fine art, theatre, music and literature. The press and the radio would also be affected. A huge exodus of actors, actresses, film directors, performers, entertainers, musicians, artists and writers followed, and many emigrated to the US. On 21 April ritual slaughters were banned; it was the first of many restrictions on the Jewish religious practices.

A limit on the numbers of Jewish students was introduced on 25 April and many were forced to leave their studies. Those who remained faced continual harassment in classes. Literature was targeted at the beginning of May 1933. Goebbels encouraged students to purge university libraries of 'un-German' books and his ministry circulated lists of Jewish and liberal authors and poets, many of them internationally acclaimed. Students collected books from libraries, synagogues and private homes on 10 May 1933 and stacked them outside their universities. Torch-lit processions led crowds to the pyres and they watched the books burning while speakers denounced the writers.

SA troopers boycott a Jewish-owned store which has closed for the day. (NARA-242-HB-00732)

293

Burning books outside the University of Berlin.

The banner calls for world peace and an end to Jewish world domination. (NARA-242-HB-14152)

The main parade took place in Berlin where the Students' Battle Committee burnt 20,000 books in front of the university library. As the flames lit up the night sky, Goebbels proclaimed that 'spirits are awakening, oh, century; it is a joy to live!' Although his ministry limited press coverage on the book burning, the international press denounced it as a barbaric act.

The next targets were Jews who had been naturalised in Germany's eastern territories before the First World War, particularly Polish Jews. Their citizenship was revoked on 14 July, leaving them stateless and vulnerable to deportation.

The Nazis also started their indoctrination of Germany's youth. On 13 September, their views on race theory were introduced into the school curriculum. Meanwhile, a wide range of local anti-Semitic bans were introduced across the country, slowly affecting everyday life. Customers stopped using Jewish-owned businesses, either through choice or harassment. On 17 September the Reich Agency of German Jews was organised to administer new laws and legislation relating to Jewish issues. Community elders were appointed to local Jewish Councils, called *Judenrate*, and they had to act as mediators with the Nazi administration.

The Nazis continued their attacks on culture on 22 September when the Reich's Culture Ministry excluded Jewish artists from the Reich Chamber of Visual Arts. Publishing houses and bookshops also had to exclude Jewish writers. Jews were banned from farming on 29 September and Aryan farmers profited from their confiscated lands.

The press was targeted next and on 4 October the Editor's Law was introduced, banning Jewish editors from working on newspapers and magazines. Jewish journalists were also prohibited from contributing to newspapers and magazines on 17 October. Jews were then eliminated from the economy, limiting their ability to work and earn money. The German Labour Front had replaced the trade unions by July 1933 and while membership was mandatory, the work-shy were being imprisoned in concentration camps by the end of the year. On 24 January 1934 Jews were banned from the German Labour Front and they had to stop working for Aryan-owned industries, factories, businesses and shops. It forced them to look for work within their own community where jobs were scarce. After 17 May, Jews were no longer entitled to health insurance, excluding them from the country's health service.

For twelve months there were few changes but the next law targeted young men. Conscription became compulsory in March 1935 but two months later a law was introduced stating that potential conscripts had to prove their Aryan heritage. The law effectively split German youth into Aryans who had to join the armed services and non-Aryans who could not. In May 1935 mixed marriages between soldiers and non-Aryan women were banned. At the same time Jews were banned from applying for German citizenship.

By the summer of 1935 the German people were becoming dissatisfied with the regime and the Nazis decided it was time to start encouraging national anti-Semitism to give them a new focus. A new trend for displaying anti-Semitic posters and signs began across Germany. 'Jews Not Welcome' signs appeared above village name plates while similar signs appeared in urban public areas, including shops and restaurants.

Stickers notify the customer that the doctor is Jewish and that visits are forbidden.

THE NUREMBERG RACE LAWS: SEPTEMBER 1935

Ministers and party leaders discussed the effects of the Jews pogroms on the German economy on 20 August 1935. Dr Schacht, the Economics Minister, believed that arbitrary attacks against Jewish businesses were harmful to Germany's fragile economy; he believed that Jews should be contributing to the economy. Adolf Wagner, the NSDAP representative, agreed that the attacks were undermining the economy, but he wanted to exclude Jews from it altogether. Wagner won the argument. The meeting resulted in two race laws drafted by Wilhelm Stuckart, a lawyer from the Ministry of the Interior. The Reich

Order Police harass an elderly Jew.

Citizenship Law defined citizens of pure German blood and others, dividing society into two on racial grounds. The Law for the Protection of German Blood and German Honour forbade intermarrying between the two groups.

Nazi leaders stressed that the legislation had to be consistent with the party programme at the Nuremburg Rally three weeks later. Jewish experts from the Ministry of the Interior were flown to Nuremberg to finalise the race laws. Hitler announced them and later Hermann Göring explained them to the thousands of people gathered at the rally on 15 September 1935. They came into immediate effect.

THE REICH CITIZENSHIP LAW

The law determined who was a citizen of the Reich and who was not, dividing the population into two groups which could be treated differently by law. It effectively stripped Jews of their German citizenship. While citizens of pure German blood were known as Reich Citizens, subjects of the state were known as Nationals. Promised Reich citizenship papers were never introduced, but the main articles of the law are given below:

Article 1.1   A subject of the State is a person who belongs to the protective union of the German Reich, and who therefore has particular obligations towards the Reich.

Article 1.2   The status of subject is acquired in accordance with the provisions of the Reich and State Law of Citizenship.

Article 2.1   A citizen of the Reich is that subject only who is of German or kindred blood and who, through his conduct, shows that he is both desirous and fit to serve the German people and Reich faithfully.

Article 2.2   The right to citizenship is acquired by the granting of Reich citizenship papers.

Article 2.3   Only the citizen of the Reich enjoys full political rights in accordance with the provision of the laws.

THE LAW FOR THE PROTECTION OF GERMAN BLOOD AND GERMAN HONOUR

The law was split into three parts and the important sections are listed below. Breaches of the law were punishable with a fine, hard labour or imprisonment: The first part prevented citizens and Jews from marrying or having sexual relationships with each other, and it came into effect immediately.

Section 1.1   Marriages between Jews and citizens of German or kindred blood are forbidden. Marriages concluded in defiance of this law are void, even if, for the purpose of evading this law, they were concluded abroad.

Section 2   Sexual relations outside marriage between Jews and nationals of German or kindred blood are forbidden.

The 35,000 mixed-race marriages between Germans and Jews were known as 'blood dishonours' and they were annulled by the Public Prosecutor. They would be soon pressurised into getting a divorce by the authorities. Further cohabitation between German Aryans and Jews was classified as a criminal activity called 'race defilement' and perpetrators were denounced in the press. After July 1938 the Marriage Law allowed couples to have their marriages annulled under racial grounds; it placed a huge strain on many marriages.

The second part of the law banned Jews from employing Germans as domestic servants and it came into effect on the 1 January 1936.

Section 3:   Jews will not be permitted to employ female citizens of German or kindred blood as domestic servants.

This was included in response to lurid claims about Jewish employees having sexual fantasies about their German servants. The third part of the law referred to displaying flags on houses and businesses and it came into immediate effect.

> Section 4.1 Jews are forbidden to display the Reich and national flag or the national colours.
>
> Section 4.2 Jews are permitted to display the Jewish colours.

This piece of legislation worked alongside two others laws. One declared that the Swastika was the national flag and the second made it an offence not to display the national flag on national holidays. Flags were being used to visibly divide the population.

THE NUREMBERG RACE LAW AUTHORS

WILHELM STUCKART (1902–1953)
Stuckart fought with the Free Corps before joining the NSDAP in 1922. He became the party's legal advisor for the Wiesbaden area in 1926, but he continued to work as a judge until he was forced to resign in 1932. A year later he was appointed State Secretary in the Prussian Ministry of Education and a member of the Prussian State Council by the Nazis. By March 1935 he was the State Secretary in the Reich Ministry of the Interior.

HANS GLOBKE (1898–1973)
Globke became a civil servant in 1929, working as deputy to Aachen's police commissioner. When the Nazis came to power, he became an adviser to the Prussian Ministry of the Interior. Although Globke never joined the NSDAP, he worked on the legislation to dissolve the Prussian State Council and coordinated the rest of the parliamentary bodies.

Swastikas hang from every window in the centre of Nuremberg. (NARA-242-HB-15080a80)

DEFINING RACE

The Reich Citizenship Law did pose the question: who was a Jew? After further discussions, the party leaders wanted the legislation to apply to the 200,000 'individuals of mixed race', or '*Mischlinge*'. On 1 November the question was answered in a memorandum published by Dr Bernhard Losener of the Ministry of the Interior.

Anyone with three or four Jewish grandparents was a Jew. Anyone with two

A Jewish man and an Aryan woman are paraded through the streets with placards denouncing their relationship.

Jewish grandparents was a First Degree Half-Jew and they were considered to be Jewish if they had married another Jew or if they practised the Jewish religion. They could still be treated as a Jew, if and when it suited the authorities. Anyone with only one Jewish grandparent was a Second Degree Quarter-Jew and they were considered to be Reich Citizens when it suited the authorities. Family researchers were often employed to help classify individuals. Relationships with Jews were also discouraged by classifying any babies born out of wedlock as Jewish.

APPLICATION OF THE RACE LAWS

Senior Nazis often applied the Race laws to suit their own needs. False rumours of Jewish ancestry were used to discredit or remove opponents from office. Theodor Duesterberg, one of the leaders of the Steel Helmet ex-serviceman's organisation, was accused of having a Jewish grandfather during the March 1932 presidential elections, and he came a poor fourth. Hitler apologised to Duesterberg when he became Chancellor in January 1933, in the hope of getting his support. Duesterberg refused to accept and the rumour was resurrected. Accusations of Jewish ancestry were used in the political infighting and the party spent time discrediting rumours directed at Adolf Hitler, Reinhard Heydrich and Adolf Eichmann.

Jewish ancestry could also be ignored when it suited the Nazis. Hermann Göring declared 'I decide who is or is not a Jew' when he was challenged about appointing non-Aryan technical experts for the Luftwaffe. Erhard Milch, one of his chief assistants, had a Jewish mother. She was forced to sign an affidavit declaring that he was the illegitimate son of his father and another Aryan woman.

POST-NUREMBURG POGROMS
OCTOBER 1935 TO OCTOBER 1938

The severity of the laws against the Jewish community increased dramatically following the introduction of the Nuremburg Laws. The first decrees pertaining to the National Citizens Law and the Law for the Protection of German Blood and German Honour were introduced on 14 November 1935, and they gave the definition of Jew. At the same time Jews were denied the right to vote and they were not allowed to hold public office. The marriage of Jews to non-Jews was also prohibited. Meanwhile, Jewish children were forced to use separate school playgrounds and locker rooms. Many left because of segregation in the classroom and bullying in the playground by members of the Hitler Youth. They joined new Jewish community schools and had to contend with poor facilities, large classes and the lack of trained teachers. Many parents sent their children abroad to live with family.

In February 1936, the Gestapo was placed above the law and many Jews were targeted by the organisation as they came to terms with the new race laws. There was a brief period of respite in August during the Berlin Olympic Games but anti-Semitism resumed as soon as they were over.

Businesses continued to be targeted and the Security Service produced false documents to denounce businesses, allowing the Gestapo to act. After October 1936 revised tax demands were issued to Jewish companies and as Jewish banks were forced out of business, it was difficult to continue trading. In January 1937 there was a campaign to force Jewish businessmen to sell up to Germans at a fraction of market value. Those who refused to sell were threatened, attacked or arrested. After the autumn of 1937, Jewish businesses had to display signs declaring Jewish ownership.

Week after week small businesses closed and by 1938 the number of Jewish owned businesses had fallen from 150,000 to 40,000; it continued to fall as rival businesses used blackmail and denunciations to close them down.

In April 1938, Jewish businessmen were also banned from investing their money in Aryan enterprises. They also had to register all their investments with a treasury office two months later.

Domestic Jewish property was targeted next. Any property worth more than 5,000 RM had to be registered in April 1938. It was a tiny amount of money and virtually every property had to be registered. At the same time directives were issued regarding the confiscation of all Jewish property. Wealthy Jews had to register their personal finances with a treasury office in June 1938. They also had to register with their police districts, so they could be targeted for arrests and fines in future police raids.

Steps were also being made to undermine the powers of community leaders. In March 1938, Jewish cultural organisations were no longer considered to be legal entities with civil rights. They had to be registered as a legally-formed association, placing their leaders at great risk.

The summer of 1938 saw attacks on two of the largest synagogues in southern Germany in Munich and Nuremburg. In both cases neither the government nor the public reacted. On 15 June police across the country carried out a 'social action' arresting 1,500 Jewish men and women with previous convictions, no matter how minor. Most were released within a few days. Some police forces were also issuing guides on how to carry out non-violent harassment. Segregation was increased in September when Jews were banned from attending cultural events.

A display in the 'Eternal Jew' exhibition.

Employment restrictions continued and Jews were prohibited from working in any office across Germany in January 1937. The number of doctors had been limited since April 1933 but they were banned from practising in hospitals, clinics and public health institutions in March 1938. They were only allowed to work with Jewish patients in July and all medical certification was cancelled at the end of September. Lawyers were targeted next in another two step process. They could only act as 'Jewish Consultants for Jews' after September 1938 and all legal licenses were cancelled at the

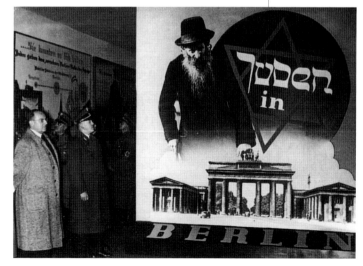

Refugees left to fend for themselves at Zbaszyn railway station.

end of November. Pharmacists, dentists and vets were banned from practising in January 1939.

Between November 1937 and January 1938 an exhibition titled 'The Eternal Jew' ran in Munich. It featured photographs and cartoons depicting the Nazi view of Jews, and the Jewish-Bolshevik conspiracy for the world. Over 5,000 people visited daily and the Secret Police reported that the exhibition resulted in an increase in anti-Semitic crimes.

Emigration had been an option in the early days of the Nazi regime, and over 35,000 Jews left Germany in 1933, but they had been forced to leave their money behind. The Haavara Transfer Agreement allowed 50,000 to emigrate to Palestine, alleviating international criticism, and the Gestapo charged a huge fee for a place on their transports. The SS Jewish Affairs Division took control of emigration in 1935.

In October 1938, all Jews had to hand in their passports. A complicated procedure prevented many from acquiring a new passport and replacements were stamped with a large letter 'J'. While steps were being taken to stop German Jews leaving the country, the Nazis rounded up 16,000 Polish Jews on 27 October and transported them to the border. The Polish government refused them entry and they were held in a temporary refugee camp at Zbaszyn where they would spend the winter in deplorable conditions. The trains stopped when the Polish authorities started deported German Poles. The action would have deadly repercussions for the Jewish communities across Germany a few days later.

KRISTALLNACHT, THE NIGHT OF BROKEN GLASS
9–10 NOVEMBER 1938

HIRSCHEL GRYNSZPAN (1921–1940?)

Grynszpan was the son of Jewish Polish-Russian immigrants. He left Germany in 1936 and headed for France, spending the next two years on the streets of Paris. At the beginning of November he learnt that his family had been evicted from their Hanover home, had their business and possessions confiscated, and had been taken to the Polish border. The seventeen-year-old wanted revenge and on 7 November 1938 he entered the German Embassy in Paris, armed with a revolver. Although he intended to assassinate the German ambassador, Grynszpan shot and mortally wounded the Third Secretary, Ernst von Rath.

While the Nazi leaders monitored the diplomat's deteriorating condition, a nationwide campaign of terror against the German Jewish population was being planned. The NSDAP leaders were in Munich for the Putsch anniversary when Rath's death was announced on the night of 9 November 1938. Orders to start the attacks were issued immediately. Grynszpan was eventually charged with murder in France but he was never taken to court and he disappeared in 1940.

THE ORDER FOR ANTI-JEWISH DEMONSTRATIONS

Hirschel Grynszpan.

The head of the Security Service, SS-Gruppenführer Reinhard Heydrich, issued specific instructions for attacks by the SA and the SS. The attacks had to maximise damage against Jewish communities but not affect Aryans. Plans to safeguard Aryan properties were arranged with the local Gauleiter or Circle Leader and the Order Police were not to interfere unless the guidelines were broken.

Jewish business and apartments could be vandalised but they were not to be looted. Synagogues could also be ransacked and their archives had to be handed over to the Security Service. Synagogues could be set on fire and the local fire brigades would be on standby to stop fires spreading to adjacent buildings. The Criminal Police, the Security Service and the Reserves were alerted to provide assistance.

The police had orders to arrest as many male wealthy Jews as their prisons would hold. The police had orders not to ill-treat prisoners and they had to hand them over to concentration camps. They were not allowed to arrest foreign Jewish citizens, the elderly or the infirm.

THE ATTACKS ON JEWISH COMMUNITIES

The mobs generally ignored Heydrich's orders and many attacks got out of hand. They

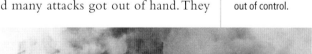

A synagogue burns out of control.

smashed their way into properties and dragged Jews out of their beds, and then abused or attacked them as they were dragged off to prison. Officially over 100 Jews were killed and hundreds more were injured. Around 300 committed suicide as the mobs broke down the doors of their homes. The total of people who died was probably over 1,000. Another 30,000 were arrested over a week-long period and sent to Dachau, Buchenwald and Sachsenhausen concentration camps where they were harshly treated. Although they were released soon afterwards, it was a brutal warning.

Across the country any building connected with the local Jewish community was attacked, including over 1,000 synagogues. Records were seized, religious artefacts were smashed and the buildings were set on fire. Jewish schools and cemeteries were also vandalised. Thousands of Jewish-owned shops and businesses had their windows smashed and were ransacked. The following morning, streets across Germany were littered with broken glass, resulting in the name 'Crystal Night', *Kristallnacht*, or 'the Night of Broken Glass'.

THE NAZI RESPONSE TO THE ATTACKS

On the day after the attacks, a law was introduced banning Jews from buying, possessing or carrying knives, truncheons or firearms, leaving them defenceless. While Jewish communities cleared up the damage, the government referred to the attacks as spontaneous outbursts. On 12 November, Göring told senior Nazis that the Jews were going to be held responsible for *Kristallnacht* and that Hitler had made it clear that 'the Jewish question will be now, once and for all, coordinated and solved one way or another.'

SS troops remove everything of value from a synagogue.

Jewish communities were forced to pay for the damage to their own properties, at a grossly exaggerated value of 25 million RM. A fine of one billion RM was also levied for the assassination of von Rath. Remaining businesses would be sold at a reduced rate or confiscated. Six million RM of insurance payouts were also given to the state to help cover the cost of repairing the businesses. The total amount of money raised topped two billion RM.

Over the next three days further restrictions were placed on Jews. Adults were prohibited from attending all public meetings, including movies, concerts and cultural performances, while all children were expelled from schools. A month later they were stopped from using sports fields or swimming pools, and there were plans to complete segregation in universities, hotels, restaurants, public places, parks, beaches and holiday resorts.

Although President Roosevelt recalled the US Ambassador from Germany and made a public condemnation against the attacks, the Nazis were satisfied by the lack of reaction and interference by European countries. It gave them the confidence to step up anti-Semitic laws.

POST-*KRISTALLNACHT* POGROMS
NOVEMBER 1938 TO SEPTEMBER 1939

The pressure on the Jews intensified enormously after *Kristallnacht*. The new laws violated their human rights, restricted their personal freedom and limited their ability to work and save money. They could be arrested for the smallest infringement, subjected to harsh treatment in custody and they were likely to be sent to a concentration camp. Hitler also made a deadly prediction in the Reichstag on 30 January 1939 when he stated a war would result in the 'extermination of the Jewish race in Europe'.

On 1 January 1939 identity cards became compulsory for all Jews over the age of fifteen. On the same date men had to add the name 'Israel' alongside their signature while women had to add the name 'Sara'; failure to do so would result in their arrest. It meant that Jews had to declare their religion every time they were stopped on the street or they had to sign papers. All tax concessions were also removed.

In January 1939, Göring instructed Reinhard Heydrich to speed up emigration and the Reich Centre for Jewish Emigration was set up. 110,000 left over the next eight months, paying extortionate fees. Meanwhile, countries around the world were limiting the number of Jewish immigrants they were prepared to accept. While Britain would accept children on an adoption scheme, it was reluctant to let adults enter the country unless they had a desirable trade. Meanwhile, in May hundreds of passengers boarded the USS *St Louis* in Hamburg heading for Cuba. They returned to Europe four weeks

The broken windows of a looted shop.

later having being refused residency. Himmler also suggested deporting Jews to the island of Madagascar; the proposal was probably just one of his many impractical ideas.

One serious attempt to organise mass emigration of Jews had been under discussion in Evian in France, since the summer of 1938. The Intergovernmental Committee for Political Refugees, chaired by the American, George Rublee, wanted to allow German Jews to transfer their ledger credits abroad so that their emigration could be linked with the promotion of German exports. Hjalmar Schacht, president of the Reichsbank, raised the matter on 2 January 1939, and while Göring and Ribbentrop argued over who was in charge of the plan, Hitler gave Schacht permission to discuss the emigration of 150,000 adults and 300,000 children over the next three to five years. The plan considered those aged between 15 and 45 who were fit to work. Jews would place 25 per cent of their assets in a cash fund and it would be used to ease their emigration; the money would then be transferred to the Reich. At the end of the month, Schacht was dismissed following an unconnected argument with Hitler over the financing of Germany's rearmament. Rublee resigned a few days later and the plan was dropped.

Personal freedom was severely restricted at the end of November 1938. Jews had to hand in their driving licences and they were banned from using public transport. They also had to hand in radios and carrier pigeons. Following the invasion of Poland on 1 September 1939, Jews were subjected to a night curfew, restricting movement to 5am to 9pm in the summer and 6am to 8pm in the winter.

A series of laws announced in April 1939 had cancelled tenancy rights, eviction protection and rent agreements, leaving landlords to freely evict Jewish tenants. At the same time preparations were being made to form Jewish ghettos in cities. 'Jewish Houses' were also being allocated in towns and villages where families could be forced to live together in mini ghettos.

The squeeze on employment also continued and in January 1939 a decree stopped Jewish dentists, veterinarians and pharmacists from practising. Six months later the public sector was completely aryanised when Jews were banned from working in any government job.

Businessmen were also subjected to further laws and in December 1938 a number of directives were issued aimed at completely removing Jews from economic life. After two years of trying to coerce Jews into selling their businesses, owners were forced to sell them to Germans at vastly reduced prices. Anyone who refused was held in a concentration camp while their business was confiscated. In February 1939, Jews were forced to hand over, or sell at a reduced value, all their gold, silver, precious metals, jewellery and art works. Bonds, stocks and shares also had to be sold at a low rate. Anyone failing to do so would be arrested.

The combination of laws meant that the 400,000 Jews left in Germany could neither own a business nor work for a German, limiting them to menial tasks in their own community. The ban on holding savings or valuable items reduced them to abject poverty. They were also facing having to move into over-crowded ghettos. They had been forced out of economic life, segregated in every day life and banned from leaving the country. If any believed it could not get any worse; they were terribly mistaken.

AUSTRIA AND CZECHOSLOVAKIA

On 12 March 1938, German troops crossed the border into Austria. Although the majority of Austrians welcomed the Anschluss with open arms, the persecution of Austrian Jews started immediately. It had a massive impact on Jewish communities. Men and women lost their businesses and jobs. Children were forced out of school and had to adapt to segregation. Anti-Semitic abuse, violence and humiliation were rife.

Adolph Eichmann opened the Central Office for Jewish Emigration in Vienna in August 1938 and over 100,000 Jews emigrated over the next six months. Many parents were forced to send their children overseas while they battled with the authorities for emigration papers. Czechoslovakian Jews had to deal with a similar situation when German troops entered their country.

THE EXPERT ON JEWISH AFFAIRS

ADOLF EICHMANN (1906–1962)

Eichmann worked as a travelling salesman in Vienna and joined the Austrian Nazi Party in April 1932. He came to the attention of the police for taking part in pro-Nazi activities and he joined the Austrian legion-in-exile in Bavaria in July 1933. He started work as a file clerk with the Security Service in 1934 and Heinrich Himmler later appointed him head of the Jewish Questions Office in Berlin. After learning a little Hebrew, Eichmann visited Palestine in 1937 hoping to contact Arab leaders but he was immediately ordered out of the country by the British Mandate Police. He was promoted to assistant of the Security Service for the Danube area on his return.

Eichmann worked in Austria following the Anschluss heading the office for Central Office for Jewish Emigration after August; he covered Czechoslovakia the following year. He also organised forced emigrations to Poland in March 1939 and by October he was the main advisor on emigration. In December 1939, Eichmann became head of Subsection IV-B-4 of the Reich Central Security Office, and the expert on Jewish affairs in the Third Reich. He would go on to coordinate the Holocaust and the deaths of over six million Jews.

OTHER ENEMIES OF THE STATE

Although the Jewish communities were the main targets for the Nazis, other minorities attracted similar attention. Laws were introduced against homosexuals, gypsies and Jehovah's Witnesses and 'offenders' were dealt with severely under a range of new laws.

HOMOSEXUALS

Homosexuality had been outlawed since 1871, but Germany developed a liberal approach after the First World War and there were numerous calls for the law to be dropped, particularly in cities. Homosexuality undermined the heterosexual ideals of the Nazis, but they usually turned a blind eye to the activities of their own leaders while the party's rank and file was subject to severe punishment. The Nazi hierarchy also preferred to expose someone when it suited their own causes. Homosexuality was rife amongst the SA leaders but their activities were ignored for years. Ernst Röhm and Edmund Heines were executed during the Night of the Long Knives, having been previously allowed to act as they wished. False rumours of homosexuality were also used to remove people from office. The army's Commander-in-Chief, General Werner von Fritsch, was forced to resign following accusations.

The homosexual community was subjected to decrees on public indecency following the Reichstag fire in February 1933, exposing them to a range of punishments including castration. Yet again standards were inconsistent and while some bars were closed down, many homosexual actors and actresses were given unofficial immunity.

In June 1935, the Nazis declared homosexuals to be 'national pests'. They also revised the Reich Penal Code criminalising all forms of sexual contact between homosexuals, making it far easier to arrest a suspect. In 1936 the Reich Central Office for the Combating of Homosexuality and Abortion began a national registration scheme and over the next six years it collected information on over 50,000 suspected homosexuals; many were arrested.

The office also began to purge the Hitler Youth. A night curfew was introduced in 1937 to curb community activities, while repeat homosexual 'offenders' were placed under invasive police supervision. The laws were extended to Austria and Czechoslovakia following their occupation.

Around 10,000 offenders were eventually sent to concentration camps where the pink triangle insignia on their uniforms singled them out for humiliation. Some chose to become concubines to get protection. Persecution of lesbians was less severe but many were forced to leave their jobs and they lived in fear of being denounced by their neighbours. Repeat offenders were usually imprisoned in Ravensbruck concentration camp.

GYPSIES

The 26,000 Gypsies in Germany had always been under surveillance, but the intensity increased under the Nazis. Camps were raided, families were moved on and individuals were arrested for begging or criminal activities. The NSDAP looked on them as an inferior race and the Research Centre for Racial Hygiene was opened in Berlin shortly after the party took power. Its research classified gypsies into four groups:

German gypsies	the Sinti
Hungarian gypsies	the Roma
Bohemia-Moravia gypsies	three groups descending from Gelderari, Lowari and Lalleri
Balkan gypsies	

They were classed as a 'foreign race' under the September 1935 Nuremburg Laws. After 1936 they were forced to move into government-controlled residential camps but the guards were usually hostile and the conditions poor. Those who failed to use them were held in concentration camps. The occupation of Czechoslovakia and Austria increased the number of gypsies living in the Third Reich by 30,000.

Under a decree called 'Combating the Gypsy Troubles' announced in December 1938, they had to register for an identity card which defined individuals as either having pure gypsy blood or mixed blood, 'mischlings'. The Nazis targeted inter-race gypsies, leaving pure blood ones alone; they also banned inter-race marriages. In the round-ups that followed, foreign gypsies were exiled while the rest were banned from travelling in large groups.

JEHOVAH'S WITNESSES

A branch of the Witnesses, the Earnest Bible Researchers, started practising in Germany in 1927. There were 30,000 members by 1933 and the organisation declared their political neutrality in October 1934, refusing to attend meetings or use the German greeting. It was banned in April 1935 after refusing to swear allegiance to the Führer. Despite persecution as enemies of the state, members refused to abide by the restrictions placed upon them and they continued to practise their religion. Thousands of members were arrested, tried by Special Courts and sent to concentration camps. They still refused to conform and were subjected to severe punishments.

AFRICAN-GERMANS

A small number of African-Germans, the offspring of mixed race relationships from the colonies, were sterilised.

CHAPTER TWENTY-THREE

RESISTANCE

Between 1931 and 1939 there were several plots to overthrown the Nazis and a number of attempts to assassinate Hitler. The threat of torture by the Gestapo, or execution for treason, meant that most plots rarely went beyond the preliminary discussion stage. The main attempts to destabilise the regime are given below.

REVOLTS

THE STENNES REVOLT: APRIL 1931

Walther Stennes (1895–1989) was a Free Corps leader before he joined the SA and he quickly rose to become head of the Berlin SA. Stennes supported Gregor Strasser and he

Crowds wait in the road outside the Berghof in the hope of catching a glimpse of Hitler.

became increasingly disillusioned by Hitler's leadership. He was also angered by the party's poor treatment of the SA rank and file, many of whom were living in poverty. Resentment reached boiling point in September 1930 when members refused to protect Goebbels, preferring to heckle him when he spoke at the Berlin Sportpalast. They went on to beat up his bodyguards and smash up his office. Hitler dismissed the SA commander Franz Salomon for failing to take action, asked Ernst Röhm to return from Bolivia to take command.

The peace was short-lived. By February 1931, the SA were getting out of hand on the streets and Hitler ordered Röhm to curb their activities. Stennes denounced the order as a betrayal of the party's principles and he refused to take disciplinary action when Berlin's SA men mutinied. Goebbels had to step in to stop the revolt spreading.

In April 1931, the government placed a blanket ban on public demonstrations to try and restore peace on the streets. At the same time Stennes became aware of his impending dismissal and he called a meeting of SA leaders. Although they pledged their support they were unable to help due to a lack of funds. Stennes and many other SA leaders were expelled from the party for insubordination. While Goebbels accused Stennes of being a police spy, Göring used SS men to restore order in the Berlin SA.

Stennes narrowly avoided arrest following the Reichstag fire with Göring's help and he was smuggled out of Germany ahead of the Night of the Long Knives. He went on to organise the Black Front with Otto Strasser in Prague. Stennes later went to China and served as the commander of Generalissimo Chiang Kai-shek's bodyguard.

THE HALDER PLOT: SEPTEMBER 1938

Franz Halder (1884–1972) was senior quartermaster of the Reichswehr and the Wehrmacht from 1926–1938. He became Chief of Staff in August 1938 after General Ludwig Beck resigned in protest at Hitler's plan to occupy the Sudetenland. Halder was already aware that many senior army officers disagreed with the Nazis' interference in military matters and the brutality of the SS. He was also aware that many would not act due to their oath of loyalty to the Führer. Although Halder was prepared to organise a military coup to remove the Nazis, he was opposed to assassinating Hitler.

A three-deep cordon of SS troops stand in front of Hitler's podium. (NARA-242-HB-05837)

Halder enlisted Generals Ludwig Beck, Erwin von Witzleben and Kurt von Hammerstein-Equord in the plot, and they were joined by the heads of the Abwehr, Admiral Wilhelm Canaris and General Hans Oster. Halder also enlisted Dr Hjalmar Schacht, the ex-president of the Reichsbank. The group planned to stage a military coup in Berlin when Hitler gave the order to invade the Sudetenland. They would install a military regime, arrest Hitler and certify him insane.

Indecisive leadership and poor organisation stopped the plot getting beyond the

discussion stage. Attempts to contact London failed and Neville Chamberlain was unaware of the plot when he started negotiating with Hitler in September 1938. The signing of the Munich Agreement on 30 September ceded control of Sudetenland to Germany, bringing the plot to an end.

THE BEER HALL PLOT: NOVEMBER 1939

Hitler attended the annual Beer Hall Putsch commemorations in Munich on 8 November 1939, two months after Germany invaded Poland. His welcome speech in the Bürgerbraukeller for the Nazi Old Guard was much shorter than usual and he left the hall early. Twenty minutes later a bomb exploded on the platform, the roof collapsed and seven members of the Old Guard were killed; another 60 were injured.

Hitler immediately offered a reward for information leading to the capture of the conspirators. Johann Elser, a carpenter, was arrested on suspicion of setting the bomb as he attempted to cross the Swiss border. Evidence implicated him and he admitted

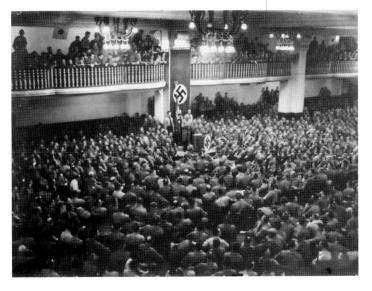

Hitler makes his annual speech in Munich's Bürgerbraukeller. (NARA-242-HB-17023)

setting the bomb under torture. He was held at Sachsenhausen and Dachau concentration camps but senior Nazis did not believe that he had acted alone; some were convinced that the British Secret Service was involved. He was finally murdered in Dachau in April 1945.

UNDERGROUND RESISTANCE MOVEMENTS

The Nazis had effectively smashed political opposition across Germany by July 1933. Leaders were held in concentration camps, some had fled the country, and others had been murdered. Established political parties had been banned and it was against the law to form a new one. Only a few political activists continued a secret battle to undermine the Third Reich.

Although there were one million members of the Social Democrat Party, groups were quickly closed down. Groups printed newsletters, posted fliers at night in the street and left leaflets in workplaces. They also smuggled information out of the country and brought back leaflets and newspapers. However, groups' attempts to undermine the regime were disjointed and they argued over policy while the Gestapo tracked them down; thousands were arrested.

The Communist Party had 180,000 members and although they were more determined, they persisted in opposing the Social Democrats. Cells continued across the country but they struggled to keep holding meetings or producing leaflets. One by one the Gestapo infiltrated them and members were tortured to expose their comrades.

UNDERGROUND NEWSPAPERS

The Central Committee of the Communist Party was an underground resistance movement of Communists, Social Democrats and trade union leaders, who printed and distributed anti-Nazi newsletters. The Gestapo had infiltrated the group by 1935 and arrested hundreds of members in coordinated raids across the country. Only a few escaped to Spain in 1936 and they joined the Thälmann Brigade in the Republican's fight against Franco's fascists. The rest were sentenced to death in mass trials.

Walter Schmedemann formed the Eilbek Comrades in Hamburg in 1934, and members printed an underground newspaper while running courier services to Czechoslovakia and Denmark. The Gestapo again infiltrated the group and in 1935 they arrested over 60 members; Schmedemann was one of the few to survive torture.

The leader of the group New Beginning, Walter Loewenheim, soon realised it was fruitless to carry on an active resistance to the Nazis. The group continued to publish the *Green Otto* newsletter with the support of exiled members in Switzerland and Spain, but they made little political impact. The group managed to evade detection by the Gestapo, and it smuggled information on German rearmament to foreign contacts.

Heinrich Himmler discusses what action to take. (NARA-242-HB-12071)

THE KREISAU CIRCLE

An early group of dissenters calling themselves 'Stand Against' were too fragmented to organise a coup. Many members joined the Kreisau Circle in 1933 and they met at Helmuth von Moltke's estate in Kreisau in Silesia. The Circle was dedicated to creating an open society with equal justice for all and a return to Christianity.

Helmuth von Moltke (1907–1945) was a lawyer who helped victims of the Nazi regime with legal assistance or emigration. He was also a legal adviser to the German High Command. Martin Gauger (1905–1941) was a lawyer who had been forced to resign after refusing to take the oath of allegiance to Hitler. He became a legal adviser for the Confessional Church. Hans von Trott zu Solz (1909–1944) worked for the German Foreign Office.

Attempts to get support for the group had failed because the American State Department and the British Foreign Office both suspected that it was working for the Gestapo. Although the group had many ideas for Germany's future they did not issue any plans until 1943.

THE WEDNESDAY CLUB

This group of right-wing academics, industrialists and civil servants gathered every Wednesday in Berlin to discuss history, art, science and literature. Members included the diplomat Christian von Hassell, who had been recalled from Rome following disagreements with Ribbentrop, and Johannes Popitz, the Prussian Minister of Finance, who secretly advocated the return of the monarchy. They often contemplated organising resistance but plans never went beyond the discussion stage.

YOUTH RESISTANCE

There were many scattered youth resistance groups across Germany during the early years of the Third Reich; many had adopted the Edelweiss flower as their emblem, including the Edelweiss Pirates. They enjoyed hiking and camping and sometimes mixed with political dissidents, deserters or escapees from concentration camps who were in hiding. The groups were usually poorly organised and were closed down one by one by the Secret Police. The SS-controlled Reich Main Security Office set up a dedicated youth section in 1939 and offenders were sent to Neuwied youth concentration camp.

INDIVIDUAL OPPOSITION

Although opposition to the regime was extremely dangerous, a few determined individuals took a stance against the Nazis.

CARL GOERDELER (1884–1945)

Goerdeler was the Mayor of Leipzig and he was appointed the Controller of Foreign Exchange and Reich Price Commissioner in 1934. Although he welcomed the Nazis, he became disturbed by their increasing anti-Semitism and rearmament. He drew unwelcome attention from the regime after he refused to fly the swastika flag over the city hall and failed to have a statue of the Jewish composer Mendelssohn removed. He was sacked in 1937 and travelled to Britain, France and the US to warn them about Hitler's intentions. His suggestions for returning territories to Germany to help the country recover went unheeded. He also tried to organise resistance amongst his contacts across Germany.

WILHELM LELISCHNER (1888–1944)

Lelischner was the deputy chairman of the German Trade Union Association when the Nazis seized power in 1933. His criticism of the NSDAP led him to be arrested and tortured along with other prominent trade unionists when the German Labour Front closed them down in May 1933. Lelischner organised trade unionists in a futile resistance against the Nazi regime after he was released.

HERMANN RAUSCHNING (1887–1982)

Rauschning joined the NSDAP in 1932 and became Hitler's trusted confidant on the Danzig Free State. Although the Old Guard denounced him as a latecomer, the NSDAP won the Danzig Volkstag election in May 1932 and he was appointed the President of the Danzig Senate. By August 1933 he had negotiated a treaty concerning future relations with Poland but he was becoming disillusioned with the National Socialist form of government. Rauschning lost the 1935 Danzig elections when he stood against the Nazis, and he was forced to escape to Switzerland. He went on to expose the Nazis' ruthlessness in a series of books.

DR JOSEPH ROMER (1890–1942)

Romer was a First World War veteran and commander of the Oberland Free Corps. He and his supporters became fanatical opponents of the National Socialists, working with activists at both ends of the political spectrum. Details of his activities are obscure but he was arrested following the Reichstag fire and again in 1934. Romer immediately re-established his resistance contacts after he was released from prison.

CARL VON OSSIETZKY (1889–1938)

Ossietzky became an active pacifist after serving in the First World War and he became the editor of the pacifist newspaper *The World Stage*, in 1927. He was briefly jailed in 1931 for accusing the Reichswehr of secretly building an air force in contravention of the Treaty of Versailles. Ossietzky continued to speak out and he was rearrested and held in a concentration camp following the Reichstag fire. He was awarded the Nobel Peace Prize in 1935 and Hitler responded by ordering Germans to refuse future prizes. Ossietzky died of tuberculosis in Oranienburg concentration camp in 1938.

VERBAL OPPOSITION

Freedom of speech was suspended in the Reichstag Fire Decree. Anyone making statements against the state, derogatory remarks about the party leaders or even jokes about the Nazi regime could be arrested. They could be tried for treasonable behaviour, a crime that was punishable with death. Most opposition speakers were imprisoned following the Reichstag fire in February 1933 while others went into exile. Two important speeches were made during the first two years of Nazi rule; the Marburg Speech in June 1934 and the Konigsberg Speech in August 1935.

MARBURG SPEECH

On 17 June 1934, Vice-Chancellor Franz von Papen spoke out at the University of Marburg, requesting a return of civil rights, freedom of speech and an end to the lecturing of the German people. He also questioned the state of Christianity under the Third Reich and condemned the effects of the Nazi coordination and propaganda on German society.

Papen was applauded but a news blackout kept the speech out of the press and off the radio, while Hitler ridiculed him when he heard about it. Edgar Jung and Erich Klausener helped Papen to write the speech and both were murdered two weeks later during the Night of the Long Knives. Papen's secretaries were also killed and the Vice-Chancellor was lucky to escape with his life.

KONIGSBERG SPEECH

Dr Hjalmar Schacht, President of the Reichsbank and the Reich Minister of Economics, delivered a speech condemning indiscriminate attacks against Jews on 18 August 1935 in Königsberg, East Prussia. The speech was again subjected to a news blackout and it did not appear in the press or on the radio. It only appeared in the Reichsbank publication which had very a limited circulation. A month later the Race Laws were announced during the Nuremberg Rally.

FUNERAL DEMONSTRATIONS

During the early days of the Third Reich, thousands of mourners would gather at the funerals of anyone murdered by the Nazis. It was the only safe way to demonstrate solidarity against the regime. Eventually, individuals executed for treasonable activities were buried or cremated in secret to prevent demonstrations and stop their graves becoming shrines.

INDEX

Abwehr, *see* Foreign Intelligence Office
Adolf Hitler Donation of the German Economy, 79
Adolf Hitler Schools, 201
Adolf Hitler-Spende, 66, 81
African-Germans, 306
After Work Organisation, 158
Agricultural Auxiliary Service, 205
Ahnenerbe, *see* Society for Research and Teaching of Ancestral Heritage
Air Protection Police, 131
aircraft specifications, 268–272
air force, German, 240, 25–253
airships, 152–153
Amann, Max, 58, 63, 71, 171, 172, 175, 179
America, *see* United States
Anti-tank guns, 263–264
architecture, 186–188
Arco-Valley, Count, 11
armoured cars, 262–263
armed forces, German, *see* Reichswehr and Wehrmacht
army, German, 239–240, 243–244
    division organisations, 245, 247–249
art, 181–182
Artaman League, 14
Aryan Clause, 168, 170, 179, 182, 184, 293
aryanisation, 97, 124, 126, 145, 166, 179, 229, 233, 287
atomic bomb, 168
Attack, The, 32, 172
Austria, 14, 16, 30, 47, 49, 54, 55, 58, 68, 73, 80, 89, 107, 119, 133, 137, 146, 165, 166, 176, 201, 211, 214, 220, 221, 223, 224, 225, 226, 227, 228, 229, 230, 244, 249, 253, 277, 288, 304, 305, 306
    Anschluss, 47, 55, 80, 93, 119, 133, 137, 152, 166, 172, 226, 227, 228, 229, 230, 231, 235, 241, 249, 252, 254, 304
    Homeland Protection Party, 226
    Fatherland Front, 226, 227
    Central Agency for Jewish Emigration, 229
Austro-Hungarian Empire, 55, 226
autarky, 69, 145, 146
Auto Union, 215, 216
autobahns, 87, 131, 146, 147, 150–151, 155
Axmann, Artur, 210
Baeumler, Alfred, 199
Baltic Coast, 206, 235
Bamberg Party Congress, 31, 32, 52, 67, 169
Banse, Ewald, 17
Barova, Lida, 170
Baumer, Gertrud, 191
Bavaria, 11, 13, 14, 18, 25, 29, 30, 33, 40, 40, 81, 82, 111
Bavarian Free Corps, 13–14
Bayreuth Music Festival, 122
Beauty of Labour, 99, 159
Beck, General Ludwig, 231, 244, 308

Beneš, Eduard, 231, 232, 233, 234
Berchtesgaden, 32, 60, 62, 224, 227, 232, 253
Berchtold, Joseph, 279
Berghof, 60, 62, 63, 66, 227, 231, 253, 280, 307
Bergmann, Gretel, 214
Berlin uprising, 7, 8, 11, 14, 25
Best, Werner, 41, 284
Bismarck, Otto von, 93
Black-Red-Gold Banner, 35
Blitzkrieg, 55, 224, 246, 247, 257, 258
Blomberg, Field Marshal Werner von, 85, 86, 98, 100, 104, 107, 110, 130, 223, 224, 239, 240, 241, 242, 243, 254
Blood and Soil, 14, 67, 144, 162, 177
Blood Flag, 117, 119
Blood Purge, 13–14, 22, 32, 47–48, 57, 69, 83, 100–103, 132, 134, 137, 143, 154, 175, 226, 240, 253, 275, 276, 281–282, 287, 289, 305, 308, 313
Blunck, Hans, 179
Bodelschwingh, Reich Bishop Fritz von, 100, 162
Bock, General Fedor von, 247
Bonhoeffer, Dietrich, 162
Bormann, Martin, 19, 40, 63, 71, 76, 79, 98
Border Control Police, 129
Bouhler, Philipp, 61, 71, 106, 185, 196
Boxheim Documents, 42, 284
Brahms, Johann, 184
Brandt, Dr Karl, 61, 196
Brauchitsch, Manfred von, 215
Brauchitsch, Walter von, 110, 243, 244
Braun, Eva, 59, 60
Braun, Otto, 27
Braunau-am-Inn, 49, 228
Breker, Arno, 181
Brest-Litovsk, Treaty of, 7
broadcasting, 131, 144, 176
Brown House, 15, 59, 76, 77, 102, 103, 121, 186
Bruckner, Wilhelm, 22, 61
Brüning, Chancellor Heinrich, 36, 37, 40, 41, 46, 48, 94, 99
Buch, Walter, 71, 83
Burckel, Joseph, 230
Cabinet of Barons, 41, 47
Cabinet, Hitler's, 85–86
Capital punishment, 123, 127
Carraciola, Rudolf, 215
Cartels, 17, 146, 147, 148, 149
Cartel Tribunal, 99, 148
Catholic Centre Party, 28–29, 35, 36, 41, 46, 47, 86, 93, 94, 99, 112
Catholic Church, 164–165
Central Intelligence Office, 129
Chamber of International Law, 125
Chamberlain, Houston, 17
Chamberlain, Neville, 231, 232, 236, 254, 309

Chancellery of the Führer, 106, 185, 196
Christian festivals, 115–116
cinema, 182–184
Circle of Friends of the Economy, 142
Civil Service, 70, 82, 84, 99, 112, 124, 198, 220, 292, 293
Coburg, 35, 203
College of Three, 109
Commercial Economy Organisation, 99, 148
Communist Party, German, 11, 12, 25–26, 27, 35, 36, 74, 76, 87, 89, 90, 112, 221, 236, 310
concentration camps, 26, 39, 84, 90, 95, 97, 125, 127, 129, 134, 135–140
    administration, 138
    locations, 135–137
    prisoner categories, 138–139
    regime, 139–140
Concordat, 99, 100, 164, 165, 166, 220
Confessional Church, 100, 162, 293, 311
Confessional Synod of the German Evangelical Church, 162
Constitution, 8, 9, 27, 37, 43, 85, 88, 93, 94, 95, 100, 151, 162
Conti, Leonardo, 195
Coordination, 97–100
Councils of Trust, 99, 157
Courts of Honour, 157
County Police, 131
Counterespionage Police, 129
Czechoslovakia, 8, 27, 32, 68, 107, 130, 133, 137, 146, 176, 201, 223, 224, 225, 226, 235, 237, 252, 257, 288, 304, 305, 306, 310
    Munich Agreement, 55, 231, 232, 234, 309
    Sudeten German Party, 230, 231, 234
Daladier, Edouard, 232, 236
Daluege, Kurt, 131, 282
Danzig, 8, 55, 73, 74, 225, 235–237, 312
Darré, Richard Walther, 71, 86, 106, 107, 144, 145, 280, 281, 285
Dawes, Charles, 10
Dawes Plan, 11, 151
Day of National Solidarity, 120–121
Degano, Alois, 62
Democratic Party, German, 27, 99
Den Bruck, Arthur van, 17
Diels, Rudolf, 130
Diem, Dr Carl, 212, 214
Dietrich, Joseph, 57, 102, 196, 280, 287, 288, 289, 309
Dietrich, Marlene, 182
Dietrich, Otto, 57, 71, 91, 102, 143, 169, 173, 175
Dimitrov, Georgi, 89, 90
Doenitz, Karl, 251
Dollfuss, Engelbert, 226, 227, 230
Dorpmüller, Julius, 107, 108, 152
Dressler-Andress, Horst, 179
Drexler, Anton, 12, 15, 16, 19, 67
Duesterberg, Theodor, 13, 86, 298
Duty of Service, 157
Eagle's Nest, 60, 63
East Prussia, 44, 235, 237
Eastern Aid Scandal, 44
Ebert, President Friedrich, 9, 11, 22, 25, 30, 39, 45, 105
Eckart, Dietrich, 12, 15, 16, 18, 62, 171
Economic Chambers, 148, 149
economy, 141–148
    Defence, 146
    Hitler's views, 141
    under the Nazis, 145–148
    income and expenditure 148
    War, 109, 144, 146
Edelweiss Pirates, 311
Education, 197–202

Egk, Werner, 184
Ehrhardt Brigade, 14
Eichmann, Adolf, 229, 298, 304
Eilbeck Comrades, 310
Einstein, Albert, 166, 168, 185
Eisner, Kurt, 11
elections, Presidential 25, 26, 39, 47, 298
elections, Reichstag
    May 1928, 33–34
    September 1930, 36
    July 1932, 41
    November 1932, 43
    March 1933, 91
Elser, Johann, 309
Eltz-Rühenach, Paul von, 85, 86
Emergency Association of German Science, 166, 167
Emergency Pastors League, 162
Emergency Work Programmes, 155
Enabling Act, 27, 47, 53, 85, 93, 93, 94, 95, 107, 112, 124
Engel, Johannes, 153
entailed estates, 144
Entailed Farm Law, 144
Epp, General Franz von, 13, 19, 65, 71, 112, 171
Equord, General von Hammerstein-, 100, 243, 244, 308
Ernst, Karl, 102, 103, 276, 305
Esser, Hermann, 16, 31, 56, 169
Ethiopia, 217
Expansionism, 68
Farben, I. G., 137, 146, 149
Factory Protection Police, 131
Falkenhayn, General Erich von. 45
family, 189–191
Faulhaber, Cardinal von Michael, 165, 166
Feder, Gottfried 15, 16, 18, 67
Fiehler, Karl, 71, 113, 114
Fighting League for German Culture, 179, 181
film, 182–184
Fire Protection Police, 131
Fleischer, Tilly, 214
Flick, Friedrich, 79, 81
Foreign Intelligence Office, 241, 243
Fountain of Life, 69, 285
Four Year Plan, 80, 109, 1111, 144, 146–147, 150, 151, 229, 231, 254
France, 7, 8, 10, 22, 32, 50, 54, 55, 64, 81, 150, 151, 216, 217, 219, 220, 221, 223, 224, 225, 226, 230, 231, 232, 236, 237, 246, 249, 250, 252, 260, 300, 303, 312
Franco, General Francisco, 58, 221, 224
Frank, Bernhard, 63
Frank, Hans, 72, 108, 125, 185
Frank, Karl, 234, 235
Free Corps, 9, 11, 12, 13–15, 19, 21, 25, 31, 47, 51, 65, 66, 69, 116, 125, 144, 195, 231, 239, 243, 276, 281, 286, 297, 307, 312
Frick, Wilhelm, 22, 23, 36, 37, 44, 56, 71, 85, 86, 88, 91, 94, 98, 103, 106, 107, 109, 123, 124
Friedeburg, Hans von, 250
Fritsch, General Werner von, 108, 109, 110, 130, 223, 224, 241, 243, 244, 247, 254, 305
Fritzsche, Hans, 174
Froelich, Carl, 179
Frontbann, 23, 66, 274, 276
Führerlexikon, 71, 93
Funk, Walther, 107, 109, 110, 111, 143, 144, 148, 169, 241
Fürstner, Captain Wolfgang, 215
Furtwängler, Wilhelm, 184
Gall, Leonhard, 61
Garmisch-Partenkirchen, 212
Gauger, Martin, 310
Gau areas, 74
Gauleiter, 73

Gempp, Walter, 90
Gendarmerie, 131
General and Interior Administration, 133
Geneva Disarmament Conference, 93, 218
George Circle, 18
German Academic Exchange Service, 181
German Armament Works, 150, 287
German Association of Cities, 113
German Local Authorities Association, 112, 114
German Civil Service, 71
German Communal Congress, 71
German Excavation and Quarrying Company Limited, 150, 287
German Girls League, 190, 203
    history, 209–210
    organisation, 209
    activities, 209
German Labour Front, 70, 74, 77, 98, 115, 149, 154–155, 157, 158, 188, 191, 192, 201, 229, 294, 312
German Law Academy, 105, 125
German Law Front, 125, 126
German Police Comradeship Organisation, 131
German Reich Committee for Sports, 210
German Reich League for Sports, 210, 211, 212
German Research Community, 166, 167
Germany Society for Military Policy and Science, 199
German State Party, 27
German Students' Society, 71
General German Trade Union Federation, 154
German Women's Bureau, 191
German Women's Order, 191
German Women's Work, 71
German Workers' Party, 10, 12, 15, 16, 17, 51, 57, 67, 125, 156, 171, 203, 273, 291
Gestapo, 32, 90, 97, 127, 128–130, 132, 133, 135, 137, 157, 163, 181, 229, 237, 281, 282, 284, 299, 300, 307, 310, 311
Gleichschaltung, see Coordination
Globke, Hans, 297
Globocnik, Odilo, 229, 230
Goebbels, Dr Joseph, 31, 32, 33, 36, 55, 56, 58, 66, 71, 72, 74, 76, 81, 82, 83, 84, 86, 88, 91, 94, 98, 102, 103, 106, 107, 109, 110, 114, 117, 124, 130, 143, 152, 155, 164, 165, 169–170, 172, 173, 175, 176, 177, 179, 180, 181, 182, 183, 184, 185, 186, 187, 192, 193, 195, 212, 214, 228, 231, 274, 292, 293, 294, 308
Goerdeler, Carl, 311
Göring, Hermann, 18, 21, 32, 40, 43, 44, 63, 66, 76, 85, 86, 88, 90, 94, 97, 102, 103, 106, 108, 109, 110, 111, 112, 118, 122, 124, 127, 128, 129, 130, 147, 152, 170, 177, 223, 232, 233, 242, 243, 252–255, 273, 274, 280, 295, 298, 302, 303, 308
Graf, Ulrich, 58
Graf Zeppelin airship, 152, 153
Great Britain, 4, 7, 10, 54, 55, 60, 64, 119, 216, 217, 218, 219, 220, 221, 223, 224, 225, 230, 231, 232, 236, 237, 249, 250, 252, 303, 312
Greece, 214
greetings, 84
Grimm, Wilhelm, 71
Grimminger, Jakob, 117
Groener, Wilhelm, 40
Gruber, Kurt, 204
Grynszpan, Hirschel, 121, 300, 301
Gumbel, Emil, 200
Gürtner, Franz, 85, 86, 88, 103, 106, 107, 123, 125–125
gypsies, 139, 213, 305, 306
Hácha, Emil, 233, 234
Halt, Karl Ritter von, 212
Hammerstein-Equord, Kurt von, 244
Hanfstaengl, Ernst, 52, 58
Hanisch, Reinhold, 50

Hanke, Karl, 169
Hansa towns, 112
Harrer, Karl, 12, 15
Harzburg Front, 11, 13, 29, 38, 143
Hassell, Christian von, 311
Harzburg Front, 11, 13, 29, 38, 143
health, 194–196
Heer, see German army
Heiden, Erhard, 279
Heines, Edmund, 57, 102, 204, 305
Held, Heinrich, 29
Helldorf, Heinrich von, 274
Henlein, Konrad, 230, 231, 234–235
Hereditary Health Courts, 195
Hermann Göring National Works, 150
Hess, Rudolf, 18, 23, 57, 63, 65, 66, 71, 72, 76, 83, 86, 98, 101, 102, 107, 108, 109, 110, 177, 225, 227
Heydrich, Reinhard, 97, 111, 127, 128, 129, 131, 132, 133, 134, 237, 280, 281, 282, 285, 291, 298, 301, 303
Hiedler, Johann, 49
Hierl, Konstantin, 15, 51, 156
Hilgenfeldt, Erich, 192, 193
Himmler, Heinrich, 14, 20, 57, 60, 69, 72, 97, 101, 102, 110, 117, 127, 129, 130, 132, 134, 138, 145, 274, 279, 280, 281–282, 283, 284, 285, 286, 288, 290, 303, 304, 310
    Circle of Friends, 81, 131, 287
    Himmler, Operation, 237
Hindenburg airship, 152, 153
Hindenburg, Oskar von, 44
Hindenburg, President Paul von, 11, 13, 22, 23, 25, 30, 37, 39, 42, 43, 44, 45, 46, 47, 48, 53, 54, 86, 88, 91, 92, 94, 95, 101, 102, 104, 141, 152, 153, 240, 242, 243
Hindesmith, Paul, 184
Hitler, Adolf
    aides, 57–58
    author, 63–64
    Chancellor, 53
    childhood, 49–50
    citizenship, 55–56
    dictator, 54
    diplomat, 54–55
    doctors, 61
    friends, 58–59
    military service, 50–51
    party leader, 52–53
    party member, 51–52
    residences, 62–63
    romantic attachments, 59
    youth, 50
Hitler Youth
    activities, 207
    history, 203–206
    organisation, 204, 206–207
    Young Folk, 207–208
Hohenzollern, Crown Prince Wilhelm, 48
Hohenzollern, Prince August, 48
Hoffmann, Heinrich, 58–59
Hoffmann, Henny, 59
Holy Roman Empire, 93
Homosexuality, 134, 137, 138, 139, 193, 214, 244, 276, 285, 291, 305
Hönig, Eugen, 179
Höss, Rudolf, 19
Hossbach, Colonel Friedrich, 223
Hossbach conference, 55, 218, 241, 242, 244
Huhnlein, Adolf, 215, 278
Hugenberg, Alfred, 11, 29, 30, 38, 44, 52, 85, 86, 91, 99, 106, 142, 171, 174
Hungary, 8, 89, 232, 233, 234
Illustrated Observer, 16, 172
Imperial insignia, 119

Industry Club, 79
Inspector for Highways, 111
Interest Slavery, 16, 141
Investigation and Settlement Committee, 83
Iron Front, 39
Italy, 219–221
    Rome-Berlin Axis, 54, 221, 227
    Pact of Steel, 221, 236
Japan, 133, 168, 222, 225
    Berlin-Rome-Tokyo Axis, 222, 225
Jehovah's Witnesses, 135, 138, 192, 291, 305, 306
Jewish Councils, 294
Johst, Hanns, 179
Jung, Edgar, 102, 103, 303
Kaas, Monsignor Ludwig, 28, 29, 93, 94, 99
Kadow, Walther, 19, 66
Kahr, Gustav Ritter von, 19, 20, 22, 29, 103
Kaiser Wilhelm II, 7, 9, 101
Kaltenbrunner, Ernst, 230
Kapp, Wolfgang, 14, 15, 23
Keitel, Field Marshal Wilhelm, 109, 110, 237, 241, 242, 243
Kempka, Erich, 57
Keppler, Wilhelm, 43, 79, 80
Kerrl, Hans, 107, 108, 164
Kesselring, Albert, 253, 255
Kirdorf, Emil, 79, 80, 81
Klausener, Erich, 102, 103, 303
Klintzsch, Hans, 273
Koerner, Paul, 109, 147
Konigsberg Speech, 312, 313
Korner, Ludwig, 179
Krauch, Carl, 149
Kreisau Circle, 310
Kriegsmarine, see German navy
Kristallnacht, 57, 114, 121, 137, 166, 198, 300–302
Kroll Opera House, 85, 91, 93, 94, 109, 183
Krupp von Bohlen, Gustav, 79, 81
Kubizek, August, 50, 58
Labour Charter, 157
Labour Maids, 156
Lagarde, Paul Anton de, 17
Lammers, Hans, 66, 91, 105, 109, 110
Landsberg-am-Lech, 23, 24, 30, 57, 62, 63, 84, 114, 120, 279
Laubinger, Otto, 179
Laws
    Against the Establishment of Parties, 112
    Against Habitual and Dangerous Criminals, 157
    Protection of German Blood and German Honour, 296–297
    Protection of Individual Trade, 149
    Reconstruction of the Reich, 113
    Reduction of Unemployment, 98, 155
    Reich Citizenship, 296
    Restoration of the Civil Service, 112
    Secure Unity of Party and Reich, 113
Leadership Principle, 56
League of Nations, 8, 10, 54, 217, 219, 249
Lebensborn, see Well of Life Registered Society
Lebensraum, see Living Space
Leber, Julius, 27
Legitimate Power, 41
Lehnich, Oswald, 179
Lenk, Gustav, 203, 204
Lelischner, Wilhelm, 312
Lewald, Theodor, 210
Ley, Robert, 66, 72, 154, 155, 159, 201
Liebknecht, Karl, 11
Leibstandarte-SS Adolf Hitler, 57, 102, 121, 275, 280, 281, 282, 287, 288, 289
Linz, 50, 58, 137, 228, 230
literature, 185–185

Lithuania, 8, 235, 237
Litvinov, Maxim, 236
Living Space, 17, 69, 285
Local authorities, 113
Locarno Treaty, 10, 58, 217, 218
Loewenheim, Walter, 310
Lossow, General Otto von, 19, 20
Louis, Joe, 211
Lubbe, Marius van der, 88, 89, 90, 124
Ludendorff, General Erich, 7, 16, 19, 20, 21, 22, 23, 30, 31, 45
Luftwaffe, see air force, German
Lutze, Victor, 72, 101, 102, 182, 275, 276, 277
Luxemburg, Rosa, 25
Maginot Line, 246
Malicious Practices Act, 97
Marburg Speech, 103, 107, 313
Marx, Wilhelm, 39
Masurian Lakes, 45
Matteotti, Giacomo, 220
Maurice, Emil, 18, 57, 63, 273
Mayer, Helene, 211, 212, 214
MEFO bills, 146
Mein Kampf, 23, 52, 57, 62, 63, 65, 73, 143, 175, 179, 180, 181, 186, 210, 291
Meissner, Otto, 39, 105
Memel, 235
Mendelssohn, Felix, 184, 312
Mercedes Benz, 215
Meyerbeer, Giacomo, 184
Milch, Erhard, 254, 298
Ministerial Council for the Defence of the Reich, 66, 109, 110
Ministries
    Aviation, 108, 109
    Communications, 86, 107
    Culture, 98
    Defence, 107, 241
    Ecclesiastical Affairs, 107, 164
    Economics, 16, 107, 147, 241, 254
    Finance, 83, 107, 141, 142
    Food and Agriculture, 30, 107, 142, 145
    Foreign, 57, 107
    Interior, 87, 105, 124, 130, 138, 295, 297
    Justice, 107, 125, 134, 226
    Labour, 107
    Public Enlightenment and Propaganda, 143, 169, 180
    Science, Education and Culture, 107, 197
Ministerial Council for the Defence of the Reich, 66, 109, 110
Molotov, Vyacheslav M., 225, 236, 237
Moltke, Helmuth von, 310
Morell, Theodor, 61
Mosley, Sir Oswald, 60
Muchow, Reinhard, 74, 153, 155
Municipal Police, 131
Müller, Friedrich, 17
Müller, Heinrich, 129, 130
Müller, Chancellor Hermann, 36
Müller, Reich Bishop Ludwig, 100, 162
Müller, Renate, 59
Munich, 10, 11, 29, 30, 55, 81, 82, 111, 112
    Beer-Hall Putsch, 19–21, 26, 41, 55, 62, 83, 117, 120, 120–121, 171
    trial, 23
music, 184–185
Mussolini, Benito, 54, 58, 165, 219, 220, 221, 222, 224, 226, 228, 232
Napola Schools, 201

National Authorities, 105
National Health Main Office, 195
National Labour Day, 98, 115
National Socialist Freedom Party, 23
National Socialist Monthly, 172
National Socialist organisations
    Doctors' League, 194, 195
    Farmers' Association, 144, 145
    Flyers' Corps, 277
    Former German Students of League, 71
    German Students' League, 70, 200, 210
    German Technology League
    German Veterans' Organisation, 13
    Information Service, 132
    Labour Offices, 154
    Lecturers' League, 70, 199
    Legal Officials League, 70
    Motor Corps, 215, 278
    People's Welfare Organisation, 70, 190, 192–194
    Physical Exercise League, 71
    Relief Fund, 40
    School Children's League, 199
    Shop Cell Organisation, NSBO, 153
    Sports League, 210
    Teachers' League, 70, 198
    War Victims' Welfare Service, 70
    Women's Organisation, 70, 191
National Vocation Competition, 159
Nationalist Party, German, 29–30
navy, 240, 249–251
    strategy, 249–250
Nebe, Artur, 132
Neithardt, Judge Georg, 23
Niemöller, Pastor Martin, 162–163
Netherlands, 48, 54, 89, 221
Neubauer, Alfred, 215
Neurath, Konstantin Freiherr von, 85, 86, 94, 98, 107, 108, 110, 111, 217–218, 223, 224, 225, 234, 241
Neudeck estate, 44, 45, 46, 47, 102
Nietzsche, Friedrich, 17
Night of the Broken Glass, *see* Kristallnacht
Night of the Long Knives, *see* the Blood Purge
NSDAP
    25 Point Programme, 67, 115, 161, 291
    Army Politics Office, 71
    Agriculture Office, 71
    awards, 83
    calendar, 115–116
    business donations, 79–81
    corruption, 73, 144
    discipline, 83–84
    Economic Council, 141
    female vote, 82
    finances, 76–81
    Foreign Affairs, 71
    headquarters, 75–76
    influential groups, 17–18
    influential individuals, 17
    Law Division, 125
    membership, background, 82
    membership donations, 77–78
    membership, size, 81
    organisation, 73
    Organisation for Foreigners, 74
    Party School for Orators, 82
    Political Organisation, 71
    racial theories, 69
    Reichstag Parliamentary Party, 71
    targeting voters, 82
Nuremberg
    race laws, 125, 295–297

rally grounds, 119–120
Oberfohren, Dr Ernst, 90
Oberlindober, Hanns, 194
Obersalzberg, 52, 59, 62–63, 66
Office for Agriculture, 144
Office of the Reich Chancellery, 105
Office of the Presidential Chancellery, 44, 105, 106
Ohlendorf, Otto, 133
Ohnesorge, Wilhelm, 107, 108
OKW, armed forces high command, 242
Olympic Games, 120, 186, 212–215
    summer, 212–215
    winter, 212
Ondra, Anny, 59
open air medleys, 121–122, 185
Order Castles, 155, 201–202
Orfl, Carl, 184
Ossietzky, Carl von, 312
Oster, Hans, 243, 308
Owens, Jesse, 214
Palestine, 304
Papen, Chancellor Franz von, 27, 28, 29, 39, 41, 42, 43, 44, 45, 46–47, 48, 53, 79, 85, 86, 91, 101, 103, 107, 164, 226, 230, 274, 313
Party Foreign Affairs Department, 71, 181, 218
People's Army, 274
People's Car, 159, 160
People's Court, 90, 97, 127, 129
People's Observer, 13, 16, 19, 118, 58, 171, 172, 173, 180, 203, 281
People's Party, German, 27–28, 99, 112
People's Party, Bavarian, 22, 29, 99, 112
Pietrzuch, Konrad, 42
Poelzl, Klara, 49
pogroms, anti-Semitic
    Austria, 304
    Czechoslovakia, 304
    March 1933 to September 1935, 292–295
    October 1935 to October 1938, 298–299
    November 1938 to September 1939, 302–304
Pohl, Oswald, 137, 138, 281, 286, 290
Poland, 8 55, 68, 119, 137, 137, 160, 165, 175, 216, 217, 221, 224, 225, 232, 233, 235, 236, 237, 243, 244, 246, 250, 252, 254, 255, 258, 259, 260, 262, 269, 303, 304, 309, 312
    invasion of, 247–249
Police
    Criminal Police, KriPo, 97, 127, 131, 132, 133, 285, 301
    Order Police, OrPo, 127, 131, 284, 295, 301
    Security Police, SiPo, 97, 98, 127, 128, 129, 132, 133, 134, 285
Polish Corridor, 44, 55, 235, 236, 237
political meetings, 37–38
Pope Pius XI, Achille Ratti, 165
Pope Pius XII, Eugenio Pacelli, 164, 165
Popitz, Johannes, 311
Popov, Blagoi, 89, 90
population, German, 111
Porsche, Dr Ferdinand, 215
Positive Christianity, 161, 162, 164
Potsdam, 91, 205, 210, 244
press, 171–175
    NSDAP, 171–173
Privy Cabinet Council, 109, 110
private industry, 148–149
propaganda, 176–177
Protection Echelon, *see* SS
Protestant Church, 161–162
Protestant Reich Church, 161–162
Protocols of the Elders of Zion, 180, 291
Prussia, 9, 13, 22, 27, 32, 34, 40, 44, 48, 74, 93, 111, 112, 128, 162, 164, 205, 235, 237, 281, 282, 313

public companies, 149–150
Raabe, Peter, 179
Race and Resettlement Office, 145, 280, 283, 284, 285, 286
radio, 175–176
Radio Police, 131
Raeder, Erich, 108, 109, 223, 243, 251
Rahl, Mary, 59
railways, 151–152, 159
Railway Police, 131
Rath, Ernst von, 121, 300, 302
Raubal, Angela, 38, 57, 59, 60, 62, 66, 103, 130
Rauschning, Hermann, 312
Red Front Fighters, 26, 35, 40
Reich Agency of German Jews, 294
Reich Broadcasting Company, 144
Reich Chancellery, 61, 105, 110, 224
Reich Chancellor's Office, 66, 104
Reich Committees, 108
Reich Culture Chambers, 144, 179, 180
Reich Defence Council, 109, 110
Reich Family League, 71
Reich Federation of German Industry, 142
Reich Food Estate, 144
Reich Groups, 148, 149
Reich Labour Service, 71, 155, 156, 189, 193, 201
Reich Land Service, 205
Reich Leaders, 71–72
Reich Main Security Office, RHSA, 98, 128, 129, 132, 133, 134, 200, 281, 282, 285, 311
Reich Master Forester, 111
Reich Party Day, 116–119
Reich Physicians' Chamber, 194–195
Reich Press Chamber, 173, 175, 179
Reich Propaganda Office, 176
Reich Protectorate of Bohemia and Moravia, 111, 234
Reich Radio Chamber, 176, 179
Reich Socialist Lecturers' Alliance, 199
Reich Student Council, 200
Reich Teachers' League, 198
Reich Treasury Office, 111
Reich Youth Office, 111
Reichstag, 9, 18, 25, 36, 37, 38, 41, 43, 73, 86, 91, 93, 94, 99, 103, 111, 112, 241
Reichstag fire, 87–88, 112, 125, 132, 135, 253, 274, 280, 305, 308, 312
Reichstag Fire Decree, 47, 135, 312
Reichstag fire trial, 89–90
Reichrats, 9, 68, 112, 113
Reichsbank, 11, 27, 72, 109, 143, 144, 146, 148, 303, 308, 313
Reichenau, General Walther von, 101, 248
Reichswehr, 13, 14, 15, 20, 42, 46, 47, 48, 53, 69, 100, 172, 199, 239, 241, 242, 243, 247, 255, 274, 276, 308, 312
Reinhardt, Fritz, 82, 83, 99
religion, 161–166
Renteln, Adrian Theodor von, 204
Rentenmark, 11, 142
Rhineland, 8, 54, 74, 82, 152
    Operation Winter Exercise, 115, 217, 219, 232, 239, 279
Ribbentrop Bureau, 218, 225
Ribbentrop, Joachim von, 44, 107, 109, 110, 170, 218, 222, 224–225, 233, 236, 237, 241, 303, 311
Riefenstahl, Leni, 59, 118, 182, 183, 215
Röhm, Ernst, 18, 19, 20, 22, 23, 40, 54, 72, 76, 83, 86, 100, 101, 102, 103, 108, 118, 137, 171, 175, 183, 274–275, 276–277, 305, 308
Rome-Berlin Pact, 54, 221, 227
Romer, Dr Joseph, 312
Roosevelt, President Franklin D., 168, 302
Rosenberg, Alfred, 18, 23, 31, 44, 71, 91, 98, 132, 161, 165,
171, 172, 179, 180–181, 184, 199, 217, 218, 291
Rossbach Group, 14
Rublee Plan, 303
Russia, see Soviet Union
Rust, Bernhard, 197–198
Saar, 8, 54, 145, 218, 219, 230
Salomon, Franz Pfeffer von, 4, 84, 274, 276, 308
Saxony-Anhalt, 40
Schacht, Hjalmar, 11, 27, 36, 72, 107, 108, 109, 141, 141–143, 146, 147, 241, 295, 303, 308, 313
Scheel, Gustav, 200
Schemm, Hans, 198
Schellenberg, Walter, 133
Scheuermann, Fritz, 179
Schickelgruber, Alois, 49
Schirach, Baldur von, 59, 63, 72, 111, 201, 204, 205, 206, 209, 210
Schlageter, Albert, 19, 66
Schleicher, Chancellor General Kurt von, 32, 39, 40, 42, 43, 44, 45, 46, 47, 48, 53, 103, 172
Schlieffen Plan, 22
Schlosser, Rainer, 179
Schmedemann, Walter, 310
Schmeling, Max, 152, 211
Schmidt, Paul, 57–58
Schmitt, Kurt, 86, 106, 107, 142
Scholtz-Klink, Gertrud, 191–192
Schools, 198–199
Schreck, Julius, 57, 279
Schroeder, Kurt von, 44, 79
Schultze, Walther, 199
Schumann, Robert, 184
Schuschnigg, Dr Kurt von, 226, 227, 228, 230
Schutzstaffel, see SS
Schwarz, Franz, 71, 77, 279
Schwerin von Krosigk, Lutz Graf, 85, 86, 94, 96, 98, 106, 107, 141–142
Science, 166–168
Second Revolution, 54, 69, 100, 274, 280
Secret Cabinet Council, 66, 110, 218
Secret State Police, see Gestapo
Security Service, 32, 76, 98, 127, 128, 129, 130, 132, 133, 134, 164, 200, 241, 280, 281, 282, 284, 285, 299, 301, 304
Seeckt, General von
Seisser, Colonel Hans von, 19, 20
Seldte, Franz, 13, 85, 86, 106, 107
Self-coordinator, 75, 123
Severing, Carl, 124
Seyss-Inquart, Arthur, 108, 227, 228, 229
Sharkey, Jack, 211
ship specifications, 264–267
Siegfried Line, see West Wall
Slovakia, 233–234
Social Democratic Party, 27–28, 90, 124
Society for Research and Teaching of Ancestral Heritage, 290
Sonderkommandos, 286
Sovereignty Bearers, 73
Soviet Union, 7, 23, 26, 47, 50, 55, 68, 90, 133, 212, 214, 217, 222, 223, 225, 231, 232, 235, 236, 237, 239, 240, 251
Soviet-German Non-Aggression Pact, 235–236
Spain, 243, 253, 270, 272, 310
civil war, 221–222
Spann, Othmar, 17
Spartacist League, 11
Special Court, 97, 127, 163, 306
Speer, Albert, 61, 63, 118, 119, 120, 159, 186–188
Sperrle, General Hugo, 221
sport, 210–212
SS
    administration, 283–284

business enterprises, 286–287
Combat Troops, 287, 289
Death's Head Troops, 137, 281, 287, 288, 289
history, 279–281
legal offices, 284
organisation, 279–281
Race and Resettlement Office, 286–287
security offices, 284–285
uniforms, 282–283
Waffen SS, Armed SS, 287, 289
Stadelheim prison, 83, 102
Stalin, Marshall Josef, 55, 235, 236, 237
state governor, 112, 126, 284
Starhemberg, Ernst, 226
Steel Helmet, 13, 38, 48, 86, 87, 199, 203, 205, 274, 298
Stempfle, Father Bernhard, 57, 103
Stennes, Walther, 32, 274, 276, 307, 308
Sterilisation Program, 195–196
Stinnes, Hugo, 79
Stock, Gerhard, 214
Storm Division, see Sturm Abteilung
Stosstruppen, 35
Strasser, Gregor, 15, 23, 31, 32, 44, 52, 67, 71, 101, 103, 132, 154, 155, 307
Strasser, Otto, 19, 31, 308
Strauss, Richard, 179, 184, 214
Streicher, Julius, 16, 19, 21, 66, 120, 172
Strength through Joy, 99, 120, 155, 158, 160, 185, 186
Stresemann, President Gustav, 9, 10, 11, 27, 28, 35, 48, 217
Stuck, Hans, 215
Sturm Abteilung
history, 273–275
organisation, 275–276
Stuckart, Wilhelm, 297
submarine specifications, 267–268
Sudetenland, 55, 57, 68, 73, 74, 230–231, 234, 235, 243, 244, 252, 254, 261, 287, 308, 309
occupation of, 232–233
Supreme Party Judge, 83
Syrovy, General Jan, 232
Swastika, 14, 17, 37, 69, 100, 115, 118, 119, 152, 161, 163, 164, 282, 297, 311
Switzerland, 11, 27, 29, 32, 80, 217, 291, 310, 312
T–4 Programme, 196
Tanev, Vassili, 89, 90
tanks
development, 257–258
specifications, 258–262
Tannenberg, 45, 46
Tannenberg League, 23
Technical Emergency units, 131
Temples of Honour, 22, 76, 116, 121
Thälmann, Ernst, 25, 26, 39, 310
theatre, 184–185
Thierack, Judge Otto-Georg, 127
Thingspiel, see Open Air Medleys
Third Reich, definition of, 93
Thorek, Josef, 181
Thule Society, 18
Thuringia, 13, 32, 36, 56, 74, 111, 117, 124, 276
Thyssen, Fritz, 79, 80
Tiso, Jozef, 233
Todt, Fritz
Torgler, Ernst, 26, 89, 90
tourism, 159, 169
trade unions, 28, 38, 48, 53, 79, 82, 98, 115, 125, 154, 204, 218, 230, 232, 294
Traffic Police, 131
transportation, 150–153
Triumph of the Will film, 118, 183
Troost, Paul, 61, 76, 182, 186–187

Trott zu Solz, Hans von, 310
Trustees of Labour, 157
Tschammer und Osten, Hans von, 210, 212
Turkey, 47
USCHLA, see Investigation and Settlement Committee
Udet, Ernst, 253, 254, 255
Uhlenhaut, Rudolf, 215
Ukraine, 63, 223, 234
Ulbricht, Walther, 25, 26
unemployment, 35, 36, 46, 79, 82, 86, 98, 119, 123, 127, 148, 151, 155, 156, 190, 192, 193, 220, 226, 230
United States, 7, 10, 11, 35, 64, 133, 169, 176, 182, 184, 211, 213, 214, 303, 311
Unity Valkyrie, Mitford, 59, 60–61
Universities, 199–200
Vatican, 29, 100, 164, 165, 220
Verdun, 7
Versailles, Treaty of 7–8, 10, 13, 14, 45, 54, 67, 69, 81, 86, 197, 199, 217, 218, 229, 236, 237, 239, 249, 251, 257, 264, 265, 266, 312
Vienna, 47, 50, 58, 74, 80, 133, 172, 179, 226, 227, 228, 229, 230, 304
Vienna Fine Arts Academy, 50, 179
Viking League, 14
Völkisch movement, 18
Voting under the Nazis, 93
Wagener, Dr Otto, 274
Wagner, Adolf, 102, 295
Wagner, Gerhard, 195
Wagner, Richard, 59, 60, 118, 122, 184
Wagner, Siegfried, 60
Wagner, Winifred, 59, 60
Wall Street Crash, 11, 35, 45
War Reparations, 10, 19, 46, 218
War Veterans' Aid Organisation, 193–194
Warlimont, Colonel Walther, 241
Water Police, 131
Weber, Max, 22, 27
Wednesday Club, 311
Wehrmacht, 210, 231, 232, 234, 236, 241, 242, 243, 246, 257, 258, 262, 308
Weimar, 8
Weimar Republic, 8–9
welfare, 192–194
Well of Life Registered Society, 69, 285
Wels, Otto, 27, 94, 99
West Wall, 151, 256
Wever, Walther, 252, 253, 255
Wessel, Horst, 36, 38, 120, 169, 169, 183, 204, 207
Wiedemann, Fritz, 57
Wild Camps, 134, 135, 274
Wilson, President Woodrow, 8, 217
Winter Support Programme, 192–193
Witzleben, Erwin von, 308
Woellke, Hans, 214
Wolff, Karl, 173, 281, 283
Woman's Labour Service, 191
Women's Order of the Red Cross, 191
women's organisations, 191–192
Work Books, 157
Works Councils, 99
Workers' Educational Camp, 139
World Committee for the Victims of German Racism
Young, Owen D., 11
Young Plan, 11, 13, 29, 35, 36, 38, 52, 143
youth organisations, 202, 203–209
Youth League, 203, 204
Youth Protection Chamber, 199
Zander, Isbeth, 191
Ziegler, Adolf, 179
Zweig, Stefan, 184, 185